BANKING ON CHANGE

BANKING ON CHANGE

Helena Dolny

VIKING

VIKING

Published by the Penguin Group
27 Wrights Lane, London W8 5TZ, England
Penguin Putnam Inc, 375 Hudson Street, New York, New York 10014, USA
Penguin Books Australia Ltd, Ringwood, Victoria, Australia
Penguin Books Canada Ltd, 10 Alcorn Avenue, Toronto, Ontario,
Canada M4V 3B2
Penguin Books (NZ) Ltd, Cnr Rosedale and Airborne Roads, Albany, Auckland,
New Zealand
Penguin Books India (P) Ltd, 11 Community Centre, Panchsheel Park,
New Delhi – 110 017, India
Penguin Books (South Africa)(Pty) Ltd, 5 Watkins Street, Denver Ext 4,
Johannesburg 2094, South Africa

Penguin Books (South Africa)(Pty) Ltd, Registered Offices:
Second Floor, 90 Rivonia Road, Sandton 2196, South Africa

First published by Penguin Books (South Africa)(Pty) Ltd 2001

ISBN 0670 89691 8

Typeset in 10.5 on 12.5 Sabon
Cover design: Mouse Design
Front cover photograph: Elizabeth Sejake, *Sunday Times*
Back cover photograph: *Sunday Times*
Printed and bound by Interpak Books, KwaZulu-Natal

For those who continue to seek a chance to make a difference

CONTENTS

ACKNOWLEDGEMENTS

To the late Barney Simon, a brave and visionary South African theatre director. Over decades the plays he produced consistently provoked responses as they touched the central nervous system of issues facing our society. He wrote: 'I hope my work can celebrate the gift of life without forgetting the abuse of life' and 'Without confrontation . . . there is just blur. Only do dangerous things, there is so little time.'*

At a personal level, his remark to me some years ago, 'You *can* write. You *must* write', provided that nugget of self-confidence that sustained me whilst I wrote. An aspect of his brilliance lay in his capacity to get others to explore their talents.

To my friends, family, comrades (you know who you are). You've been there for me – beyond my expectations. My daughters Tessa and Kyla – you carried yourselves wonderfully as you dealt with the repercussions of my public trauma affecting your own lives. I am proud of you.

To those who travelled the road with me (they know who they are) and put their shoulders to the wheel to steer the Land Bank in its new direction. Thank you. Some of you, who I associated with the 'old' regime, gave me your warmth, shared your culture, and laid to rest what I thought was a deep-seated prejudice.

To others, marginalised by the power play of politics, who inspire me with your determination to find a new space which lets South Africa, in some way, continue to benefit from your talents.

To those who persist with interrogation – What's being done? Who benefits? – as our country determines its new direction.

Lastly, the writing of this book was not a lonely endeavour. A group of people generously gave their time to read drafts of various chapters, were unsparingly critical and constructive in their comments and engaged in debate. The final product is so much better than it would have been without your input. Thank you.

---

*Mary Benson (1997), *Athol Fugard and Barney Simon. Bare Stage, A Few Props, Great Theatre*. South Africa: Ravan Press.

PROLOGUE

A telephone call interrupted a family holiday in July 1999 and shattered my sense of well-being.

'Helena, you are all over the newspapers, the television, and the radio. It is terrible.' The main national daily newspaper's lead story took up the entire top half of the front page under the headline: 'Serious allegations against Slovo's widow.'* Alongside was a very large photograph of me. The first paragraph set out the allegations: 'Dr Helena Dolny, Land Bank managing director and widow of the late Joe Slovo, has been accused of corruption, mismanagement, racism, nepotism and trying to more than double her salary.' The newspaper account continued: 'The allegations are contained in a report written in May by the former chairperson of the bank's board, Bonile Jack, and which has been handed over to President Mbeki.'

That phone call marked my entry into a six-month public imbroglio. It didn't end the day that I 'resigned' and left the Bank on New Year's Eve, 2000. My start to the millennium was marred by a state of trauma that continued to live with me like an intrusive companion that I could not shake off. Up to then my life had unfolded seamlessly. I had moved from one place, one job to another with a minimum of effort. The reverberating events that took place meant that my life would never be the same again. I knew that whatever I chose to do in the longer-term future would be influenced by those months. I had been in the middle of an undertaking and it had been interrupted. There was now an unexpected hiatus. I gave myself six months to take stock. The challenge

---

*P Hamnca in *The Star*, 15 July 1999.

I faced was to transcend the emotion of the events and to move on. It might prove harder than anything I'd ever taken on before.

I was numb for the first few weeks of the new year. I left home periodically, joining family or friends on holiday. Mostly I read, slept and engaged listlessly. Ten weeks passed aimlessly.

Intermittently people talked to me about writing a book. 'The tragedy,' an adviser to the Bank told me, 'is that the Land Bank is a success story that people don't know about – and the scandal has distracted attention from that success. It's one of the best examples of positive change and business turnaround in post-apartheid South Africa. The story needs to be told.'

A friend in politics suggested that I write not only about the Land Bank's transformation, but also that I put on record an alternative account of the events that led to my departure from my post. During the months of the imbroglio, my board of directors instructed me not to engage with the media on anything except strict business issues. It was a bitter irony that this should have happened in our newly achieved democratic state, won by a struggle in which a plethora of battles to defend freedom of expression had played an important part. The purported rationale was to avoid trial by media. That trial went ahead anyway, fuelled by information and misinformation liberally supplied by detractors, resulting in newspaper articles which I read with dismay, felt damaged by, and was bound by my employers not to comment on.

I had an unusual amount of time available, disposable, for introspection. I decided I would like to try to capture the excitement of what it was like to be part of an intense economic and social change process in those first years of South Africa's fledgling democracy. It constitutes a part of our contemporary history, and I felt enormously privileged to participate in this particular slice of it.

However, I was also mindful of the fact that writing such an account could have adverse consequences. Many events which make headline news are quickly forgotten in public memory. The act of publishing would be one of reminder, possibly resulting in renewed hostility and attack. I concluded that a contribution to a debate on issues that confront many of us in our daily working lives was more fundamental than any personal discomfort.

I vacillated. I was drawn by the challenge to write but also intimidated. It would be difficult to convey the energy and passion of the transformation process, combined with the dispassionate truth of a story about business change and the problems encountered. Those nights I slept long restless hours, dreaming unpleasantly, waking chilled and troubled. As people talked to me about writing, I began to map out the possible contents of the different chapters. As my thoughts crytallised into tangible shapes, my dreams got worse. I began to rethink the persuasion to write. Perhaps it would be healthier to get another job and fill my head with a new set of daily problems that would squeeze out the sleep-world intrusions of my recent past.

A friend pointed out that I had the unexpected gift of a six-month sabbatical. I had always enjoyed writing. I would be turning my back on this opportunity if I were to plunge myself into new professional work. The writing experience would create a framework for reflection. The friend took the argument further: Did I not know that people who suppressed traumatic events often became physically sick as a consequence? As for the dreams, they were precisely an indication of a subconscious at work trying to assist a healing process; I should learn to work with my dreams and not run away from them.

Three days later, I walked into a bookstore and as I stood at the counter waiting to pay for my purchase, my eyes fell on a leaflet about a workshop to be held that very weekend. The topic was 'Writing as Healing'. I was curious, and there was nothing in my life that I could not cancel. The synchronicity was the final push towards the decision to write.

Finally, as I began to draft the book outline, an acquaintance who is a sociologist commented: 'If you're going to write, you have to include a personal chapter about where you're coming from. What's happened is that you've become a public figure but not a human figure.'

CHRONOLOGY

1997	Cabinet adoption of Strauss Recommendations
April 1997	Appointment of Land Bank 'transformation board'
May 1997	Helena Dolny appointed new managing director
July-December 1997	Transformation consultation process
December 1997	National consolidation conference
January 1998	Truth and Reconciliation Commission business hearings
January-February 1998	Work redesign process in Land Bank branches
March 1998	Launch of 'new' Land Bank – new logo and new suite of products
October 1998	Industrial unrest – first strike in the history of the Land Bank
November 1998	Board approval of principles of new remuneration policy
January 1999	Decision to start social accountability project
March 1999	Board approval of new salaries
April 1999	Appointment of new board of directors
June 1999	Appointment of new Minister of Agriculture
July 1999	Press coverage of the 'Jack letter'
July 1999	Appointment of Katz investigation team
August 1999	Katz report to Land Bank board
October 1999	Dolny charged with misconduct
November 1999	High Court hearing
December 1999	Dolny resigns from the Land Bank

ONE

WHAT DRIVES MS DOLNY

Where are you coming from?

I was loath to begin 'Once upon a time I was born . . .' but Justice Malala's article 'What drives Ms Dolny' published in the *Sunday Times* in late 1999* set me off on a train of thoughts about what to cover in a book, and how much of myself to insert into it.

'*Where am I coming from? Where am I going to? I am a child of immigrants who has herself migrated.*' That was a mantra that was played over and over again at the Johannesburg 1995 Art Biennial. I sat for a long time looking at a work by Mohini Chandra, a child of migrants and, like myself, a first generation immigrant to the UK. Her artwork pursued the discovery of an identity influenced by migrations between countries and the different cultural influences of each place. I was drawn by the work to such an extent that I twice revisited it. The artwork was a set of tea chests, lit diffusely, placed in the centre of a white, container-like room; the floor was covered lightly with wood shavings. The tea chests were covered with faded photographs and stickers of journeys, and the softly spoken mantra played over and over again. Its rhythm, like a heartbeat, followed you as you walked through the other exhibition rooms. '*Where are you coming from? Where are you going to?* swung backwards and forwards in my head like a pendulum. I can still hear it.

I am a child of immigrants who has herself migrated. A person is ultimately a composite complexity, constantly being shaped and reshaped; an essential self that's influenced by life's experience, by people, by chance,

---

*Justice Malala, 'What drives Ms Dolny', *Sunday Times*, 12 September 1999.

by what we make of chance. Maybe each of us has, as Mohini puts it, 'an ever-changing self-identity' over time, a response to different events in our lives. But surely there's a central core that drives our responses? That's what I decided to try to identify in so far as I would write about myself.

The 'what ifs' in my life have been huge. What if I'd gone straight from school to university? What if I hadn't decided that a boat ticket from Cape Town to Southampton was a better option than a flight from Lusaka to London? What if I hadn't been on a train journey when reading *Cry, the Beloved Country*, Alan Paton's novel set in apartheid South Africa? What if Ruth First, anti-apartheid activist and former colleague, hadn't been assassinated by a letter bomb one afternoon just as I was about to leave my office on my way to hers? What if I had started walking to her office two minutes earlier?

I wasn't able to package a neat response to Malala's question, 'What drives Ms Dolny?' Instead I found myself mulling over certain events in my life that seemed to me to have had such significance that I consider them 'defining moments'.

Mines, mills and ethnicity

My father, Antoni Dolny, was Polish, Catholic and the youngest of fourteen children. He was Antek to his Polish friends and Tony was his immigrant identity. My mother, Regina Maria Mathilda née Klohs, also Catholic and second oldest of seven children, considers herself Czech. She was born in a region that in 1938 became known as Sudetenland, which many people think of as more German than Czech. She explained to me that my grandparents' birth certificates were Austrian, those of herself and the other first four siblings were Czech, whereas the younger two siblings had German birth certificates – all this in spite of their being born in the same village. But my mother's upbringing was strongly influenced by progressive Czech policies, such as the laws concerning women's property rights – hence her strong self-identification as Czech.

My parents, separately, found themselves in displaced persons camps in what became West Germany after the end of the Second World War. The British were recruiting labour and offered free sea passages to men and women willing to work in the mines or weaving mills. My parents met each other in a small northern English town called Accrington. He was working at a mine, and she in a weaving mill. As they fell in love, they found themselves to be most at ease speaking German. There was too much difference between their mother tongues for them to converse freely using those. Later, as a young family, we spoke German at home. In our Slavic household it was the language most comfortably used between all of us. At least it was when I was still very small.

Most of our early family life took place in the large kitchen at the back of the terraced house – 'joined-up houses' as my South African sister-in-law called them on seeing streets of them for the first time. At one end of the kitchen was the Rayburn stove that heated the water. It was only lit in the evening, apart from Monday as laundry day and Saturday as bath day. On either side of the stove my father had installed built-in kitchen cupboards which my mother was pleased with. The top part housed the unbreakable grey pyrex dinner service and had sliding doors. A huge clothes drying rack hung from the high ceiling in front of the stove area; it had ropes and pulleys to raise and lower it. In the far corner opposite the gas stove and the sink there was an extremely large earthenware jar. Different things fermented in it at different times. There were days when my father skimmed off the brown cream foam that rose to the surface as his home-brewed beer fermented. Other times it would be filled with thinly sliced cabbage that my two brothers and I had stamped on with our bare feet in a galvanised metal tub to soften it before it was transferred to the earthenware jar. Muslin-covered stones weighed down the wooden lid as the fermenting progressed until my father declared it to be ready for bottling in the specially prepared Kilner jars, hot from their recent washing and with rubber rings to fit inside the clamped glass tops. The walls of the cellar were lined with shelves full of jars of jam, chutneys, pickled gherkins, pickled onions, sauerkraut, home-made wine and home-brewed beer.

The gas stove was our rescue point on icy winter mornings. I was quite old before we got carpeting. The linoleum floors were freezing if you couldn't find your slippers. We three children would rush downstairs to the residual warmth of the kitchen. The Rayburn was never stoked to keep it going through the night; that would have been too expensive. It was the only time we didn't sit at the table to eat. Instead, we lit the gas stove and left the oven door open. Then we sat around it, eating our cereal with our feet on the edge of its insides.

The kitchen table wasn't only used for eating. It had a pull-out leaf that made it longer and then we used it for ironing. After supper, when everything was cleared away, it became the homework table. In winter, when the cellar was too cold to work in, my father would bring up his tools and sit by the table mending shoes or doing woodwork. There was no counter working space; on my mother's rare baking days an oilcloth was spread over the table and the surface used for kneading and cutting biscuit shapes. Eventually the table would be covered with hot cakes and we would wait anxiously for them to cool. My father loved the taste of poppy seed cake, even though it meant putting up with seeds that bothered the spaces between his gums and his false teeth. My mother's favourite was the plum cake of her Czech childhood. I liked the plaited sweet bread eaten with butter best of all. On my father's happiest days, when he'd drunk some of his home-brew, he would play the accordion or a harmonica and occasionally sing; he had the most beautiful baritone voice. We children couldn't understand the words of his Polish songs, so he'd sing Frank Sinatra for us, and my mother would smile. He'd tell jokes and stories, all blended together in my head now, how he'd saved his cigarette ration coupons in the displaced persons camp, how he'd swapped them with the American soldiers for a watch, and later for the harmonica.

It was on a summer, jam-like making day when we were in the kitchen that something memorably unpleasant happened; it must have been a weekend afternoon if my father was home. We heard footsteps running up the cobbled backstreet. My elder brother Roman, just over seven years old, came into the backyard and threw the bolt. That was a strange thing to do. We never locked the door except last thing at night. He burst through the kitchen door and started to tell us that he had had a fight with the Morley boys next door. They'd called him a German pig and he was angry. We were sitting around the kitchen table listening to his story when we heard banging on the front door and loud shouting voices. The sounds were muffled by the walls and we couldn't make out the words.

We all went into the hallway, my mother carrying my baby brother Martin. I held on to my father's hand. Roman kept close by. The flap of the letter box was thrust wide open. Lips and teeth stared us in the face, and the words 'You German pigs' were shouted over and over again.

The irony was that their war experiences had made my parents both anti-Nazi and anti-communist; they had suffered at the hands of both. My mother had described her fear as Nazi soldiers stamped through the farmstead home, their leather boots marking the polished floor. They ransacked the house and made a bonfire of grandfather's books which were considered to be too liberal by the invaders. My father had spent his teenage years through the war labouring on German farms. He had kept the fifteen centimetre square cloth with the black capital P on it which he had been forced to wear every day during those years. But my parents were not anti-German. The Russian soldiers, as victors at the end of the war, did not behave any better. Scarred by wartime inhumanities, my parents were now wary of political extremes. My mother has alluded to brutal experiences, but the memories remain too awful, raw and painful and she's refused to give details to her children.

So my parents were heartsore about the incident of the voices that jeered through the letter box. They had been born in different countries. My mother had seen her village community torn apart by the Nazi insistence on each family drawing up their family tree in order for them to categorise which persons had or didn't have German blood in their ancestry. Life had taught my parents to be fearful of the possible damage wrought on communities by ethnic division and intolerance, and this was basic to their upbringing of their children.

The Morley-Dolny brothers' fight was a landmark in my childhood. English became the day-to-day language of the household; German continued only for our prayers. *Vater Unser der du bist in himmel.* Later, when we had forgotten our childhood German, our parents would revert to it for those private conversations when they didn't want us to know what was being said between them. The 'defining moment', however, was not so much the language change, but the acknowledgement of the hurt and damage that can be exacted through cheap recourse to crude ethnic hostility.

Whilst I've been writing I've talked with my brother Martin asking what he remembers of things which only lurk in my memory.

'Martin, when a journalist refers to me as 'a young Englishwoman' why do I have such a gut rejection of the description? Yes, I remember the tweed-coated, chauvinist sons of the British gentry who did the same agricultural economics course at Reading University, and who teasingly asked, "You're from Lancashire, isn't that where they still take baths in tin tubs?" But, besides this, I remember you and your friends singing an alternative version of the National Anthem at your school speech night. Where did this antipathy come from?'

'Helena, it's so obvious, how could you have forgotten?' my brother replied. 'Besides the fact we got called Poles and Krauts when we were kids, you were brought up as Roman Catholic in a town full of Irish Roman Catholics, forty miles from Liverpool where there was a strong support base for the IRA. Remember when we were teenagers and going to pubs or the Working Men's Club, like the one we went to with Dad down the road on Wellington Street? Well, it was still the days when people stood and sang "God Save the Queen" at closing time, except that where we grew up, half the people didn't stand. They sat and kept quiet.'

When I thought more about it I realised that until I'd gone to university I hadn't met many English people. My parents sent us to a Catholic school; on 17 March, St Patrick's Day, there were very few who couldn't wear shamrocks as the sign of an Irish heritage. My childhood memories are dominated by the strong ethnic traditions of different immigrant groups. My parents' social life was strongly linked to the Polish community, and my school life was ruled by Irish Catholicism. At the bottom of the hill on which we lived half-way up was the Pakistani community. The ethnic group that I cannot remember with any real clarity is the English, most probably because of the religious divide in schooling.

As children we were treated with curiosity by those friends who were not Eastern European. They were curious about the food we ate, the cabbage rolls stuffed with meat and rice, the sliced cucumber with buttermilk dressing. On the days when school friends visited we wanted the meals to be as plain as possible, brown stew with mashed potatoes and peas. We children eventually left home with an abiding sensitivity stemming from our own experience of being treated as different, and with a respectful curiosity about other lives and other cultures.

A sense of class

When I was seven or so my mother was hospitalised for a hysterectomy. At the time my brothers and I were ten, seven and four years old. The doctor could not imagine my father coping with work as well as the cooking, shopping, washing and cleaning for a month. As an immigrant family we did not have relatives, apart from my father's brother. But because of a family feud they hadn't spoken to each other for years. The social worker suggested that foster care might be the best for us; I was sent to one home and my two brothers to another.

The people who cared for me for a month showed me every kindness; my brothers were less fortunate. Mary and Edwin Castlehouse lived on a council estate in the village of Chatburn, a few miles from Accrington. Mary was a cleaner and her brother Edwin had a job at the sewerage works. Their warmth and sympathy to my parents' plight left me with the knowledge that human decency belongs to anyone and everyone, irrespective of their social standing. One of 'Aunty' Mary's cleaning jobs was at a big country house owned by people called the Whittakers. I was taken there one day on a half-term holiday. I wandered open-mouthed through the house. There was a split-level lounge with a grand piano standing splendidly in one part. The floors were parquet. There were stairs leading to passageways with children's rooms which were empty because they were away at boarding school. There was a rose garden, and bowls of fresh flowers filled the house.

'How come they have so much money?' I asked quietly.

'Cotton ginneries in Rhodesia,' was the answer I was given.

'What's a ginnery? Where's Rhodesia?'

And so I was told about a hot sunny continent called Africa where most people were black and cotton grew in fields.

'The people are really black,' I was told, 'not dark like the Pakistani community or the Italians, but very dark brown' – like the West Indian bus conductor I had met on our local bus routes.

It was difficult to grow up in England in the sixties without a sense of class. My impressions were abnormally skewed as ordinary English people did not figure much in my childhood and the ones I did meet, like Mrs Whittaker, fell into the caricature of being better off and speaking English as though they had marbles in their mouths. The landed gentry who did the same course as me at university compounded the caricature.

My school friends even drew fine distinctions about differences within classes. In my first year of secondary school I was friendly with a girl named Anne. She invited me to her house and suggested that I stay over, as she lived in a neighbouring town. Her mother asked me lots of questions, checking out the foreign child that her daughter was befriending. When I returned the invitation Anne spluttered and blushed. 'My mum says I shouldn't be friendly with you.' 'Why?' I asked, puzzled. I'd been on my best behaviour. What could I have done to offend her mother? 'She says that your family are too posh for me. You live in your own house and we only live in a council house. And, besides, you use posh words.' Apparently I'd used the word 'hectic' and that word meant Anne's mother thought that I thought I was a cut above the ordinary and so she banned our friendship.

The sensitivities cut both ways. My junior school friend was Clare whose parents were schoolteachers. They lived in a bigger house higher up the hill and went on holidays to France. No one else I knew at junior school in the 1960s went on regular 'continental holidays'. Her mother seemed mean-spirited to me and gave me back-handed compliments that let me know that I came from a 'down-the-hill', less well off household.

My mother sews beautifully. We lived in a mill town and the markets were full of 'seconds' material. My mother would scour the stalls for good quality 'fents', as the off-cuts were called. They often came in pieces and you had to find two or three to get enough to make a dress. One day, as a ten-year-old on a visit to Clare, I wore a shirt-waister that my mother had just finished. She'd been hard put to get the bodice made up, and had puzzled over what to do with the small remaining pieces, otherwise I would have to have only a skirt. She solved her problem through decorative French pleats, the folds of which disguised the joined pieces; she prettied the seamwork with some white scalloped edging. 'So clever, your mother, to do so well with so little,' was the remark made by Clare's mother, which I took as cutting.

I didn't especially dwell on these incidents as they happened. It was only years later when I was a researcher in rural Mozambique that the work I was doing caused me to think about the class origins of my parents and my upbringing.

Admittedly I grew up in the strangest household in post-war Britain. My father, who came from a poor Polish peasant background and had only four years of secondary schooling, had become a factory worker. My mother, the daughter of a well-off farmer, made the transition from being the fiancée of a young man completing his medical studies who she'd met at the *lycée* to becoming a mill worker after arriving in England from the displaced persons camp. After twelve years of almost full-time motherhood she began a nursing career from scratch. My parents' relationship was one in which warmth and affection plastered the cracks of class differences; we were surely the only family in our working-class neighbourhood whose dog was pretentiously named 'Rigoletto' after my mother's favourite opera. My dad always accepted his 'place in life', fitting in with that strong English tradition; he felt favoured to enjoy the material benefits of post-war economic prosperity which were in sharp contrast to a hungry childhood. He was grateful; he felt that England afforded him the possibility of offering more to his children than he could have if he had remained in Poland. My mother, on the contrary, had fallen in status, lost her language, her culture, her place in the community; what she gained was an escape from political extremes.

I was constantly reminded of my dad by the men in rural Mozambique who were part of my daily working life. In 1977, when I'd begun working in agricultural cooperatives in Gaza province, Ruth First, then the research director at the University of Eduardo Mondlane's Centre for African Studies (CEA), asked me if I could help with the data analysis of the questionnaires that students were bringing back from Inhambane province. This was the CEA Mozambican Miner Project, later written up by Ruth in a book called *Black Gold.** The response of the South African regime to Mozambican independence was to cut the number of workers recruited by the Witwatersrand Native Labour Association ('Wenela'). The reduction in income transfers from South Africa was strangling a rural economy that had evolved on the basis of these transfers. What would happen to the artisans who built, weaved and thatched – that is, were paid to do the things that the absentee worker

*Ruth First, *Black Gold: The Mozambican Miner*, 1983.

had not been there to do. Now the workers were back, unemployed, and there was no money to pay anyone to do anything.

The CEA wanted to design a skills recognition and registration system. It advocated, in policy terms, that FRELIMO* needed to consider an industrialisation project that would use the skills of the returned migrants. Failure to do so might have serious social consequences. Indeed, it has been argued that a few years later RENAMO,[†] the opposition to FRELIMO, found it easy to recruit its members in the three southern provinces whose social fabric had most fallen apart due to economic decline.

The CEA work gave me a more analytical class consciousness. The questionnaire analysis meant filling in data columns, recording the information on ownership of means of production: 'Do you have hoes, how many? Oxen? How many? A tractor? Do you hire labour? How many contracts have you done on the mines in South Africa? What was your worker classification on the mines?' In the end we categorised families as poor peasants, middle peasants and rich peasants (kulaks) and debated the worker peasant class formation. Do men revert to peasant consciousness in their rural homes? How deeply changed are they by industrial experience?

The following year, 1978, I visited my parents and asked them questions about their lives in Poland and Czechoslovakia. How much land did they have? What animals and machinery did they own? Did they hire labour? As children, did they have to work on the farm? My father's answers classifed his family as 'poor peasants'. He was the youngest of fourteen. They did not have enough land to support the family; his brothers and sisters were hired out at harvest time to bring in extra money. Their house was a modest peasant home, a packed earth floor covered with wood shavings. The eating utensils were wooden, and the children slept on straw covered with canvas sheets. Cabbage with potato was the staple diet with a bit of meat on occasion, and potatoes in sour milk for supper in summer. I learnt that my grandfather also fished; he sold the bigger fish and brought home the small spiny ones. I understood then my father's refusal to eat fish that had not been filleted – the bones were a reminder of childhood poverty.

The farm that my mother grew up on was one of the largest in the district, and when she speaks of her childhood the power of property, who married who, who brought what land with them into the family

*Frente de Libertaçao de Moçambique.
[†]Resistencia Nacional Moçambicana.

on marriage, features strongly. There were two big houses built side by side; her grandparents lived in one and her parents and their seven children in the other. The two-storey stone house was well furnished, the yellow block-printed wallpaper that she remembered in her grandmother's sitting room still hangs in what today is a ruin of a house. There were shelves of books, polished wooden floors covered with patterned rugs. My mother told of cherry wood being cut and stored in the attic, ready to make the furniture that would be part of her dowry. There was an out-building that housed the tractor and implements. Up to thirty workers were hired at harvesting time. A tractor in the 1930s! – that confirmed for me my mother's kulak status.

My mother's work was to help bake the bread to feed the workers. 'On Saturdays we baked many loaves – rye, not wheat. To start the leavening we used a piece of dough which we had kept in an oiled cloth from the time before. We had big wooden vats to mix the dough. We shaped the loaves and left them to rise in wicker baskets.' When I asked what she ate as a child, she said: 'Barley porridge in the mornings, we called it *kasha*. At lunchtime we had our main meal; there was always potatoes, vegetables and meat – either salami or cured pork. Supper was a "junket" of stewed apples or plums with milk or cream. We did sweet-baking for special occasions, like apple strudel with raisins – that was before the war. But soon after the war started there was nothing like raisins available any more; the shops in Pribor were cleared out in a matter of weeks.' Later I asked why I couldn't find Pribor in my atlas. 'That was our Czech name for the town,' she replied. 'After Hitler came many towns were given German names.'

So it was only at the age of twenty-four, and because of the research on the Mozambicans who had worked on South African mines, that I had the curiosity to ask my parents these questions. It was the first time that I took real measure of the huge differences in their upbringing. 'Awesome', as my children would say; I am awed by the impact of levelling caused by war and migration.

It made me think of how tenuous life's circumstances are, how one should never take anything for granted, because events can happen beyond one's control that can change everything from one day to the next.

Work and motherhood

My mother would not differentiate household tasks between boys and girls. She distributed chores equally. My brothers and I shared cooking, cleaning and ironing. She'd grown up with an elder brother and four younger brothers and what she hated most as a young girl was ironing one shirt after another, endlessly. She decided I would not suffer the same fate, and insisted on domestic literacy for everyone; it was very poor training for me in later life when I had to come to terms with the fact that most men have a low level of domestic skills.

My mother had a part-time job even after my elder brother was born but she suffered from ill health and after my birth she didn't return to factory work. I have more romantic 'mother-at-home-making-jam' memories than my two siblings. But after my younger brother started school my mother began to fret. She'd lose her temper if you annoyed her – I mean, *really* lose her temper. You had to be careful to duck a flying plate if you really pushed her over her limit. She felt confined and was tired of the family always being short of money.

In the early sixties the British government advertised a process of equivalency tests for people whose education had been interrupted by the war. If you passed the exams there were professional training opportunities; for women the chance was to begin a nursing career. My mother told my father that she'd like to try for the exam. 'Why can't you go back to the mill like everybody else?' he asked. 'If you take up nursing the hours are unsociable, three months' night duty a year, as well as the studying. You won't be home in the evenings. We won't have holidays at the same time.'

My mother said that she needed to do something that made her use her head, otherwise she would go mad. She was bright. Her father had supported her efforts to go to *lycée* and stood up for her when her own mother had argued against it – 'What does the girl need to go to *lycée* for when she's going to be a farmer's wife?'

We lost our mother as we'd known her when she passed the exam. She worked 'earlies' (7 am to 4 pm) or 'lates' (4 pm to 11 pm), and when she was at home in the evening she was often studying. She still sewed, ironed and mended, but at night when we were asleep. My younger brother says it's my father that he remembers as being at home for us. It's true that it's my father who watched us at the athletics track. It's my father who always knew if we were upset about something that had happened at school because he was home in the evening. It didn't matter how hard my mother tried, the irregular hours really cut her part in family life.

My father loved my mother and knew he'd married out of his class. He was handsome. She was very attractive. He felt simple and uneducated beside her, and was amazed that she, with her cultured upbringing and airs and graces, had fallen in love with him. I've always thought that's why he acquiesced to her taking up nursing. If she hadn't taken up a profession he would have lost her in a different way; she would have resented factory work so much that it would have destroyed them. It wasn't easy for him. As a student nurse my mother earned little. 'Your father earns the bread, and I earn the jam,' she used to say proudly when we enjoyed the extras that her salary afforded us. But twenty years later my mother was in charge of a small hospital earning a salary far more than my father's wages. This was hard for my father to swallow. One had a sense of him being proud of his wife, and yet his own pride was dented; the male ethos about being the breadwinner in those small northern industrial towns runs deep. There was something stoic about my father's acceptance of the way things turned out in his marriage.

We resented our mother working as a nurse. If she'd had a job in the factory or as a shop assistant that would have been acceptable. I was envious of my best friend whose mother finished work at 4 pm, and who had her family's supper on the table an hour later. I wanted a mother like that. I didn't want to be a latchkey child, as those school-children who unlocked the doors to let themselves into their empty homes were called. I wanted my mother to be there.

As an angry teenager I vowed that if and when I were to be married and had children I would find work such as teaching, so that I would be at home in the evening and during the school holidays. As a young woman in my twenties, in a different frame of mind, I had to revisit this earlier resolve. My mother's pursuit of equality within a relationship had rubbed off on me. She'd also made me realise that there was something about choosing satisfying work that was more important than getting a job just to earn money.

It was really only at university, with exposure to the thinking of the women's movement, that I came to terms with my mother's decision to want a profession. I asked her why she hadn't talked to us as children to explain her feelings, instead of leaving us resentful with our lack of understanding, but she sighed and said her generation didn't talk to their children in the way we now tried to with ours. And then she said something that stuck with me: 'Remember that your children grow up and leave you,' she said. 'Sometimes you do something for yourself because you feel you have to. It may not be in the best interests of your children.'

Face to face with colonialism

When I finished secondary school in 1972 I opted for a year out. I had passed my 'A' levels, which qualified me for a university place. Affordability was not an issue; post-war Britain provided grants for tertiary studies. I'd started the 'year off' as a naïve school-leaver simply wanting to take a break before starting a university course of English literature and philosophy. My mind took a pounding during that year. So many concepts that I'd grown up accepting were challenged, one after the other, taking knocks like skittles in a bowling alley.

As I hadn't been especially interested in earning money, I had applied to do voluntary work through the Voluntary Service Overseas (VSO) organisation. Their offer of a year in Zambia as an assistant teacher at Lwitikila Mission was gratefully accepted. I shared a house with Mary, a fiery, red-haired, independent-minded agronomist. She had also been brought up as Roman Catholic near Birmingham, but the red hair was the sign of her Irish ancestry peeking through. My housemate had already been teaching there a year; she was a graduate from Reading University. She was sociable and welcoming to hitch-hikers passing through (some of them Vietnam war-resisters), who were glad to spend a few days off the road, in sight of beautiful mountains, enjoying clean water, food, books, music and conversation. I'd never thought of questioning the 'rightness' of the American involvement in Vietnam before.

But more immediately, I was being challenged within the community. On Wednesday afternoons I joined the bicycle brigade 'literacy group' that rode out to nearby villages. We sat on straw mats or low carved wooden stools under the cool eaves of the huts, going over the literacy materials prepared by the Zambian Department of Education. Many of the words referred to everyday items: the Chitenge wrap-around cloth, oil, sugar. One day an old woman asked me: 'And when is Independence going to finish?' She wasn't a subversive, she was simply reflecting on the fact that things were cheaper in the old colonial days. But she made me think about changing governments and the material differences that are felt by people who are at a level of poverty where the pride of independence doesn't compensate.

Some of my new friends made me question the content of the teaching material. Shane, the son of an Australian sheep farmer, taught at the secondary school for boys in the nearby town of Mpika. His two-year stint was part of a Commonwealth deal; many non-African Commonwealth students would complete their postgraduate teaching diploma at the University of Zambia, and then be allocated to teach for a minimum of two years in a secondary school. This was part of the Commonwealth contribution to solving the problem of shortage of national secondary schoolteachers after so many decades of colonial rule.

But Shane objected to quite a lot of the content of the curriculum. In the second-year English lessons I was entrusted to give, we were covering abridged versions of the classics – *Lorna Doone*, *Jane Eyre* and so on.

'So how do you think the kids relate to these stories? When they say here that the person knelt and she placed a sword on his shoulder and she knighted him, what do you think they make of it?' He would edit materials or even bunk the teaching of certain lessons.

'The kids have exams to pass,' I protested. But his questioning of the colonial content struck a chord. What was then just a gut reaction that he was right later took on more substance when I was at university and reading the works of Franz Fanon, Amilcar Cabral, Walter Rodney and later Edward Said.

And then there were the 'kids', the pupils. Many of the girls doing O-levels were in fact young women, older and more mature than I. They'd started school quite late, at seven or eight years old. And their schooling was sometimes interrupted. They were 'only girls' and the affordability of their schooling often took second place to that of their brothers. In the senior forms, many were already nineteen or twenty years old. The Form Fives were given an essay topic: 'Who do I want to be like when I grow up?' One of them wrote a piece: 'When I grow up I want to be like Angela Davis . . .' My housemate Mary came home enthusing about what a good essay it was. I was humbled. Firstly, I had to ask who Angela Davis was. Secondly, I had to acknowledge that Florence Chilanga in the back of beyond at this missionary school in Zambia knew much more about what was happening in the big wide world than I did. As a volunteer teacher I really didn't have much to offer – those 'kids' could leave me behind any day.

Losing religion; discovering spirituality

The mission station, run by the order of White Brothers and Sisters, had a huge church in the grounds with spires and stained glass windows, ready to host the converts in the community. It was quite a contrast to the humble surroundings of what is a relatively poor agricultural area; the Bemba men went off to the mines on the Copperbelt leaving the women and children to cultivate food crops. The school history department had a teacher with an unusual interest in Bemba culture, and she was supported by a Father Corbeil who had collected material for decades. There were two 'museum' rooms in the form of traditional rondavels in which the artefacts Corbeil had collected were displayed with the catalogued descriptions of their use. Perhaps it was his influence which resulted in a more than ordinary interest in and respect for African culture among the teachers at the school.

One day the girls organised a presentation of dances in the school's outdoor amphitheatre. Before each dance they told the story of its time and place in the planting or harvesting seasons, or in the life cycle of boys and girls growing up and celebrating puberty. Yes, a 'display' of such dances takes them out of their ceremonial time and place. They were beautiful and you could watch as if in a trance, a voyeur into someone else's culture. I'm thankful I had that chance to be let inside; it opened my mind. In my last two years at school I'd felt queasy with the arrogance of Catholicism – that it purports to be the 'one, true, holy and apostolic church'. As schoolchildren we were made to pray for misguided Christians like the Anglicans, that one day they might see the light and join us Catholics again. But now my queasiness took on another dimension: in the face of such obvious African spirituality, why did missionaries think that their religion was superior and that they were right to seek 'conversions'? I gained respect for another culture and spirituality, but lost it for the religion that had moulded me. It was that year, on the mission station, that I stopped going to church. It took me years to become accepting of the sustenance that so many people draw from the daily practice of their faith.

When I returned to England I was invited to have tea with the teacher who had most nurtured me as a secondary school pupil. She had given three of us extra lessons for what was referred to as 'Special English', a course set at a higher level than the A-level university qualifying exam, intended to benefit those who were considering studying English at university. I anticipated the reunion somewhat nervously. I was going to tell her that I would no longer be studying English at university; the year away had made me change my mind. I explained to her that I thought I might want to return to Africa, but if I were to do so, I would prefer to have a more practical skill to offer. She was deeply Christian. After listening to me she commented: 'First we must feed the bodies, only then can we feed the minds.' I was relieved that there was no expression of anger, regret or disappointment, but her words sank like a stone. I'd moved away from her world. The *raison d'être* of her life and logic was informed by a proselytising Christianity that African spirituality had taught me was unacceptable.

Racism: the South African wake-up call

Towards the end of that year which marked the real transition from schoolgirl to adulthood, I had to decide about the journey back to England to start my university studies. I sat on the veranda of the Mpika rest-house, listening to the 'Gumba-Gumba' juke box, drinking beer, comfortably mingling with a mixed-race group of people. I watched the sun go down over the bush; an indigo sky pierced with stars quickly replaced the evening orange. I thought about the two offers from VSO – a direct flight from Lusaka to London, or a ticket on the *Windsor Castle* from Cape Town to Southampton. I couldn't bear the idea of a dramatic transition. If I were to fly, within twenty-four hours I would switch from the wide warm African landscape and come in to land at Heathrow airport looking over concrete suburbia dotted with bits of wet green and blanketed in cold grey light. I opted for the Cape Town ticket.

I had to fly from Lusaka to Johannesburg's then Jan Smuts airport. The British Council prohibited their VSO volunteers from travelling overland through Zimbabwe, which was then still called Rhodesia, because there was 'trouble' there. I knew nothing about South Africa, really nothing. I simply wanted to go home the long way round and have ten days on a ship to create a transition time. I'd kept up correspondence with two girls who I'd met on the VSO orientation course and we decided we'd travel together. I went along with their suggestion that we catch a train from Johannesburg to Durban and then hitch-hike along the 'garden route' to Cape Town. The suggestion meant nothing to me. Mpika with its four grocery shops, its prison, post office and petrol pump was not exactly the place to look for tourist brochures.

My journey through South Africa is remembered as a series of shocks.

The first shock is seeing Johannesburg from the air as we come in to land. Here I am, the young woman who'd rejected the idea of a direct flight from Zambia's capital to London, who so badly wanted a transition journey. Yet I am now staring at a huge city with tall buildings and industrial suburbia full of sandy-coloured mine dumps. I'd been to Blantyre, Dar Es Salaam, Lusaka, Mombasa and Nairobi – I thought I knew what African cities looked like. I am wrong.

My second shock is inside the airport. I need the toilet. I look for the female signs and go to the door of the first one I see. An attendant stops me. 'No,' she says, 'these toilets are not for white women, only black women, you have to go to those over there.' So strange. Who thought up this system? I've grown up with different schools for different religions but, after that, if you need to use public amenities, I'm used to the same deal for everyone!

The third shock is Johannesburg railway station and the train that is standing ready to leave for Durban. It doesn't just have signs for first class and second class, but also has signs about black and white. This is weird; there seems to be some twisted thinking around here that I can't fathom. I'm used to class differences; those who have money travel 'posh' and those who are ordinary travel second-class. I'm used to being second-class along with everyone else in my mixed neighbourhood of English, Irish, Pakistanis and Eastern Europeans.

My fourth shock is the residence for young women in Durban. My friends told me that we were booked into a type of young women's hostel. I'm used to the European youth hostels – a clean bunk bed for the night. The Durban hostel, I discover, is more like a residence for young *boere meisies* (farmers' daughters) who are doing secretarial or other studies in town. We arrive and cause a stir; I guess we look different. We are three young women, each of us carrying a rucksack and a rolled-up sleeping bag.

There is a pleasant dining room with long tables. We take our trays and queue for our food. Our table becomes surrounded by inquisitive young women.

'Where have you come from?'

'Zambia.'

'What have you been doing there?'

'Teaching.'

'Who've you been teaching?'

'Schoolchildren.'

'What kind of schoolchildren?'

'Secondary school children.'

'No, but what *kind* of schoolchildren?'

'What do you mean, what *kind* of children?'

'White kids or *kaffir* kids?'

It is the first time in my life that I recall hearing the word *kaffir*. We calmly explain that we have been working at mission schools and that the schoolchildren were black. The next mealtime we find ourselves isolated. I guess we were labelled as – what will be another new word for me – *kaffirboeties*. I am shocked to the core. I try to work out why I should be so shaken; it's not as though my childhood was lacking in the experience of bigotry. I can remember incidents of 'Paki-bashing' being reported in the local newspaper when I was a teenager, so why should the racism be such a shock to me? I think it is because of how sharply it contrasts with the relaxed racial environment that I have just left. Perhaps it is because they are young people, my own age, and that especially after the 'flower-power' sixties I have expectations that young people are more flexible and less prejudiced than older ones. This incident proves not to be the only time I hear the word *kaffir* spoken, and the next time is to be all the more shocking.

My fifth shock happens while travelling on the garden route. We leave Durban and plan to take several days hitch-hiking to Cape Town.

Our ground rules are that we will not split up. We also have large rucksacks. This means that we tend to get lifts from lone businessmen who are driving big Mercedes or BMWs, hardly a cross-sectional sample of South Africans. One particular lift, however, is from a different kind of lone male, a white policeman. He picks us up outside East London and drops us in Port Elizabeth. In a guttural Afrikaans-accented voice he says: 'So you're coming from Zambia, hey? Black bastard *kaffir* Kaunda! Give me a gun and a chance and I'd shoot him any day.' My convent upbringing projected policemen as 'good' citizens who work to maintain peace, law and order. I am shattered.

My last shock is the Cape Town Natural History Museum. I stare at the models and display of artefacts. In contrast to the humble but deeply respectful Bemba museum in Mpika, this Cape Town museum denigrates the lives of those referred to as *hottentots* and *bantu*, placing people among the wildlife.

I'd had enough. I wanted out. I could not wait for the days to pass until the boat left. I didn't want to enjoy the beauty. I could not seem to be able to. Everything was too interfered with by the ugliness of what was in people's heads: greediness and a racism that had the stamp of government approval. And there was an apparent oblivion to the ugliness. The inhumanity and unfair division of the spoils seemed to be accepted without question by the whites. I was not exactly meeting anyone who could tell me otherwise, at least not anyone who might speak of feeling differently with a stranger who's just passing through.

On the boat my head spun round and round. Zambia had prodded an awareness and respect for a different culture and set of values and South Africa was a dreadful way to end a year of journeying. Maybe I would want to go back and work in another African country – but next time I would make sure I had some real skills to contribute. At some moment in those next ten days, as I lay in the narrow bunk of a cabin on the *Windsor Castle* cruise-liner, I resolved to scrap the idea of studying literature and philosophy and to switch to agriculture. I preferred to forget South Africa. I'd never want to go there again. But now that I had been disturbed I wanted to know more. I read books. I went to anti-apartheid meetings at Reading University. I learnt about other anti-colonial struggles. I donated blood for freedom fighters. Eventually, I joined a solidarity group called Committee for Freedom for Mozambique, Angola and Guinea-Bissau.

One Sunday evening after a weekend away, I sat on the Paddington to

Reading train engrossed in the book *Cry, the Beloved Country*. A man greeted me as we arrived in Reading and converged at the exit of the same carriage. He said he recognised me from the university squash courts and did I want a game? And, by the by, what did I think of the book I was reading? He was a good-looking guy in a Paul Newman sort of way, with a judo black belt. I was to learn that he was in his early thirties, a shop steward of the branch of the union at the place where he worked. His continuing involvement in politics was especially appealing; I was surrounded by students whose interest was fleeting and dilettante.

He was also the first progressive white South African that I'd met. Ed Wethli's family connections with anti-apartheid activities led to his leaving the country in 1968 after a tangle with the police. He was a poultry specialist and worked on one of the university's research farms. We met just before the 25 April coup in Portugal in 1974. The next year we got married. In 1976 we packed tea chests with books and a few belongings and left for Mozambique. We were in love and heady with excitement that change in Southern Africa was about to speed up. I was twenty-two years old.

Seven years later I walked on the beach in Maputo reflecting on the time I had spent so far in Mozambique. It was 17 August 1983, a year to the day since the assassination of Ruth First. My life had become dominated by the pervasiveness of South Africa – both my working life and my personal life. The rural cooperative training centres that I'd worked in, alongside crèches, schools and health centres, were targets of attack by the Pretoria-backed RENAMO rebels. Joe Slovo, chief of staff of the African National Congress (ANC) liberation army, had us doing errands for his Special Operations sabotage units, mapping the sites of power stations, driving cars with weapons and money hidden behind door panels and other out-of-sight crevices. Ed and I both had British passports and could travel easily in and out of Swaziland and South Africa. Ruth First, who had been a mentor to me, now lay in the cemetery alongside other comrades massacred in 1981 in Matola by an apartheid hit squad. My husband and many of my friends were South African; every day of my life was affected in some small way by the liberation struggle. I resolved to join the ANC, if they'd have me. That day I typed up my application – as the wife of a South African I was eligible for membership. That day was decisive. I'd reached the point where I couldn't imagine living in England again. Southern Africa was home for now and one day – Joe always said 'within five years' – home would be South Africa.

Three years later, towards the end of 1986, now divorced with two young children, I walked along the Maputo beach once again. This time I was walking with Joe. I had a small pink file card in my jacket pocket – I still have it – on which there were two columns: one headed 'for' and the other 'against'. We were discussing my move to join him in Zambia, and whether or not we should get married. That day, once again, another life-shaping decision was made. And as a friend later wrote to me, not only was I to marry again, but also, as he put it, 'I hear you've tied your knot with South African history.'

Working lives

I can begin to see the influences that led to the shaping of my values, and the roots of my strong sentiments on different issues: class, race, religion, women's rights. The last is an issue that has surfaced over and over again. I've been told that I'm sharp in my criticisms of men; I feel it is a direct consequence of accumulated negative experiences that would be tedious to catalogue. Just one suffices as an illustration.

When I was waiting to hear if and when Ed and I were to work in Mozambique I applied to do a master's degree at Wageningen University. They turned me down without an interview. Later, when my degree examination results were out and I had an upper second class and best student award to my credit, I felt bold enough to enquire what their reasons for rejection had been. The man who spoke to me replied: 'But your application form said you were married. Perhaps then you might have become pregnant while studying.' I was indignant. On what basis were they to make this judgement? I would not have accepted a study place if I did not expect to be able to complete the course.

It was hard to accept that people have the power to make decisions that affect your destiny, that you have no control over their chauvinism and little recourse to challenge. It was a harsh welcome to the problems of shaping a career as a married woman, even before having children!

By the time I started the job as managing director of the Land Bank in 1997, twenty-one years into a working life, there was one major issue that consistently captured my attention. I was attentive to the environment people worked in, how work was organised, and the conditions of service and systems of pay for manual and professional workers. Environment, for me, was more than green and safety concerns – it was about how people relate to one another in the workplace; in Marxist terms, 'the relations of production'. It was my childhood observations of my father's work experience that sparked my initial interest.

My Polish peasant father had become a factory worker in England, but in the early years of my childhood he still toyed with the idea of taking a bond on a piece of land. In time he settled for his factory life. He joined the union and went round the factory collecting the union dues. He liked the sociability, and the 'commission' he earned gave him extra income, but in truth he was not a loyal trade unionist. He would hold forth at home, voicing his complaints during a 'work to rule' or a strike; quite often he did not agree with union tactics. He was always sceptical about going short on pay, or getting strike pay, in the hope of a pay hike that might not materialise. There were arguments among workers about whether it was better to be paid for the amount of time worked or for the quantity of work done, i.e. 'piecework'. My dad wanted to work fast and to be paid according to output. He reckoned he could earn more this way; he did not appreciate the trade union persuasions that this pay system led to a higher rate of industrial accidents.

His attitude changed somewhat after he was seriously injured at work. At the English Electric factory he and his friend John Plachta worked as semi-skilled 'slitters'. They worked on machines dealing with huge rolls of metal from which shapes were cut out for aircraft manufacture. The machines were old and wobbled; wooden padding needed to be placed 'just so' to keep the metal from sliding. Gloves were provided for workers handling rolls of steel, but they were short gloves to the wrists only. One day a sheet of metal buckled and came off the rollers; my father tried to stop it but the metal sheet veered towards him, slipped out of his gloved grasp, and cut his arms half-way between his wrists and the insides of his elbows. The cuts were severe, with much loss of blood and damaged nerves. He was off work for several weeks and we felt the pinch of the loss of regular overtime pay that was built into our family budget. The union complained about safety conditions; long gloves became standard issue, and due to union efforts my father was eventually granted some workman's compensation.

Although my dad accepted his lot, it was hard for his children to watch what happened to him during his working life. He would put 'efficiency' ideas into the suggestion box at the factory and proudly receive the miserly five pounds that the owners awarded for those suggestions that were taken up. For a few pounds' 'reward' he may well have increased company profits by thousands. He should have been an engineer. My mother still has the press that he designed and had made up in the factory workshop. It is ingenious and incorporated a lid that can be lowered by turning it round a central screw. It is ideally suited to the making of sauerkraut – that early winter activity of pickling cabbages in true Eastern

European tradition that happened every year throughout my childhood.

For many years my father had pride in his work. His job as a slitter demanded hand-setting of blades and the wastage levels depended on team precision. My dad's team were proud of their low wastage levels. This pride took the most terrible knock when a new management changed the teams and it was no longer possible for him to achieve the same targets with the new combination of personnel. His personal pride suffered in doing a job less well than before, but the biggest blow was the realisation that the bosses didn't really care. As long as wastage was below 7 per cent it didn't matter that my dad's team achieved 6,5 per cent as opposed to the one to two per cent that had been their earlier norm. My dad felt devalued. Not only had his pride in the quality of his team's work been taken away, but the lack of respect shown by management further devalued his own sense of self-worth.

There was worse to come. In his early fifties he was made redundant. The Wilson government cancelled contracts for fighter planes and the development of the TSR2 supersonic jet fighter which would have secured local jobs was aborted. After that, although there was some change to product line in the factory, it was downhill all the way in terms of cut-backs to the workforce. No one wanted a semi-skilled immigrant factory worker topping fifty. He considered himself lucky to get a job eventually as a storeman at Walker's Steel. He hated every day of the few years he spent there. The warehouses were bleak and cold. He missed the cama-raderie of his team mates from the machine-work days. He fretted and his unhappiness resulted in angina, early retirement and a relatively young death.

I promised myself that if ever I was given the opportunity, what would matter to me would be to make sure that conditions existed for people to develop to the best of their potential. It's always felt as though it's something that I owed to my father – to make sure that people, if they wanted, might have the chances that he didn't.

It influenced the way I saw things in Mozambique and what I put my energies into. My first job as a newly qualified agricultural economist in 1976 was to join the state farm department's planning team. I was unable to accept a top-down planning approach that ignored the practical knowledge that workers had to offer. I hated the time I worked as a state farm planner – I lasted less than a year. Later, as a university researcher, I wrote up the interviews with state farm workers in Tete province on the Mozambique-Malawi border: 'We know that potatoes are not going to grow in this lower field. It gets too wet. But no one listens to us. So we'll plant and get paid, but there won't be any harvest.'

I was rescued by a Mozambican who'd quietly noted my unhappiness and offered me a transfer to the agricultural cooperative department that he was in charge of. I had four years of the most satisfying work imaginable. First, I was given the chance to develop a simplified accounting system, the learning of which was to be accessible to people in cooperatives who were just finishing literacy courses. My second task was to develop a planning process which started from the principle that those doing the work have knowledge that must be used in the planning process; only the cooperative members themselves could decide what work norms they would use for daily planting, weeding and harvesting tasks. Failure to use self-determined norms had earlier resulted in economic failure. The district office would send tractors to plough up the eighty hectares of land to be planted with rice (the quota prescribed in fulfilment of a national plan), only sixty were weeded and still fewer were harvested – but the overhead costs were for eighty.

The quest for a simplified accounting system was provoked by my boss's dissatisfaction with the Bulgarian bureaucratic control approach. The Bulgarians in charge of technical assistance in Gaza province insisted on a three-tier bureaucratic system – cooperative, district office, and provincial headquarters. The cooperative members were merely expected to fill in dockets or receipts in a minimum of four copies. The original copy went to the buyer or seller, one stayed on site in the cooperative, one went to the district office, and one to head office in the provincial capital where a chief accountant did the real accounting and final reconciliation of figures.

I was committed to the idea that each cooperative would have a group of members who understood their own accounts. I designed and piloted a step-by-step, learn-as-you-go system, training six people in each cooperative. We began with school exercise books but eventually achieved the competence to use the conventional ledger. My motivation was double-edged. There was the interest in people being in charge of their own affairs and understanding their own accounts. But the quest to create a group who had shared knowledge was also an insurance attempt to make rips-offs more difficult. There were too many stories about the corruption that had harmed many of the Ujamaa cooperatives in Tanzania a decade or more earlier.

My commitment to an accounting system that empowered people got me into trouble with the Bulgarians. They mounted a campaign against the step-by-step approach. They argued that the system did not offer adequate controls; and, importantly, the state would not be in full possession of information. They were true products of Eastern

European style socialism. My sense was that the real reason was different, the truth of the matter was that they were protecting their jobs and their status. The new approach, if generally adopted, meant that the role of senior accountants would change to a training and support function; the role of masters over subordinates would be redundant.

The Bulgarian technicians played dirty, even suggesting 'technical incompetence' in the design of the new system. Surely they, white-haired men in their fifties with thirty years' experience, knew better than this young woman? An 'experts' meeting was called, involving bankers from the People's Development Bank. It was a stressful experience. The meeting would, of course, be conducted in Portuguese. My husband Ed told me that I began to rehearse my presentation in Portuguese in my sleep, desperate to be articulate in a language which was not my mother tongue. The simple system withstood the test of scrutiny – but face-saving was required for the maintenance of international relations and technical assistance agreements. The step-by-step approach began to be taught in eight of Mozambique's nine provinces; Gaza – the province which was the focus of the Bulgarian technical assistance programme – maintained the bureaucratic disempowering process.

There were times I felt ashamed to be a member of the elite national team and the authoritarian zeal which it was sometimes party to. One particular occasion burns in my memory. Nampula province was 'on my beat' of national oversight responsibility. Early one grey drizzly morning, I travelled with the district extension officer to visit Samora Machel Cooperative. Our land rover lurched into the village and came to a halt beside the co-op cotton field that needed weeding. There was no one there – it was raining after all. The technician started up the vehicle again and drove round the village, jumping out, banging on doors and shouting 'Today, today is the day for collective work. *Venha ca*! Come out!' It still makes me shudder to think of it. The old power relationship of the district technician who, in colonial days, would have played his wage-earning role in ensuring forced cotton production, was being replayed. There was no connection with Marx's concept of 'transformation of relations of production' as taught to us every Saturday morning when, as state employees, we attended compulsory political education classes. There seemed little point in berating the man; at that point in time that was how he understood his job should be done. I returned to Maputo and, together with my colleagues, drew up a proposal for the training of district level cadres.

Over the years the weight of those experiences accumulated and influenced my receptiveness to stories told by his cousin Bella to my late husband Joe, in Lithuania in 1989. Every afternoon for a week we sat in a coffee house in the seaside resort of Palanga and they conversed in broken Yiddish, each reaching into the recesses of their childhood memory for a language they had not used for forty years. Some afternoons we were joined by her son Josef, who fortunately spoke English and patiently translated. She reflected on various mistakes she felt she had been party to as a loyal communist for more than half a century. She said the worst mistake was the lack of attention to the working conditions and the pay system. 'It didn't matter if you worked well or if you worked badly, you took home the same money.' She attributed to this mistake, more than any other, the manifest demotivation and economic decline of the Soviet Union.

This set of experiences probably resulted in my having an out of the ordinary respect for the place of work in people's lives. I made a pledge to myself to try to avoid the abuse of any authority entrusted to me, and a pledge to create possibilities where people could push their potential if that's what they wanted. Last, but not least, there was an emerging acknowledgement of the link between performance, pay and the importance of people feeling their contribution is appreciated.

An eclectic composite

Malala's question, 'What drives Ms Dolny?' and the 'Where are you coming from?' mantra set me off on a journey of retrospection that focused on identifying the roots of the values I held most dear and that would bear influence on the way I approached my job at the Land Bank. I consider myself to have been very fortunate in the range of experiences that life has offered me, and I'd like to think that I've sifted what I could out of them towards strengthening a composite, if eclectic, whole person.

When I was appointed as the new head of the Land Bank there was the usual flurry of interviews that occasion such events in this relatively small country of ours. Don Robertson did a 'Newsmaker of the Week' feature article in the *Sunday Times* under the heading 'Pragmatic "leftist" at the head of the Land Bank'.* Robertson noted the contributing influence of my family background. He wrote: 'Dolny's mother was a Czech and her father Polish so she grew up in a home both anti-fascist and anti-communist. She was brought up in England with subsequent exposure to non-democratic socialism in Mozambique and Eastern Europe, and she ended up with strong criticisms but also admiration

---

*Don Robertson, *Sunday Times*, May 1997.

for the elements of different economies.' He reports me as saying: 'So, for example, I think incentive systems are essential, but so is redistribution and democratisation and I remain, at heart, essentially committed to democratic socialism.'

Robertson questioned me on the fears expressed by senior executives of the agricultural industry about the continuity of the Land Bank's business with regard to white farmers, who also accused me of having socialist ideals. I responded: 'They obviously feel threatened because I have a leftist background. I can assure them, though, that I am a pragmatist, and I will take the best from the capitalist world and the best from the socialist world.'

The journey of taking stock of 'Where are you coming from?' has been intriguing. I did so many things and took so many personal decisions instinctively rather than consciously locating the pulse of what was driving me. It's only now that I'm standing back and recalling the events that I consider to have influenced me to the extent that I think of them as 'defining moments'. A sociologist friend comments: 'You had this marginalised immigrant upbringing, and a rooted class con-sciousness. Working in Mozambique meant you engaged with people like Ruth First and Joe Slovo, and were exposed to people who had extraordinary social commitment. Joining the South African political struggle was an inclusive act; you became a participant.'

It's strange listening to or reading someone else's packaging of oneself. But I guess the feeling of being a participant was very true and was valued by me. The ANC effort seemed to subjugate the ugliness of race, ethnicity, religious and class difference. Once I was an official member of the ANC what I liked best was my right to attend an ordinary members' meeting – and given my dislike of most political meetings, this says something about my gaining a sense of belonging that mattered more! What seemed to count in that exile period was the contribution you made towards a common goal irrespective of whether that offering was big or small: giving accommodation, undertaking courier tasks, clipping newspapers. Perhaps I had the luxury of naivety; but for me, whatever the fears, those were halcyon days, and they are warmly remembered.

TWO

FROM FREEDOM CHARTER TO COMPROMISE

Shaping a personal future

I spent a lot of time and effort working out what I could do in Lusaka when I moved there at the end of 1986. I was about to marry Joe Slovo, the chief of staff of Umkhonto we Sizwe, the military wing of the African National Congress. To my mind, he did not have a long life expectancy. The eighties were a period of serial assassinations as well as over-the-border raids into the Frontline States. Joe's wife, Ruth First, had been killed by a letter bomb in Mozambique. Joe Nqabi was killed by a car bomb in Harare. Dulcie September was killed in Paris. Joe happened to make me extraordinarily happy. For that all too rare experience of such intense joy, I was prepared to throw in my lot and make the most of whatever time came our way.

But I needed to 'be my own person'; it sounds so trite but it was true for me. I'd grown up with a very strong mother and left home at a time when feminism was on the ascendancy. I could have looked for employment in Zambia as an agricultural economist, but I had made my own political commitment when I joined the ANC in 1983. If anything happened to Joe, my life needed to be grounded. I needed to be doing something that was meaningful, that gave me my own reason for living in Lusaka, and that I would carry on doing whatever might happen.

I drew up a PhD research proposal after discussions with Pallo Jordan, head of the ANC research department, and with the advice of Harold Wolpe. Harold was Joe's lifelong friend and comrade, but at that stage I knew him only as the author of a work on 'The Articulation of Modes of Production'. It sounds so esoteric in retrospect, but those of us trying to understand what makes things tick in rural areas considered it a seminal work.

In selecting a topic for my PhD I wanted to look forward. I wanted to study something that might have application in a post-apartheid South Africa. We settled on the topic of land markets and land prices with a view to their relevance in a post-apartheid transition.

I'd lived for ten years in Mozambique where land was nationalised, and serious efforts had been made to organise state farms and cooperatives. Zambia, however, had nationalised land as a natural resource but provided for the marketable transfer of land improvements. I'd observed, with professional and political interest, the outcome of the Zimbabwe-UK Lancaster House talks that ended with Britain promising a significant monetary contribution towards land purchase for redistribution. The Lancaster House agreement envisaged a land reform process in which Zimbabwe's post-independence leaders would, as government, have the first option to buy land for redistribution as and when it came on to the market, and at prices determined by a 'willing seller, willing buyer' situation.

'A country that denies its history also denies its future' is a quote from Seretse Khama that I've heard in discussions with South African historian Luli Callinicos. The way she spoke made me understand the importance of delving into history when looking towards the future, and trying to work out the most appropriate strategies for moving forward. That was what I set out to do through my doctoral thesis. If I succeeded, so I thought at the start, then I might have something useful to offer in a new South Africa. What policies had been tried by government in the past to foster agricultural development, and for whose benefit? What worked, and if it did, why? And what hadn't worked, and for what reason?

The Zimbabwe settlement provoked my interest in the concept of market prices and the notion of a fair price. Where did prices come from? What influenced the changes – outside the extremes of war? After all, the land price of a battlefield falls to zero! More seriously, what effect, if any, do tariffs, subsidies and fixed price policies have on land prices and their movements over time?

In pursuit of a shared understanding

There was one more push in following my heart to Lusaka to live with Joe and begin my doctoral studies. The additional challenge would be to see if I could be part of getting the ANC to take land issues more seriously, from its top echelons down to its rank and file cadres.

During the ten years I lived in Mozambique countless ANC comrades had passed through the house; many of them stayed around for several days whilst in transit to either Swaziland or Lesotho. In all those years it was only ever Ebi Ebrahim who engaged in a serious discussion about the rural areas. Ebi was the only comrade who asked questions about Mozambique's post-colonial agricultural development and tried to relate it to South Africa's impending future.

Joe was one of the worst offenders. He more than once walked in on a heated discussion taking place at his home between myself, his wife Ruth and other colleagues from the Centre for African Studies. 'Talking fertilisers again,' he would say with the intention of being humorous rather than derogatory, but you couldn't capture his attention to engage him in the debate. His head was too full of maps and images of power stations, oil refineries and the logistics of smuggling weaponry over the border for sabotage attacks.

As head of the ANC's military Special Operations unit, his pre-occupation was with details such as the purchase of exactly the right fabric for Alma Vally, a South African dressmaker, to make up fake overalls to be worn by the comrades who would carry out the sabotage of the Koeberg nuclear power station. There was a worrying time factor. The plant was not yet operational and the ANC ethos that innocent civilians should not be harmed was strong; the sabotage had to take place before the plant was finished and activated. The fact that Joe once engaged in debates over the consequences of what was referred to as 'colonialism of a special type' belonged to his years of exile in London. In a Southern Africa that was in turmoil in the late seventies, the focus was on the seizure of power; you could remind him, to no avail, that more than one revolution had been compromised by a conservative peasantry.

The rank and file had even less interest in rural issues than Joe, if that were possible. Many comrades who transited through the house that Ed and I lived in on Rua M S Muthemba were township youths and they would use the word 'peasant' between themselves as a term of insult when they considered someone's behaviour uncouth or their way of thinking unsophisticated. Hence the challenge emerged: of the work to be done in Lusaka, I hoped to be part of an attempt to foster a different level of engagement and respect for rural issues and rural people.

After some months in Lusaka, when I'd found my feet and worked out the who's who and pecking order of my new environment, I tried to set up a reading group on land issues. It was a dismal failure. Less than a handful of people were interested in working their way through thirty-something pages of an academic paper and debating its relevance to post-apartheid policy formulation. It led, however, to the beginning of a friendship with Sahdhan Naidoo, the son of legal activist Phyllis Naidoo; he ran an ANC farm that each week provided a box of fresh produce to ANC households. I also got to know Bongi Njobe, who'd recently completed horticultural studies in Bulgaria but who preferred to work with the Women's Section of the ANC.

I was by now on the board of directors of a Canadian development agency and travelled to Canada three times a year for meetings. Marlene Green, a Dominican Canadian, put me in contact with a network of 'popular educators'. Several of them had worked in Latin America and were influenced by Paulo Freire's ideas on how people learn and how analysis informs a social change strategy. In Canada they worked with the trade union movement but one of their major clients was also government, as they specialised in running workshops on race issues in schools and in the workplace, much needed in the inner city of Toronto.

Many young comrades in Lusaka were despondent about the ANC's 'political education' approach. Like the reading group I'd started, the political study meetings were unsuccessful; they tended to be academic, dogmatic, and boring. A few like-minded young comrades got together and founded the Popular Education Working Group (PEWG) and wrote up a project to get funding for our training by the Canadians.

Sahdhan and I began to prepare a motivation for a workshop, run on popular education principles, as an alternative to the many academic seminars that were becoming fashionable.

We motivated that an ANC in-house workshop was much called for to channel the products of earlier international seminars and to examine their implications for future ANC research policy deliberation on rural issues. We lobbied and got Pallo Jordan's support. Furthermore, it was felt that an in-house workshop would allow broader participation between those involved in theory and those with practical experience.

Barb Thomas, a member of the Canadian popular education network, spent three days in Lusaka assisting us to design a workshop that intended to accomplish the following:

- analyse the status quo of power relations in the countryside;
- pinpoint the gaps in our knowledge and therefore identify the priorities for further research;
- identify the connections between our analysis and the effective mobil- isation strategies;
- develop a strategy to broaden the numbers of comrades engaged in the debate on rural issues.

We spent a great deal of time during the second half of 1989 fund-raising and organising. We raised enough money to bring together thirty people who were scattered in different countries. The dates were set – 5-9 February 1990 – and venue and travel bookings began.

Then something devastating happened. Sahdhan and Moss Mthunzi were gunned down on the farm. It seemed that there was a quarrel between comrades; one of them had reached for a gun. Some said Sahdhan was a hothead – it was not the work of an agent. But ten years later the Truth and Reconciliation Commission established otherwise – Sahdhan's killer applied for amnesty, revealing that the price tag per assassination was R2000 (worth some US$500 at the time).

I was faced with a dilemma. Sahdhan's death meant that now, more than before, I needed Bongi Njobe to make a commitment. She was ambivalent. The Women's Section was to hold a big conference in Amsterdam in late January 1990 and it was unclear whether she would return in time. Fortunately she did, and in the last week of January, beginning February, she joined the twenty comrades taking part in a five-day training session on popular education. The agricultural workshop would take place the following week, and the trainers were to remain to give us professional support.

It was an unforgettable week. The work was energising and spirits were high. Older comrades, like Regina Nzo, the wife of the ANC Secretary General, came alive in a way that we'd never seen before. We could now imagine her as the young woman involved in health education who had been drawn to politics.

On our last day of training, 2 February 1990, Sue Rabkin of the underground department arrived with a radio; later that morning F W de Klerk, the apartheid regime president, was to make a speech. It was difficult for us to focus our attention on the final training session – people were watching the clock. There are photos of the group crowded around Sue, listening intently, frustrated by the crackle of radio interference. The photos taken minutes later show faces of joy, euphoria, everyone hugging, and then dancing. De Klerk's announcement meant that we were 'unbanned'. We were going home. Exactly when we didn't know, but we were going.

'Breaking new ground'

The unbanning changed everything. It coloured everyone's discussions. It also gave the agricultural workshop an immediate, tangible relevance. People had discussed post-apartheid policies in the abstract for years; now everyone was asking themselves the questions: 'What will I be doing when I go home? What will the ANC be doing? What will be the outcome of negotiation discussions?'

Pallo's opening speech at the agricultural workshop expressed the many questions that flooded people's minds. As he began to talk people fell silent, listening attentively. He cut a tall striking figure, his trademark scent of patchouli drifted faintly over the conference room. There was always gravitas in his delivery. He was revered among comrades. His intellectual prowess was something they were proud of; the progressive intellectual debate had too long been dominated by whites. Pallo made people feel that, given the opportunities, black intellectuals would come into their own. He was also respected because he had survived some of the worst of the ANC's own abuse of its comrades. Someone had tried to label him a spy, and he'd spent time detained in a pit. He seemed to rise above harbouring any bitterness. He expected no special privileges as a member of the ANC's higher echelon. When I first met him in Lusaka he was living in spartan conditions in the building that housed the ANC's library in the suburb of Makene. All of this meant that comrades listened to him with a special pride.

> This workshop occurs at a moment in our country's history pregnant with possibilities and hope. It will be some time yet before we can fully measure the impact of the unbanning of the ANC, the South African Communist Party and other people's organisations. Despite this, one could confidently predict that, as with the political space created by the legalisation of the African trade unions, the restoration of legal status to these people's organisations offers us new opportunities for major advances, even if they do not lead to negotiations.
>
> It has perhaps become unfashionable in these times to speak of the seizure of power by the oppressed. Yet I would insist that this is a perspective that the National Liberation Movement cannot abandon. The seizure of power, freed of its more vulgar conceptions that invoke images of armed masses storming the Bastille or the Winter Palace, I would contend, remains valid even at a time when the prospect of a negotiated settlement appears more realistic than ever. I would submit also that, in the event that such negotiations succeed, the National Liberation Movement will be compelled to implement policies which entail the seizure of various economic assets, presently the monopoly of the dominant white group, regardless of the actual modalities of the transfer of power.
>
> It is our hope that this workshop will assist us in defining the shape and content of such policies in relation to the rural areas of our country. The majority of us come from the urban areas, which is where our movement has historically had its main base of support. Few of us are conversant with the rural areas of the country. We must stress that by

rural areas we refer not merely to the so-called Bantustans or homelands but also to the vast tracts of land in the Karoo, the Maize Triangle, in the Northwestern Cape, the vast sugar estates in Natal, the commercial orchards of the Transvaal and in the Hex River Valley.

One part of our workshop was dedicated to an analysis of social stratification in South Africa's rural areas; the intention was to use it as the basis on which to discuss the expectations of alliances between different social groups that would assist a progressive transition process. Pallo set the tone, confirming the importance of such an exercise by offering his own analysis of the characteristics of the rich, middle and poor peasantry of black South Africa.

Pallo is an inveterate historian, a symbiosis of training and disposition. He was at pains to point out that not only did many of us hail from an urban background, but also that rural struggles were often less frequently written about.

> History and historiography in class societies almost always focuses on the contributions made by the articulate sections of society who are able both to record their own actions and ensure that they pass into the store of human knowledge. When dealing with the masses in South Africa's rural areas, we are addressing the part played in the history of our country by the least articulate. Until recently, little was written on the struggles of the people in the rural areas. A recent collection of papers is titled 'Hidden Struggles', indicating how obscure these generally are. This often conveys the misleading impression of quiescence of the rural masses. With the exception of those instances when rural unrest has burst into revolt, urban dwellers rarely are concerned to record the struggles of rural people.

Pallo described the differing nature of rural struggles, giving the workshop participants more than they had bargained for in an opening address. He described the 'Jacquerie' – sporadic attacks on landlords; 'banditry' – acts of armed resistance romantically associated with Robin Hood and William Tell; and the 'Peasant War', of which the classic examples, as Pallo reminded us, were the peasant wars in Germany at the time of the Reformation and the Taiping Rebellion against the Manchus in nineteenth-century China. His purpose in inserting this historiography was to lead us to the following:

> All the major revolutions have to one degree or another incorporated some or all three of these elements of rural struggle. With the exception of the Russian Revolution, all revolutions that have occurred during this

century have been peasant wars. The transformation of South Africa will inevitably also involve the rural masses. We shall, as a movement, harness the energies of these masses to the extent to which we understand their needs and demands that a democratic dispensation will place on a post-apartheid government.

Pallo's specialisation and contribution to the theoretical writing informing political debate among the cadres of the Liberation Movement had focused on the national question. Again, the workshop participants were alerted to the import of that debate on the proceedings that were about to take place.

The notion of the national question being based on the land question was first employed by Karl Marx in relation to Ireland . . . As in South Africa, the dominant colonial power in Ireland shared the same territory as the colonised, distinguished not by race, but by religious affiliation. As in Ireland, so in South Africa, dispossession of their land was the cardinal national grievance which could give coherence to a revolutionary strategy.

Among our tasks during the next few days will be to examine whether this is still applicable in South Africa today. At a glance one may say that much has changed since . . . The majority of blacks are no longer peasants; the black working class has emerged as the most combative contingent among the forces of revolution; millions of blacks, formerly employed in the labour intensive commercial farming sector, have been displaced by mechanisation and dumped in impoverished rural townships; though it still has an emotional appeal, the land question has not in recent years been a rallying call to mass struggles.

He concluded with a reference to a relatively recent ANC position on the potential of the rural areas in conducting a people's war, as well as offering some reflections on the added complexities resulting from the complicity of some chiefs and bantustan bureaucracies with their apartheid masters:

Though the profile of the land question and the rural areas as sites of struggle has declined since the 1960s, as recently as 1985 the Commission on Strategy and Tactics at the Second National Consultative Conference in Kabwe (Zambia), noted the significance of the rural areas for a strategy of people's war. The accents in which we speak today may have altered slightly in view of recent developments, I would none the less contend that this is an option that cannot as yet be foreclosed.

A complicating factor in the solution of the land question is the role Pretoria has assigned to the chiefs and bantustan bureaucracies. Land, its

availability and the manner of its distribution are central concerns of the
African population of the bantustans. The conflictual relationship the
bantustan system has interposed between chiefs and their subjects under-
mines all efforts to forge unity among the disparate social and political
forces opposed to apartheid. Are the collaborationist chiefs deserving of
the allegiance of their subjects? Should this institution itself be retained
in a post-apartheid South Africa? What impact would the retention of
these people have on a future policy regarding the distribution of land?

The issue of struggle and its continuity must be the central focus of our
workshop. If today we can point to the prestige our movement enjoys,
both at home and abroad, this is the outcome of struggles, not least those
waged by people on the land. In the coming period it will be our strength
on the ground and our ability to wield it wisely that will determine whether
the promise of a peaceful transformation becomes a reality or an un-
realisable hope.

Before the next session began, we stood for two minutes in silence to
honour the memory of Sahdhan Naidoo, who would have been a co-
facilitator. We then directed our energies to complying with Pallo's
closing words: 'Comrades, let us get down to work!'*

Mapping the status quo

We wanted to create a common basis for discussion. We'd decided to
experiment with an approach of pooling the knowledge of the participants as an alternative to circulating an academic paper. We'd taped
together several sheets of flip chart paper and stuck them to a large
wall. Armed with felt-tipped pens we began to get people to draw what
they knew about South Africa's rural areas, black and white.

People's references to their family history quickly allowed us to put
land dispossession on the map. Although most participants came from
urban backgrounds, they had knowledge of what had happened to their
grandparents – the loss of land and the forced removals which were
compounded by population growth, causing ever more people to live,
impoverished, in the confines of a deteriorating land area. The conservationist attitude to black people keeping too many cattle seemed
outrageous. Was the question one of too many cattle, or was it rather
one of too little land? In a country where sixty thousand white farm
owners had access to eighty-seven per cent of the land while millions of

---

*African National Congress, 1990. 'Breaking New Ground', ANC Research
Department. 'A report on an in-house workshop on the political, economic and
social issues of South Africa's rural areas'. Lusaka, Zambia, 5-9 February 1990.

black households were crammed into the remaining thirteen per cent, it surely was not possible to question the logic that there was a need for redistribution.

A huge white octopus was drawn at the top right hand corner of the wall. This represented the white state, the powerhouse of decision making of the apartheid regime. Its tentacles reached down and its eyes looked over the smaller black octopus that it had spawned. The black octopus represented the bantustan administrations, run by rent-seeking groups of Judas Iscariots, ready to betray their own for the thirty pieces of silver offered by their white rulers. The chiefs were drawn in, close to the heart of the black octopus.

The picture mapped out for the black areas was bleak. People were arriving with their goods and chattels as a result of forced removals – just as in earlier decades sharecroppers had walked huge distances with their families and animals, their carts piled high with implements, looking for a white landlord who might enter into a deal with them. There were also people leaving the black areas: men looking for work on the mines, men and women looking for work on white farms or as domestic workers in white households. The spectre of black unemployment loomed large.

The black land area showed a woman, her back bent over a hoe. A man wearing a trilby represented the better-endowed landowner trying to making a go of a commercial farming business without having the same access to credit, transport, technical assistance and marketing deals as his white counterpart.

There was some discussion of the schemes set up by bantustan development corporations intended to increase the numbers of the rural bourgeoisie willing to collaborate with the apartheid state. There was scepticism about some of these schemes; there was emerging evidence of indebtedness among the farmers. Those who seemed to benefit most were the black bureaucrats and technicians.

The white farmer was operating under different conditions. Each tentacle of the white octopus was named as one of the components of a state apparatus set up to secure white economic success in contrast to black subjugation. There was the law, with its judiciary ensuring that legalised injustice prevailed in its racist application. The security forces were depicted as working hand in hand with justice. Participants placed a question mark next to the leg of the octopus representing the church. While the Dutch Reformed Church was seen as inextricably linked to the repressive regime, a powerful Christian dissent had begun to emerge. Beyers Naude, S'mangaliso Mkhatshwa, Frank Chikane and Allan Boesak were clergy well known for their opposition to the immorality of apartheid.

Another leg of the white octopus wrapped itself around banks and big business linked to multinational corporations. The role of the state in fostering Afrikaner big business has been well documented.* In recent years information has been revealed about the lengths that the state was prepared to go to in order to rescue Afrikaner private sector business when it got into trouble.

There was a similar nurturing of the white commercial farmers. The racism in differential support to white and black farmers was now more than a century old. White farmers were beneficiaries of credit, state provision of seeds, stock registration, dipping tanks and subsidies to erect stock fencing.

In the period after the Anglo-Boer War white farmers had lobbied the government about the conditions they faced for getting inputs and marketing their produce. They wanted government-financed central depots. The outcome was the parliamentary passing of the Cooperative Act which granted special rates for both financial and technical assistance to groups of farmers who formed a cooperative society.

After the depression of the late 1920s and early 1930s, price support schemes for whites only were introduced. Participants cited the 1937 Marketing Act which obliged farmers (quid pro quo for price certainty) to sell produce through a fixed channel at a fixed price. Control Boards were set up to manage this process: the Egg Marketing Board, the Meat Marketing Board, the Maize Marketing Board – there were twenty-one of them in their heyday in 1978. They acted as a safety net in a country which is mainly semi-arid and where intemperate weather conditions are a regular occurrence. These institutions also provided numerous employment opportunities – 'jobs for the boys' – for Afrikaner families.

Much of the farming appeared to be profitable only at enormous cost to the state. By 1970 state subsidies to agriculture devoured the lion's share of the national budget at R108-million – the estimated equivalent of R2,8-billion in the year 2000. The state exacted taxes and levies on the gold mining industry to cover this expenditure before they started borrowing internationally to finance their internal deficit, landing the country with a foreign debt that would be part of our apartheid legacy.

Marq de Villiers's book *White Tribe Dreaming* described the commitment to farming of the boer trekkers in the then Orange Free State. There was a mythology that 'the Afrikaner will never leave his land'. The figures of the Central Statistical Office (CSO) told otherwise. For my

---

*For instance, by Dan O'Meara in his book *Volkskapitalisme.*

doctoral thesis I'd spent hours poring over the CSO annual publication, 'Transfers of Rural Immovable Property'. White farm owners, at sixty thousand, numbered less than half of what they had been after the Second World War.

Tessa Marcus, one of the workshop participants, had done research for what was to become a book on the super-exploitation of workers on white farms.* She analysed the concentration of capital in farming; fifteen per cent of the farmers were responsible for more than eighty-five per cent of the value of produce. Some participants were familiar with the academic work of Mike de Klerk, a Cape Town based academic, that brought us up to date with the extent of indebtedness despite subsidies. Bankruptcy was on the increase. There had been 144 in 1985, 412 in 1987, and by 1988 as many as three thousand white farmers were on the verge of sequestration.

All in all, the picture of what we would inherit as the starting point for post-apartheid rural transformation did not look at all rosy. Black farming had largely been destroyed and bantustans had become labour reserves. How many people would want the chance to become farmers? How many would prefer jobs? We realised that there was a gap in our knowledge about trade and the terms of trade. It was expected that a post-apartheid South Africa would reintegrate into a world economy, but we didn't know enough to fathom the implications of this. The mapping exercise effectively pooled what different people in the room knew, and provided a basis for a discussion on research priorities.

Exploring transformation

We moved on to explore the socio-economic dynamics of post-apartheid transformation. To avoid abstract discussion we had designed a role-playing simulation exercise. It proved great fun in unleashing debate and amateur dramatics; it was also extremely sobering in identifying the obstacles to any radical transformation of the countryside. It was an eerie insight into trends that would play themselves out in the reality of our future.

We created a scenario set in the forthcoming transition period of negotiations and as a location chose the maize farming area of the then Western Transvaal. The details of farming conditions and employment outlined in Mike de Klerk's master's thesis[†] provided a gold mine of local level information. Participants received a fact sheet on the Western

---

*T Marcus, *Modernising Super Exploitation*, 1989.
[†]M de Klerk, 'Seasons that will never return', 1984.

Transvaal and were then divided into six groups, unequally in keeping with the demographics of the real world. Each group was given a definition of the role assigned to them, including details of particular concerns and interests. It was intended as a guide, not a limitation to the boundaries that might be explored by role play. Three people became representatives of the new transitional government. Three represented white farm owners. Three represented the banks. The large groups of participants represented, firstly, full-time workers, mainly men, with a divided outlook. Some emphasised the right of their ancestral claim; others did not want to own land – they wanted better wages and conditions of employment. Another group represented casual workers, mostly women and children who migrated seasonally from nearby Bophuthatswana. There was a disparate group of unemployed men and women with a varied history. Some had been removed from so-called 'black spot' areas where they had been freehold farmers. Others were farm workers made redundant with the advent of mechanisation, especially the use of combine harvesters.

There was also an input on negotiation strategies: coercive, exchange bargaining or a coalition approach. And then the drama was almost set to roll. The content of the preliminary briefing was drawn from the many future policy discussion papers circulating at the time. These ranged from internal documents produced by ANC comrades to those coming out of reformist policy think-tanks at the Development Bank of Southern Africa and a private sector financed unit called the Urban Foundation. The prelude to the briefing began:

> The new government has a policy of a mixed economy. It is also committed to the Freedom Charter, which states that 'our people have been robbed of their birthright to land', that 'the people shall share in the country's wealth' and that 'land shall be shared by those who work it'.*
>
> The government is considering a variety of possibilities of how production might be reorganised in the interest of people but there is also concern that there should be a transitional approach to change to ensure that production is maintained and that food supplies are secure. The farming options they are considering range from state farms, production cooperatives, family farms or the continuation of commercial farms with improved wages and living conditions.
>
> For the Western Transvaal region, the transitional government has received 'Recommendations' from the Ministry of Agriculture technicians that the investments made to achieve large-scale, high productivity farming should not be lost, but that some reorganisation of cropping patterns is advisable

---

*See R Suttner & J Cronin, 1986.

in the interests of improved land care. The technicians have also recommended that some of the less productive farms should be taken over
and the land redistributed to Africans who have farming skills and proven
entrepreneurial capacity.

The new government is highly sensitive to the regional differences and
is aware that any action it takes will be controversial. It is concerned not
to make decisions in Pretoria without consultation. The government has
initiated a process of consultations to take place in the different farming
regions to hear representations from different interest groups, and to present
its own concerns.

There will be a consultation meeting with all interested parties tonight.

Preparatory time leading up to the 'consultation meeting' was divided
into three sessions. Firstly, people focused on identifying their own group
interests, agreeing on priorities, identifying information needed, checking
what help might be available, and the resources required to back up a
position. The second session was dedicated to identifying the interests of
the other groups, a discussion on what their expected response might be,
and whether or not it might be wise to explore an alliance with another
group. This session provided some lively interaction. The last part was
the preparation of the position to be taken at the evening meeting; people
were late for supper as they fine-tuned the introductory speeches that
they would make as the prelude to an open debate.

People's energy electrified the air as we gathered in the conference
room that evening. The three persons representing the transitional government were in charge and had placed themselves up front and arranged
the room very formally. The spirits of people were visibly dampened as
the proceedings began. I can't remember which comrades were allocated
this role, all I remember is the shock we felt as they played it out. They
were high-handed, officious and full of self-importance. What took people
aback was that the briefing had indicated a 'consultation meeting', that
the new transitional government 'is concerned not to make decisions in
Pretoria without consultation'. Yet within minutes of opening the meeting,
before anyone else spoke, the officials announced 'measures' which it
'intends to implement immediately'. There was almost a walkout. The
'officials' had to back-track and calm people down and try to convince
them that, in spite of their opening remarks, they would listen seriously.

Each of the groups then spoke. They all added an impromptu preface
criticising the transitional government representatives as having said
they were coming to listen and yet they had opened the meeting
announcing a position. The presentations were interesting, surprising
in some ways, disappointing in others. We'd expected an alliance

between the farm worker and the seasonal worker; this didn't happen. There was a divide between those who wanted jobs and those who wanted land. What woke people up was the power of the bankers – even in this role play situation. They were smooth-talking and intimi-dating. 'We are YOUR bankers, and we have met to consider the new situation. We have noted the government's statement and will consult with our lawyers on the legal implications of the proposed measures.' They emphasised the importance of title, their belief in the free enterprise system and the importance of a 'market-orientated, hard-working community'. In the debate that followed they held their own – a clear indication of things to come.

It was February 1990. We were unbanned. Our leaders would now seriously start negotiating the conditions under which a transfer of power would take place. What had become clear was that the conditions of transfer would fiercely debate property rights. At the time of colonial conquest there had been a 'winner takes all' stand as celebrated in Van Riebeeck's report in 1660. When the Khoi people had resisted dis-possession, Van Riebeeck wrote:

> The reasons advanced by them . . . for making war upon us last year . . . that our people had done much injury, and also perhaps stolen some of their sheep and calves etc., in which there is also some truth . . . they had cause for revenge, they said, upon people who had come to take and occupy their land which had been their own in all ages . . . keeping them off the ground upon which they had been accustomed to depasture their cattle . . . we were at length compelled to say that they had entirely forfeited that right, through the war that they had waged against us, and that we were not inclined to restore it, as it had now become the property of the Company by the sword and by the laws of war.*

The ANC and its liberation movement partners were not, however, regaining power as the result of a victory 'by the sword and by the laws of war'. It was therefore an outstanding question as to the terms on which a sorely needed economic redistribution process would take place.

Homecoming

In 1990, after the unbanning of the African National Congress, Joe and I settled in Johannesburg. I split my time between finishing my PhD and working for the ANC Land Commission. On completing the

---

*M Wilson & L Thompson, 1969, p.65: Van Riebeeck report to Chamber XVII in Holland in 1660.

doctorate I looked for a job that would give me the opportunity to work in rural South Africa – I now had too much book knowledge and needed to get some down-to-earth practical experience. I found a job with a national non-governmental organisation (NGO) that provided improved water supplies and agricultural support. Once people had a bit more water they, especially the women, were often interested in the chance of making more intensive use of their homestead land.

I learnt a lot about ordinary people's lives in rural settlements, and the fragile economy of rural households with limited access to land. It was ironic that while South African households appeared comparatively well off compared to their Southern African neighbours in their quality of housing and acquisition of consumer goods, the tough reality was that their livelihoods were not as robust and sustainable. So much depended on salary remittances, or a pension. A lost job meant real crisis; in Mozambique, Zambia and Zimbabwe people had more and better land to fall back on in hard times.

I'd been working for the NGO for two years when our director, ever optimistic about imminent inflow of additional funds, over-committed himself in terms of staff recruitment. We zoomed towards a cash flow crisis and crashed the barrier into bankruptcy. I took up freelance consulting; it provided less financial steadiness but more flexibility that was welcome for personal reasons.

After the elections in May 1994, Joe was appointed Minister of Housing. My expectation of his death at the hand of an apartheid assassin had come to nothing. Death's calling card had arrived by way of bone marrow cancer, diagnosed in mid 1991. In early August 1994 his remission came to an abrupt end. 'Mr Slovo, I'm afraid your kidneys are beginning to be affected. With careful diet and lots of water you might delay the need for dialysis' was the gist of the diagnosis. At intervals the blood platelet levels fell, and I sat for hours over weekends at Cape Town's Groote Schuur Hospital monitoring the speed with which blood travelled its slow red way down the tubes into a narrowing vein. Out of hospital, I watched with envy and admiration as Joe judiciously applied his energy to his ministerial responsibilities; if anyone has ever mastered the art of effective delegation it was he.

I struggled through this period. I left my daughters with my ex-husband and travelled wherever Joe was travelling. I had a laptop computer and the policy work I was doing involved many solitary hours of writing, and only the occasional meeting. I sat alone at a desk in a damp thatched house on the parliamentary estate, the cold winter rain of the Western Cape beating against the windows. Clumps of arum lilies were planted near the house. I looked out over these towards the huge manicured grounds of the estate, so unlike the homeliness of my own garden. In my mind arum lilies are symbolically linked with death – funereal flowers. I wanted to pull them out of the ground, one by one, and every single one of them. I made myself do no such thing. I needed to come to terms with an impending death; accepting the presence of the lilies was part of that process. When Joe came home, depleted, he didn't have the energy to talk; he wanted to sit in comforting silence. That fast flow of freeway conversation and quick wit was grinding towards a halt. I was miserable, but to speak of one's own misery with a dying partner seemed a mean and selfish thing to do.

The thing about dying is that there are no firm deadlines. You've been told that remission is over, but how much time before that 'final curtain': four months, six months, ten months? It's a guessing game. Meanwhile I felt pulled every which way. I was a mother who missed her children. I was a professional for whom work was one of life's necessities. I was a wife with a dying husband with special needs.

It was suggested to me that I have a session with an art therapist. There was concern that I wasn't talking about what was going on inside my head; perhaps drawing would free up some expression. But I froze and could not bring myself to draw. The studio had shelves of artefacts. You could choose something you identified with and talk about that instead of drawing, if you wished. In the end I chose a rubber octopus and arranged it in a sandbox, unfurling the tentacles one by one. Finally, they lay outstretched and radial like the spokes of a bicycle wheel. If they were to be pulled any harder they'd reach breaking point.

Clearly, I needed a regular job if I was to maintain my equilibrium – I needed an interactive professional existence that would offer me some out-of-the-house outlet in the months ahead. I'd been approached to lecture at the Wits School of Public and Development Management. They were prepared to schedule my classes so that I would need to be in Johannesburg for only two nights a week. I'd be able to see my children – and hopefully Joe would endure my short absence. I was also named as a member of the Presidential Commission on rural financial services – the Strauss Commission, as it became known. I'd worked on rural credit policy in Mozambique and was excited at the prospect.

The viability of my own survival scheme was never tested. In early December 1994 we went to a beach house at Cinza in the Eastern Cape with my two girls and my mum. We were supposedly on holiday and yet both of us flew separately to Johannesburg for work commitments – Joe for a cabinet meeting, and myself for the first meeting of the

Strauss Commission. That week Joe fell on the path leading from the slopes of the sand dunes to the beach. For another person it could have been a fall softened by sand; for Joe, whose bones had been rendered fragile by disease and the effects of cortisone, it was the catalytic incident. His right collarbone was broken. He now needed physical help for the ordinary tasks of daily living: dressing, eating, and he hated this dependency. There was a speedy deterioration towards 'all systems closing down'. He died a month to the day after the fall. He'd always said that once he couldn't work, couldn't enjoy life, there'd be no point in fighting to stay around.

Afterwards, wrapped up in grief, the working life that I'd hung on to with such tenacity now seemed irrelevant. I felt so tired. I just wanted to sleep, drift around the house, sort through photographs and sit silently in a trance of memories. I requested leave of absence from Wits, and from my responsibilities as a co-ordinator of one of the Strauss Commission task teams. Two months' leave became four and then five. I assembled Joe's unfinished biography, and spent days writing: the crafting proved calming. I considered myself lucky; I thought about people who didn't have the financial cushioning of 'death benefits' and wondered how they held themselves together after the one week of compassionate leave that goes with the normal conditions of employment.

It was hard for my children. 'Mum,' said Kyla, then ten years old, 'when Joe died you told us you'd have more time for us. It's true, you have more time, but you're not here – you're in your head somewhere.'

When I surfaced things had changed. My comrade friends advised me not to go back to the university. '*Sekunjalo*,' they said. 'Now is the time.' They argued that, at this critical juncture of policy implementation in our new democracy, people with my skills should be in the public service. I became adviser to the then Minister of Agriculture, Derek Hanekom. I was instructed to divide my time by three, a third to the Strauss Commission, a third to parastatal restructuring in the Eastern Cape, and a third troubleshooting in communities facing a logjam on land issues.

Negotiated settlement: both a miracle and a raw deal

Two main objectives drove the liberation struggle: the unacceptability of unequal wealth distribution and the inhumane denial of franchise for all races. Our political settlement is viewed by the world as a miracle of negotiation. It achieved one objective – political franchise – but circumscribed the conditions for achieving the second. A cornerstone of the settlement agreement, which led to the elections and political transfer of power, was that current property rights would be respected.

When the African National Congress agreed to relinquish its pursuit of the armed struggle as the path to power, it relinquished the possibility of repossession of economic resources 'by the sword and by the laws of war'.

It might be said that the leaders were 'struggle weary' after years of exile, incarceration, and a massive people-based resistance that was damaging to economic development. My late husband was one of the team of negotiators. I know his thinking was profoundly influenced by what had happened in Angola at the time of and after the elections in that country. He was of the belief that if the MPLA* had been prepared to consider the – albeit distasteful – possibility of power-sharing with the opposition then the subsequent decades of a country destroying itself and its resources in an ongoing civil war might have been averted.

We are number two in the world's ranking of countries with the greatest internal economic inequality. Yet the outcome of a negotiated settlement, influenced by a world order which made the Van Riebeeck style takeover less tenable, is that South Africa's economic transformation now depends on governmental ability to create policies and influence the direction of investment to secure redistribution.

The redistribution process is further circumscribed by government dedication to fiscal restraint. The apartheid regime prolonged its tenure through borrowing to finance its war machine and spend on its favoured constituency. The democratically elected government vowed not to follow the same path of economic irresponsibility. They pursued a policy of debt repayment leaving only modest budgets available for redistribution. The challenge would be to convince people of long-term commitment and find acceptance for the slow gradualism of their chosen approach.

This gradual reform perspective influenced the five years of debate leading up to the democratic elections. In May 1990, in response to the unbanning, the intelligentsia of the Congress of South African Trade Unions (COSATU), left-leaning academics, and the ANC gathered in Harare to deliberate on post-apartheid economic policy intentions.

Thirty-five years had passed since the Freedom Charter proclamation: 'The land shall belong to those who work it.' There were huge differences of opinion on the approach to the land question. Mike de Klerk was deeply concerned that black farmers should not get land reform deals that were laden with the potential for bankruptcy. His land reform vision focused on the reintroduction of wide-scale sharecropping; the proposal

---

*Movimento Popular de Libertaçao de Angola.

met with the objection that the racial power relations would remain the same. The 'wabenzis', the aspirant bourgeoisie of the liberation movement, began to creep out of their closets with confidence following the collapse of the Soviet Union. Masiphula Mbongwa, who was to become deputy director general of Agriculture, presented a policy vision in which the poor would have a constitutional right to one hectare of land alongside flourishing black large-scale capitalist farmers. The idea that the majority should be consigned to everlasting poverty was distasteful to participants.

Later that year, in October 1990, the ANC Land Commission organised a policy workshop, this time in Johannesburg, in which the activists outnumbered the intellectuals. A popular understanding of land nationalisation was expressed by community leaders and rural activists: 'The whites came and nationalised the land and shared it between themselves, now the blacks must also nationalise the land and give it back to the people.'

The ANC needed to do some fancy footwork to satisfy the diverse interests in its broad alliance. The stated commitment to fiscal restraint limited the chances of the landless or land-poor aspirant farmers getting the same deal enjoyed by many colonial settlers – i.e. land and money for inputs and expenses to tide them over until the first harvests were complete. The policy decision of the Government of National Unity in 1994 was to provide a grant allocation of up to R15 000.

There were, however, a series of other government services that could be used to support black economic empowerment. A great deal of effort was put into parallel policy formulation that would result in improving people's access to technical assistance, or a reorientation of research spending to reflect the priorities of poor farmers' needs rather than those of hi-tech agribusiness who could afford their own research. Improved access to credit was also considered as important to facilitate empowerment. The Ministry of Agriculture and Land Affairs conceived of and duly won approval for the establishment of a Presidential Commission on rural financial services to deliberate future strategy.

Rural finance: the thin end of a large wedge

I have no illusions about credit. It seems to fall into the classification of 'one man's meat, another man's poison'. It can be a powerful resource to be used by people attempting to change the economic basis of their lives; it may also contribute to the very undoing of their attempts. Credit is expensive, especially South African credit, and the stories of indebtedness and bankruptcy among black farmers who bought freehold and failed to service their bond are more than a century old.

And yet during the tenure of the apartheid regime, black people had been denied easy access to credit. It would be important for the new South African state to address access to rural financial services, not only its geography but also the conditions for loan approval. Comparative studies indicated that innovative thinking and some risk-taking would be necessary if access to credit were to change fundamentally. South African financial institutions seemed to be obsessed with property ownership as a precondition for the approval of a loan application. In our neighbouring states land was nationalised, thus negating the possibility that saleable freehold could provide the backing for a loan. In many countries in Latin America and Asia tenancy prevailed as the dominant form of agricultural production, and yet tenants had access to credit.

The Presidential Commission on rural financial services was tasked to investigate fully the prevailing conditions in rural areas. Furthermore, it was to use the government development objectives as expressed in the Reconstruction and Development Programme (RDP) as its lodestar and 'make recommendations for policy, legislative and institutional measures to improve financial services for rural households, farmers and other entrepreneurs'.*

The Commission was given twelve areas in which they were expected to solicit research, analyse the information and draw up recommendations. The following issues were to be incorporated:

- the needs and aspirations of rural people, including an assessment of the current and potential demand for rural financial services;

- a review of the current sources of rural credit and other financial services and the extent to which they are meeting this demand. This review will scan the legislative framework, the motivation and effect of such credit and other financial services. This should include an analysis of the policies and practices of the diverse institutions involved in the delivery of rural financial services;

- broadening the participation of rural people in rural financial markets by proposing diverse financing mechanisms to ensure access to financial services with an emphasis on savings mobilisation;

- central, provincial and local interrelationships in terms of institutional structures and financial arrangements;

- financial mechanisms to facilitate the acquisition and development of land within the framework of a land reform programme;

---

*Terms of Reference, Strauss Commission, Report RP 108.

- the position of women to be attended to as priority beneficiaries of public sector activities;
- complementary and interactive roles of civil society and the state sector;
- mobilisation as well as the application of financial resources;
- the impact of related policy frameworks on rural finance within the wider spatial framework of South Africa and Southern Africa;
- recommendations to structure a monitoring and evaluation system regarding the provision of rural financial services;
- capital retention in rural areas;
- methods of expanding the backward and forward linkages in the rural and broader economy.

Parastatal and private demarcation

At the end of several months of work, the Strauss Commission reached its preliminary conclusions and published an interim report to solicit public response. The recommendation was that the Land Bank should become a multisectoral bank to serve the rural poor as well as those commercial farmers who would be considered as marginal clients by private sector banks.* In the circles of the banking world it was said that it was unrealistic to expect the private sector to concern themselves with the financial needs of poor people. Their business was considered as 'high volume, low value, nuisance transactions'. Furthermore, the private sector should not be deprived of profit-making opportunities as would occur if state-owned development finance institutions were to begin to compete for the high value business of coveted prime clients.

My problems with this line of argumentation were threefold. Firstly, I have never bought the argument that the role of the state is to do only that which the private sector considers not sufficiently profitable. Assessments of the privatisation process in the UK and the United States have noted the vulnerability of the position that the state finds itself in post-privatisation. It has no yardstick to measure whether there's efficiency in the sector, and sometimes private sector efficiency is wildly overstated. For example, on the proposals to privatise state-financed hospitals operating under the National Health Service in the UK the sceptics of wholesale nationalisation have argued for partial privatisation. The idea is that you keep enough of the business under the aegis of the state so that you can never be held to ransom on the delivery of a critical service. In this way you also maintain your own yardstick on comparative

---

*Strauss Commission Interim Report, RP 38, 1996.

efficiency and will be able to gauge whether or not quotes submitted in response to calls for tender are reasonable or a rip-off.

Secondly, I thought the relegation of parastatal banking activity to marginal white commercial farmers and emergent black entrepreneurs and land reform beneficiaries curtailed the potential of the state being able to leverage a development ethic among a broader range of rural producers. This is an issue of vision. The vision can be limited to the buying and selling of money at various rates for different activities – or the vision can contemplate a wider developmental purpose. Parastatals, whose shareholder is less likely to have profit as the dominant objective, have this special opportunity which is rarely pursued by conventionally run private sector businesses.

My third doubt was not in the realm of debates on economic philosophy but concerned a lack of confidence in the institutional proposition. The preliminary recommendations suggested that the Land Bank should be transformed to be all things to all people in rural areas. I doubted whether it was realistic that this apartheid institution was transformable to the extent implicitly expected. It would have to be capable of giving customer service to South Africans of all races, rich and poor, and would need diverse language skills among its staff if it were to discontinue the normal patterns of prejudice and discrimination. Furthermore, having been only a specialist agricultural bank, would it really be able to develop the skills necessary to deal with other business fast enough?

I had had the opportunity of having discussions with a couple of the Land Bank senior personnel; people who would have been categorised as *verligte* – enlightened – into the bargain. So they were – when compared with many of their colleagues! Their vision of a Land Bank in the new South Africa reminded me of the kind of bar/bottle store commonly operating in 'white areas' in the time of apartheid. The saloon bar was for whites, and then round the side, with a separate entrance, there were over-the-counter sales to blacks.

The *verligte* approach within the Land Bank anticipated the creation of a new post, a third general manager position. They assumed that this new appointee would be black, and that he or she would run a separate arm of the Land Bank business. On this basis they had already purchased the neighbouring four-storey building which had formerly housed the Citrus Board. If separate business premises was the perspective for the Pretoria head office operations, I wondered how the retail branch network would operate – hence why the image of white bars with the round-the-corner sales to blacks came to mind.

Out of curiosity I asked about the demographics of Land Bank employees. The response was: 'We are approximately thirteen hundred people, some four hundred people in the head office and the others spread over the twenty-five retail branches. The split is roughly a third, a third, a third.' This didn't make sense to me so I asked my informant if he could explain further. 'One-third white male, one-third white female and one-third black,' was his ready response. I listened with amazement; the implicit racism was totally unconscious and unintended. So, are black people gender neutral, I thought of asking. 'The white men are mainly technical, the white women mainly administrative and the blacks are sundry staff,' he continued to explain helpfully.

I had real fears that Afrikaner patriarchy and patronage would prove so deep and so strong that it would be impossible to truly transform this institution. But leaving aside racism and gender issues, it was obvious that a new black clientele would need staff with different skills, not just language training but people with a broader approach to agriculture. The Land Bank employees had only ever dealt with large-scale commercial farmers, the majority of whom were mono-cropping maize and wheat, or raising cattle. Among black rural families, especially the entrepreneurs, farming was sensibly just one among a set of economic activities that secured a risk diversification strategy. And how would loan officers deal with different farming practices, how would they calculate projected returns on the inter-cropping of maize with pumpkins and beans? I felt that current employees probably had a fairly poor understanding of the socio-economic dynamics of black rural households. And what about the new clientele? Would black farmers forgive the Land Bank its racist past and accept it as the bank for all farmers of all races?

My gut feeling was that privatisation of the Land Bank should be seriously considered. Its sale could be expected to bring at least R1,2-billion into the state coffers; that money could be used to set up a new operation from scratch. Only Steven Goldblatt, in our personal conversations, shared an understanding of the enormity of the envisaged transformation proposal and sympathised with my view on privatisation.

I wondered why privatisation was so far from the minds of the commissioners; it seemed to be outside the boundaries of their mind-maps as options were considered. I realised that I was the only commissioner who had lived in neighbouring countries in which I had experienced institutional restructuring in a post-independence situation. No other commissioner had this experience.

The arguments in favour of retaining the Land Bank as a principal role player in the revamping of rural financial services were set out.

- There were several hundred professionals who had technical skills and experience – these should be put to the service of all South Africans.
- The Land Bank was the only national-level development finance institution (DFI) that had an established retail network – this was advantageous.
- The Bank had market standing as having been prudently and professionally managed; it had thus earned a good double-A risk rating. This affected the price at which it sold its bills on the money market, and again this rating was seen as a favourable asset.

Eventually the concession was made to give more attention to the transformation issue and a task team was designated to draw up some guiding principles for change management. A major modification to the recommendations of the preliminary report as a result of feedback was the reconsideration of the proposal that the Bank should become the 'rural bank' lending for any kind of business undertaken in rural areas. Popular and institutional opinion was that the Land Bank should remain focused on farming but start agribusiness financing as well.

Some of the arguments were nothing more than a 'get off our turf' position taken by the other DFIs, which were not laudable or especially convincing. From the point of view of risk management, the multi-sectoral approach was safer – besides which none of the other DFIs had any retail network. My support for the proposal that the Land Bank should remain focused on agriculture was pragmatic. If the Bank was not going to be privatised and therefore needed to transform, then at least it made more sense that, for the moment, it should stick to the business sector with which it was familiar.

After twenty-one months of deliberations the commissioners signed the final report in September 1996, and it was handed over to the President's office. Cabinet ministers approved the recommendations without alteration.

The Land Bank's new mandate

The Strauss Commission formulated sixty-five recommendations, several of them directly or indirectly pertaining to the Land Bank. The first recommendations, however, dealt with the roles of the state and the need for it to 'accept its unequivocal responsibility to facilitate as well as to co-ordinate the provision of a balanced range of trustworthy financial services to the rural people of South Africa with special attention to women and their legal disadvantages'.

It is the opinion of the Commission that this responsibility in the context of land acquisition finance would best be addressed through the appointment of a commercially oriented parastatal institution to champion the cause of the rural communities in the above context.*

Another recommendation dealt with the market relationship between the state and the private sector and the role of civil society.

State activity should seek to complement and gear private sector engagement, enhancing efficiency through supporting the market. The corollary is that the state, in supporting rural people, must recognise the strengths and weaknesses of existing local level institutions. Currently these institutions are not able to contribute to the aims of rural reconstruction on a national basis without appropriate and active support.†

The study of international best practice pointed to the success of multi-sectoral finance. The South African approach still favoured specialisation. There were and continue to be five national-level development finance institutions. The National Housing Finance Corporation had already earmarked funds for rural housing. The Development Bank of Southern Africa (DBSA), which previously had a multisectoral approach in its lending for projects supported by the bantustan leaders, now had a singular focus and was to fund infrastructure in both urban and rural areas. Khula Enterprise Finance was a newly established parastatal with intentions to provide wholesale finance for Small, Medium and Micro Enterprises (SMMEs) in both urban and rural areas. The Land and Agricultural Bank of South Africa was to continue to specialise in agricultural funding. The Post Office, with its extensive network of more than two thousand branches and agencies, made some of us dream of electronically serviced community centres providing information as well as online transactions for rural financial services. The possibilities for synergy with the Land Bank were seductive; but Strauss realistically referred to these ideas as 'blue sky' – the business jargon for long-term potential.

The Commission's review of current legislation identified the need to rectify the unconstitutional discrimination of customary law against women. It also noted the need to bring in line the Land Bank's legislation with that of the commercial banking sector. The Commission recommended that the preferential creditor status of the Land Bank should be reviewed. I didn't especially agree with this one – but there is a need

---

*Strauss Commission Recommendation 1, Report RP 108, p.4.
†Strauss Commission Recommendation 4, Report RP 108, p.4.

to compromise when you're in a consensus-seeking group. 'Choose your battles,' Joe used to tell me. My reservation was that if the Land Bank was being designated to deal with the bottom end of the market, and expected to restrict itself to business that the private sector didn't want to touch, it would not share the same 'level playing field' with the commercial sector in terms of 'spreading risk', hence the merit of its continuing privileges. It always seemed to me that some of the commissioners from the private sector defended their interest here. While they undertook the role of concerned citizen in their service on the Commission, their largesse was restrained when it came to anything that they thought interfered with private sector rights to make money. Up to now private sector banks had been the beneficiaries of the following neat, unwritten, gentleman's agreement: The private sector would deal with the top end of the market – the category one farmers. The Land Bank would deal with new entrants and middling farmers classified as category two until they were considered as worthy private sector bank clients. They also handled the commercial banks' referrals, the dropouts from category one. Category three, a stratum of strugglers trying to avoid sequestration, were handled by the Department's Agricultural Credit Board.

One battle worth fighting was the issue of gender equality. Our new constitution with its emphasis on a non-racist, non-sexist democracy made it easier to push through recommendations intended to benefit women. The Commission stated that it 'believes that the contractual incapacity of any competent adult is both an abrogation of human rights and an impediment to the functioning of financial markets'. But gender rights would probably have little impact unless sexist attitudes were also to change. The Commission therefore recommended 'that the state fund a gender awareness programme for staff employed in the retail financial sector to change their attitudes to women as potential clients. This is particularly important in terms of retailers working with land reform beneficiaries, the majority of whom are women.'*

Besides the consideration of attitudinal impediments towards quality assistance for the poor and/or female applicants for financial service, the other problem areas would be information and language. The Commission's Recommendation 33 was 'that all rural financial service providers should give consideration to the employment and training of a high proportion of staff with the linguistic skills and cultural sensitivity necessary for developing business with previously unbanked rural

---

*Strauss Commission Recommendation 32, Report RP 108, p.13.

clientele'.* Whilst language would be important, communication skills and products needed to be available. Hence the Commission Recommendation 34 was that 'rural financial service providers should develop new communication products, and design simpler, user-friendly facilities aimed at the female and lower income market'.

My favourite recommendation was Number 29.[†] I took pleasure in coining its title as 'Sunrise Subsidies'. I'd been on the receiving end of considerable flak from friends about how angry they were with my late husband for having advocated the 'sunset clauses' that ensured civil service job security for five years, a compromise that facilitated a negotiation breakthrough. Hence the satisfaction of outlining the sunrise subsidy recommendations: a graded entry to repayment, a flexible repayment system, a discount subsidy for timely repayment, and a minimalist insurance scheme.

Many of the sixty-five recommendations were general but fourteen of them referred specifically to the Land Bank. They dealt with the need to maintain capacity while changing focus (Recommendation 43),[‡] hence requiring both political support and an infusion of new personnel. The collateral rules would need to change. Capacity building would be required if the Land Bank were to expand its activities through using up-and-coming new retailers.

The overhaul in the Land Bank's business was expected to be fundamental. Recommendation 51 states: 'The Land Bank must adopt a developmental approach to its business, including attempts to influence the type of production loans financed. The development criteria for lending should include a "good practice ethic" in terms of clients applying the legally required health and safety standards and the Basic Conditions of Employment Act.'

In terms of making a public statement of the mandate to change, the Commission recommended (Recommendation 52) that 'The new board of the Land Bank should consider whether there should be a name change to assist the public to recognise its changed role.'

The Land Bank: a view of a change process

The point of departure was that far-reaching change was required in the Land Bank if it was to deliver on the recommendations. However, a catechism of commandments from government, as the sole share-

---

*Strauss Commission Recommendation 33, Report RP 108, p.14.
[†]Strauss Commission Recommendation 29, Report RP 108, p.12.
[‡]Strauss Commission Recommendation 43, Report RP 108, p.16.

holder, in and of itself changes nothing. The commissioners spelt out a vision of restructuring to support their decision on the transformability of the Land Bank. They canvassed several institutional change experts as well as undertaking an in-depth literature review of conditions that have proved determinant in securing a business turnaround and institutional transformation. The following set of guiding principles for institutional change was proposed:

- The transformation process should not be viewed as a rehabilitation exercise; rather the goal of transformation is to facilitate change, which will enable the pursuit of excellence . . .

- It is essential that a vision statement should be drafted prior to any transformation initiatives being undertaken. The vision statement should state clearly what the objectives are, the activities to be pursued and for whose benefit.

- Political backing is critical to the transformation effort. The acceptance and open support of major political entities and (role) players . . . is a sine qua non for its success.

- Appropriate enabling legislation for the statutory bodies concerned is essential to the success of the transformation initiative.

- The mandate would need the wholehearted support of the board of directors to the extent of requiring an entirely new membership.

- The effectiveness of a new board will require the concomitant appointment of a new chief executive officer. The managing director is appointed by the appropriate Minister and given the delegated authority to implement the vision and strategy as articulated by the board.

- An effective, committed executive team will be required to support the efforts of the new board of directors and managing director. The executive must form a team of diverse and complementary skills.

- Maintenance of capacity should be an objective. As most of the (South African) institutions being transformed, or targeted for transformation, are going concerns one crucial aspect is the maintenance of capacity in these institutions.

- A vision that is not communicated has no impact; it is a set of worthless words – a dream transcribed onto paper. The vision must, from its inception be stated unequivocally to all within the institution. Employees at all levels must be enrolled into the new vision and modus operandi.

- It is imperative that the organisation be restructured as a whole, rather than new functions merely being added on as stand-alone entities.

- The institutional transformation may require staff restructuring. The management and staff at all levels needs to be reviewed; those who subscribe to the vision should be retained, if their expertise and function remains relevant. A staff transformation programme must keep staff comprehensively informed of all developments to ensure that inevitable insecurities are minimised.

• There must be a measurable transformation process with targeted delivery. Changing priorities must be identified in terms of operational impera- tives. The structure of the institution must support revised targets, functions and priorities within a time frame.

• The new mandate will not be possible without a major commitment to capacity building of existing employees as well as the recruitment of new staff with appropriate skills. Staff will be required to take on additional responsibilities for which they will require training.

• The new functions may require additional funding for establishment costs; this funding should be committed before the process begins. Sources and terms of new funding must also be examined to ensure the ongoing sustainability of the institution.

• The time frame within which certain changes are expected should be set out and agreed to. It is important that not too long is spent on the planning phase before starting implementation. Gaining momentum at the outset of the transformation process is vital to all concerned and to the success of the process as a whole. Within a short period of time (approximately six months) the restructuring of the organisation must be finalised. The following eighteen months should be used to achieve staff reorientation and goals of recruiting new staff. Thus, the first twenty-four months must witness the substantial transformation of the organisation.

A new job and boardroom takeover

Those days of quietness in between and after the Christmas and New Year celebrations are often my stocktaking time. This particular year-end of December 1996 and beginning January 1997 was unusual. The context for the 'Where are you going? What are you doing with your life?' annual personal checklist was changing. My older daughter Tessa had just finished secondary school and was leaving home. My younger daughter Kyla had decided to live in Pietermaritzburg with her father for a couple of years; he was being treated for cancer and she wanted to spend more time with him.

One evening I sat sipping whisky on the balcony of a block of flats near the water tower at the top of the hill in Yeoville, Johannesburg. There was a breathtaking view of a spectacular sunset over the city skyline – the colour all the more vibrant, I'm told, because of the levels of air pollution that we live with. I hadn't seen my host, John Sender, for several months. He's a fellow agricultural economist – a professor at the School of Oriental and African Studies who had completed several semesters of teaching and research at Wits University. There was the pleasure of the easy flow of 'shop-talk' stemming from our common professional roots. Part of the conversation concerned the final outcome of the Strauss Commission, and the Agriculture Minister's frustration that the Finance Minister was distracted by a falling rand and not preoccupied with advertising for a new managing director for the Land Bank or the appointment of a new board. Then John asked me a question that unsettled me: 'Why don't you apply for the post of Land Bank managing director when it's advertised?' The gist of his reasoning was: 'As Minister's adviser you're playing the role of troubleshooter. Today it's Tsitsikamma, tomorrow it'll be Makatini Flats. I'm not saying you're not good at it – you are. But why don't you get yourself a real job, one where you can stand back and see what you achieve over time.'

I went home to mull over what he had said. It seemed strange for me to consider applying for the job. I'd argued that I didn't think that substantial change in the Land Bank was possible. I had preferred the 'privatise-take-the-money-start-something-new' option. It would be a job and a half for whoever took it on. But someone was going to be doing it. John's expressed confidence in my capability made me confront the possibility seriously. The fact that I wasn't going to have daily parental responsibilities for the next couple of years meant I felt able to consider a more demanding job.

I met up with my brother Martin and told him about the conversation with John. What did he think? I didn't like his answer. It needled me. 'You've been Joe Slovo's widow, now you're Minister Derek Hanekom's adviser. Why don't you try being Helena Dolny for a change?'

Getting the job was by no means a straight dash for the home run. From the newspaper advertisement I noted that two headhunting firms had been appointed. Neither of them contacted me to request a CV. The message was clear enough; the search was on for a black professional. This seemed fair as a preference in keeping with the national political objective of ensuring that black people took over the reins of steering the economy. I felt despondent but decided I'd send in my CV anyway. At least I was a woman, albeit a white woman – and thus belonged to the category of the previously disadvantaged.

Some of my friends thought I was mad. I spent several hours in a car the weekend prior to the interview travelling to and from a first-time fishing expedition. Two of my fellow travellers worked in private sector banking. The first half of the journey was spent trying to dissuade me from pursuing this possible career option; having failed, the second part of the journey was spent coaching me to do my best at the interview.

I made it through to the shortlist for the second interview. The panel was made up of government representatives from the Ministry of Finance, and a representative from the Ministry of Agriculture and Land Affairs. The haves and the have-nots were represented: the commercial farmers' South African Agricultural Union (SAAU) representing the first, and the chief official of the South African Plant and Allied Workers' Union representing the latter. The head of the National Land Committee represented the land reform and broader farm worker constituency. A change management expert was also on the panel and, finally, the outgoing acting managing director, Mr Freddie van Staden.

The shortlist included two very senior black professionals employed by provincial development parastatals. A third black professional was Bonile Jack, a senior employee at the Independent Development Trust, a large, not-for-profit, rural development agency. Jack had postgraduate qualifications as well as having held the position of director general of Agriculture in the Ciskei. An internal candidate was the general manager of finance at the Land Bank – a lifelong employee. And there was me.

I was nervous on the day of the final interview. My office at the Ministry was only a few blocks from the Land Bank. I decided that I would walk and breathe deeply to calm myself. The highveld sky opened up in a sudden thunderstorm and I arrived on the front steps of the Land Bank on the run from the rain. My hair was bedraggled – my attempts to protect it with a writing pad weren't very successful. I was wearing a blue suede suit – not the kind of material from which you can easily brush off the raindrops. As for my feet – the water was squelching through my toes inside my shoes.

Land Bank security gruffly asked me what I wanted. I explained that I had an interview on the eighth floor. They obviously reckoned this was a tall story. The hotline of gossip meant that everyone knew that interviews were taking place for the position of new managing director – but surely not a woman?

The secretary in the managing director's office confirmed that I was expected and I was escorted along the dark corridors. Lettie Kleynhans, the acting managing director's secretary, was kindness personified. She immediately took me to a bathroom where I could dry myself down, and gave me hot tea.

The interview was somewhat shorter than I expected. I did not interpret this positively. Perhaps they had their preferred candidate and now had to fulfil the requirements of interviewing everyone who had been invited. Months later I met one of the interviewing panellists and remarked how insecure I'd felt, especially when the interview had been so short. 'But you were so articulate and concise,' was the response, 'and you convinced everyone of how clear you were in your understanding of what needed to be done.'

Meanwhile the Minister of Agriculture and the Minister of Finance had selected a new board of directors. They were to start their two-year term of office on 1 April 1997, and I would start on 1 May 1997.

The board of directors was a major switch-over. The outgoing full-time board members comprised commercial white farmers, as well as Bonile Jack and Daphne Motsepe who had been asked to join as non-executive directors during the tenure of the Strauss Commission.

There were three carry-over appointments from the old to the new board. Van Staden, the outgoing acting managing director, agreed to stay on – it seemed important to secure some institutional memory. Izak Cronje, a respected farmer from the Free State, was asked to stay for the same reason. Bonile Jack had served almost two years as a board member; his familiarity with the work of the Strauss Commission and prior knowledge of the Bank were considered important.

The new board members were:

- Dennis Creighton, former general manager of Nedbank, financial manager at SERVCON housing solutions, a company dealing with housing finance at the lower end of the market;
- Evan Matthews, chairman of the African Farmers' Union (AFU), a black farmers' association in the Western Cape. Originally trained as a meat inspector, he now ran his own farm;
- Totsie Memela, regional manager of Peoples Bank in North West Province, a member of the Strauss Commission, and a member of the ANC's underground in exile;
- Murray Michel, an adviser to the Minister of Finance;
- Kate Moloto, the transformation manager at the Development Bank of Southern Africa, who shortly afterwards became the head of Ntsika, a parastatal providing training support for the small business sector;
- Ugandra Naidoo, a senior lecturer in accounting at the University of Durban Westville, the first black to come in the top ten in South Africa's examinations for chartered accountants;
- Kate Philip, the chief executive officer of the Mineworkers' Development Agency, a not-for-profit organisation born out of the 1987 strike

when the trade union pledged that it would support retrenched miners in rural areas who were establishing new business ventures.

On the evening of the first meeting of the new board at the end of April 1997, the Land Bank organised a press conference at cocktail time, attended by Derek Hanekom, the Minister of Agriculture and Land Affairs. The Minister's intention was to introduce the board members to the public and give a reassurance that the traditional business of the Bank would continue. I was invited to give my 'inaugural speech'. I had been practising for almost ten days. I was determined to speak in three languages – English, Zulu and Afrikaans. Friends had made tuition cassettes. I repeated the speech over and over again to reach a minimal level of competence so as not to embarrass myself.

I thanked the staff of the eighth floor who had set me at ease with their warm welcome and helpfulness – '*gerus gestel deur u warm verwelkoming en behulpsaamheid*' and expressed my hopes that in the future I would be able to continue to depend on this help: '*Ek vertrou ek in die toekoms daarop sal kan bly reken.*' I also hoped that the employees now felt more at ease with me because of the manner in which I had handled some of the press criticisms and fears that followed my appointment.

The English-Zulu speech marked the change of power and commitment to a new non-racial future: 'The doors of the Land Bank shall be open to all, it cannot be like a white-owned rural bottle store with a side entrance for blacks' was what I had proposed as a start. Totsie Memela put together a more elegant speech, and accommodated me by choosing words whose pronunciation I was capable of getting right as a novice in the language.

Ibhangi kufuneka lishintshe.	The Bank must change.
Kudingeka ushintsho oluljulile. Olungagijima nje phezulu.	We need meaningful change. The change we seek must not just be at the top. It must be at grass-roots level.
Thina ke kuyofuneka samkele wonke umuntu kudingeka sakhe usiko olusha.	We must embrace all our people and build a nation.
Luyadingeka ushintsho	We need change that will unite all

oluhlanganisa wonke amasiko amalimi nezizwe zonke zomzansi Afrika.	our people, all cultures, all languages.
Kusobala-ke ukuthi kuyodingeka sifundisane sincede wonke umsebenzi ngezifundo zolwimi olusha.	It is clear that it is necessary that we should support workers to take on the new values we have adopted.
Ngiyathemba ngiyoba ngowokuqala ukuba yisibonelo.	I hope to be both an example and a witness.
Sekunjalo! Jwale ke nako! Isikathi sobumbano nokwakha Ibangi elisha – a new bank.	Now is the time! The time for unity and development. The Bank must become a new bank.

In retrospect it was ironic that I, the only person on the Strauss Commission who wanted privatisation of the Land Bank to be seriously considered, should end up as the person appointed to drive its transformation.

It was not going to be easy from whichever way I looked at it. I was quickly made aware of unhappiness among some black professionals that I had been the successful applicant. One of my fellow candidates was in an airport departures lounge waiting to board a Cape Town to Johannesburg flight. The newspaper that day had carried the announcement of my appointment. A short remark was uttered with bitterness: 'You see, Joe Slovo still has influence from beyond the grave!' The speaker did not know that the listener was an acquaintance of mine.

Another avenue of conservative criticism (this time white) was the Afrikaner agricultural business community. Dr Piet Gouws and Mr Dries Bruwer issued statements opposing my appointment. Gouws said I 'had a communist background which did not bode well for the commercial farmers' capitalist and free-market views'. Bruwer warned I would make a 'socialist input . . . aimed at ruining commercial farmers'.* The *Landbouweekblad* did the first of a series of cartoons. They had me as Helen of Troy, riding a chariot and brandishing a whip, with Derek Hanekom, dressed in armour, showing the way though the open doors of the Land Bank fortress. The humour appealed to me, although I

---

*'EPAU (Eastern Province Agricultural Union) to keep an eye on new Land Bank head', *Daily Dispatch*, 9 May 1997.

wasn't sure about the role model I was supposed to emulate.

More seriously, I had become aware of divergence between the Minister and the Deputy Minister. The appointment of the Strauss Commission had been driven by Minister Hanekom who took a close interest in its deliberations. The Deputy Minister supported departmental officials undertaking a somewhat parallel process. Masiphula Mbongwa, then chief director, worked with his Dutch mentor Gerard van Empel and issued reports 6 and 7 of the BATAT series on Finance putting forward departmental views. Van Empel opined that the Land Bank retail branches in the provinces should be integrated into the Provincial Development Corporations (PDCs). My view was the opposite. The PDCs were running at huge losses. There could be a mutual benefit if the PDCs were to integrate into the Land Bank, thus diversifying the racial composition of senior professional staff, as well as bringing their experience of dealing with black clientele.

Leading up to the cabinet approval of the Strauss Commission recommendations there were two very different press releases prepared from within the same Ministry. The statement* issued by the Minster of Agriculture and Land Affairs, Derek Hanekom, read:

> In short, the Final Report recommends that a Development Council should assume co-ordinating responsibility for the financial aspects of rural development. It proposes that the Land Bank should continue to play a significant role as financier of commercial agriculture and related activities, but that it should broaden its clientele through becoming the institution most responsible to the need of land reform beneficiaries and emergent entrepreneurs . . .
>
> I would like to take this opportunity to commend the Chairman of the Commission, Dr Conrad Strauss, and all the members of the Commission for a task well done. This report will no doubt assist and guide government in creating an enabling environment for rural participants and in expediting the task of rural development.

The press release prepared earlier by the Deputy Minister of Agriculture, Ms A T (Thoko) Didiza, was a commentary on the Interim Report that had been issued for public comment, and her views did not substantially change when the report was finalised. Her commentary, probably drafted

---

*Media Release: 'Statement by Mr Derek Hanekom MP, Minister for Agriculture and Land Affairs: Final Report of the Commission of Inquiry into the Provision of Rural Financial Services', 23 October 1996.

by Mbongwa and approved by the director general Bongi Njobe, stated:

> The Deputy Minister of Agriculture, Ms Thoko Didiza, commended the
> Strauss Commission. She however expressed certain reservations regarding
> the preliminary report.
>   The National Department of Agriculture (NDA) had been involved in
> the deliberations of the Commission with the belief that its work would
> assist the Department with what it regards as the main problem, namely
> providing services to the lower end of the financial market in the rural
> areas. The problem has three elements: the lack of collateral security, the
> high cost of service provision, and limited credit-worthiness. Although
> these issues are discussed, the Deputy Minister is of the opinion that the
> preliminary report does not adequately address the problem of filling the
> gap at the lower end of the financial market as it tends to focus more on
> the national institutions and institutional issues that are far removed from
> the problem on the ground.*

The Deputy Minister also expressed a different approach to the view
taken by the commissioners on the need to dismantle the department's
Agricultural Credit Board. The department's officials were reluctant to
relinquish this power base.

There seemed a lack of confidence, among certain officials, that the
Land Bank could become an effective delivery vehicle 'on the ground'.
I sympathised. I'd held the same views. Nevertheless, and more importantly, in taking on the job I had persuaded myself to believe that change
would be possible. I was indeed 'banking on change'.

---

*Press release by the Deputy Minister of Agriculture, Ms A T (Thoko) Didiza:
'Commentary on the Report by the Strauss Commission', 20 June 1996.

THREE

'BE REALISTIC: PLAN FOR A MIRACLE'

– Bagwan Shree Rajneesh

Stepping into the unknown

My new office was huge with wall-to-wall carpeting. Parallel to the wall furthest from the door was the largest glass-covered wooden desk that I had ever seen. It presided over the spaciousness of the entire room. Anyone granted an audience might have been intimidated by having to walk the distance between the door and the two visitors' chairs placed in front of the desk. The managing director's upholstered executive-status chair had a high back and wooden armrests – the overall effect was rather throne-like. I could not sit on the chair, but had to perch on its edge, lost in its space and discomfort. It was also impractical for my purposes. I wanted a swivel chair, adjustable in height and without protruding armrests that interfere with the elbow room needed when using a keyboard.

The walls were panelled with dark wood, another symbol of status. Only certain offices in the Land Bank had wood panelling – the others were painted a dreary beige. One dark panel of wood was actually the door to a cupboard that contained a safe. I was told that it was for any documents that I did not want to leave on my desk overnight, and also that a gun had been stored in it in the old days of needing to be prepared for possible terrorist attack. Another internal door led to a personal cloakroom; after all, the managing director could not be expected to share a bathroom with minions.

But there was no keyboard. When I asked for a computer I got strange uncomprehending looks. Why would I need a computer when I had two secretaries and a dictating machine? The puzzled looks also stemmed from an experience that the managing director did not draft documents but was provided with drafts that had worked their way up through the seniority levels of the Bank for comment or signature.

It was mid 1997, and I was seated in the head office of a publicly owned bank which turned over billions of rands a year, part of a financial services industry where investment in technology is one of the highest items of expenditure. Not one of the most senior managers was computer literate. Their offices were adorned with a dictating machine and a personal secretary. When the building and supplies department finally delivered a laptop to me it didn't have a modem. The idea of wanting to access a web site or of communicating through e-mail was not on their agenda of needs.

I began to liken myself to ET, the extraterrestrial being in the movie of the same name. My spaceship had come to rest in this Land Bank that was quite unlike anything that I had ever before experienced. Perhaps if I'd arrived after a stint in South Africa's corporate world it might have felt less strange. I would have been more used to the patriarchal business environment dominated by pale males.

But my experience was that of working in the Ministry of Agriculture in Mozambique, in the ANC Land Commission, in the NGO sector. I was used to a professional world in which my boss was likely to be black, and the majority of my peer group colleagues were black. Here I was surrounded by whites everywhere, and almost every single one of them a man. The sixty-nine most senior staff were all white men, the personal assistant was a white man, the drivers were white men; the only female in my working vicinity was my secretary Lettie. It all felt so very strange, a world unto itself; and we were already three years into the new South Africa. People's description of the Land Bank as a 'bastion of apartheid' was more apt than I had expected. I had had no direct involvement in this world before; I really had stepped into the unknown.

My office overlooked the gardens in front of Pretoria's City Hall – but the large office windows were shrouded with swathes of net curtain that were grey with age. As I sat at the desk during my first week my feelings of isolation were accentuated by the spaciousness. Flowers arrived from a friend and their scent and colour broke up my sombre environment and cheered me – they are remembered as special among all the flowers I've ever received in my life.

There was nothing to be done but to roll up my sleeves and give it the best shot I could muster with as much help as I could find. That's what I'd pledged – two years to secure a successful change process or lobby again for the privatisation option. I needed to do some serious business homework and start mapping out a way forward. But first of all I needed to do something to turn the office into a more hospitable working place.

I rejected the glossy catalogues of cherry-wood office furniture and asked to tour the basement storerooms. It wasn't that I didn't like the beautiful cherry wood – I've long coveted such a desk for my study at home – but I was conscious that we were a publicly owned institution and wanted to discourage any tendencies towards conspicuous consumption. In the storeroom I found tables that I could use to make an L-shaped work corner, as well as a table and chairs for meetings so that I could sit around a table with people rather than look at them from the other side of a huge desk.

The throne went down into the basement together with the reclining armchair. I'd forgotten about that item of privilege; each manager who enjoyed a certain rank had a reclining armchair in his office ready for that lunchtime nap. I unhooked the net curtains and discarded them. Natural light from the south-facing windows filtered weakly into the office. I brought a portable CD player from home in expectation of some long evening stints. My office began to feel a little more comfortable.

Stocktaking: a chronicle of findings

The Auditor General's (AG) Performance Report on public entities provided a composite review of work undertaken during the business year of 1996, and was issued by the Government Printers as a document for public consideration in mid 1997.* The Land Bank was one of several entities reviewed. The report provided a concentrated synopsis of the business of the Land Bank, as well as raising areas of concern:

(1) The Land and Agricultural Bank of South Africa (Land Bank) performs its financing function in terms of the Land Bank Act, No 13 of 1944, and operates as a legal entity. The Land Bank is not managed or directed by any state department and is accountable directly to Parliament through the Minister of Finance. The operations of the Land Bank are controlled by a board which consists of a chairman, who is also the managing director of the Land Bank and at least six, but not more than ten members, who are appointed by the Government.

(2) During 1995 the Land Bank granted 5 027 loans, totalling R1 001,9 million, to producers . . . Individual producers' total debt, as at 31 December 1995, in respect of long and medium-term loans as well as

---

*Auditor General's Report RP39, 1997, pp.8-13.

seasonal loans, amounted to R4 549,2 million. An amount of R14 416,7 million, including R14 296,9 million in short-term seasonal debt, was made available during 1995 to agricultural operations, control boards and statutory institutions. At 31 December 1995 the outstanding debt under these loans amounted to R4 477,7 million.

The direct farmer-client lending was mostly for bonds and medium-term loans to purchase machinery and equipment. Land Bank seasonal credit to commercial farmers was transacted via the cooperatives who received loans for onward advancement on a wholesale basis.

The section of the AG report titled 'Shortcomings in Management Measures and Examples' presented a litany of disturbing business issues.*

Issue (1) Management has not in all cases set formal goals in respect to the maximum time for each phase of evaluating and granting long-term advances to farmers. The Land Bank has also not benchmarked its loan application process against that of similar institutions in order to establish acceptable norms for the completion of the process.

Issue (2) No formal objective or target has been set by the board regarding the ideal ratio of own funds to borrowed funds (capital adequacy). Actual reserves in December 1994 totalled R1 370 million, exceeding the requirement of the Banks Act, No 94 of 1990, by more than 100 per cent.

Issue (3) The Land Bank had no formal strategic plan to address the financing needs of the agricultural sector in South Africa. The number of loans to farmers has declined over the last thirteen years, while the Land Bank share of the total agricultural financing market has remained constant.

Each of the issues raised was substantiated with data. Despite the Land Bank's advantage of being able to offer highly competitive interest rates, the number of loans and new applicants for both the long and the short-term loans had declined from 34 492 in 1986 to 26 771 in 1995. The AG report made the point that whilst the Land Bank had expanded the client catchment range of sourcing its business to include part-time and category one commercial farmers, its percentage of the overall agricultural financing remained at approximately 45 per cent.

Issue (4) The Land Bank did not have a formal plan to communicate the benefits of Land Bank financing to the agricultural sector.

---

*Auditor General's Report RP39, 1997, pp.10-11.

Substantiation of this issue was provided.

- Apart from the annual report, no documentation was made available to the agricultural sector setting out the requirements, terms, conditions and benefits of the Land Bank's financing.

- In September 1995, a one-page information pamphlet was produced, setting out the two types of loans the Land Bank offered. The pamphlet was primarily intended for use when communicating the Land Bank's functions to politicians and prospective farmers and did not give sufficient detail about the Land Bank's products.

- The Land Bank relied on organised agriculture to provide invitations to address farmers on the Land Bank's activities. There was no action plan or strategy to ensure that all sections of the agricultural community were addressed.

Issue (5) The methods used to determine staffing structures did not adequately address economy and efficiency issues. The internal Human Resources Department was not able to measure branch productivity and did not objectively ensure that the right number of people were employed per branch or for the Land Bank in total.

- No benchmarking or comparison between branches in relation to the number of loans or applications was done. Overall staff utilisation and effectiveness were not monitored and there was no scientific exercise to determine an optimal personnel structure to ensure that staff were utilised in the most economical manner.

- In 1995 Land Bank branches were overstaffed by between 34 and 38 per cent in comparison with 1985.

Issue (6) Strategic personnel management issues were not formally considered at board level. Specific goals and objectives were not set for existing strategies and therefore the performance of the Human Resources Department was not monitored on a regular basis.

- A total of 64 affirmative action appointments (59 per cent of the total appointments) were made up to the end of 1994. These constituted approximately five per cent of the personnel of the Land Bank. The affirmative action policy document did not, however, quantify any predetermined objective in this regard.

The Board's affirmative action policy limited affirmative action appointments (with the exception of a proposed black general manager) to entry level. Combined with a policy of only promoting from within, this would have the consequence of middle and senior management posts only being filled by affirmative action appointments in fifteen years' time.

My own findings confirmed the AG's report, but more sharply. First of all I was told that the pattern of recruitment of black staff had mirrored the ebb and flow of the progress of settlement talks at Kempton Park. When the talks were in progress blacks were actively recruited; but when the talks stalled so did the 'affirmative action' at the Land Bank.

The attitude towards recruitment at entry level reflected a decades-old practice of men and women joining the Land Bank after they had completed matric. They would then, on the basis of the same secondary school qualification, begin very different career paths in the Bank determined by gender discrimination. Van Staden, the outgoing acting managing director, proudly told me during the month of overlap that we shared that he was now sixty-five; he had started in the Bank at the age of eighteen, and expected everybody to start off as he had done with a stint in the Registrations Department. The inflexibility astounded me. One of the first retail branches I visited was Middelburg. I found two professional black employees on the staff, both doing low-level administrative tasks yet both were graduates with B Juris qualifications. The waste of talent in the Land Bank was to take my breath away over and over again.

> *Issue* (7) The Land Bank had no predetermined objectives in respect of interrelated variables such as operating expenditure, annual profit, interest margins, and interest rates in relation to market rates, growth and the risk exposure in the loan book.
>
> – In 1995, no budgets were prepared for operating and administration expenses. These expenses were monitored against prior year expenditure. Zero-based budgeting was not used. Decisions on interest rates to be charged were made primarily with reference to the projected profit for the year. Information on past margins and current interest rates of competitive products was not provided as part of the management information and there was no fixed policy on interest rate margins.*

I needed serious advice and support to tackle these issues. I did not think that I could undertake the job at the Land Bank without access to a mentor operating in an advisory capacity.

Japie Jacobs, better known in the Bank as Dr Jacobs, was a septuagenarian who had enjoyed enormous standing under the apartheid regime. He had presided over government commissions; for years he had been

---

*Auditor General's Report RP39, 1997, p.11.

senior deputy governor of the Reserve Bank and adviser to the Minister of Finance. He, more readily than most, accepted the political changes of the 1990s and was invited to join the business and labour discussion forums. In 1990 when he was asked to become a part-time adviser to the Land Bank, he readily accepted the position. I was glad that he did not opt to resign when I was appointed. I appreciated his continuing presence which gave me a sense of security that the oversight of the financial markets and their effect on the Land Bank's treasury and its balances was in extremely good hands. But whatever Dr Jacobs's qualities, I also needed someone with an integrated expertise that combined institutional change and business analysis.

I approached Claude Peyrot, who was a consultant to the European Reconstruction and Development Bank and also to the Development Bank of Southern Africa. I'd met him when I was a Strauss commissioner, and I now requested his availability to advise me on a regular basis over the next two years.

Claude operated like bush fire in a wind, spreading himself rapidly and covering ground at an enormous rate. He also operated like a bush telegraph, picking up information at speed and processing it into a coherent analysis. He occasionally made a mistake in character judgement, but his business analysis and 'next steps' advice was always spot on. His personality both exuded and solicited confidence. I wished I could have placed an invisible camera inside his shirt pocket so that I could monitor his technique and try to learn the essence of his approach. He had a field day on his first 'sounding' mission to the Bank; he had never before been anywhere quite like it.

His analysis was even more sobering than that of the Auditor General's office, because Claude confronted the core issue of the business profitability and made an assessment of its future in a wider global competitive environment. His words were like a cold shower intended to wake everyone up from an all too comfortable sleep. We made multiple copies of a twenty-minute video in which he presented his business appraisal to be shown to all employees in both head office and the branches. 'This is not a bank. This is an administrative factory,' were Claude's first cutting words. Then he went further, again using a no-holds-barred approach: 'Your retail business is losing money. It is the wholesale finance that is keeping the Bank afloat. It is imperative that you change your business approach, otherwise you are going to go out of existence.' This was his conclusion after a review of the Bank's business figures, markets and productivity.

Claude Peyrot was concerned that most staff saw change at the Bank as politically motivated and failed to understand the business imperative for change. Staff needed to be injected with a sense of urgency, he advised. They needed to be provided with information about the financial reasons that required that the Bank transform itself to survive in a new environment. He related this in particular to increasing deregulation in banking and to the influence of globalisation. Together these opened the way to local and international competition. Trends favoured general banks at the expense of specialist banks.

Claude also stated that if the Bank were a privately owned enterprise and he was being asked to advise the shareholder on what to do with the business, he would advocate closing all of it down except the wholesale business which was done by less than five per cent of the staff. Claude accepted the shareholder's intention, as expressed in the mandate covered by the cabinet-approved Strauss Commission, that the Land Bank had a special role to play in extending rural financial services to the previously disadvantaged. However, acceptance of such a decision did not exempt the Bank from revamping itself to start operating with business ethics. There was a need to 'get real' and leave behind the administrative factory approach of people with a civil service rather than entrepreneurial approach to business. He sensed an advantage in that the Bank had many younger employees, but was concerned at the absence of market awareness and marketing activity. The stumbling blocks, forecast Claude, were 'outdated systems, the inward-looking culture, and the lack of urgency about change'.

Outdated systems included a five-year lease agreement for an ICL mainframe of which the average usage was less than fifteen per cent. Someone, somehow, had persuaded the Bank that it needed a machine of mighty capacity; it was the equivalent of someone renting a combine harvester to deal with a smallholding of mealie cobs. I could not understand the agreement to hire a machine so much more expensive than we needed. And why five years? The turnover in computers and software meant that I, who have minimal knowledge of the IT industry, would have been reticent about signing anything more than a three-year commitment. And this hasty agreement had been amended at the very time when I was in overlap with the outgoing MD. When Claude and I asked for a copy of the agreement we found that there was not one on the premises and we had to arrange for it to be delivered from the ICL offices.

Not only were the systems using outdated 1970s COBOL-based programs, but there were also fiefdoms of computers programmed so as not to be able to interface with one another. Hence the agricultural economists were able to build their own little empire. We tendered for an external computer company to do an independent assessment of our needs. They recorded both the manual and computer input of the business process. One item, the now infamous 'registration', was done four times; once manually at the branch and once into the data bank. Head office repeated the operations. I groaned as I learnt these details.

Yet when a client phoned to make an enquiry about his current balance (the number of female clients at the time was minuscule), the employee who took the call had to say they would call back. The employee then went to the filing room where rows of dark green filing cabinets with brass handles housed the brown cardboard files, tied up with pink ribbon; these cavernous rooms were the only place where the information could be found. It was not available online.

The depth of staff experience and level of technical skills, as presented to the Strauss Commission, had been exaggerated. There were of course many competent people at the Bank, but they operated within a very strict set of inflexible rules. The range of business loan requests that the employees had been exposed to was also limited and there was no experience in the Bank of working in an innovative environment where the ethos would be to find the 'how to' rather than the prevalent tendency towards 'can't do'.

The staff organogram for dealing with loan processing at a branch also reflected the organisation of the workflow. It was a highly segmented process. Each workflow segment was then constituted into a mini section staffed by a hierarchy of junior, senior and supervisory employees. The majority of staff knew one discrete piece of the entire loan approval process, but never had a vision of the overall production line. The branch manager, assisted by a couple of seniors, then took responsibility for all loan approvals irrespective of size. Staff moved around over the years from section to section, but the process did not afford them the opportunity to apply accumulated skills. The system was rigid in that experienced loan clerks who had for years assisted clients to fill in application forms complained that they would often recognise the conditions for rejection of an application but were not permitted to make an input. The loan processing would advance until completion and only then be considered by the branch manager's committee. There was, according to the loan officers, considerable wastage in the systems.

The culture of the Bank was not only inward-looking but comprised both highly visible and less visible systems of hierarchy, racism, and gender discrimination. The visible symbols were probably fairly normal for the South African corporate world. There was a transition from office-sharing to having one's own office, the acquisition of the reclining armchair on obtaining a certain rank, the personal secretary, to the final prize of personal cloakroom and waiting room when you reached one of the top three positions.

I was regaled with stories of how Land Bank people in positions of authority behaved; of how when the managing director got into the lift no one else was permitted to enter except the security officer/driver. It took me weeks to realise that status and hierarchy even played themselves out in the dining room arrangements. I'd take my tray and sit at a different table each lunchtime so as to have a chance to talk to a variety of Land Bank staff, unaware that I was disturbing an unspoken order and creating invisible waves. I learnt later that the most junior employees sat nearest the serving counter, and the most senior sat at the far end, where the extra windows made it the most pleasant part of a long narrow room. Moreover, the men who had reached a certain rank did not take a tray and join the queue. They sat, and were served by waiters.

I noticed that not many black employees chose to eat in the ninth floor canteen. I thought that might be because it served 'European' style food, perhaps considered unpalatable even if it was subsidised to sell at R3,85 a plateful. I discovered that a separate dining room was in operation on another floor of the building. Here staff classified as 'sundry workers' (people such as messengers, cleaners and gardeners – who were one hundred per cent black) could get a plate of *pap*, *vleis* and gravy (maize meal porridge with meat) free of charge. Again, I had to pinch myself to convince myself I was not dreaming – it was, after all, a full three years since the elections.

White patriarchy reigned supreme. It wasn't long before I noticed that all the women and sundry staff wore uniforms – but not any of the white men – from the most junior to the most senior. The explanation was that women and sundry workers occupied the less well-paid jobs, so the provision of uniforms represented a saving for them. Two of the women had made it to the title of senior director and were positioned at numbers seventy and seventy-one in the bank's hierarchy – but they still wore uniforms. The men had, however, decreed that on Fridays the women could choose to wear their own clothing if they so wished. Even this dispensation had limitations – the white tribal patriarchy enjoyed laying down the law – and up until a few months before my arrival Friday's own clothing choice did not extend to the wearing of trousers! By now I could imagine the eleven elderly white male deputy general managers gathered in Conference Room One on the ninth floor deliberating whether or not to grant women employees the right to wear trousers on Fridays.

The pecking order of the career ladder in the Land Bank was extremely well developed. It comprised seventeen titled positions, each with three 'notches' – interim grades of seniority within each position. A school-leaving entry level as a clerk at position number forty-two could eventually lead through forty-one promotions to appointment as managing director – as had happened with my predecessor, Mr van Staden. In the next few months of internal consultation workshops, younger Bank employees repeatedly expressed sentiments that promotions were often linked less to merit than to years of service. Favouritism was alleged to play its part, as well as a tendency for members of the different Land Bank clubs to support one another's promotions – they called it the *boetie-boetie* system. The 1997 appointment of an externally recruited managing director was the first in the history of the Bank since 1912.

Women, however, were less fortunate, although they at least had the opportunity of administrative service work, an option closed to black employees until as late as 1993. Very few women escaped from the tripartite categorisation of Madam Clerk: Grade I, Grade II or Grade III. Apart from the gender-based obligation to wear uniform, there was further discrimination against married women in that they did not have the same rights to medical aid. There were several interconnected families in the Bank, man and wife, and their siblings. A ruling was in force that if the husband of a female employee was offered promotion to a managerial position, the woman was obliged to resign. The intention was to avoid any awkwardness for employees having to work with the boss's wife.

Men also had other privileges, as I discovered unexpectedly. One Thursday afternoon some problem came up on which I wanted quick advisory input from the senior managers. I no longer remember the reason for the meeting, that part of my memory having been effaced by the effect of learning the reason why it could not take place.

'Lettie, could you ask V, W, X, Y, Z if they could possibly come to my office, and please apologise for the short notice.'

None of them could be reached in their offices. It transpired that they were attending a meeting of the Land Bank Golf Club. It was two o'clock on a Thursday afternoon. The news, as conveyed, implied that a hallowed meeting was in session, not to be interrupted. I was not discreet in my reaction which was, firstly, that I expected social club meetings to happen at lunchtime or after hours and, secondly, that I expected that if the women had wanted a club meeting the same privileges would *not* apply. It was a spontaneous response on my part and it provoked hostility.

In retrospect I realise that at that time productivity was low, they were not busy; they probably wondered why I was being so uptight about the issue. It might have been better strategy to have followed the advice given to me by Conrad Strauss to 'take up golf' and to have joined the Golf Club. It was only a year later that I was to read the Sun Tzu classic *The Art of War* which contains that thought-provoking sentence: 'The supreme act of war is to subdue the enemy without fighting.'

In that first period, however, the incidents and discoveries had a cumulative effect. Within a few weeks of my immersion into Land Bank matters I began to harbour a modicum of anger. The Auditor-General's report and Claude Peyrot's analysis, added to my own observations on workplace culture, provided a depressing overall scenario. The discovery that an addendum to the multimillion computer deal had been signed behind my back in my first month of tenure provoked not only indignation but also mistrust towards certain staff. When I finally received a laptop – without a modem – I wondered whether the omission was a genuine mistake born of ignorance, or whether certain people were trying to get under my skin. Late at night, in that Kafka-esque citadel of the state's farm loan administrative factory, aka the Land Bank head office, it was possible to imagine all manner of demons.

I felt that the Strauss commissioners had not been able to take full measure of the status quo. Would they have reached a different conclusion if they had been in full possession of the facts? It seemed that the new board of directors and I were being asked to lead an institutional transformation process that equated with amateurs being asked to join an expedition to climb Everest. I was not sure that the obstacles were not insurmountable. There's an African saying, 'You don't try to eat the elephant all at one sitting'. We were going to have to find a process that allowed us to tackle issues in bite-sized chunks, whilst keeping in mind the overall objective of ingesting the whole elephant.

It was around this time that I made a Sunday morning foray to the flea-market in Rosebank, Johannesburg. I was with my daughters and we were looking for a gift for a friend. We were not in a hurry, there was time to look at the many craft stalls. We stopped at one that sold fridge magnets. I bought the one that appeared to be appropriate to what I was trying to do in my professional life. The words painted on the magnet were: 'Be Realistic: Plan for a Miracle'.

A breath of fresh air

Claude's advice was that I needed to get out fast, needed some space to think, needed exposure to a different way of doing things, and to the current debates on institutional transformation. I would drown if I had to tread water in the deep end of this stagnating pool on a daily basis. I took two weeks out and travelled to London, visited City Bank and a branch of a North African Bank. I spent time with tutors who ran the banking and finance departments at the University of London's School of Oriental and African Studies. In France I spent a week with the second largest French bank, Credit Agricole, first at their Paris head office and then in an agricultural region visiting their provincial office and several branches.

Every minute that I was not in a meeting, or being tutored, I spent reading the business literature on institutional transformation. I scoured the bookstores and offices of friends on a treasure hunt for a jewel, something that resonated with the situation I was in and gave me clues as to how to map out a process of change. There are literally dozens of books, a confusing variety, and I felt a reasonable scepticism about how much one could learn from books as compared to learning by doing and listening to those who have experience. A friend who had finished a course at Harvard the year before passed over several volumes, among them the transcript of a book that was about to be published.

Leading Change by Kotter was where I found the resonance and guidance for the task of institutional change at the Land Bank – and I'd use much of the same approach again if faced with another change management challenge.

Kotter begins his book by arguing that change is the permanent condition of our business environment. We have outlived a period when a company could revamp itself and then settle down to years of stability in which tinkering at the edges to make minor adjustments could secure business longevity. He states:

> Although some people predict that most of the reengineering, restrategizing, mergers, downsizing, quality efforts, and cultural renewal projects will soon disappear, I think that is highly unlikely. Powerful macroeconomic forces are at work here, and these forces may grow even stronger over the next few decades. As a result, more and more organizations will be pushed to reduce costs, improve the quality of products and services, locate new opportunities for growth, and increase productivity.*

Globalisation would ensure that there would be no islands of immunity from these macro-economic drivers. That's exactly what Claude Peyrot

---

*Reprinted by permission of Harvard Business School Press. From *Leading Change* by J P Kotter, Boston, MA, 1996, p.3. Copyright © 1996 by John P Kotter. All rights reserved.

had tried to convey to Land Bank staff, most of whom thought the reasons for change were only politically motivated; they could not yet see that the bureaucratic machine they were part of had reached the end of its depreciation period and was on the verge of obsolescence.

Kotter begins by outlining the eight major mistakes that are often made in an institutional change process:

Error #1	Allowing too much complacency
Error #2	Failing to create a sufficiently powerful guiding coalition
Error #3	Underestimating the power of vision
Error #4	Undercommunicating the vision
Error #5	Permitting obstacles to block the new vision
Error #6	Failing to create short-term wins
Error #7	Declaring victory too soon
Error #8	Neglecting to anchor the changes firmly in the corporate culture

Kotter substantiates each identified error with real world examples, and then proceeds with the classic conversion approach to problem solving, the 'don'ts' are replaced by a contrasting set of 'do's'. The error 'allowing too much complacency' provides the rationale for Command #1 in Kotter's 'Eight-Stage Change Process':

Stage #1	Establishing a sense of urgency
Stage #2	Creating the guiding coalition
Stage #3	Developing a vision and strategy
Stage #4	Communicating the change vision
Stage #5	Empowering broad-based action
Stage #6	Generating short-term wins
Stage #7	Consolidating gains and producing more change
Stage #8	Anchoring new approaches in the corporate culture

The process recommendations are then unpacked one by one with the opening caveat:

> . . . major change will not happen easily for a long list of reasons. Even if an objective observer can clearly see that costs are too high, or products are not good enough, or shifting customer requirements are not being adequately addressed, needed change can still stall because of inwardly focused cultures, paralyzing bureaucracy, parochial politics, a low level of trust, lack of teamwork, arrogant attitudes, a lack of leadership in middle management, and the general human fear of the unknown. To be

effective, a method designed to alter strategies, reengineer processes, or improve qualities must address these barriers and address them well.*

The Land Bank appeared to have more than its fair share of these characteristics.

Kotter also made what for me was a most helpful observation in the circumstances, iterating how he saw the roles of leadership and management differently:

> Management is a set of processes that can keep a complicated system of people and technology running smoothly. The most important aspects of management include planning, budgeting, organizing, staffing, controlling and problem solving. Leadership is a set of processes that creates organizations in the first place or adapts them to significantly changing circumstances. Leadership defines what the future should look like, aligns people with that vision, and inspires them to make it happen despite the obstacles.†

It might be that my title was 'Managing Director' but the focus of my job for the immediate future had to be leadership rather than management.

The first five steps of the eight-stage change process seemed daunting, and possibly insurmountable. I felt very much alone. There was no sense of urgency. There were no communications personnel, and an empowering broad-based action plan seemed a far-fetched possibility. Most importantly, although there was a clear mandate outlined in the cabinet-approved Strauss recommendations, there was no vision as to how this would translate itself in practice.

It was the days spent with Credit Agricole that helped to clear the blurred outlines into a focused vision. Credit Agricole boasts an institutional historian, one of the personnel who I met for a lengthy discussion at their Paris head office. 'The Land Bank, as you describe it,' (and my descriptions were fairly diplomatic – I had no wish to be a poor ambassador and wash dirty linen with foreign associates) said the historian, 'is reminiscent of Credit Agricole at the end of the Second World War.'

I gulped at the implication that we had half a century to catch up on. He then detailed a fifty-year continuous change process. They had created provincial networks. They had different categories of branches, dealing with different levels of business, each staffed accordingly with

---

†Ibid, p.25.

the appropriate skills level. They had financed themselves through a savings drive. They had diversified their business. A second wave of major change began in the early seventies. They had recruited new blood into the institution as well as spending ten per cent of the salary bill for ten years on staff training programmes, far outstripping an industry norm that regarded a three per cent skills development budget as high.

My visits to the branches were revealing. They were staffed by as few as four to eight people, very different to the Land Bank branches which were generally made up of twenty-five to forty-five people. An online computer link-up to the provincial data processing unit provided up-to-date information on transactions and balances.

There were no secretaries; everyone was computer literate. In spite of a branch handling thousands of accounts, a loan officer handled enquiries from clients who needed a written response, with designated responsibility for a client portfolio. Complaints tended to be handled by the branch manager who saw himself as responsible for public relations, marketing, engagement if necessary in local politics, as well as for oversight of the business plan. 'Himself' is used advisedly – very few professional women were to be seen. Affirmative action with regard to gender did not seem to have figured strongly in the Credit Agricole change process.

Loan officers were graded, although there was one overall job description, and they handled a loan from A to Z. The internal process of grading was based on demonstrated competence and determined the level of loan that an officer could handle. There were also specialisations: agriculture and a sort of 'private banking' service for large account clients.

Credit Agricole's rural accessibility was enhanced by their use of agents and 'mobile banks'. The latter were not mobile in terms of an on-the-road trailer, but consisted of teams of people who would move around from rural town to rural town on market days and open up for business. The improved accessibility afforded by the mobile teams was comple-mented by Credit Agricole's *Agences Verde* a 'green-for-go' agency system. These were businesses, registered and working on a commission basis, where one could make the simple deposit and withdrawal transaction without going to a branch. Agencies included not only shops but also restaurants. I had already noted that the South African post office was using agents, often spaza shops that offered a service over extended hours. The idea of the Land Bank using a similar system merited exploration. The Bank had only twenty-five branches; investment in bricks and mortar to build more branches was definitely not the answer.

It was a successful operating model. It captured my attention as providing answers to tackling the accessibility issue, the segmented or divisional approach to workflow, the role of the branch manager, the required levels of business skills and computer literacy. However, the Land Bank did not have fifty years in hand to make the changes. A fast-track approach would be needed.

The board *bosberaad* and the think-tank workshop

In June 1997 the recently appointed board of directors booked into Zebra Lodge, a country retreat, for a two-day workshop – *bosberaad** as it would commonly be referred to. The group's objective was to familiarise themselves with the business of the Bank and get to grips with the transformation issues. This meant that the agenda was extremely varied between current business and creating time for thinking conceptually about institutional change.

Current business included having to consider a management resolution proposing to spend more than R20-million on refurbishing buildings. Another issue dealt with a R2-million contract for new uniforms for women and sundry workers. This agenda item derailed our time management. Everyone was so shocked by the implicit discrimination of the uniform practice. Abolition was out of the question – that would constitute a wage cut. There was also the consideration of corporate image. The outcome of the debate was that corporate wear should be stylish, optional, and also available to all male staff!

An overview of how the Land Bank functioned included examination of the financing of its loans, the Land Bank Act, the Auditor General's performance audit findings, its approach to human resources management, staff grading and salary structures.

We arranged for two external inputs. In one session invitees from the Gauteng public service commission and the Development Bank of Southern Africa (DBSA) gave an overview of different job grading systems – Paterson, Peromnes, Hay and JE Manager – and explained their similarities and differences. The Land Bank had just completed a second two-year study on the restructuring of its salaries and we wanted to consider what was referred to as the McGee proposal on an informed comparative basis.

The second presentation covered an assessment of DBSA's transformation process – what were the lessons learnt that the Bank could usefully adopt for itself. As a finale to the two-day meeting the board drew up its own guiding principles for transformation. These were:

---

*South African term for an extended meeting usually held off business premises.

- Vision led
- Thorough consultation
- Sustainable transformation
- Transparency
- Personal choice
- Fairness and justice
- Gender affirmation
- Affirmative action
- Inclusivity
- Empowerment

The Board also gave a directive: '. . . and it must be FUN.'

To kick-start the process, to design its operational nuts and bolts, it was decided that another workshop should be held. It became known as the 'THINK-TANK' workshop. It was to be attended by myself and three non-executive board members tasked with the responsibility of special support to the change process. A broad cross-section of staff would be invited: both senior and junior, men and women, technical and non-technical, and with careful attention to race representation.

It was difficult to settle on the names of participants. Over and over again in my first few months at the Bank I would ask for nominations for some task team, or representation at some meeting or other, and almost invariably I would send back the list of nominations with the comment that white males were over-represented. I needed nominations with more women and 'people of colour'. The two unions with a membership base at the Land Bank, the South African Society of Banking Officials (SASBO) and the South African Commercial Catering and Allied Workers Union (SACCAWU), were invited, and indeed each sent an internal delegate; the SASBO regional officer also chose to attend.

The use of the eighth floor of the Land Bank was about to change dramatically. For more than four decades since the head office had been built, the eighth floor accommodated the eight executive board members, the adviser, the two general managers and the managing director. The only other mortals whose presence was permitted were the secretarial, messenger, and catering employees. There was a large spacious salon used previously as the Board Dining Room which, when not set up for eating, was furnished with huge comfortable easy chairs. It had a well-supplied bar and a music system in one corner. It became the Indaba Room, intensively used for meetings, consultations with stakeholders and training sessions. The eighth floor became the engine room of change activity as task teams were set up and met frequently over the next few months.

That first cross-sectional THINK-TANK workshop was history in the making. In the absence of internal skills we employed an outside company to assist with facilitation of the entire change process. We needed an agency committed to a methodology that would promote the development of common values and ideas. We scoured around for a firm with a reputation, experience and availability to appoint as our transformation consultants, and contracted the Guild of RGA (Reconstruction, Growth and Alignment) whose associates had several years' experience of working with companies undertaking institutional restructuring.

There was no organisational development experience within the Bank. In fact, the supplies department had to purchase flip chart stands and paper and felt-tipped pens for the workshop for the first time in its history. No one had used them as a work tool before.

The transformation consultants used a 'Where from? Where to? How are we going to get there?' approach to a meeting that began late one afternoon and finished on the afternoon of the second day. The format gave us a warm-up session to start people thinking, an evening mealtime for informal interaction and then an early start to a day of serious brainwork.

As an ice breaker and a technique to set the discussion rolling on the 'Where are we coming from?' component, the transformation consultants, Steve Hobbs and Pam Pretorius, subdivided the group of twenty-four people. Each group was asked to draw the animal that they felt most closely resembled their own personal experience of working in the Land Bank.

In the early part of this meeting I sat back, my responsibility lay in the second section – the vision for the future. For this first session I needed to be a listener and hear what employees said about their workplace. We were all both shocked and amused by the results: shocked because of the harsh honesty, and amused because people dealt with the issue with a sense of humour. A feeling of 'WOW!' and laughter pervaded the room; the ice was broken.

One group drew a rhinoceros standing in water with small fish swimming between its legs. Their rationale was that, first of all, it was an African animal that dates back a long while, but hasn't evolved greatly. It was like the Land Bank in that it had a thick skin – impervious to criticism; its small ears represented the Bank as short on listening skills. The other features were: poor eyesight/narrow vision, demarcates its area, a limited diet, a threatened species, and moves very slowly, except when angry. The numerous small fish represented a staff who currently felt they could not make any real impact on the behaviour of the rhinoceros.

Another group drew an ostrich. The Land Bank, they said, put its head in the ground when it saw trouble coming. It catered to an elitist group, serving limited products to an exclusive market. It was a conservationist in terms being an efficient utiliser of limited natural resources. Its long neck, they argued, represented inherent potential: if it would only pull its neck out of the sand, it could contemplate the world from a vantage point.

A third group drew a tortoise. The slowness of this creature, they said, reflected the way the Bank went about its business. The hard shell represented 'a rigid and inflexible construction', meaning its impermeability to criticism and unwillingness to be more adaptable. Moreover the tortoise had short legs and poor eyesight; it did not have either the height or the broad line of vision to see what future lay before it. Lastly, the tortoise's strategy of self-defence was to retreat into its shell rather than tackling and resolving a problem; it maintained a low profile and could boast longevity.

It was a tough workshop. We broke into groups and brainstormed issues around Land Bank products, workplace culture and human resources policies. People were confronted by criticism that they themselves generated. It was both a cause for anxiety as well as a process of creating a collective determination to change.

Visioning

I gave an introduction to the workshop, drawing on the clauses of the Strauss Commission that informed the new mandate of the Bank. I also referred to my own hopes about what kind of working culture should be aspired to – a place where people spoke without fear, a place where employees could confidently cast constructive criticism, where creative thinking and innovation would be rewarded, and so on. I supported decentralisation of some functions. I felt that branches, at the leading edge of client service, needed to become centres of empowerment seated within a cross-culture of learning between branches.

There are people who remain sceptical about the value of vision and mission statements as a tool. The scepticism is warranted if the vision is perceived as 'hot air' and there is no visible 'walk the talk'. Kotter* argues that the absence of vision can damage a business through fruitless expenditure on disconnected or inappropriate activity. Without a vision it would be difficult to decide what gets priority, proportionality of

---

*J P Kotter, 1996.

spending, sequence of effort, or to secure the interconnecting synergy of various components of the change effort.

My intervention was counter-balanced by Claude's sobering message: 'You are working in a failing business.'

John Sender, a professor with years of research experience on farm worker conditions – especially those of women workers – asked people to think about the business from an alternative starting point. The issue at stake was defining the 'broad goal' which, in his view, was 'a positive impact on very poor people in rural areas', many of whom could be characterised as landless women farm workers with irregular incomes, poor living conditions and low quality nutrition? He threw out some ideas to get people's minds engaged with his direction of thinking.

What can the Land Bank do to improve employment and the living conditions of the rural poor? He noted: some crops require much more labour per hectare than others and there could be incentives for certain cropping patterns. Irrigated land uses much more labour than rain-fed farming – therefore an incentive scheme for irrigation linked to disincentives for irresponsible water use could be contemplated. Better wages would improve people's lives – the Land Bank, proposed Sender, could in the manner of its lending influence farmers. He suggested we investigate the adoption of a Code of Good Practice whereby, for example, the Land Bank would have special rates for farmers who had good employment practices. He mentioned that certain companies, especially export buyers, were adopting such a code to determine from whom they were prepared to buy.

When contemplating delivery to the new mandate clients, he reminded people that the best practice literature indicated that a repayment record was more important than levels of collateral, so we needed to consider the design of a product that would establish repayment commitment. He suggested joint ventures to offer endowment policies to farm workers through the farm-owner client. He proposed linking up land reform beneficiary projects with supermarket chains to get the best deal out of a marketing agreement.

A subgroup then spent time debating employees' views on workplace culture and the human resources policies that would be required to support such change. Another group looked at Land Bank products, and their appropriateness to clients' needs. Another group began an evaluation of internal 'back office' systems, since the cry of murder was on the lips of many employees as soon as they got space to complain about bureaucracy.

By the close of the two-day session we had set up five task teams, each to be co-ordinated by one of the persons present, and had generated lists of names of employees who were thought to have the skills and willingness to be co-opted on to the teams. The task teams were New Products, Human Resources, Office Systems, Communications, and Finance.

Many people responded with both their heads and their hearts to the vision of a new Land Bank that was being dangled before them. It offered the possibility of a break with an oppressive history. They also realised, perhaps for the first time, that to continue along the lines of the past was tantamount to committing business suicide and putting their own jobs at risk. I learnt in those first months not only the extent to which the apartheid system had denied opportunities to black South Africans, but also about the culture of internal repression even within the institutions run by Afrikaners and for their own benefit. There was a psychological culture of control, and age-based hierarchies. It had left little room for creative challenge, especially from the younger generation. It did not make for a thriving business environment.

But we had made a start; we had mapped out a process and a programme for the rest of the year. For the first time in three months I felt a little lighter, felt that perhaps there was a chance for the change process to work after all. In terms of Kotter's eight-stage process,* we had made progress on the first three:

Stage 1   Establishing a sense of urgency
- Examining the market and competitive realities
- Identifying and discussing crises, potential crises, or major opportunities

Stage 2   Creating the guiding coalition
- Putting together a group with enough power to lead the change
- Getting the group to work together like a team

Stage 3   Developing a vision and strategy
- Creating a vision to help direct the change effort
- Developing strategies for achieving that vision

---

*Reprinted by permission of Harvard Business School Press. From *Leading Change* by J P Kotter, Boston, MA, 1996, p.21. Copyright © 1996 by John P Kotter. All rights reserved.

To make further progress we had to tackle the issue of communication, referred to by Kotter as Stage 4:

Stage 4   Communicating the change vision
            • Using every vehicle possible to constantly communicate the new vision and strategies
            • Having the guiding coalition role model the behaviour expected of employees

To make a start on this issue, a communications task team was set up at head office. A black staff member, Hope Babili, who had a personnel management diploma and human resources degree was found in the registrations department; naturally she felt her talents and qualifications were being wasted. She teamed up with Letitia Erasmus, a bright spark who had managed to study for her degree whilst underemployed doing administrative work at the Bank. We used a short-term consultant for guidance whilst we pursued the idea of setting up a new and fully fledged Communications Department.

Consultation: bottom-up, inside-out, top-down

One of the issues to be tackled was how to design a process that would be inclusive of some 1300 employees spread over twenty-six locations. There were twenty-five branches in the nine provinces and the head office in Pretoria. The design of the internal process also had to be married to the proposal for proactive external consultation. One of the strengths that the transformation consultants brought to the design was an emphasis, born out of their experience, on the need for a consultative stakeholder approach with special attention to external stakeholders, existing clients, potential clients, civil servants, farmers' unions and non-governmental organisations.

We decided on a process of internal branch workshops complemented by workshops with external stakeholders. There would be nine provincial workshops and one head office workshop with both internal and external participation. The process would then culminate in a national consolidation conference to be held at Klein Kariba in December 1997. The conference, with countrywide internal and external delegates, would be attended by the board members designated with special responsibility to support the transformation process. Over and over again, the external presence prevented the workshops from the tendency to lapse into introverted navel gazing.

The internal branch workshops included a review of the Land Bank as a place to work. There was a session in which the transformation consultants got people to discuss what they were proud of as employees and what they were sorry about. They were proud of stability, reliability, and the fact that the Bank was supportive to customers in times of difficulties and not just a fair-weather friend. An issue that caused discomfort in the 'sorry session' was race.

'The young white man is called *Meneer* . . . from his first day of employment. I am referred to by my first name.'

'I have a matric certificate but I am a "sundry worker".'

'I have a driver's licence and do the gardening but am not allowed to drive the garden rubbish to the dump – only the white man is allowed to drive.'

Discomfort around religion also had a place.

'Up until two years ago, if you wanted a job at this branch you were asked for a Dutch Reformed Church testimonial.'

Some staff members asked why the corporate wear was European style; why could there not be an accommodation for, say, the Indian staff who might prefer to wear saris, made up in the corporate material.

Another part of the workshop focused on decision-making culture, and discussed adult-to-adult working relationships rather than the parent-child systems that are prevalent in authoritarian workplaces. Videos from other countries showed more participatory workplaces, interviews with factory workers, and discussions on business productivity changes as a result of changed systems. People were challenged not to regard change as a risk, but rather as an opportunity.

We used internally produced videos as an alternative to communication through circulars. There was already the video in which Claude Peyrot had put forward his business appraisal. The communications task team canvassed a list of burning questions arising in staff discussions from branch to branch and Hope and Letitia organised the production of a video in which they interviewed me on these issues. The questions were internally focused – on job security, and fear of affirmative action.

There was a session which tried to move people from their internal focus: 'How do we wish to be perceived by the customer?' It always generated a list of positives: flexibility, speed of response, a diverse range of products to suit needs. The facilitators introduced the concept of the score-card and suggested it be used with external stakeholders and in the provincial workshops. If developed in the future, it could provide a measuring tool for progress on delivery issues.

I did not get to many of the twenty-five branch workshops, but was persuaded of the importance of making it to at least part of every single one of the nine provincial workshops. This was becoming a real on-the-road job – but it was effective in inducing some fence-sitters to take a leap forward. The face-to-face interaction with staff was a winner, even if they didn't like what I had to say. I'd be told: 'I've worked in this bank for twenty-seven years. I've never seen the managing director in person, let alone spoken to one, and still less ever expected that I would be sharing a lunch table.'

The list of external stakeholders consulted in the process was lengthy: clients, agribusiness, NGOs, farmers' associations, government department representatives. Agribusiness raised the issue of their assuming the role of intermediaries in the field so as to improve our outreach. The clients mostly raised issues on products. Why could we not have a flexi-bond instead of a new loan application for every single new need? What about our financing of agribusiness? What about insurance? Questions were asked about the Bank's future intentions to provide wholesale finance to or partner provincial development finance bodies. There were concerns expressed about the composition of the new board of directors. The old board had strongly represented the white farming constituency. The newly appointed and very diverse board did not offer constituency representation. I was at the Mpumalanga provincial workshop when this issue came up. The discussions bore fruit. My defence that the board was chosen because of its skills to support a transformation process was heard and accepted. On the other hand, the idea of provincial advisory forums based on constituency representation was born.

Claude Peyrot co-ordinated the first of a series of monthly Transformation Progress Reports presented to the board in August 1997. He organised each task team to provide not only a summary but a set of overheads. Most of the team leaders were nervous; their Land Bank experience meant they were not used to public speaking, let alone making a presentation to the board of directors; speech and presentation training needed to be added to our capacity building list of requirements.

Claude's brief to the board covered his assessment of a process that was on the move and beginning to bring people on board. A schedule had been mapped out so that preliminary recommendations would be ready for discussion at the national consolidation conference in early December.

Key interim findings were: a high level of anxiety internally, languages as an important marketing issue, and the need to reassure the present client bases of the Bank's continued commitment. It was also noted that fifty per cent of our clients undertook rain-fed cultivation, and that we needed to revisit our risk and pricing strategy.

The board was primed on what the recommendations resulting from the work of the task teams, as well as the provincial review process, might cover:

- Defining a 'product plan' for implementation in 1998, including targets on client numbers and financial volume.
- Proposals to redefine the field network and scope of operations.
- Creating support for new intermediaries to reach the historically disadvantaged clients.
- Proposals for decentralisation of some head office functions to the branch network – the unhappiness about potential redundancies was noted.
- Proposals to change the decision-making approach included the formation of a strategic management team working with the MD which would replace the deputy general manager caucus.

What the Bank had in its favour was its manageable size. There were 1300 people spread over twenty-six locations. It was feasible to contemplate the implementation of decisions on new proposals simultaneously. An overall objective of twenty per cent improvement in efficiency was proposed. All resources set free by efficiency gains were to be redeployed towards sales and marketing. The human resources grading of jobs and new salary proposals were expected to be completed for implementation in March 1998. At the October 1997 board meeting Peyrot and the task team leaders confirmed progress towards implementation as being on track.

A conference to consolidate

A national consolidation conference was held at Klein Kariba in early December 1997. It was the culmination of the consultation process. There were ten representatives from each province (seven internal Bank representatives and three persons drawn from the external stakeholders in each province), and some twenty-five from head office. There was a cross-section of some forty external stakeholders nationwide. It had been a nightmare compiling the final lists, requiring a delicate balancing act of weighing up the mix of race, gender, skills, commitment, and constituency. At one moment it seemed such an impossible task that the best solution might have been to put the names into a hat and do a draw. But people had specialised in their contributions to task teams, and as the conference was a working occasion rather than a celebratory jamboree, the balancing act was necessary.

There were three board members in attendance – Bonile Jack, Izak Cronje and Evan Matthews. It was they who'd taken on special oversight of the transformation process and they attended most of the sessions in spite of their business commitments. Izak, as always, and in spite of the fact that he was recovering from a recent heart attack, was there one hundred per cent of the time, giving one hundred per cent of himself unstintingly. I admired him for the transition he'd made from the old board to the new without ever being a Judas to his constituency, and also for the personal integrity he showed when faced with the discomfort of discussing some of the previous board's problematic decisions.

The conference began with a 'Futures Fair'. Everyone came with artwork that for them epitomised the process and aspirations of the transformation journey. The first 'warm up' hour allowed people to wander around and share impressions. Each group then gave the background to the display they had prepared. Many included designs for a new Land Bank logo intended to symbolise the changes. People then divided into small groups to present their input into the Mission, Vision and Value statements.

Four parallel theme groups, each with two subgroups, operated for the major part of the conference. The Delivery Group dealt with products, partners, and provincial decentralisation. The Organisational Design Group focused on workplace redesign at branches, the restructuring of head office, and the revamp of the delegation of powers that should accompany decentralisation and branch empowerment. The Human Resources Group looked at policies on job grading, approaches to salary packaging, the internal rules and procedures, and affirmative action. The last group considered the inputs of the mission, vision and value presentations as well as identifying tangible goals for progress on race, gender and leadership culture.

It was a starry night in high summer when people took after-supper time out. Klein Kariba has huge pools fed by hot springs. There was a massive turnout at the pool, the most mixed race and gender group that the majority of the people present had ever been part of. There was some lazy swimming, but mostly there was lounging about in the shallow end, laughter and relaxation after a hard day's work following on weeks of preparation.

In the morning people were crisp and ready to go. The working groups carried on through the whole day, finishing up with preparations for a presentation to plenary the next morning. That night, with the work tucked under their belts, people let their hair down. They were exuberant. We grilled meat, and hired a disco with a special request that they bring a wide variety of music to cater for our different tastes. That was the night that many of us learnt to do an Afro-American square dance with slave origins known as the 'bus stop'.

Derek Hanekom, Minister of Agriculture and Land Affairs, attended the final presentation. His presence was a bonus for the participants, especially when they got positive feedback. He commented on the high levels of energy displayed, and the quality of the work, and criticised us for not getting media coverage of what was really a magnificent occasion. His closing speech* touched on eight topics.

- The first covered the need for the Bank to have the ability to carry out its owner's (government's) objectives.

- The second topic concerned the issue of autonomous governance, that the Bank, although state-owned, should not be subject to government interference in terms of its operations. Cabinet, he stated, had appointed a board to oversee the Bank on its behalf.

- The third topic was the need for the board to be in touch with clients, which would be achieved by each board director becoming a member of the provincial advisory forum. This link would make the board unique.

- The fourth topic outlined the delivery objectives: 'Servicing the poor is part of social responsibility or upliftment. We need continually to assess whether the Bank contributes to economic growth, eradicates poverty and creates a vibrant rural economy.'

- The fifth topic addressed the preference to avoid subsidised interest rates, in spite of pressure from clients. Historical economic analysis indicated their ineffectiveness in the longer term.

- The sixth issue addressed government support. The self-sustainability of the institution was important – government was not expecting to offer additional capital to the Land Bank. Hence, 'a low interest rate may be popular (but costly) and short-lived if the financial institution cannot break even'.

- The seventh point suggested that special funds be earmarked and ring-fenced for loans to risky clients who it was felt should be given a chance. This should be the domain of the Bank: 'The Department of Agriculture should stop dealing with credit as soon as possible. The department has not done well at this and the government acknowledges its failures. It has chosen the Bank to do what the department failed to do.'

- The last topic dealt with expectations of the Bank as an institution: 'This Bank should become an institution of excellence. People need to stop

*Land Bank Prospectus 1998, p.16.

asking whether we need it and see clearly that government has decided that we want the Bank. But if the Bank does not assist the government to achieve the objectives of the RDP then government does not need it. It is a special institution because it is addressing particular needs.'

Implementation: a public commitment

The first few weeks after the New Year of 1998 were spent preparing for the public launch of the 'new' Land Bank, planned for each of the provinces and including a national celebratory evening at Gallagher Estate, a conference-banquet centre midway between Pretoria and Johannesburg.

An advertising agency designed an inspired triptych-like invitation card. The front cover showed a picture of orange to burnt amber coloured flames with the words printed over it: 'There are rare species of plants that need to go through a fiery cauldron of heat and smoke to truly take root, spread and grow.' Inside there was a packet of seeds of the everlasting flower *Syncarpha vestita=Helichrysum vestitum*, and a description of the conditions required for their germination: 'Devastating fynbos fires are needed for the regeneration of the species. The heat and smoke from these fires trigger *Syncarpha*'s germination process. In the absence of fire the species will eventually die out.' The second part of the triptych read: 'The Land Bank has been through an intensive transformation process, and is standing on the threshold of exciting times in agriculture. We would like you to join us as we take the next leap forward . . .'

This time the Minister didn't make it. We'd settled on a Wednesday evening during a time of parliamentary sittings, and there was a conflict with cabinet sessions in Cape Town. Bonile Jack, the chairperson designate, read both his and the Minister's speech; the latter reconfirmed the shareholder expectations. Thenjiwe Mtintso, then head of the Gender Commission, was the special guest of honour, and reconfirmed the expectations that the Land Bank would cater to the needs of rural women with special sensitivity.

My own speech addressed the nature of transformation and the alignment of institutional leadership behind a vision. I tried to make it serious, but with some humour befitting the occasion. Like so many others engaged in economic restructuring in the post-1994 period, I'd grappled with identifying the essence of 'transformation'. Restructuring was happening in every corner of South Africa – in the private sector, in public companies, and in the civil service. The ethos we'd tried to pursue in our attempted transformation was more than restructuring. 'Downsizing', 'rightsizing' was not what we wanted to achieve. There's a difference between transformation and reformation. Were the changes in the workplace real or cosmetic? Where they superficial or deep-slice? Did the changes reflect some of the aspirations inherent in the stated political ethos of the new South Africa, i.e. black empowerment, gender justice, and workplace democratisation? The quality of achievement on these three issues would determine the extent to which genuine transformation had occurred.

Lastly, I discussed the word 'transformation' – a word that is misused, abused, and over-used but, significantly it seemed to me, a word which in its true essence embodied an idea of metamorphosis. When we speak of someone 'transformed', we acknowledge that the essence of the person remains, but that something fundamental has happened to him or her that has provoked a deep change. The everlasting flower that had been chosen as the symbol of this occasion represented the attempt at a holistic metamorphosis as well as acknowledging the associated trauma.

I tried to identify the critical success factors in our process. There had been a mandate that had generated a vision with clear goals, a consultative approach that secured the release of people's energy, and a clear business analysis that pushed the sense of urgency. Beyond that, the more important basic input was simply 'graft', the dedication of many people putting in the hours, under time constraints, to create the synergy to make the inputs of the task teams come together as a whole. For those of us who'd been fortunate enough to attend the national consolidation conference at Klein Kariba, that was part of the magic. Suddenly we could see all our work as pieces of a jigsaw puzzle slotting into place. In reality, few businesses approach change holistically; we liked to think we were one of those that did. Our efforts in the last ten months represented a serious start to becoming an institution of excellence.

I covered the changes to product design and the new products that were ready to be rolled out into the market, I spoke of the new strategic management team and its commitment to bring the change project to maturity in the coming months. We considered ourselves a team of talented individuals with diverse and complementary skills. We also knew we had weaknesses and needed to hone our support skills to go the extra mile together. I referred to our recent reading of a management book, *Flight of the Buffalo*,* and showed a slide of strong buffalo stampeding in a disorganised charge. Then I showed a slide of geese in flight, in formation. Geese rotate their leader so as to give respite to what is otherwise too arduous a commitment, of always being the one

---

*J A Belasco & R C Stayer, 1994.

in front breaking the resistance of the air. They take care of their weak through careful placement within the formation. As a team they are able to fly further than any one of them could fly alone – that's what we needed to learn. The last slide went back to the buffalo, except this time they were in a V formation, like the geese. That was what we aspired to, a strong and interdependent supportive leadership. The audience laughed; the slides of the geese and the buffalo caught their sense of humour.

I had the honour of unveiling the logo representing the new corporate identity. It was based on the submission by the Vryheid branch and developed by the advertising agency. The logo is an orange sun rising above two sets of contours, one brown, one green: 'The rising sun . . . epitomises hope. Orange is a colour with high memorability, brilliance, and warm, exuberant physiological effects. The brown and green lines describe the topography of a valley with its hidden river, as well as plough lines. The green appears in the foreground; the crop ready to be reaped. The colours, though bright, are complementary to one another and give the logo a refreshing earthy quality.'*

As the unveiling took place, the lights dimmed almost to nothing – the focus was a spotlight on the logo itself. Simultaneously the Land Bank employees in the banquet hall rose from their chairs and made their way to the sides. The sound of African drums filled the building, with a voice-over that was deep and resonating: 'The Land Bank has changed. The doors of the Land Bank will be open to all.' The lines of personnel, each person carrying a candle, began to move towards the centre at the back of the hall. Pairs of employees then made their way up the centre aisle; the moving candle flames marking their slow procession forward in the darkness. When they reached the podium they placed their candles on stands in front of the logo, as a symbol of commitment. The candlelight cast its soft shadows on faces, and it was a time of suffused emotion. Even those who'd voiced objection to the idea of a symbolic ritual admitted that they'd felt a lump in their throats as they were moved by the ambience of the occasion.

The commitment ceremony brought to a close the first phase of transformation. A lot of people had been won over during the consultation process. It was an exciting, creative period, but the real test would be implementation. That would be the measure of both capacity and commitment.

---

*Land Bank Prospectus 1998, p.27.

FOUR

REINVENTING ROBIN HOOD: DOING BUSINESS WITH A DEVELOPMENT ETHIC

What constitutes development?

> The questions to ask about a country's development are three: What has been happening to poverty? What has been happening to unemployment? What has been happening to inequality? If all three of these have declined from high levels, then beyond doubt this has been a period of development for the country concerned.
>
> – *Seers, 1977, p.3*

The Land Bank is classified as a development finance institution, one of five such public finance enterprises of which the South African state is the sole shareholder. Each has been attributed a sectoral responsibility: agriculture, housing, industry, infrastructure and small business development.

But the Bank had never asked itself what it was about the way it did its business that merited its being described as developmental. Historical self-perception was simply that its role was to ensure financial benefits to whites as a select population group, in keeping with the government's racially based land and agricultural policies. How the loans were used in terms of environmental impact, employment opportunities, or the labour conditions on farms was not considered.

What best constitutes a rural development strategy for the early twenty-first century in South Africa is influenced by history and is perhaps less simple to define than in other post-colonial situations. The legacy of social engineering undertaken by the apartheid state led to a reluctance towards supply-driven, top-down land redistribution wherein the state would acquire massive areas of land and redistribute it either to the landless unemployed or entrepreneurs with a land shortage.

There were also other concerns. Firstly, redistribution should not be damaging to the overall productive capacity of agriculture; it should therefore take place hand in hand with adequate support services.

Secondly, decades of coercion into wage labour employment through the use of devices such as the hut tax and the poll tax had resulted in the so-called bantustans becoming labour reserves rather than places of productive employment. Proletarianisation rooted itself, in spite of people maintaining a residential foothold in the rural areas. Many now expressed a preference for a paid job as a better alternative to trying to eke out a living on a relatively small land area subject to irregular weather conditions.

Thirdly, a paradox had emerged in the former bantustans; while people spoke of a shortage of land, this demand coexisted side by side with unused land. The reasons given for why land was unused were various. People said they were dependent on money transfers to finance agricultural production. With increasing unemployment and a fall in remittances there was less money available to pay for inputs, for ploughing, or to hire labour. The capacity to exploit a land resource fully depended on people's ability to access a combination of inputs. Finally, the common history of blacks leaving their original land areas as a result of forced dispossession rather than voluntary urban migration led to a political demand for land. This was an inescapable emotional reality quite apart from any economic considerations.

All these factors considered together led to a preference among the new Land Affairs policy makers for a demand-driven approach to land redistribution, with stringent planning requirements to ensure the land would be used productively in the future and not lie fallow as an idle asset. A policy to promote increasing employment opportunities on commercial farms, or the encouragement of contract farming as a redistribution option, as had been argued for by some researchers, was not explored.

Clearly a rural finance policy which increased people's access to borrowed money to spend on inputs was integral to the creation of an enabling environment. The rub would be the cost of borrowing weighed against the possible returns for using the money on other investments. Rural finance could be enabling but it was certainly not a panacea, and if awarded badly the consequences would be contrary; the access to credit would increase people's economic vulnerability rather than improving their economic resilience.

The mandate given to the Bank by the state, as embodied in the cabinet approval of the Strauss Commission recommendations, was 'Transform to Deliver'. The Bank must not in the future be vulnerable to any accusations that it was the stumbling block to effective use of land resources due to a lack of access to credit, as had been the complaint of the better-off black farmers during the apartheid era.

Transformation was needed to provide a more appropriate customer service and to tailor product design to the needs of the new potential clients. However, the continued viability of the Bank had to be a major concern. It was clear that the government was not interested in rescue operations requiring the injection of additional taxpayers' money into failing state enterprises. The implementation of the mandate required a self-sustaining strategy. It would be regarded as irresponsible to achieve an institutional transformation that secured the approval and disbursement of massive numbers of loans with huge risks attached that might not be repaid. We needed to avoid a situation where poor credit practice resulted in insolvency, not only that of our clients, but ultimately our own.

This was a discussion I would have with black farmers' unions again and again over the next two years. We needed to stay in business to do business, and if we did not sell our money at a certain price, and make loans that we believed were recoverable, we would not be around to do business with anyone. Over and above this, the question we would grapple with, and answer, over the next two years, was exactly what would be different in our approach as moneylenders that would merit the Bank's being referred to as a development finance institution. Taking on clients that the private sector banks considered as high risk might turn out to be a dubious developmental activity, although we were committed to giving people the chance that they hadn't had before. This in and of itself was not enough; there had to be more to our development character.

The big issue to confront would be the morality of our lending to the commercial sector. When I read newspaper reports about farm worker abuse, it crossed my mind that the farmer in question might be a Land Bank client, and I wished otherwise. In the longer term the aspiration was to find ways to leverage our loans, to create an incentive for a commitment to a certain code of conduct, or desirable environmental criteria. The pursuit of such a strategy, if successful, might make a bigger impact on development and the lives of farm workers than the loans made to aspirant black entrepreneurs.

Commercial farmers and farm workers are the dominant feature of our South African rural economy, occupying by far the greater part of the land and responsible for most traded produce. We have long left behind the rural landscape that is romanticised, and still of economic importance in other African countries, represented by images of villages peopled with self-sustaining small-scale farmers producing cash crops as well as food. A development strategy that ignored the dominant commercial sector, and considered development only as the loans given to black farmers would be short-sighted. The Bank was a major player in the agricultural financial market, granting loans to about one third of South Africa's white commercial farmers. The potential impact of a developmental approach in our lending to these customers was significant.

Captain of a sinking ship

Those were longer-term dreams. First we needed to get the Bank's business into shipshape condition.The analysis of the Bank's current business situation was worrisome. Only three out of twenty-five branches brought in more money than they spent. Claude Peyrot and I had also asked the Bank's wholesale finance unit to give us a breakdown of their clients and expectations of what funds we needed to set aside to provide for cooperative insolvency. It turned out that at least two huge bankruptcies were on the cards: Vleissentral and Northern Transvaal Cooperatives could easily cost us a couple of hundred million rands to cover our losses.

The long and the short of it was that the Bank survived by making money out of its treasury activity, through interest accruing on the wholesale loans, and because it didn't pay tax or dividends and was able to use all its surplus towards cross-subsidising loss-making operations as well as topping up its reserves.

I regretted that the Strauss Commission business analysis had been so weak. The Bank was not as robust as had been made out. In addition, the claim of a large staff complement possessing skills that could be applied more widely, whilst not untrue, had been exaggerated. Most of the loans granted were for land bonds, grain and cattle farming. There was not a huge variety in the business. This meant that the skills that loan officers had developed were limited.

There were some factors that might just make it possible for the Bank to become shipshape and seaworthy for the future. As Claude had pointed out:

- There were many younger staff who might be willing and able.
- The productivity at branch level was appallingly low compared to the commercial banking sector. The staff numbers involved in maintaining the portfolio and granting new loans were excessive; some branches

had figures as low as four loans per person per year in terms of handling new applications. This largesse in staff numbers should mean that there was unused capacity that could be tapped; the possibility of training and marketing to attract new business could be contemplated.

- The interest rates charged to the farmers in 1997 were several percentage points below those of the commercial banks. This was considered to be our 'competitive advantage'. However, the income from wholesale lending was cross-subsidising the rest of the banking operations. Surely we would be able to persuade farmers of our need to increase lending rates without there being a mass exodus of customers?

- It might just be possible to bring down expenditure.

- There were criticisms of our inheritance of a network of branches that were well placed to serve the white commercial farming community, and hence not geographically well located to service the new black clients. The fact remained that they constituted a well-established infrastructure that could serve as a springboard for a different future.

Although I felt like the captain of a ship that had a damaged hull, it did not feel as though I should resign myself to the inevitability of its sinking. The above factors all offered possibilities to be explored before accepting the inevitability of business decline. The changes, however, needed to be both fundamental and long lasting. Cosmetic activity that achieved no more than the effect of rearranging the deckchairs on the Titanic would be a waste of energy. What was required was change that would secure business sustainability as well as transformation.

The price of money

The Bank, contrary to popular belief, did not get its funds from the government; twenty years had passed since the last injection of taxpayers' money. It had originally been capitalised by the state, and its R1,7-billion reserves would revert to the South African government in the event of its privatisation. But on a day to day basis, it borrowed the money it required for its lending operations on the capital and money markets. Its R1,7-billion in reserves provided the capital adequacy required by banking regulations, as well as persuading money market dealers and credit rating agencies that it was a sound financial institution with adequate backing.

The buying price of money was the result of macro-economic factors beyond the control of any single institution. Much depended on the state of the economy, the financial markets, and also on Reserve Bank policy. When the world financial markets went awry in the latter part of 1997 the price of money to be obtained for on-lending went up and up. Our treasury dealers had no influence over the cost of money that they solicited for the Bank to on-lend to clients. The dealers worked in a strange kind of shop. They sat in front of computer screens that told them the different prices of bonds and bills that people were buying and selling. They were given supply and demand figures of how much money the business needed, or what payments were forthcoming because of the Bank's own maturing bills, i.e. reaching the due date of their repayment.

The selling price of the money lent to Bank clients depended on combining a minimum of four considerations: the initial cost of funds, the cost of delivery, an estimate to cover risk, and a margin to secure a surplus above the inflation rate.

Up to then the Bank had not worked out a logic to its retail pricing. Its wholesale pricing was competitive with the general market rate for bulk finance. The retail pricing for loans to individual farmers, however, was in certain instances several percentage points below those of the commercial banks, and always had been. Nobody questioned the rationale; it was assumed to be the right of the favoured white farmer to benefit from this lower rate. There were hidden consequences that came to light; the fact that twenty-two of twenty-five branches ran at a loss had not been a consideration in the pricing discussions, because nobody had ever carefully worked out the expenditure and income accounts of running the branches.

The problem was that the Land Bank Act had stipulated that the Bank should try to avoid running at a loss – running the institution with a business ethic had not been part of the mandate. It was only in the eighties when government generally cut back on subsidies that the Land Bank interest rates even began to approximate the commercial banks' rates. But in terms of internal accounting, the Bank's own funds were not costed, and the comparative efficiency of different parts of the business was not analysed.

The issue was how to revamp the business while keeping the white commercial farmers and their institutions as its customers. When I'd been appointed to the Bank, there were many negative comments in the Afrikaans press. I shouldn't be trusted, was the gist of some of them; I was the widow of a communist, even if I had never myself been a party member. It should be expected that any reassuring statements I made concerning continued commitment to our white commercial clients deserved the same amount of trust one would place in a Trojan horse. They concluded that I should be treated as a potential traitor, and every move the Bank made under my directorship should be watched carefully for signs of betrayal. Any upward price adjustments were going to be difficult. It was now clear to me that our retail prices needed to increase and the gap between our interest rate and that of the commercial banks needed to narrow.

I regretted the suspicion that I was a Trojan horse character. I was committed to maintaining, and even expanding, our commercial portfolio. The continuity of that portfolio was essential to our emerging vision of running a development bank that was viable with long-term sustainability. A very important consideration was also the intention that the Bank might find a way to leverage a developmental sensibility within the commercial farming sector. But there was no justification, to my way of thinking, to continue to cross-subsidise the retail operations from the income of the wholesale business. On what basis did one justify continued subsidies to the historically privileged, when the needs of the disadvantaged were paramount?

The instability of the world money markets in late 1997 and early 1998 turned out to be a blessing in disguise. Every time the commercial banks put up their rate so did we. When the rates eventually reached their peak and started to come down, we dragged our feet in making our reductions. We brought down our rates later, and when the commercial banks brought their rate down by a whole percentage point, we brought ours down by only a half. In this way we were able to achieve a relative increase in our rates over a period of several months.

When the rates did not come down apace with those of commercial banks the farmers complained. They also said that it was unacceptable that they should pay higher interest rates because of the need to subsidise the new mandate clients. We were able to respond that, irrespective of the new clients, the retail business had been running at a loss; and that the price increases were reasonable. We pointed out that the annual statements of commercial banks showed that almost half their revenue derived from bank charges and commission. Even if our prices had floated closer to those of the commercial banks, our service charges were minimal, and that had to be taken into account when making a true comparison between bank costs.

When we started to lose our prime retail clients we knew we needed more finesse in our strategy. We didn't need to reinvent the wheel; we simply needed to copycat the practices of the commercial banks. They did not have a single rate for all their commercial clients; they made distinctions between customers. There was a general prime rate, and then some people or businesses qualified for prime minus one, or prime minus two, depending ·on the volume of the business and the risk attached. We had named our standard commercial rate as 'gold'; we now set about devising two cheaper rates: 'gold premium' and 'platinum', also using volume and risk as the basis for client categorisation. The strategy worked; we regained the business that we'd lost for a while.

To subsidise or not to subsidise?

While our interest rates might still have been lower than those of the commercial banks, they were still high in terms of payback commitments; this was a direct consequence of the price we ourselves paid for the money.

The resentment among black commercial farmers was latent but potent. The rural poor were not vociferous in expressing their displeasure about interest rates, but the rural bourgeoisie were. For the rural poor access to credit was more often than not a need for funds to cover emergencies, whereas aspirant entrepreneurs considered the rate of interest as a make or break factor in whether or not they would succeed in building up their enterprise. They felt they merited special conditions. White farmers had been backed by decades of subsidies to secure their commercial establishment. The black farmers' union argued that if subsidies had been available to whites then they should be equally available to blacks in the new non-racial, non-sexist, democratic South Africa which pledged to settle historical injustice and put black economic empowerment on a firm footing. The issue was emotive, and no amount of reliance on economic rationale could satisfy the plaintiffs. Trying to explain how subsidies backfire and often promote undesirable side effects that cancel out the potential benefits was as successful as trying to light a match in a hailstorm.

The issue of subsidies was one of the focal points of study undertaken by the Strauss Commission. The effect of subsidised credit on land prices was also a matter that I had to pay some attention to when completing my doctorate on land markets.

It seems very attractive to have a subsidised bond. Every single one of us is acutely aware of the difference that a couple of percentage points can make on the outflow of cash we need to provide for interest repayments. What is invisible and insidious in the nature of a subsidy is that the existence of the subsidy causes increased demand for the product and influences a price increase. In terms of a farm purchase, while you may be getting a subsidised bond, you end up paying more over time for the land than you would have done if the subsidy had not existed to distort prices in the first place.

This is not to say that subsidies can never have the desired effect, but to do so they need to be extremely well designed, targeted, with a defined time frame and exit strategy. Otherwise the consequences are highly undesirable. A study on the effects of subsidies on the farm profitability of wheat production in Europe initially showed that the farmer's profit per hectare of wheat increased.* This increase in the returns on wheat meant farmers decided to produce more of it. Overall production went up, as did the demand for the inputs required: land, labour, seed, fertiliser and machinery. The increased demand for these inputs put upward pressure on their price, especially for those whose supply is inflexible, such as land. Within twelve years the extra profit originally derived from growing a subsidised crop was absorbed into the price of land used for wheat growing. The farmers' profitability gradually declined to the pre-subsidy levels. And there was one ghastly consequence: the farmer was now reliant on the subsidy to produce even the former modest level of profit.

There's a lot of ill-informed and sometimes cheap criticism of so-called 'inefficient farmers' who cannot survive without subsidies. The issue is more complex than may appear to be the case at first sight. For one reason or another, government introduces a subsidy. When that subsidy is removed the input costs, which have adjusted upwards over time as a result of the subsidy, initially remain the same. The farmer is stuck between a rock and a hard place as profits are squeezed. It is not so easy to adjust the mix of farm activities.

Subsidies would seem to be a treacherous policy option. When government introduces them, like bees to honey, they attract an increasing number of users. The subsidy bills accumulate; government and taxpayers complain. The reduction of subsidies cuts the knees from under the producers and their economic viability is crippled, sometimes permanently.

The apartheid government found itself in a cleft stick with regard to farming subsidies. It supported their reduction as part of economic deregulation that would promote only the survival of the fittest and free the state of a strangulating subsidy burden. On the other hand it was about to sell out its white rural constituency in political terms as a negotiated settlement and transfer of power loomed as a real possibility. In 1988 there was an allocation of R309-million to maize farmers, as well as R900-million as state guarantees on carry-over debts, and R400-million to keep insolvent farmers on the land. This sweetener was not enough. Four years later, political sabre-rattling about insurrection

---

*Food Studies Group, Oxford, UK, 1996. Unpublished mimeograph 'Effects of farming subsidies'.

coinciding with a drought caused the state to run up the country's debt bill still further. As a compensatory swansong, the state provided white commercial farmers with a soft landing into the post-apartheid economy. There was a final handsome handshake offered to commercial farmers on the eve of the political settlement in 1992. Parliamentary approval was given for a budget award of R3,8-billion. R3,25-billion was specifically allocated to summer grain farmers, a final pay-off to a key National Party constituency. The grain farmers were to receive R375 a hectare, comprising R175 to reduce debts accumulated with their local cooperative, R100 to cover the cost of the failed crop in the 1991-92 season, and R100 to be retained by cooperatives as an advance on production credit for the next season's crop. It was possibly the biggest refinancing exercise in our history for a target population group. But the farmers were not the only beneficiaries; the private sector banks and the Land Bank all benefited indirectly, as farmers were able to reduce the level of their accumulated debt.

Try explaining to black entrepreneurs that subsidies are a catch-22 against this background of financial largesse which benefited whites almost exclusively! Emotions invaded the discussions. It just seemed to be grossly unfair. White farmers had received massive subsidies and now, when the time had come for black economic empowerment, government policy was against them.

We spent months trying to design a 'grace period' investment product. The idea was based on a sliding scale of interest rates for black entrepreneurs, starting low and increasing year by year to the normal commercial rate. The problem, according to our calculations, was that unless the unpaid interest in the early years was written off, the repayment burden in later years was still crippling. In a policy environment that was against subsidies there seemed to be no way out.

The one subsidy that we did introduce, and for which I incurred some knuckle rapping from my political masters, was our introduction of a Special Mortgage Bond for first-time buyers of farm land by those citizens classified as historically disadvantaged. The final interest rate we settled on was ten per cent. We hived off a part of our reserve funds for this purpose, and our calculation of the interest rate was based on a desire not to devalue too much the real long-term value of the money. The decision was made in spite of my awareness of the price distortion arguments. The rationale, however, was that some kind of overture was essential as a sign of goodwill, and that the number of such purchases in terms of annual national land transactions was relatively small. It was a targeted subsidy and its magnitude should not affect overall land prices. The black farmers' union appreciated a product clearly designed to address their concerns.

My other outstanding reservation about selling money at interest rates that were lower than those of other financial institutions concerned the customer commitment to the repayment schedule. People, in general, borrow money from a variety of sources. The interest rates differ. A house or land bond has a different rate to the interest paid on vehicle finance, which in turn has a different interest rate to a credit card or overdraft facility. The observations on repayments to the Department of Agriculture's loan scheme, run by the Agricultural Credit Board (ACB), was that the repayment record was poor on two counts. Firstly, it was run by a government department. There was generally a lukewarm commitment to repaying government, and an attitude that it was possible to get away with non-payment. Secondly, the ACB's interest rate, raised from eight to fourteen per cent, was still the lowest in farming financial markets. If ACB credit was part of your debt portfolio, one thing was certain: it got paid only after all the other higher interest accounts had been paid.

The common sense lesson to be learnt was that if you don't want to be last in line to be repaid, then don't offer a lower interest rate. And yet our edge on interest rates was at that time our most competitive advantage, more decisive in attracting customers than our continued commitment to follow a policy of leniency in hard years. A comparatively lower interest rate brought customers through our doors, but we needed to attract timeous repayment. We decided once again to learn from our competitors. We opted for a system of financial penalties for late repayment.

If we weren't going to be offering subsidised credit to the historically disadvantaged, then what was it that we were going to put on the market that would not be available from any of the private sector banks? We settled on three product approaches that would make a difference to three market sectors: aspirant black entrepreneurs, black economic empowerment agribusiness ventures, and last but not least, the rural poor, especially the women.

Supporting black entrepreneurs: challenging the collateral fetish

The first new product was a tailor-made line of production credit that benefited the up-and-coming smaller-scale farmers. The most common stumbling block for black entrepreneurs was the collateral requirement of most banking institutions, including the Land Bank.

The requirement for normal lending for medium-term loans to

purchase equipment and machinery was that the value of the applicant's assets should be double the value of the loan being requested. A further criterion was that the total amount of debt that they needed to service should not be more than fifty-five per cent. For example, if someone had assets of R100 000, the Bank considered R55 000 to be the maximum debt ceiling.

Obviously if you own freehold land the estimated market value of that land is counted in your asset portfolio. But what about the thousands of black producers who farm on land that has common property status and to which they have usufruct rights? There were many black entrepreneurs in the former bantustan areas to whom chiefs had awarded land use rights for up to two hundred hectares, but the land could not be counted as a monetary asset for the purposes of evaluating the loan assessment because it was not saleable. Yet without the possibility of buying machinery and equipment, the productive potential of farming operations on the land area could not be realised.

It is a South African fetish to be so bound to the requirement of land as collateral. In other southern nations, where tenants paying rents to landlords comprise the majority of producers, credit institutions have long adjusted to evaluating loan applications on the basis of farming track record and payback potential. This was obviously the route we would have to go, otherwise thousands of black entrepreneurs would continue to have their loan applications turned down.

We changed our rules. Our standard commercial product had been the 'gold' loan; we designed two other categories, 'bronze' and 'silver'. We had a creative lapse in finding appropriate names, and incurred some criticism. The 'bronze' loan allowed a person to borrow up to R50 000. The security lay in the item purchased, and a farming business plan that indicated the positive cash flow that would cover repayment. Proof was required of access to land and/or grazing rights. A twenty per cent deposit was required, which we later thought should be reconsidered; it created a barrier that some people just could not overcome.

Implementation was a trial and error experience. We had to work out how to avoid abuse of the facility and how not to be tripped up by our own rules. There was the client who was awarded a loan to buy a light utility vehicle; it was reported that he had walked down the street with the money to a furniture store and paid off his outstanding account. There were medium-term loans awarded for the purchase of second-hand tractors. Logically, the clients then made an application for seasonal production credit, and were told that the amount they requested would take them over the limit of their debt ceiling. The farmers rightly queried the sanity of having awarded them an investment loan if we were then not going to award the production credit required to make the money out of the machinery to pay off the debt.

The 'silver' category of loans was an intermediate product between bronze and gold. It required assets as security, but rather than the two to one requirement of the low-risk gold clients, the silver loan worked on a sliding scale. The security required varied from fifty per cent of the value of the loan to one hundred and fifty per cent, depending on the amount borrowed.

There was obviously a higher risk involved in making these loans as opposed to the safe, fully secured loans historically granted by the Bank. Increased risk means a higher expectation of default, which in turn means that the price charged on the money lent out should be higher than normal to cover the expected higher rate of losses. This was another tough conundrum. The higher-risk people who most need cheaper money were being told in no uncertain terms that their higher-risk status meant they should pay more. They were asked to understand that this was not only a fact of life but that they should consider themselves fortunate to be given the opportunity to borrow at all. Our attempt to deal with this issue was to charge a higher interest rate due to the risk estimation, but with the possibility of a bonus incentive for on-time payments that brought the interest rate down to the normal commercial rate charged to the low-risk gold clients.

We still hadn't fully escaped from the collateral fetish, but we were making progress towards a 'payback' capacity assessment. We were clear that fine-tuning adjustments would be needed but, at least in the first two years, the uptake by black clients of the new products seemed to indicate that we had designed a credit facility that was more appropriate to their needs than had been previously available.

In February 1999 we were asked to account for our progress to the parliamentary portfolio committee on agriculture; the figures were later updated as we provided our annual briefing to investors and rating agencies. The increase in the pace of delivery was phenomenal. In 1997 the Bank approved 3 348 loans. In 1998 the figure almost doubled to 6 302 loans. In the first six months of 1999, the Bank records indicated that 9 944 loans had been granted. As many loans were granted to black entrepreneurs in the first quarter of 1999 as in the whole of the previous year. Of the total number of loans handled by the Bank in the first six months of 1999, sixty-six per cent were to the historically disadvantaged. We had picked up 5 356 clients in the silver and bronze categories. The credit outlay was R88,9-million. On our balance sheet, which was a snapshot of an institutional history representing decades of lending to white farm purchase with debt outstanding around R4-billion, the amount was minuscule. However, that fact does not negate the phenomenon that two-thirds of new loans granted were to black farmers, excluding the micro-credit scheme, and as new clients this would have accounted for an even greater percentage of staff time. It seemed as though we were doing something right – and this without counting our 25 000 new micro-finance clients. The facts challenge accusations that the Bank continued to service whites at the expense of a true focus on black business.

There were a couple of additional opportunities that we put in place for black entrepreneurs and land reform beneficiaries. In 1997 I had noticed that we were selling several insolvent farms at auctions at a loss, and that the buyers had all been white. It seemed to me that if the Bank was to incur such loss, it should at least be to the benefit of black entrepreneurs. The board approved a new policy that black entrepreneurs would have first option to buy the Bank's bought-in properties. The South African Agricultural Union (SAAU) complained, but was ignored.

We also put in place the possibility of bridging finance for land reform beneficiaries who were playing a waiting game for the release of money from the Department of Land Affairs for the purchase of farms.

Lastly, we were approached for bridging finance by the Homeless People's Federation for agri-villages. They found themselves in a lose-lose situation. They couldn't get rural housing subsidies for people because a qualifying requirement was the possession of land with security of tenure. But they couldn't acquire such land because they didn't have money for its purchase. It took more than a year to sort out an agreement, but in the end we did it.

We really had fun trying to use the Bank's money creatively to solve problems that people were facing on the ground. Slowly but surely, Bank employees began to adopt a 'can do' approach to their work, rather than the old 'have never done, can't do' approach that had been the dominant attitude.

Equity finance for black economic empowerment

We had begun to succeed in making it easier for people to borrow. The problem, however, with selling money is that unlike the marketing of consumer goods, you have not really made your sale unless you get your money back. Monitoring the arrears, turning the screws on people behind with their payments, is the unpleasant side of the business. Interest rates were high in relation to the average rate of return prevailing in the agricultural industry. I worried about emerging black entrepreneurs becoming insolvent as so many white farmers had done before them.

The first years seemed to be the most critical period when people started a new business. Yet many agricultural investments have low returns in the first years – the herd is being built up, the fruit trees are growing but not yet at the point of bearing fruit; the income stream is dismal – and yet the interest payment on the investment is still required.

The answer to this problem is every cash-strapped entrepreneur's dream. You need someone to back you; someone who believes that you will make it and is willing to put their money into the business. A longer-term view of reaping rewards is needed and the absence of harassment for a quick return. Richard Branson, in his autobiography, describes having a hard time with his bankers on several occasions. He carps that they had a short-term view focused on the income stream from interest repayments and a tight attitude to overdraft limits; he observes that if the banks had an equity share in the business, their behaviour as financiers might well be different.

The Land Bank Act of 1944 had, by 1997, been amended several times and was by now a document designed to deal with ad hoc problems rather than representing a coherent statute to assist the implementation of business or political strategy. In 1997 the Act did not yet permit equity finance as an activity to be undertaken. But in 1998 several amendments to the Act were presented to parliament, pending a total overhaul of an archaic piece of legislation passed in 1944. My concern was that the amendments should enable the Bank to pursue the implementation of the Strauss Commission mandate that included an equity investment facility.

The amendments were passed in June 1998. There were two remaining obstacles – the recruitment of appropriate expertise into the Bank, and the money to make equity investments. The second was easier to resolve than the first.

One of the special privileges of the Bank, as a public entity, was that it did not pay tax on its surplus revenue. The Banking Council of South Africa complained vociferously about such privilege, referring to it as 'unfair competitive advantage' and 'unlevel playing fields'. These criticisms seemed a bit rich coming from an industry that had benefited enormously from the Bank's existence. The Bank had often provided a safety net to those farming clients who the commercial banks decided were too risky to continue to carry. I did not necessarily agree with the privilege of not paying tax, but for different reasons; I thought it permitted the kind of unfocused management that had resulted in the Bank's never having paid serious attention to business principles in the past.

There seemed to be a way of killing lots of birds with one stone. We could calculate the imputed tax and dividends that would have been due on our surplus revenue if we had been required to pay it. We could then set aside that money for equity investments and other development expenditure on a yearly basis. Our investors would be happy because it would be clear that we were not putting their funds into riskier investments. The Banking Council would be assuaged because it eliminated the 'unfair advantage' of all the surplus revenue simply being added to our capital reserves. I preferred this option because it meant that there would no longer be a hidden internal subsidy to our commercial lending and we could therefore begin to measure our efficiency more accurately. On this basis a proposal was made to the board of directors and a Development Finance Fund was initiated.

Applications for equity finance started to accumulate. We put off dealing with them because we lacked capacity and instead undertook efforts to hire in people with experience. Twice I thought we might be getting close to successful recruitment, but lack of progress on a new remuneration policy meant that we couldn't entice people away from the commercial and merchant banks. Once I thought someone from Standard Bank was on the point of committing himself; he was enticed by the challenge of the job and the latitude afforded for creative work. However, after some sweet talk from one of his senior colleagues about impending promotion, forgoing the possibility of share options, and 'you never know how the politics of a state-owned bank will work out', he got cold feet and decided not to sign the contract.

Towards the end of the year we were suddenly landed with one application that we felt we couldn't defer and should pull out all stops to consider immediately – after all, we needed to cut our teeth at some stage or other. It was an application for part loan and part equity finance from the Mineworkers' Development Agency (MDA). MDA was a not-for-profit agency that had been set up with funds negotiated from the mining sector. Their focus was on rural development activity that would benefit the many thousands of mine workers who were being laid off each year. The investment proposal was captivating; it was for MDA to buy out a rural technology company, RUTEC, that produced equipment for various rural enterprises. The equity finance component required was about R5-million; it was not a lot of money in terms of risk to the Bank. We needed to gain experience; what better opportunity than in partnership with the MDA to create employment in the rural areas for redundant mineworkers?

There was just one snag. The director of MDA was Kate Philip, who was also on the Bank's board of directors. There was a section in the Land Bank Act to the effect that Bank employees or directors could not personally benefit from the Bank's credit. I asked our lawyers for an interpretation of the Act and its applicability to this situation. The interpretation we received indicated that the Act intended to rule out the possibility of private gain. It would not apply to the MDA submission. Kate recused herself. The application went through just as we all began our Christmas holidays; for some of us it was a cause for celebration that the Bank was putting its money where its mouth was and taking black economic empowerment seriously.

'Step Up' micro-credit: the women's choice

Most of the applications for bronze and silver loans were coming from black men. We wanted to market a product that would more especially be useful for rural women. The research considered by the Strauss commissioners indicated that female-headed households dominated the rural economy, and that women in charge of household budgets made trade offs between consumer needs and production activities. An intention to use certain monies for ploughing might suddenly be thwarted by a medical emergency. A modest, easily accessible credit facility might go some way to assisting women through these hiccups, and reduce their dependence on borrowing from local moneylenders at usurious interest rates.

Our homework led us to an NGO in Cape Town that ran a programme called the Start Up Fund. It had a five-year track record. There is a line of thinking on small-scale credit that promotes a 'savings first' philosophy. It is premised on the wisdom that good savers make good borrowers. More recent research challenged the validity of this approach in South Africa, and suggested that when dealing with small loans neither a savings capacity nor collateral were the key determinants of what makes a good client; more important than anything else was a demonstrated commitment to repayment.

The Cape Town NGO had designed the Start Up scheme that set out to give small amounts of credit initially, and the track record that people established through repayment would qualify them for a larger loan the next time round. The first amounts were purposely small at R250 a step, as the default rate was highest in the first two loan cycles; it seemed that those clients who graduated to Step Three and beyond were those who were most determined to establish their track record of creditworthiness.

We asked Start Up to tailor-make a Land Bank product along the same lines. It was named Step Up. Unlike the Start Up loan, which was mainly used in trading businesses with a daily turnover in townships and repayable on a monthly basis, we needed something with a more flexible repayment perspective. Loans granted through the Step Up scheme were intended for people with smallholdings who wanted credit to produce vegetables, run a small poultry activity, or plough a field and so on. To qualify for a loan, a person had to make a down payment of R50 and open a bank account in order to make withdrawals and repayments. We entered into an agreement with First National Bank and paid them for the administrative costs incurred in handling our Step Up clients. As we had only twenty-five branches in the rural areas this strategy afforded the client better geographic access to banking facilities than we could offer. The coveted prize would have been an agreement with the Post Office. They were a sister state-owned institution and offered the best geographical network of facilities in the rural areas. But they charged R3 per transaction, which was punitive on small sums of money and far more than we were to pay the commercial bank.

Step Up was a customised version of Start Up. The first loan was not to exceed R250; Step Two permitted R500 to be borrowed. On the ninth loan people could borrow as much as R5 000. They would be building up a track record and would eventually qualify for the bronze loans if needed.

In the first year the number of Step Up clients was almost two thousand a month. The interest rate we charged was two per cent a month, although later we worked out that 2,5 per cent would be more appropriate if we were to break even on the costs incurred. When we reported to the parliamentary agricultural portfolio committee in 1999 we could proudly say that we had more than 20 000 micro-finance users, of whom seventy per cent were women, and a repayment rate of eighty-two per cent. We expected that problems would emerge, and that we would have to learn through doing, but as far as we could gauge from the uptake, it seemed as though we were again getting close to delivering something that responded to people's needs.

In September 1999 we won the South African Micro-Finance award for 'Foresight'. The award was given to us as an institution, but personal credits would be in order for several branch managers and the support they gave employees dealing with Step Up. However, the behind-the-scenes champion at head office was the retail network manager Louise Colvin, whose leadership motivated many branch employees to walk far beyond any one extra mile in their endeavours.

We began to appoint agents, working on a commission basis, to cope with the increasing number of clients. Our idea was to pay a small fee to the agent who brought in a successful application, and a larger commission on repayment, thus ensuring the agent's commitment to finding quality clientele.

Foresight and hindsight were both required if this product was to have a long-term future. We detected hiccups when some clients paid the money straight back in the first couple of steps so as to qualify for a higher loan; more stringent screening would be required. We had some problems appointing trustworthy agents; in one instance a batch of applications was processed and paid out but the monies were somehow diverted. This alerted us sooner rather than later to the need to improve the criteria for appointment and tighten up loop-holes in our systems.

On a more worrying note, our mentors at the Start Up programme overextended themselves and went insolvent after running their scheme for six years. Our resilience would be greater as our programme was riding on the back of our normal infrastructure, and the monies involved (an outstanding balance of less than R5,5-million) was minuscule in terms of the Bank's composite balance sheet that totalled over R12-billion.

Whilst we were aware that we needed to take stock of our own findings and learn from others' mistakes, it was also satisfying to be running a programme that appeared to respond to the needs of the rural poor as well as those of aspirant entrepreneurs. The appointment of agents was also employment generating, another reason for gratification in an economic climate where job losses, rather than job creation, was the more normal news story.

Leveraging a development ethic

In the period after the public launch of the 'new' Land Bank, with its new logo and its new products tailor-made to suit the needs of different sectors of the historically disadvantaged, the challenge was to respond proactively. Branch directors sent staff to rural communities or organised sessions with potential clients to explain the different loans. There were reports of potential black clients queuing up outside several branches, a definite first in the history of the Bank.

There was a political need to be seen to be responding to black clientele and that was the major focus of the effort from March 1998. But another aspect weighed on my mind, and needed consideration as to what could be done about it in practical terms. There was a need to remember that large-scale employers (almost wholly white) and their wage workers (almost wholly black) were the core of the rural economy, and that the political and economic thrust of ensuring effective black economic empowerment should not eclipse the need for a transformative, developmental approach to the commercial farming sector.

Synchronicity played its part yet again. A pamphlet put on my desk among many other papers surfaced at the very moment when I was in a state of mind conducive to reading it. It was an eight-page brochure compiled in the UK for the Association of Chartered Certified Accountants by associates of an institute of social and ethical accountability and a research unit of the the New Economics Foundation. The executive summary of the report, 'Making Values Count: Contemporary Experience in Social and Ethical Accounting, Auditing and Reporting', stated:

> Virtuous but uncompetitive companies will not be part of our future. Socially or environmentally destructive companies must not be a part of our future. The challenge is to create the conditions where social and environmental benefits go hand in hand with competitive advantage.
>
> New tools are needed to meet this challenge and to help organisations and stakeholders manage the transition to a more open, inclusive, people-centred approach to success. This need has underpinned a re-emergence of interest in the field of social and ethical accounting, auditing and reporting, as both a management tool and a mechanism for enhanced stakeholder accountability.
>
> 'Making Values Count' explores current practice in the field, focusing particularly on the pressing need for both quality assurance and standards in an area characterised by considerable diversity. It outlines the common principles underlying contemporary practice, and also sets out the practical tools for assessing and ultimately improving quality in this emerging field.

My heartbeat quickened. I'd always thought that there should be more to auditing than the narrow, conventional financial approach that the Bank dutifully complied with.

The brochure gave an insight into the leading edge of work on devising a methodology with the intention that it should gain an international standing, alongside risk ratings such as those awarded by agencies such as Standard and Poor, and Duff and Phelps.

A standardised approach was essential to achieve this long-term goal. Various well-known companies had latched on to differing elements of what could be termed 'doing business with a social responsibility ethic'. Shell International, in response to the bad publicity it received from its Nigerian operations, had issued a statement of 'Principles and Values' and promised that a full social audit would be taking place at Shell operations the world over. I was intrigued to see a couple of financial institutions ahead of the pack – a Danish bank, a Canadian credit union. I wanted to learn more about what methodology they had used, and how effective it had been not only in terms of measurability but also in terms of providing analysis to inform discussion on changes required in the business. There were other well-known firms with brand names that were engaging in this new field of expertise, The Body Shop, the USA ice-cream makers Ben and Jerry's, British Petroleum and Nike.

There was enormous appeal in the idea of our tiny, parochial South African bank being in the forefront of this kind of social accountability initiative. Up to now we had been in 'catch-up' and 'copycat' mode, emulating superior efficiency in the commercial banking sector. It would be a real feather in our caps if we could be on the leading edge of a socially desirable and innovative business practice.

It was even more complex and comprehensive than I anticipated. The methodology focused on both internal and external business aspects. I discovered a couple of South Africans at a consulting firm, Letsema, who had worked with a UK consultant, Simon Zadek – one of the authors of 'Making Values Count'. We also undertook discussions with the monitoring and analysis outfit Business Map, as they had coinciding interests in measuring institutional change, especially with regard to monitoring the progress of black economic empowerment initiatives. By January 1999 we had done enough groundwork to be ready to make a presentation to the Bank's directors about introducing a social account-ability project for which we would need staff and an additional budget.

There were four areas of focus:

- an assessment of the company by its employees on an annual basis to measure change over time;
- an assessment of how the company used its own investment funds – for example, were the pension funds invested in companies that one could consider as having a corporate responsibility ethos;
- an assessment of the service providers and the criteria for their selection;
- an assessment of the company business and how it was run – were environmental concerns taken into account, and so on.

Although I was interested in all of these, it was the last element that most attracted me. Could we design a way of running the business that would in turn positively alter the way our clients ran their businesses?

I had heard some inspiring South African stories about uncon-ventional commercial farmers. There was the tomato farmer near Cullinan who had sectioned off an area of his farmland and subdivided it into plots. Each had a residence and an area of irrigated land. It was the farmer's retirement scheme for workers reaching pensionable age. It secured not only a place to live but also the possibility to use the land to supplement the state pension.

There was another encouraging story. A white farmer's daughter had studied psychology. She returned to the farm with new ideas, and persuaded her parents to organise an equity scheme. Shares in the enterprise were given over to workers and from all accounts productivity and profitability were high. An additional benefit was the improvement in race relations and interdependence that gave a sense of physical security at a time when South Africa's rural areas were being scarred by criminal attacks on isolated farmhouses.

Then there was one elucidating day that I spent visiting wine farms in the Western Cape. One of the farm owners had a negative attitude to the new government's labour laws. The investments he was undertaking were intended to minimise the number of employees; seven was the desired target. Just a few kilometres away I visited a farm that had an agri-village with good quality housing, and a crèche as well as a school. Asked about the possibility of redundancies in the future, the answer was: 'The workers and their families have lived on this farm for gener-ations. They have been a part of making this farm what it is today. It would be a sad day for us all if we were ever to have to lay anybody off.'

I had a counterweight collection of distasteful stories. Many con-cerned incidents of farm worker families being evicted when a farm changed ownership and the new owner had no interest in employing them. It seemed irrelevant to the new owners that the farm worker families might have lived on the land for generations, that members of their families were buried there, and that they had no other place to go. And I have yet to hear of a case where a retrenchment package was given as compensation for the loss of job and residence. There were awful stories of inhospitable living conditions, especially for temporary and migrant workers – such as a pigsty converted into sleeping quarters. The worst stories were those of physical abuse, chaining, beating, the worker being run over, the worker who was painted – an act intended to humiliate; I would shudder when I thought about the worst stories I had heard or read about.

It's true that the distasteful stories may derive from a small number of farmers and cannot be said to be representative of the industry. However, according to surveys, the statistical track record of South African commercial farmers, black and white, in terms of workers' remuneration and living conditions is dismal. Data collected on matters such as workers' access to a room with a window for ventilation and a cement floor, to ablution facilities, running water, cooking facilities or electricity is discouraging because of its indication of the very poor conditions that workers are expected to endure. A mid nineties study comparing farms in the same region, undertaking similar commercial activities, showed that the best paid workers were to be found on the most profitable farms.* This challenges the conventional argument of farmers that higher wages are not affordable.

I puzzled over what might be the role of the Bank to encourage farming that was humane in its employment practices and also environmentally responsible. Whatever strategy we might devise, it could not be based on a policing function. We would not be able to withdraw a loan facility because of someone's report that temporary workers were given sacks to use as blankets in winter.

I thought about the two wine farms I'd visited. Both were Land Bank clients, but surely one of them merited the award of a lower interest rate than the other. It might be possible to leverage a development ethic through an incentive approach. We could investigate a range of rural activities considered as desirable from an employment and environmental point of view: extending irrigation that was employment creating, investment in irrigation equipment that was more economical in its use of water, farm worker training, improved farm worker housing.

In June 1999 we set up the Bank's Social Accountability Unit. It had two main objectives. Firstly, there would be a stocktaking exercise that would ensure us a comparative base against which to measure our progress. Secondly, the 'social incentive' loan products, on which there would be a discount on the normal interest rate charged, had to be designed. Our research and development unit made estimates of the interest income that we might lose through offering such a scheme. It would be affordable through the Development Finance Fund. We should do it. After all, we were a development finance institution and this was one way of affirming our developmental character. Unlike a commercial banking institution, we were not under pressure to maximise shareholder returns. The application of business criteria as a performance yardstick in terms of efficiency of service was relevant, but in terms of our mandate as a South African public enterprise our contribution to rural development was more important.

Reaching out: the search for viable intermediaries

There was one major issue outstanding in terms of implementing the development aspects of the Strauss Commission recommendations, and this concerned the geographical improvement of access to financial services in the rural areas.

*J Sender, 2000.

As a Strauss commissioner I'd shared thoughts on the potential symbiosis of the Land Bank and Post Bank, the financial wing of the South African postal services. They had the best network in the country in terms of outreach to people residing in the deep rural areas.

When exploring how we could best service our clients while launching the Step Up micro-credit product, we knew we needed to tap into a network of transmission and payment facilities larger than our own. Post Bank did not yet have electronic transfer facilities in place, and we had struck up an agreement with First National Bank.

The Strauss Commission's vision for the Bank was that it should expand its outreach through the use of intermediaries and be instrumental in creating these.

I understood where the recommendation was coming from. I was aware of the submissions to the Strauss Commission that included feedback from the black farmers' union expressing their unhappiness that they might be expected to apply for production credit through the white farming cooperatives. There was discomfort and some hostility about this as cooperatives were still viewed as an extension of the white apartheid state machinery.

We succeeded in reaching several hundred black farmers through agreements with agribusiness agencies. Through Lonhro in Northern Province, Bank monies made it possible for black contract farmers to get credit for their cotton production. We also changed our internal rules to permit branches to deal with production credit applications. The Vryheid branch was immediately overwhelmed with applications from farmers operating on the Makatini Flats. But our small network limited our internal efforts, and there was no doubt that we needed to explore other avenues to achieve a more extended outreach.

As far as possible, in fostering an extended intermediary network, a careful assessment of experience to date was required before 'rushing in where angels fear to tread'. The Department of Agriculture had run a credit scheme for intermediaries between 1995 and 1997.* They had chosen some emergent black farmers' associations and supported them with capacity building as well as a credit line from the Agricultural Credit Board (ACB). I organised a two-day seminar with staff of the ACB for them to give us a detailed briefing on their experience. R20-million had been advanced to five private sector intermediaries between 1995 and 1997, and in late 1999 the figures on the amounts repaid still stood at zero. The briefing covered the difficulties of capacity

---

*G Coetzee, M Mbongwa & M Pheeha, 1999.

building, problems with financial control, and problems with the skills to make credit assessments. The systems in place for checks and balances had proved inadequate. All in all, we were left with the advice to travel with circumspection if we opted for this route.

Another Department of Agriculture initiative was that of 'village banks'. It had the support of the top civil servants in the department, Bongi Njobe and Masiphula Mbongwa. They initially attracted resources from the International Fund for Agricultural Development (IFAD), and then later they attracted major financial support through the bilateral agreement between South Africa and the USA.

After the first field evaluation carried out by IFAD consultants there had been scepticism about the village bank approach in some quarters. On paper it is a wonderfully attractive and laudable idea in populist terms. A community of people puts their savings into a village bank, administered for the people by the people, and the deposits can serve for reinvestment into community business activity.

I had read a hard-hitting article on the real costs of setting up local-level financial service institutions that detailed the hidden costs, and the problems of replicability. In addition, our low population density in rural areas and relatively low turnover of funds stacked the odds against ever achieving financial viability at village level. It is a hugely expensive way of running a small business, except that the 'donor funding component' masks the non-viability.

Considerable expertise in capacity building to administer what are relatively small amounts of money was a prerequisite. The first three pilot banks were in Northern Province in Kraaipan, Modimola and Lotlhekane. The community mobilisation required was demanding, and the human resources development needs were extensive. An elected liaison committee, with due regard for gender representation, had a chairperson, treasurer and secretary plus deputy positions. Project documents referred to the need for training to secure professional management, and the fact that, naturally, all aspects of internal auditing, marketing, security, and credit and investment evaluations had to be done in a professional manner.

The development of local-level financial services required the full complement in terms of operational systems. They needed a Village Bank Manual that would cover the operational systems and procedures as well as training materials. There was a need for infrastructural and transport support: the provision of safes, the collection and secure transport of cash deposits.

As much as it might be expected that a person of my background would be attracted by the populist appeal of the 'local empowerment' aspects of the village banking project, there are some serious pragmatic limitations to my populist leanings. Returns must at least look as though they have a good chance of being greater than the outlay. In this case the chances of financial viability, in real terms, seemed to approximate a cat in hell's chance of survival.

We began to explore three other avenues of improving our client outreach with due regard to replicability and costs incurred.

First we decided to make minor adjustments to our own network. We were well aware of the drawbacks of over-investing in bricks and mortar; the commercial banks were closing down some of their branches in rural towns. We began to rent premises in a few select towns and opened what we referred to as 'satellite branches' on particular days of the week, following the Credit Agricole practice in the small French country towns. We also decided that some of our branches were badly situated and could serve the rural community better if relocated. Prime examples were our Cape Town and George branches. During one week when we surveyed client visits to branches, the Cape Town branch chalked up only eight client visits. Its location next to the parliamentary gardens was not well placed to attract visits from the farming community. A proposal for four smaller branches – Worcester, Belville, Swellendam and George – using the same complement of staff emerged for the restructuring of our services in the Western Cape.

Secondly, we started to use agents. The idea first came up when I heard someone complaining about a black farmer in North West Province who was assisting fellow farmers in filling in the Bank application forms and charging a fee for his services. It seemed to me that the person had identified a marketable service that he could offer. We began to consider the idea of accredited agents who would work on a commission basis. The benefit was that they knew the community they were dealing with and had a good local knowledge of prospective clientele.

The third approach we came up with, that may or may not ever come to fruition, was the concept of franchises. Our agents' work was very limited; they did not do credit assessments. Their work dealt with the induction of the potential client and follow-up in the event of non-payment; the loan approval decisions were taken by Bank employees. The system worked for a simple mass-based product, such as Step Up, involving relatively small sums of money. But my concern was the feedback I was receiving from far-flung rural areas about potential rural entrepreneurs who were not being reached. A businessman from Bushbuckridge and another from the far northern reaches of KwaZulu

Natal contacted me to ask that their services as intermediaries be considered.

With due caution, a proposal for the criteria for intermediary appointments was drawn up, and we decided that we would get a reaction to it. We organised a one-day workshop and invited several businessmen from small rural towns and some NGOs working in the field of small business development. We worked through the proposal.

Intermediaries were to borrow rather large sums of money from us and then take on the entire responsibility for on-lending to clients of their choice, and ensuring repayment. They needed considerable security against the loan and they needed accounting skills. Our risk manager Godfrey Masilela put forward his proposal for a minimum amount of R1-million to be lent to intermediaries – provided they could comply with the stringent accounting and auditing requirements. Participants made themselves clear that something different, on a smaller and more modest scale, was required. The discussions went off at a tangent as people decided to explore other ideas. The outcome of a creative day's work was the identification of the possibilities that a franchise operation might offer as an alternative.

Unlike agents, the franchise would process a loan application, making the full credit assessment, but it would be submitted for final approval to the nearest Bank branch. However the franchise, unlike a fully fledged intermediary, would not deal directly with the monies and accounting. We would rather organise their access to a transit account that would be used as loans were approved and repayments made. I could envisage the disbursement side more easily than the modus operandi of repayment transactions. It would obviously take work to design an up-and-running system, but intuitively it felt as though the franchise option was an innovative approach worth pursuing. It held several attractions. We would use the skills and knowledge of the local community without having to worry about extensive capacity building, financial control and auditing of accounts. We would tap into the community spirit of willing members of the private sector, as well as providing them with an additional business activity. On our side, we would be fulfilling the Strauss mandate to facilitate improved access to a range of trustworthy rural financial services.

Capacity building

Capacity building. The words haunted me. It was yet another expectation of our shareholder that the Bank should undertake this activity on a major scale. I was wary about burning fingers on this one. Knowing how to drive a car does not mean that one has the skills to become a driving instructor. Similarly, the ability to do credit assessments and manage a banking operation does not mean that personnel have the skills to teach business planning and financial management to the new strata of entrepreneurs. Based on this logic I was prepared to become an addict of the 'core business focus' line of argument and try to get out of the capacity building responsibility.

'No use lending money without the parallel support in place to deepen financial management skills,' I would be told. I couldn't disagree.

There was not even the excuse of lack of funds. In June 1998 the parliamentary amendment of the Land Bank Act included the provision that any monies arising from repayments to loans made by the ACB could be transferred to the Bank. The parliamentarians went so far as to determine the possible use of these funds: loans and equity finance for the historically disadvantaged, and financing capacity building activities.

It was rumoured that the accrued funds topped R600-million. Later that year I received a ministerial request for a proposal as to how the Bank might use R350-million. I suggested using R200-million to pay off an outstanding loan from the Ministry of Finance. Another R140-million could be allocated towards loans and equity funding, and I modestly requested R10-million for capacity building.

The ministerial counter-proposal was radically different. R200-million should be used for land purchase and its subdivision into smaller units for sale to black entrepreneurs. This indicated the emergence of a new strategic approach among the land reform policy makers. R100-million would be earmarked for loan and equity finances. The remaining R50-million should be used for capacity building. It was way outside my field of competence even to begin to think about how you spend such a seemingly vast sum of money on training. I contacted the Independent Development Trust. Lulu Gwagwa had just taken over as its director. Capacity building was their core activity, and there was nothing to prevent us from outsourcing. As I explored this option with her my panic attack subsided.

I need not have worried so soon. I had forgotten how dissenting civil servants have the ability to drag their feet and find bureaucratic obstacles when they disagree with something, even a ministerial decision. By the end of 1999 we still hadn't seen the colour of the money of the ACB funds.

Symbiosis and sustainability

The Strauss Commission had recommended that the Bank should be awarded additional grant funding to support its new mandate. Recommendation 50 stated:

The Land Bank should receive direct grants during the establishment phase of its new responsibilities. These grants should be assessed at the outset and annually thereafter on a three year budget cycle. The grants should be administered through a separate line budget item at the Land Bank thus keeping apart the profit-orientated activity from the development activity. The deposit of R200 million currently held by the Department of Finance with the Land Bank should be converted into a suitable contingency reserve to meet such requirements of the Land Bank as cannot be funded out of its normal cash flow.

The idea of ACB funds coming our way stemmed from this recommendation. It seemed laudable and logical enough. However, on becoming managing director of the Bank, I was wary of it. The five years at the Ministry of Agriculture in Mozambique had made me cautious of the clashes that can emerge over control of financial resources. If we could work out a way of achieving the same end without tangling with power-hungry bureaucrats over money, that would be my preferred option. It might be better to work with less money on the basis of long-term, self-financing sustainability that made one independent of cap-in-hand begging for additional handouts.

There's a popular line of thinking most avowedly punted by the private sector that works to their own self-interest. They argue that the profitable economic activities should be reserved for the sole benefit of the private sector. The public sector, they argue, should deal with those activities that the private sector does not find sufficiently attractive either in terms of profitability or risk. They argue that public-owned companies are inefficient, and are best left to do only that which may be deemed socially necessary. There are without doubt numerous examples of public companies that have not been well run and have turned out to be a drain on the taxpayer. However, there is a dearth of in-depth analysis of the causes of failure. There has been a broad, sweeping assumption that the absence of the private sector drive for profit means that public companies are inherently doomed to failure.

The private sector views draw support from such eminent beings as Joseph Stiglitz, the former chief economist of the World Bank. He supported parastatals in so far as governments 'need to devote (their) scarce resources to areas that the private sector does not and is not likely to enter . . . Government needs to focus its attention on those areas that represent its distinct advantages, which distinguish it from private organisations.' I do not generally consider myself as lacking in humility, but on this point I would beg to differ.

My first consideration in taking on the Bank job was that the key to public companies operating differently lay in introducing clear business and development goals that were not airy-fairy but translated into measurable 'to do' items for every employee. If one could also create a more positive working environment, including material incentives for performance, there was no inherent reason why public companies should underperform relative to the private sector.

The second consideration was that I thought the Bank should not only retain its commercial business but also actually aim to make as much money as possible. A portion of the surplus revenue could then be put in a Development Finance Fund (DFF) to be used for development finance activities.

By the end of 1997 the rationale of the profit motive for this public sector institution was clear to me. That year after provisioning for bad debt and putting aside money to upgrade the entire information technology system, we were left with a measly R97-million. If the DFF was to be refuelled out of the imputed tax and dividends, we needed to make more money in order to generate a more substantial fund. The next year we focused on pricing and cost control, with the intention of still giving farmers a good deal relative to commercial banks. In 1998 we clocked up a surplus of R371-million and the figures for 1999 were R434-million. It was sweetly satisfying to watch the figures creep up, an antidote to those who had forecast our failure.

The commercial banks complained about our starting to market ourselves aggressively – this could damage the viability of their rural branches, and it was inappropriate for a parastatal to be acting in this way, so they argued. My problem was that I could not accept that the private sector expected the Bank to have a moral obligation to leave the profitable parts of the business to them. Their profits would not go to development but find their way into private shareholder pockets or investments – perhaps another lucrative shopping mall, another consumer playground for the urban affluent minority.

I heard their arguments, but I suspected opportunism. It was generally accepted that the commercial banks had overspent on infrastructure in rural towns. I also heard that merchant banks with online link-ups to clients were creaming off the top rural businesses who then no longer had any need for discussions with the local manager of a small branch outpost of any one of the big four commercial banks. I was given to understand this poaching comprised a far larger threat than our modest increase in commercial clientele. It was obvious that the world of banking was changing. Internet banking challenged the traditional concept of retail banking. This was an issue that we would also have to face.

Our business vision became crystal clear. Our primary objective was the achievement of the new mandate. The focus was on increasing outreach to the poor-resourced farmers. Internal changes would need to be made to secure this. There would be a big push to achieve effectiveness and cost-efficiency of operations; the remuneration strategy needed to be linked to the achievement of these goals. We would focus on improving the quality of our commercial portfolio, with a view to a steady revenue stream. Care would be taken to maintain the level of capital adequacy that was an important criterion in terms of our risk rating and keeping the confidence of our investors. The transfer of a portion of surplus would be placed behind what we referred to as the 'fire-wall' and into the DFF. The DFF was the pot of gold at the end of the rainbow, only better because it was tangible and we had worked out a system of annual refill. Out of it we could finance the higher-risk loan portfolio, undertake equity investments, pay over to the commercial side of the banking operations any monies owing as a result of farmers taking up the incentive to earn a social dividend, and finally pay for the capacity building activity that was needed to support new entrepreneurs.

We were enamoured with the beauty of the working model that we were putting in place. It had the potential to be a great improvement on any standard Robin Hood approach, because there were win-win possibilities in it even for the wealthy farmers. Its clarity was motivational. The quantity of the DFF would be determined by the level of surplus generated. Such surplus was, in turn, determined by the quality and profitability of the commercial farmer loan book. The two finance portfolios were thus symbiotic and essential components of the asset base of a bank with a true developmental approach to doing business.

In terms of evaluating our own contribution to 'What constitutes development?', by 1999 employees of the Land Bank could hold their heads high – whatever else might be happening in the wider economy, the Bank could confidently claim that it was following a strategy aimed to address the issues of poverty, unemployment and inequality.

Dr Jacobs, the Bank's financial adviser, met Minister of Trade and Industry Alec Erwin on the golf course in early 1998. Reflecting on the events of the first few months of my tenure, he gave his reckoning on the chance of successful change.

'You know, when she first came to the Bank and started, I thought: This is not going to bloody work. Now I have to say I think it's really going to bloody work!'

FIVE

RESISTANCE AND RECONCILIATION

There was no smooth transition towards the implementation of the new business ethic and institutional direction. Employees were mixed in their responses. Months passed in a maelstrom of emotions. We needed to seek alignment and steer staff towards a positive equilibrium.

A burst of thunder

Three hundred guests had gathered at Gallagher Estate on a warm summer's evening. Dressed in their finery, they enjoyed a glass of sherry before entering the vast banquet hall. It had been an evening for celebration, the marking of a rite of passage into a new business era.

One hundred metres away, however, on the other side of the green stakes that fenced off the estate, a crowd of some thirty Land Bank employees had also gathered, including old-guard senior managers. They had chosen their pitch carefully, so that guests had to pass through a flank of people armed with placards. The protesters were white and mainly from head office, but they had been joined by some of their branch colleagues. The placards they carried stated grievances about changes in the Bank that they were not happy with; the choice of English as the official business medium had, in particular, created an astonishing amount of friction.

They sought outside sympathy. They wanted to alert the public to the fact that the transformation process was not all plain sailing. But whatever valid grievances they might have had were lost: the stronger memory of the guests was of posters that were gross in their sentiment, appealing only to a conservative right-winger. There were insults relating to my being the widow of a prominent communist; his place in the country's history as a revered national hero meant that this placard did not win them many friends. Another poster, painted boldly, read, 'Paint her black and send her back', words of blatant racism. Their protest backfired. They were their own worst enemies. They won for me more support than I had had before, as they gave people an understanding that we had made progress whilst enduring unusual levels of hostility.

The raw anger was disturbing. Something had to be done. Some reconciliation needed to take place, otherwise there would be a long-term schism in the community of employees. I reflected on the last ten months. There had been insurgency and counter-insurgency; the way forward required that some wounds should heal.

Seeds of distrust

The first few weeks of the tenure of the new board had been a time of many unpleasant discoveries that coloured the relationship between ourselves and the 'old guard'. This comprised the older staff members, in their fifties, who had no working experience outside the Land Bank. Since joining the Bank on finishing secondary school, they had patiently clawed their way up the hierarchy to reach their own cherished positions of power.

There were several discoveries that irritated me and the board of directors. There was unease over contracts. The computer mainframe was a case in point. Why the purchase of a machine with eighty-five per cent overcapacity, and why a five-year contract, a copy of which could not be found in the Bank? Why had the old board tried to finalise the signing and sealing of a contract committing the Bank to more than R20-million refurbishment expenditure when transformation was on the cards and new decisions affecting infrastructure might be reached? What levels of obsession with centralisation of power prevailed? A four-storey building had been bought on Visagie Street next door to the nine-storey building we occupied. It had belonged to the Citrus Board. It had been stripped – there were gaping holes in walls where there had once been air-conditioners; you could wander through one doorless room to another. I could imagine an entire downsized head office in this space – and yet it had been bought as an *addition*, not a replacement.

There was the discovery of almost R15-million being held in reserve as provisioning against accumulated leave. Some employees had literally hundreds of days accumulated. Yet according to the staff administration data there was an above average level of sick leave taken. Then there was the discovery of the implications of the retrenchment package, several times greater than the financial industry norm. There was the discovery that black youngsters were being employed in their dozens. It was positive that these diploma-holders were getting their first jobs, although strange in light of the Auditor General's report on overstaffing. On the other hand, the strategy reeked of continued protection of white Afrikaner power – a commitment to employ blacks only at junior, non-threatening, levels.

It was these kinds of 'discoveries' on matters arising as a result of old-guard custodianship that provoked a hard line response, rather than any softly-softly strategic approach that might have alienated fewer people.

Cats amongst pigeons

Within the first weeks decisions were taken that gave rise to hostility even from some of those older staff members who might have been reasonably well disposed towards transformation. The IT maintenance contracts were questioned and an advertisement was placed to tender for an overall assessment of the systems. The building contract was consigned to archives to be revisited as and when there might be clarity on the implications of restructuring; both branch and head office managers were banned from hiring staff unless the post had head office approval. There was a moratorium on staff promotions, as there was distrust as to how the promotion process was handled. Younger employees referred to 'boetie-boetie' (I'll rub your back, you rub mine) practices, as well as membership of the golf club smoothing the path to promotion. There was a decision that annual notch increases would cease; the system was a personal benefit that brought no benefit to the business. With regard to the millions of rands worth of accumulated leave, people were asked either to cash it in or take it so as to eliminate the large provisioning figure on the balance sheet. Trade unions had fought battles over leave rights with good reason: holidays were meant to be taken.

The *faux pas* had been over language. At face value it was a simple, logical business decision without any baggage attached, certainly there was no malicious intent. I'd enjoyed learning languages in my life and the opening of doors to other cultures that's gained that way. While the dominant language spoken daily in the Bank was Afrikaans, it seemed obvious that within a relatively short time we would be buying off-the-shelf computer packages that would be in English. Land Bank employees would need a working knowledge of English just as lawyers have been expected to have a working knowledge of Afrikaans.

The decision on language policy was taken in July 1997 without soul-searching or any great deliberation. English needed to be the business language of the Land Bank; we were after all on the edge of the twenty-first century with expectations of accelerated globalisation. Naturally, language training would be provided to assist staff in making the transition. Important internal documents would be available in translation. As for clients, we would ask for the language of their preference. We hoped that in the coming years we would build up the African language capacity of employees. There was no sentiment at this board meeting that we were taking an earth-shattering decision.

Many Land Bank staff thought otherwise; for them the decision was an affront, an aggressive action on the part of representatives of the new political order. It threatened their Afrikaans identity, of which language was an important part. I was not sufficiently attuned to the language issue, perhaps because I arrived in South Africa as an adult. I was aware only of Afrikaans as the spark of contention leading to the 1976 student uprising as black people objected to learning in the language of their oppressor.

It was only months later when reading about the fostering of Afrikaner capitalism that I came to know about an earlier and different language struggle. The Afrikaner Bond had campaigned against the domination of English. I was unaware that the National Party under Hertzog had fought for language equality within the state, for Afrikaans to be equal to English, to the extent of passing the Language Act of 1925.

O'Meara* writes that in the 1930s

The cities of South Africa were overwhelmingly English. English was the language of the urban economy and culture. On the factory floors, in shops and banks, Afrikaans was hardly ever used but was derided as a 'kitchen language'. This was experienced by all Afrikaans-speakers as intense discrimination against both their language and themselves. Whatever their class position, simply to conduct their daily lives they were forced to use a foreign language, that of a conqueror . . . Under Bond direction . . . many campaigns (were) waged (such as) the call by the ANS (Afrikaans-Nasionaal Studentebond: Afrikaans National Student League), 'Never shop where you are not served in Afrikaans, and where Afrikaans is not accorded its rightful place on notices and signboards – and tell the trader why. Pay no accounts that have not been issued in Afrikaans, and patronise no firm that does not advertise in Afrikaans newspapers and magazines' (*Wapenskou* February 1936). The language struggle was given a firmly nationalist direction by the Bond. It was seen as part of the assertion of a separate Afrikaner identity.

---

*D O'Meara, 1983, Chapter 5, p.75.

Reading this historical account brought home to me how insensitive our approach had been. On reflection, I realised that the old guard, senior managers in the late nineties, were obviously all born in the 1940s. They would have been raised in the environment described by the historian. It would have been a core part of their childhood moulding. And with a few words, just a couple of sentences among the reams of pages that made up the board minutes in July 1997, the new board of directors, without much ado, threatened their very sense of identity.

I tend to be harsh in judging this decision as one of the mistakes that I was party to. Not because I doubt the sense of it, but because the communication of the decision did not receive the attention that I later understood it deserved. We should have been seen to be investigating the cost of language tuition; that would have created a state of anticipation. We should have planned people's release to attend courses, and therefore have been seen to be ready to invest the time and the money to ease a transition. Instead, a matter arising in the course of a board discussion, a resolution hastily drafted, and within hours of the meeting the news had spread like wildfire, conveyed as indicative of hostile intent.

Undermining traditions of power

I found that the internal workings of the Land Bank were regulated by a series of committees and periodic meetings:

> The Deputy General Managers' meeting
> The Management Committee
> The Finance and Economics Committee
> The Infrastructure Committee
> The Advisory Staff Committee
> The Annual Report Committee
> The Group Scheme Land Bank Management Committee
> The Staff Housing Committee
> The Asset Management Committee
> The Steering Committee (Computerisation)

The most powerful committee seemed to be the deputy general managers' meeting. The finance and economics committee dealt mainly with treasury issues under the firm guiding influence of Dr Jacobs.

I was intrigued by the content of the deputy general managers' meetings. The 11 August 1997 meeting originally had only three items on the agenda: Land Bank Calendars, Selection of Travel Agencies, and a proposal to streamline the administration of retail loans. It seemed a rather short agenda to merit the expense of flying in four regional managers from different parts of the country. However, at the start of the meeting the following items were added: language policy, marketing, Land Bank Act, salaries, and 'white male staff in the service of the Bank'.

With regard to language, apparently the sales section had submitted a statement of dissatisfaction. They noted that 'their mother tongue was being slighted', and that more than ninety per cent of the Bank's clients were Afrikaans-speaking and hence instructions and directives would have to be translated from Afrikaans to English and vice versa. There seemed to be little forward thinking that within the short term Afrikaner farmers would be far outnumbered as black farmers joined the Land Bank's clientele.

It was conceded that I had set up a task team to investigate how best to take the language policy forward, and that they would do their best to contribute.

One of the most conservative regional managers spoke of the rumours circulating at branch offices. I as managing director had allegedly said that white male staff members would only be considered for promotion as a last resort. If this were true, they noted, white males would feel there was no future for them and would lose motivation to work well; whereas they considered the 'loyalty and dedication' of such staff to be 'indispensable'. If these managers had not felt it beneath them to go to the Indaba Room to watch the videos that had been made, they would have heard the policy on affirmative action clearly articulated – it was not rumour at all. They would have heard an input that reminded people of a shortage of skills, and the white males' relative advantage on this score because of the discrimination that had historically been in their favour. They would have heard a statement on expectations that while others (i.e. blacks and women) would now enjoy preferential status, the need for skills should ensure opportunities for them too.

The outcome of the discussion on the McGee salary proposal at the July 1996 board *bosberaad* was to defer a decision until we were sure that the proposal fitted with whatever institutional restructuring was to take place. They expressed concern that new 'suitable officials' might be attracted to the Bank by salary offers that were higher than theirs. They decided to impress upon me the importance of maintaining the morale of the long-standing workforce and also that they, as the core group of senior officials, constituted 'a certain force' whose status should not be undermined by external appointees earning higher salaries.

It was their description of themselves as 'a certain force' in the core of the Bank's operations that provoked my sense of unease. In the 1980s a video copy of 'A Very British Coup' – a UK Channel Four production – had arrived for Joe and me in Lusaka. In essence it is a story of sabotage, about how new policies can be effectively subverted by an old-guard administration. I was fearful of the same thing happening at the Land Bank. The next meeting of the deputy general managers group was scheduled for 13 October 1997; it would never take place.

I anxiously awaited Claude Peyrot's next visit. I was still the only new external senior appointment, and the odd position of being both managing director and chairperson of the board meant there was not another person to use as a sounding board on a daily basis between board meetings. Claude advised that it was time for me to set up my own group, 'the guiding coalition' in Kotter's terminology.

By September 1997 I had recruited a human resources director, a communications director, and a risk manager; two black men and one white woman – powerful droplets of diversity into the bland potion of white male managers. At last I was no longer the only extraterrestrial!

'Keep the group tight-knit,' advised Claude. 'Select strategically.'

The selected group became known as the Strategic Management Team (SMT). It initially included the heads of operations, finance, human resources, and communications, and was later joined by the person heading our efforts to modernise our information technology systems.

'This is what is known as your "kitchen cabinet" – your inner circle, your support,' Claude told me, and wrote a brief for me on what items should comprise the normal agenda, and which criteria to use to evaluate the inclusion of other issues. The concern was to focus on strategy and avoid getting bogged down in detail and micro-management.

On 29 September 1997 I drafted a letter to senior managers. It advised of the continuity of the finance and economics committee (FEC), the establishment of an audit committee, and the formation and membership of the strategic management team. It advised of a plan to hold extended senior management meetings three times per year, and the intention to consider the launch of a branch manager forum that would facilitate their greater input into decision making. The letter concluded that 'the following committees are no longer required' – and listed every single one of them except the FEC. It was a bloodless coup intended to undermine the continuing bases of power in the head office. I knew this action would attract hostility. I told myself that I'd taken on a job to reshape an institution, not to win popularity ratings – small comfort when dealing with the unpleasant consequences of decisions that one was convinced had to be taken.

I spent time questioning myself about the intoxication of power, and the pen as an extraordinary weapon. The sharp edge of the pen's nib acted as a razor and sliced through the hair that held the sword of Damocles; the sitting target was the old guard power base. With a few words, written in less than an hour, the old guard inner circle, which had taken its members almost forty years to gain membership of, was disbanded.

There was no doubt of the personal hurt felt; some genuinely had good intentions, and hoped to contribute positively. If so, their contribution would have to find its way through other channels. The cohesion of the group smacked of a different cultural paradigm to that being fostered in the transformation process; the cohesion represented a threat, and provided the rationale for its dismantling.

At about the same time another incident caused deep reverberations. It was occasioned by an innocent action on my part, but was apparently considered deeply threatening and challenging of institutional culture. It confirmed how strongly entrenched the cultural paradigm was, and the justification of creating challenges to provoke people to think outside of their boxes.

I was told of a young man, an agricultural economist with a master's degree, stationed in the Pretoria branch; apparently he was under-employed. White agricultural economists dealt with the white clients, and the black agricultural economists worked with the black clients – so I was told. There were, however, only a handful of black clients. I asked to see the young man. Philly Moloto is of slight build and cuts an insubstantial figure. He has a quiet manner and holds himself back; in retrospect perhaps that had also contributed to his underemployment. We talked about his Land Bank work; he told me he needed less than half a day a week to do his job. Later I read his master's dissertation on the costs and benefits of vegetable growing in Mamelodi township.

I spoke to the branch manager, requesting that I 'borrow' Philly until the end of the year. I wanted him to work with the task team on new products, but I also wanted him to give a second opinion on the rejected applications of black clients that I was expected to sign off. It was the practice at the time that the managing director should assume this responsibility. It wasn't practical in the longer term, but I welcomed it then as it allowed me an insight into the workings of branch personnel and an understanding of the basis on which loan applicants were turned down. I had doubts about some of the decisions, and it offered an opportunity to raise questions. I was also able to push for a different approach to customer relations, that the letter of refusal should be comprehensive and empathetic and not a cursory statement – 'This

application has no merit.' However, the brown files tied with their
pink ribbons began to pile up faster than I could deal with them. I
needed help.

There were several empty offices on the eighth floor of head office,
eight of them to be precise. They had belonged to the eight full-time
executive board members who had been responsible for Land Bank
corporate governance. The offices had recently been vacated at one fell
swoop, as the newly appointed board was entirely non-executive except
for myself. I asked Philly to move into one of those empty offices. I
also asked Karl Ehrenberg, as co-ordinator of the task teams, to move
into another; the others remained free for the moment to be used by
consultants such as Claude.

I had begun to work late in the evenings. I now knew where the
independent switches were for the eighth floor after the daily switch
off of power that signalled the four o'clock meltdown as the staff exodus
took place. There were very few other lights on in the building during
the evening, only on the fourth floor where the IT personnel were busy
working overtime to upgrade the computer facilities.

One evening, just before nine o'clock, there was a soft knock on my
office door. A tall, youngish-looking man came in, told me he'd heard
the music filtering down the central stairwell and so knew that I was
still at work. He said that he was taking my letter to staff as genuine,
that I would try to keep an open-door policy and be available to employees
who wished to raise concerns. What bothered him, he told me, was my
flagrant disregard for Land Bank culture, my lack of respect for norms
and traditions. My invitation to Philly Moloto to move into an office
on the eighth floor typified this disrespectful attitude. I needed, he told
me, to understand how offensive this was to people. According to Land
Bank culture, the eighth floor was a hallowed and sacrosanct space
reserved only for those with employment longevity and seniority. The
young black man of my choosing had been employed by the Bank for
only three years and was still regarded as a newcomer. And to rub salt
into wounds, he was a nobody from a branch, somersaulting his way
to the eighth floor to work with the managing director. All of this was
related to me in a very non-aggressive way, meant to persuade me to be
more considerate and reasonable in my actions. I was friendly in my
response, but maintained firmly that there was a value system imbued
in the traditions that I could not accept. A few weeks later when the
risk manager, Godfrey Masilela, and the human resources director, Dan
Matsapola, took up their appointments, I pointed out the vacant offices.
Unlike my invitation to Philly Moloto, which was motivated by simple

practicality; this time my request that two black men join me on the eighth floor was deliberate.

Hate mail

The hate mail began with a series of provocations. The first related to the appointment of Dan Matsapola as human resources general manager. He left work one afternoon a few days after his appointment and found a neon orange sticker across his windscreen. The word printed on the sticker was INSOLVENT. These were the labels used when the Bank had a bankrupt client and was about to auction off the farm in order to settle the debt on the loan. The bright neon stickers were stuck on the clients' files for easy identification.

I did not know it to be a rule of the Bank (somehow it had escaped the information given during induction) that it would not employ people who had been declared bankrupt. The staff administration department had run a credit check on Dan Matsapola and found judgment against him. I asked Dan to fill me in. His explanation was that he had owned a house in Gauteng and that he'd asked an agent to handle the rental of it when he and his family moved to Cape Town when he took up a new job there. The arrangement with tenants had not worked out; some bond payments had been missed. He thought he had successfully negotiated a rescheduled payment deal with his bank, but there had been crossed communication and, unbeknown to him, the house had been auctioned, and he'd just discovered this himself. He hadn't known about the judgment against him until then.

I was possibly gullible, but I preferred to think the best of people, and I've never been so disappointed for cynicism to set in. I took that pen in hand again and wrote a letter to the staff, questioning the validity of the Bank rule, and put myself on the line.

TO ALL STAFF MEMBERS

INTERPRETATION OF PERSONNEL REGULATION

It has come to my attention that there are mutterings among the staff concerning the recent employment of a staff member who has an insolvency record.

The Bank has a set of rules and regulations – which need revision – for example, staff members who wish to be on public committees, including school committees, are supposed to seek approval from the General Manager. But the rules stand as they are until there is a proposal for revision that is accepted.

It is important to have rules to establish the grounds for disciplinary action, for example: absence without leave, theft, sexual harassment. There are other issues which are not so clear cut: insolvency is one of them. I understand that some institutions would regard themselves as 'embarrassed' were they to have an employee who has incurred an insolvency judgment.

I do not share this view. I would be 'embarrassed' by staff actions that are criminal and fraudulent etc, but it seems to me that an insolvency due to personal, circumstantial, financial misfortune is a reason for sympathy and support, and should not incur a punitive or hostile response from either management or colleagues. The existing staff regulations allow me the opportunity as Managing Director to make this more liberal interpretation and I am happy to take this space and defend my decision.

I think those who are critical of the most outstanding candidate for a job in spite of an insolvency record – a job which does not, by the by, require financial skill – should question the moral basis of their own judgementalism.

You are welcome to disagree. I would be happy to hear your comments.

Helena Dolny
Managing Director

The next thing I knew the letter had been sent to the *Landbouweekblad*, and to the Minister, with the intention to attract reprimand for my misdemeanour. A letter from the Minister's office landed on my desk: 'Your circular is brilliant.'

After this there was a salvo of anonymous insults that continued for the next eighteen months, and only ended with the completion of head office restructuring. A favourite spot for posting insults was on the mirrors in the lifts. They were mainly directed at the individuals who made up the strategic management team. The subject matter ranged from comments on people's skills to the length of a skirt, suggesting that a certain person was a whore. They were crude and intended to hurt.

Besides the lift notices, there was an anonymous vicious skit on our communication attempts. We had at one stage called for people to send in their questions on issues that were bothering them and then, as the strategic management team, we prepared a fairly lengthy and comprehensive response. A few weeks later a sarcastic imitation of the question-and-answer circular was making its rounds.

The ugliest hate mail – I didn't count the *Landbouweekblad* cartoons in this bracket – arrived in an official/*amptelik* envelope T.O.D./T.E.D.55, postmarked Middelburg, 26 November 1997. It was addressed to Me. Slovo, p/a Land Bank, Bus 375, Pretoria.

We had launched our consultation process with an advert of a group of talking piglets inviting stakeholders to make their input into the Bank's restructuring process. The correspondent had photocopied the advert and scrawled names on each of the piglets:

Joe Slovo	Dead Pig
Nelson	Flying Dying Pig
Naido [sic]	Satan's Pig
Omar	Moslem Running Pig
Mafumadi [sic]	Useless Pig
'Dr' Zuma	Ugly Caffer [sic] Pig

The outlines of five additional pigs were sketched into the hay and named:

Me Slovo	
F.W.	Traitor Pig
Catto Tswette [sic]	Pig-Balls
Hanekom	Swart Vark (Black Pig)
Nzo	Sleeping Pig

I felt that I had been placed in some good company, but the ugliness of the intent was sickening. There was so much bitterness in the defacement. Underneath the Land Bank signage, on the bottom right hand side of the page, was written 'Goodbaai!!!'

Thank goodness I also received some mail that sharply contrasted with the hate mail. It was equally emotive, but positive.

> Dear Helena,
> . . . I want to thank you for being the Bank's new CEO. You are like an angel being sent from heaven to come and open our eyes to see not only our own potential but specifically that of our colleagues irrespective of their background, age, gender or race . . .
>
> Despite any resistance that you might have experienced up to now and even more severe resistance you may incur in the future, please remain as brave and open-minded as you are because the Bank, its staff and our country really need you.

The writer continued a troubled and soul-searching letter, and in part I was a source of the trouble.

> . . . I time and time again feel that when we communicate in person that you are suspicious of me, my intent, my commitment and goodwill . . . I

have been doing introspection to try and find out from within myself where I got derailed or made a mistake.

It was one of the most difficult aspects of the job, receiving and dealing with such mail. This reaching-out letter touched me more deeply than the hate mail. I found it overwhelming that I could make an impact on someone that prompted such a troubled letter from the heart. I wasn't sure that I was equipped to respond well enough. I was also scared of becoming too close to people at work, of being totally consumed. I needed to learn how to keep my own equilibrium.

One of the lessons I was to learn was how my position attracted opposite extremes of response. Being in a leadership position means that you're often seen in caricature and, such is the art of cartoon, both your best and worst features will be wildly exaggerated. I also learnt not to categorise people on the basis of first impressions. Those who are at first overwhelmingly positive towards you may become disappointed and turn sour, whilst your worst critics may later admit that you have some good qualities after all.

But one has to accept that there will be 'bitter-enders' – the ones who will never forgive you, for you personify the upsetting of the status quo of their world. The passage of time would demonstrate that there was little chance of their coming to terms with the change; instead an embittered tolerance displayed itself because of the power relations, but without conciliation. They looked for a chance, or even half a chance, to take revenge.

These individuals would feed the rumour mill, or the press, or the Auditor General's office, trying to create a problem. They presented accounting information about the future search workshops as though they were fruitless expenditure, groups of people simply having a *jol* at a holiday resort. They raised issues about the payment of relocation allowances to the new managerial staff – a common corporate practice, never before done in the Land Bank because all senior staff were home-grown. My being driven to work was questioned for the first time in the history of the Land Bank. The previous managing directors, and managing directors' wives, had been chauffeured around for years without an eyebrow being lifted – including wives being taken to tea parties and insisting on the 'official' sign being placed visibly in the car so as to claim status. The attempts to create such problems were petty and irritating in terms of the time that was required to answer the issues. The new management's continued ability to satisfy the Auditor General's queries increased the resentment of certain individuals.

I wondered about the effect on one's psyche of working in a place where one knew some people were vigilant to detect the smallest margin of error.

The Truth and Reconciliation Commission

In the third quarter of 1997 we received a letter from the Truth and Reconciliation Commission (TRC) informing us that hearings on the role of the business sector during the apartheid era would take place. The Land Bank was requested to prepare a written submission for presentation. The matter was tabled at a board meeting. It seemed inappropriate that new staff should be charged with its preparation. Izak Cronje, a board member of several years' standing, kindly and voluntarily took on the responsibility to organise a group of senior staff to write the submission under his guidance. The senior members of the legal section spent hours on this assignment.

Four versions of a lengthy document were drafted one after the other. The first one I read can most aptly be described as a whitewash. There was an absolute refusal to confront the fact that the Land Bank, and its senior employees of some thirty to forty years standing, had been party to aiding and abetting the aims of apartheid.

I did not want to trash the hours of work put into it. My first tactic to try to get the group to revisit the substance of what they had written was through comments and questions along the lines of:

> I am not sure that the document gets to the heart of the matter (which is to acknowledge the Land Bank's participatory role in carrying forward the apartheid architectural plan). I share the following observations for your consideration.
>
> The Land Bank was a state agent for implementation of state policy in rural areas . . . there is a need to acknowledge moral responsibility for contributing to the execution of policy. For example:
> – Did the Land Bank finance farmers who were the beneficiaries of the iniquitous policy of forced removals?
> – It is understood that the Land Bank did not lend to landowners on so-called 'black spots' in areas considered as white South Africa, even though these farmers possessed freehold title and had collateral.
> – The Land Bank (although not profit-driven) did not have (and still does not yet have) a moral code of lending with regard to farmers.
>
> For your consideration.

And I signed off.

The subsequent three drafts represented no real improvement. The old-guard document was a descriptive chronology of the statutes, the operation of the board of directors, the focus of lending on 'category 2' farmers, the 1965 change in the liquid asset status of certain of the Land Bank's financing instruments and the move towards market-related costing of loan funds.

As a historical account of the evolution of Land Bank finance, Draft 4 was a careful piece of work. As a submission to the TRC, it was inappropriate. There was an absolute refusal to apply critical thinking on the matter of the Land Bank's role as a tool of the apartheid state. The idea of presenting Draft 4, unmodified, to the commissioners at a public hearing was scary. They would eat us for breakfast. We would be a laughing stock, although it wasn't a laughing matter. The submission, as such, would convince people that a blinkered view of the past persisted and that the Land Bank was not ready to move forward.

A friend came up with what I thought was a really bright suggestion. 'Employ an economic historian to spend a few days reading board documents and annual reports from the past forty years, and see what synopsis they come up with.' I phoned Wits University's history department and the terms of reference for a short-term consultancy were agreed upon with one of their established researchers – fluent in Afrikaans, of course.

The old-guard document and the historian's document were chalk and cheese.

The historian's document set out the terms of the Land Bank's aiding and abetting of the apartheid state policy. It argued that while the 1913 Land Act allocated seven per cent of the land to Africans, not all rural blacks lived in the communal reserves set aside for them. Many continued to farm as sharecroppers and labour tenants with the agreement of white farm owners.

The document noted that in 1959 the Land Bank Act was amended to allow the provision of 'intermediate term credit against the security of movables'. This should have been sufficient condition for share-croppers and labour tenants to qualify for loans, but there was a tacit understanding that blacks were not to be Land Bank clients.

The historian cited internal documents as testimony to the racial bias of the Bank.

In 1960 the Annual Report described the granting of a loan to a cooperative consisting 'mainly of Indian members' as a 'new aspect of finance'. It was clearly a rare occasion when a loan was issued to Indian farmers, who were gradually pushed out of white farming districts after the passing of the Group Areas Act in 1958, or the African farmers with private titles, whose 'black spot' farms were rubbed out by Apartheid from the 1950s onward.*

The historian logged the importance of Land Bank lending to marketing boards and other institutions that were central to the National Party's political agenda. White farmers who occupied the land of removed communities (Mapochsgronde, Steelpoortpark) readily received Land Bank loans. Loans for machinery in the sixties were a pinion of a state mechanisation drive aimed to stop the *beswartering* of the *platteland*. The increased use of machinery resulted in the squeezing out of the sharecroppers and tenants whose only option was to move to overcrowded settlements in the African 'reserves'.

The historian referred to the role of the Bank in the recapitalisation of white farmers. In the 1970s farm debt burden had increased rapidly. The debt standing in 1970 was R1,3-billion; by 1981 it was R4,8-billion. A great deal of the debt was with the commercial banks who were edgy about the increasing magnitude. In 1983 the National Party government took the pressure off the commercial banks by converting farmers' debts into Land Bank mortgage bonds repayable over a long term. The Land Bank was party to a scheme to assist less efficient, indebted farmers to stay on the land on the basis of their race.

In 1992 the Land Bank acted as the agent for another scheme that bailed out the commercial banks, the cooperatives, and the farmers. This time government assistance to the tune of R3,8-billion was couched as 'drought relief'. The historian noted that this recapitalisation took place after the unbanning of the liberation movement political organisations, and at a time when negotiations for a transition to a democratic transfer of power were under way. Land redistribution was on the cards. The effect of the government assistance to recapitalise was to prevent many bankruptcies and thus supported the market value of land. The consequence for the future was that land purchase for redistribution would be a more costly exercise.

The historian affirmed the gender bias in the handling of loan applications, again citing internal documents. The final salvo was an examination of the internal personnel issues where there was blatant discrimination against women and blacks.

---

*Land and Agricultural Bank of South Africa. Submission to the Chairman of the Truth and Reconciliation Commission, 12 November 1997.

I circulated this document to the old-guard working group. The next morning when I arrived at work there was a single sheet of paper on my desk beginning: 'We the undersigned . . .' There were three lines simply written, expressing the strongest possible condemnation of the document prepared by the historian. Within twenty-four hours the document had been shared amongst a wider group, nineteen of the top Afrikaner managers at head office who considered themselves to be the top echelon. They had signed that they 'reject this document in its totality' and, furthermore, 'The top management are of the opinion that an external person is not in a position to draft a report on behalf of the Bank.'

So what was I to do? I could not take the historian's document to the TRC as representing the views of the Bank. Its presentation, even as approved by the board of directors, would be misleading. I was in a quandary. The hearing was now only two days away. I phoned one of the commissioners and explained: 'At the Bank we have unreconciled perceptions about our history.' I proposed that I bind the two documents together with an explanatory cover letter. This would best reflect the current situation at the Land Bank and indicate the divide to be resolved if there was to be true reconciliation. The commissioner said that this would be acceptable.

The delegation to the TRC was made up of myself, Bonile Jack, senior deputy manager Karl Ehrenberg, and the regional manager from the Western Cape, Andre Jansen. It seemed important that we were a mix of the old and the new, just as the two documents represented the old and the new. We were complimented on the candour of our presentation. The chairperson, in concluding, said we were not the first organisation to find great difficulty in drafting a document, and that they appreciated that the Land Bank was currently midstream in its transformation process.

The *Landbouweekblad*, as was customary at that time, condemned almost everything I did. This time they redid their original cartoon of Helena of Troyeville under the new subtitle '*Donner net voort*' (loosely, 'Just blunder on'). The writing on the flagstaff of the chariot now read sarcastically:

Ons is jammer	(We are sorry)
Ons het wittes gehelp	(We helped whites)
Ons het stropers help koop	(We helped buy harvesters)
Ons het die rade gesteun	(We supported the boards)

Their write-up of the Land Bank presentation to the TRC read:

'In her march to the arch' at the 'Revenge and Divide Commission', the Land Bank's boss lady, Dr Helena Dolny, was only too willing to confess the 'sins' of the Land Bank.

Unlike some people who refuse to 'launch' their boats in the TRC stream, Helen of Troy just went ahead and jumped in. She rejected the 'first submission' made by the 'old Land Bank' (before '94) and headed straight for the TRC with a 'second submission' – that of the 'new Land Bank' (after '94).

In the second submission the Land Bank asks for action because it had, during the period of 'oppressive rural apartheid' and on the basis of a 'racist state policy', assisted the white farmers to purchase tractors and mechanical harvesters to the detriment of black farmers and farm workers!

Of all the ridiculous allegations. As if help to commercial agriculture did not also benefit workers, and non-whites in rural areas! In any case what else can one expect from the widow of an arch communist.*

Exasperation! We'd especially taken along the two reports, and carefully explained why, but the facts were not reported accurately. The intention to illustrate the gap that needed to be closed if reconciliation was to be achieved had passed over the top of people's heads and had fallen far out of the target range.

The union declaration of dispute

Everything that happened seemed to contribute to the build up of a crisis with the union. The Land Bank had recognition agreements with two unions: SASBO, the finance workers' union, and SACCAWU, which drew its members from the service workers. The reason for the two unions was that Land Bank service workers, all black, had not felt comfortable with membership of the white-dominated SASBO. Indeed, there were a couple of black professionals who had declined to join SASBO, preferring to join SACCAWU instead because of the racial discomfort.

SASBO does not have a reputation for being progressive; it's often described as a conservative, white-collar workers' union. On the days that COSATU, the mother-body to which SASBO is affiliated, called for a stayaway or for people to join a protest march, SASBO was rarely present. Certainly to my knowledge, between 1997 and 1999 none of the Land Bank SASBO members ever joined the COSATU protests that took place outside the Pretoria City Hall, which is right opposite the Land Bank head office building.

---

*'Land Bank's ridiculous actions', *Landbouweekblad*, 30 January 1998.

There was the strangest recognition agreement between SASBO and the Land Bank. There were some serious flaws, prejudicial to the development of a good employer-employee relationship, which are explored further in Chapter 7. It was so open-ended that there were none of the limits to the bargaining unit membership that I thought were customary. The most senior manager, including myself as managing director, was eligible for union membership.

I was warned: 'SASBO will be used by conservative elements in the Bank. It is not a matter of influence from the bottom-up; this will be top-down. The issues are not really about leave, or language. At heart, the real issue is the fear of losing power and status through your expressed intention to decentralise and reduce the management layers.'

Nevertheless I hoped for a relationship of dialogue with the union. I'd met with Ben Venter, the Pretoria-based regional secretary, soon after joining the Bank. He'd been invited to the first 'think-tank' workshop, after which he was quoted in the union newsletter as saying: 'I'm sure we'll eventually find a lot to fight about, but it's invigorating dealing with a CEO who cares, listens and wants a fair deal for all.'

It didn't take long to find a fight; certain decisions of the board created discontent among union members. At the same time, the union was itself very weak in bringing added value to the approach to transformation, and any hope I had that they would be a resource, bringing lessons and different ideas from other institutional experiences, was short-lived. Above all else, they focused on salary negotiations and the defence of benefits.

The July 1997 board meeting announced the end of the notch system of automatic yearly increments with immediate effect.

But backtracking was required. What the board had not understood was that notch increases were awarded on a person's birthday. This meant that all the people born between January and July had received their increase for that calendar year. To suspend the system mid-year was unfair to those with birthdays in the remaining months. We had to set a new cut-off date of 31 December.

Any policy change that affected employees' conditions of employment needed to be negotiated with the union. Notch increases were however 'discretionary' – a management prerogative – and the union understood the salary conundrum that needed to be resolved, and did not try to force this issue.

The board's decision that employees should cash in their accumulated leave also angered people. The payment would be liable to taxation. There still existed a tax concession on payments in lieu of leave – the only snag was that you had to get to the age of fifty-five to qualify for it. It was therefore the aim of employees to accumulate at least R30 000 worth of leave by the age of fifty-five so as to make fullest use of the concession. That explained the R15-million reserves in the balance sheet set against such future payments for hundreds of employees. But the board ruling affected the 'accepted' conditions of employment. Employees were right when they complained of decisions being taken unilaterally. Negotiations got under way, with the outcome that the Land Bank moved to the banking industry norm of allowing leave to accumulate to a maximum of forty-five days.

But the decision which sparked the first public protest was one in which the union was involved, and certain SASBO representatives were less than honest with their members when they said they had not been consulted. This one so fundamentally affected the lives of a select number of bank employees that extra special attention was paid to the consultation process (see Chapter 6). It concerned the decision to declare the current branch manager positions redundant and to redefine the job descriptions.

There was first a private discussion about the rationale for this change with Ben Venter followed by his attendance at a specially convened meeting with the persons concerned.

It was fear of job loss by the branch managers that finally stirred things up and lunchtime protests were held at head office and at several of the branches.

This time the media reports were fair. There was more readiness to acknowledge the Land Bank's business backwardness than its role in supporting apartheid. *Die Boer Farmer*, not known for its sympathies towards me, reported: 'Transformation will have its pitfalls – Dolny'.* They discussed the need for job redefinition as a necessary part of restructuring a failing business. They were fair, too, in noting the commitment that there would be attempts to redeploy people who might face redundancy due to restructuring.

The union leadership of the protest marked the beginning of an acrimonious relationship that was to last several months. The next issue to be picked up on was retrenchment packages. Meanwhile emotions ran high, and were divisive and damaging to relationships between staff. Something had to be done.

---

*A Engelbrecht, 'Transformation will have its pitfalls – Dolny', *Die Boer Farmer*, January 1998.

Alignment attempts

Many of the staff who were supportive of transformation felt that things would never really come right until the major restructuring of head office was complete and the fears and insecurities settled. This was an accurate assessment, and yet one couldn't just sit passively and witness heightened tension and worsening personal work relationships. We looked for actions that would create a more positive acceptance of change among the fearful in what was inevitably an uneven transformation process. It seemed important to respect that people deal with events in their lives at different paces. The consultation process had attracted those most ready to see the possible benefits of change; the sceptics and the timid had hung back, but they were not to be written off.

In retrospect, what we were trying to grapple with was organisational therapy, and what Edgar Schein* would discuss as the need for an organisation to develop an immune system to deal with its pathology:

> There is always, by implication, some pathology someplace. Something is not right and you are trying to fix it and improve it. There is pathology not in a sense of dead carcasses and postmortems. Rather, it is more like clinical pathology where you are working constantly with toxins and with residues the organisation creates, and you are trying to help the system to become more healthy.

The problem was to find a systematic approach on an organisational level that would filter through to people and engage them; a one-on-one counselling approach did not seem practical as the answer.

One of the conclusions reached at the end of the consultation process was that not enough time had been given to head office personnel. They represented almost one quarter of all employees and yet only one tenth of the transformation consultants' time had been devoted to them. We discussed what could be done to ameliorate people's anxiety, which was seen as the root cause of hostile action and demotivation.

The transformation consultants suggested that we rerun Leadership, Alignment and Development (LAD) seminars with a special focus on head office, before visiting any of the branches. They trained a group of brave young volunteers to take staff through four sessions. The entire head office staff was divided into fourteen groups; twelve of the sessions were run in Afrikaans and only two in English. It was felt that as far as possible people should be able to do their soul-searching in their mother

---

*E Schein & K de Vries, 2000.

tongues. Each person was given a file of readings – one hundred and sixty pages of text, as preparation and for future personal reference – in an institution that had not encouraged a culture of learning. These readings were in English.

The scope of the workshops was vast, probably too overwhelming. Session one covered the interconnection between the business and the personal, the 'crafting of shared competitive advantage', as well as the 'personal impact of change'. Session two focused on the characteristics of a changing organisation on the basis that a deeper understanding of the issues is at least one step towards acceptance of the inevitable. The third session looked at management models, contrasting the authoritarian approach which makes children of adult employees with an adult-to-adult managerial culture. This, of course, would require a different decision-making ethos in the workplace.

Another session dealt with empowerment, both personal and the styles of behaviour that empower others. Empowerment was linked to the competencies required for a business to become 'world class'. The concept of personal leadership was explored with reference to Covey and his 'iceberg model' of the relatively few characteristics visible above the waterline, compared to the many invisible, often relatively unexplored, principles and values hidden below the waterline. The importance of doing something right rather than saying the right things was key.

A session on interpersonal competencies for personal effectiveness covered communication skills, empathy, checking understanding, asking questions, supporting, giving information, summarising, confronting, listening actively. People were introduced to the basic 'Transactional Analysis' model looking at relating adult to adult, the parent ego state, the child ego state, the adult ego state. Another session looked at leadership competencies for leading through change. The alignment – personal, branch, provincial, and head office – required for effective organisational change specific to the Land Bank was also tackled. The sessions ended with a task for each person to identify their personal vision, and an identification of 'What I need to do'.

Conceptually, the approach aimed for completeness, and to provide useful tools to help people deal positively with the situation they found themselves in whether at work, home, or socially. But perhaps the completeness was just too much, the language – even when translated into Afrikaans – perhaps too theoretical. The truth of the matter was that these workshops did not give us the desired return of shifting personal paradigms. The workshops were difficult, the facilitators were regarded with scepticism. I didn't get the same deluge of envelopes containing positive feedback, as I did when we launched our next salvo, which was to employ professional counsellors.

Counselling

At one of the very first meetings of the Transformation Board, Kate Moloto had raised the issue of the possible need to be ready to provide counselling. Before being appointed as the Ntsika CEO she had been the head of the transformation committee at the Development Bank of Southern Africa, and I presumed that her advice stemmed from her experience there. We'd started to look into the provision of race aware-ness workshops earlier on, but had not yet reached a conclusion on the most appropriate company to use. The problems were deeper than just racism; it was so much more complex – traditions of authoritarianism, patriarchy, gender discrimination, the loss of sheltered employment, a personal and work world that had suddenly been shaken.

I was introduced to two counsellors, Rudolf Meyer and Gerard le Roux. They were well versed in liberation theology, and had been closely associated with Beyers Naude, who had become an outcast in the Dutch Reformed Church because of his uncompromising view that the racism practised by state and church was wrong. The employees in the Land Bank who experienced the most stress and difficulty with change were white Afrikaners. It seemed reasonable that the best chance of people crossing a personal Rubicon was if the persuasion came from people who had common reference points. The employment of professional people, external to the Bank, might also be an important factor. The valiant efforts of the LAD workshops had helped but they had not created radical shifts in people's attitudes. I suspected that there was alienation towards the imported 'foreign' materials used by our trans-formation consultants, and the fact that the workshop facilitators were in-house – brave Land Bank employees willing to put themselves on the line – actually went against them. They were judged as lay people not having sufficient gravitas or experience to be running workshops rooted in psychological theory. Rudolf and Gerard were older. This was their professional work in which they had many years of experience. They had more of a chance to be effective.

They offered both a group seminar approach and individual counselling. The counselling included, if the person so wished, a self-assessment exercise to get people to begin to realise their strengths and weaknesses and what they might endeavour to achieve in their lives.

Rudolf and Gerard told me that the first reaction at the branches was often one of suspicion and readiness to reject them. If they had been selected by head office, then they must be wolves in sheep's clothing. What hidden agenda did they have? Their association with Beyers Naude was also not a worthy credential for many of the conservative staff who were members of the Dutch Reformed Church. But there wasn't a place where they didn't in the end win people over.

Their 'Power to Change' workshop began with a focus on the stress that employees were experiencing as a result of transformation initiatives, their needs regarding career and work adaptability. There were two five-hour training sessions on work and life skills. As one of the participants wrote: 'The field they touched was scary. They made me examine myself.' Their strategy was to encourage self-truth and confrontation with that truth. They discussed the common adoption of 'maladaptive strategies and defence mechanisms' to try to cope with stress, breakdowns, changes, and crises by way of the following: rationalisation, denial, projection, repression, reaction formation (extreme opposite behaviour), displacement (focusing on the wrong problem), regression (reverting to victim or childlike reactions) and, finally, sublimation (camouflaging real problems).

They voluntarily made themselves available on a one-to-one basis to undertake a personal profile of an employee. They called it the 'Work Behavioural Analysis'. It helped identify the propensity of a person to adapt to various professional options in accordance with skills and personality traits. The analyses were discussed at length confidentially. They left reference materials for further reading:

- Understanding stress
- How to manage stress
- How to react in a distressing situation
- Transactional Analysis, 'Life Skills for the Land Bank'
- Personality analysis

They confirmed for me the power of person-to-person communication. They provided a check-list to assess whether or not communication has been effective:

- Contact has to be made at cognitive, emotional and will-power levels
- Comprehension and understanding the message brings clarity and safety
- Acceptance of the message is to be effected
- Internalisation of the contents is a way towards action on the message
- Acting upon the message is the climax of communication

Judging by the mail I received from staff and branch directors (the latter having been newly appointed to the redefined branch managerial positions), the overriding reaction to the work of the counsellors was positive. As one staff member put it: 'It is the first time in the history of the Land Bank that the head office has been interested in us as persons with our needs and supported us as human beings in our stressful situations.'

I was inundated with letters after each of the visits that the counsellors undertook a week at a time, every other week, to each of the twenty-five branches:

- 'It is so real and so practical, to some extent scary – some Sangoma magic.'
- 'Boy, oh boy. What a revelation! This was the best thing that could have happened to staff ... which can only lead to a more positive approach to everything.'
- 'It's a pity that this course was not one of the first presented, long before the road to transformation was undertaken.'
- 'The Power to Change workshop was one of the most dynamic work-shops that I have attended. It has taught me how to see things differently and to change what seems unchangeable. It was excellent.'
- 'A seminar to cherish for the rest of my life.'

The counsellors advised that a long period of 'walking with' staff would be necessary. They tried to convey the magnitude of change that people were dealing with psychologically. They referred to the 'deluge' of change in society, in business, and more especially in the Land Bank as a business. They argued that the effects on people, their jobs and their lives were huge and not to be underestimated.

Rudolf and Gerard tried to convey to the strategic management team the need for continued support: 'It is one thing to agree to change, to practise and implement it, and yet still another to structure and stabilise change as a permanent habit and continuing process, e.g. just think how long good, sincere "new year resolutions" last.'

They identified four stages of the personal and professional journey as requiring continuing counselling:

- Letting go   of behaviour that suited the old paradigm
- No Man's Land   the 'post-divorce' period of difficulty
- Setting priorities   new personal and job goals

- Motivation to move   from self-preservation to service
                              from insularity to diversity
                              from traditions to renewal
                              from passive security to creative 'daring'

This is a tough call. How much do you spend as a business on counselling support to employees? My inclination is towards spending a fair bit of money. This isn't simply compassion and humanism, but is also based on the fact that employees who are at ease will probably give more value to the business in the long run. But it's a debate; views differ.

A way of working: the best healer

Someone who 'walks with' his staff is Mmoloki Legodu, with a better business as the result of his approach. He probably got the most difficult placement of all the newly appointed branch directors. Most of the staff members at the Potchefstroom branch were fearful of a black branch director. This was the heart of the Afrikaner *platteland*. There was no experience of engaging with black people as equals, still less of black managers who would hold authority over you.

Mmoloki's personal relationship style is excellent. He quickly gained a reputation as a caring manager with a sense of fairness. A few weeks after his appointment the staff organised a social get-together around the traditional braai. In an ambience of relaxation and growing trust confessionals took place, and people told him how scared they had been of his appointment. They now considered it to have been the best thing that ever happened in the branch.

He showed sensitivity to people's personal situation outside the workplace and how this might be negatively affected by the stress and strain of work. People at head office thought he was going a bit far when he awarded the manager in charge of recoveries a weekend at a holiday resort for himself and his family. A 'Reward and Recognition' policy for the Bank as a whole, with appropriate budget, was still in drafting stage. Mmoloki wasn't waiting. He took the initiative. The manager in question had been working inordinate hours, as well as having been subjected to threats from clients who were angry at a decision to foreclose rather than grant yet another extension. His family had taken strain for several months, and a reward was in order.

Mmoloki publicly articulated his acknowledgement of staff effort, as well as what it meant in terms of his own growth. A letter he wrote to all his staff was published in *Land Bank Link*, the employee newsletter:

The Remarkable Potchefstromers

I have been in this office for the past eight months, and the experience I have gained so far from all of you is immeasurable. The reception and induction that I received from Jannie Wessels and Jannie Erasmus will be forever remembered. To all personnel, you are remarkable. You have handled the past four months of increased loan processing activities coupled with in-house training sessions with great success. You approached the past four months with great synergy, without being divided or competing against each other.

Up to this point, I can only summarise my appreciation in the following sentences:

- I have learned to trust you, and I paid by being honest with, loyal and open to yourselves and the organisation.
- You have taught me that interpersonal relationships are as valuable as the reward and information systems in an organisation.
- You have shown me that money is not all that matters in the workplace.
- You have taught me a sense of purpose beyond oneself, by dedicating yourselves to the principles of sustainable agro-financing.
- You have shown me your preparedness to sacrifice valuable family and social engagements to pursue organisational activities.

Business books are unanimous about the critical effect of the style of managers and leaders. They give countless examples of people who leave organisations that have a good reputation and good benefits because they are dissatisfied with the manager that they personally report to. There are some sober maxims that are bandied around:*

People don't change that much

Don't waste time trying to put in what was left out

Try to draw on what was left in

That is hard enough

Mmoloki Legodu's strength was to draw out some fine qualities from his staff that they had never had the opportunity to display in the Land Bank's previous working environment. It was clear that the trans-formation effort created contradictory energies: push and pull, negative and positive, attraction and repulsion. There's the trite saying 'no gain without pain', but if the transformation effort was going to be worth all the pain, then the positives needed to outweigh the negatives both

---

*M Buckingham & C Coffman, 1999, p.57.

at a personal and business level. The issue of counselling would, however, always be ancillary.

I had come to recognise that while good leadership from management makes a decisive difference, long-term fundamental change would only be secured if people's daily work environment offered them satisfaction in the tasks they undertook, their working relationships and the reward for their effort.

SIX

WORKPLACE REDESIGN

A better place of work

The new mandate given to the Land Bank had set out some clear measurables. There was another internal one that figured highly among the group of people who, in Kotter's terms, had become the 'guiding coalition' driving change at the Land Bank. The challenge was – could we make the Land Bank a better place to work? There was a firm belief that if we could change the workplace environment by entrenching a different workplace culture, perhaps some of the poison that seemed so insidious in the Land Bank could be neutralised.

One of the things that was initially breathtaking at the Bank was just how old and set in their ways people were when they were still, in biological terms, relatively young. There was the pervasive 'can't do it any other way' attitude that stifled creativity. There was backbiting and the unhealthiness of a career progression that, more often than not, depended on your being on the right side of power. There was fear of speaking out of turn, of the back-lash that might follow. It made sense to me as an outcome of people having grown up imbued with the psyche of an apartheid South Africa.

There's a niche of expertise among the social scientists called the 'sociology of work' – others refer to it as the 'ecology of work'. One of its basic tenets is that patterns of workplace relationships find their mirror-image in society at large, and that changes in the workplace culture can influence society and vice versa. While a sense of impotence may prevail about our ability to influence society at large, we felt determined about reshaping the workplace culture to make a difference to how people would work and behave towards one another in the twenty-six buildings that housed Land Bank employees.

We were starting from a low base. The Land Bank, as was, ranks as the most repressed working environment that I've ever come across. In Mozambique I'd caught a couple of glimpses of bosses displaying remnant flashes of crass authoritarian behaviour. The technicians from the socialist bloc countries created work environments that tended to be inflexible and rule bound. But South Africa, with some outstanding examples, would surely make the shortlist if there were nominations for the world's worst workplace – a reflection of the worst of the effects of an apartheid rule that facilitated and legitimised oppression. In a society where those in power classified a majority as unbefitting of equal franchise rights, it shouldn't come as a surprise that it created an unhealthy mindset that spilled over into the wider power relationships in society.

But I *was* surprised. The rigidity and inherent repression were beyond anything I had expected. Again, I had to consider that perhaps I felt like this because it was the first time I had been truly immersed in an apartheid-created institution.

The mindset that dominated the Land Bank culture put people in boxes with a limited set of tasks to be done to order, year in and year out, with little opportunity for personal development. On the day of the MD job interview, rain-drenched, I'd met Lettie Kleynhans who had, with such kindness and calmness, made sure I got dry. Lettie had worked at the Land Bank for more than twenty years, taking just short breaks after the birth of her children; such breaks meant that women lost their continuous service record and it affected their pension benefits – but that unfairness to women is another story. Lettie had already been the secretary to the managing director for several years – she was not new to the job. She did what was expected of her, as had every other Land Bank MD's secretary before her. The expectations were so limited, an insult to her intelligence, but the outcome was that she did not initially have the skills and experience to meet my needs. She had been allowed only to put through telephone calls – the idea of engaging with the caller to identify the substance of the call was not permitted. I wanted an assistant who would suss out the calls so that I could decide which ones to take personally and which ones I could refer to others. She had never drafted a letter. I could not, at first, say 'I need a letter which covers the following points' – she had always only typed letters which were dictated to her.

Her support role included looking attractive (she's tall, slender and leggy in that Julia Roberts kind of way), making tea for visitors and being at the ready, with the two general managers' secretaries, to do other service jobs.

'That was the worst thing in the old Land Bank, the thing I hated most. We had to put on these waitress uniforms and serve all these men. That would be when the MD or general managers invited guests for lunch in the special dining room.'

The one thing that Lettie could not complain about was poor pay. Her years of service together with the notch system of annual increases meant that she earned way above the market norm in the private sector.

Lettie's story was just one of many similar stories in the Bank of people bringing their brains to work and not being asked to use them.

I soon noticed that often when Lettie got stuck with a computer problem, Jurgens, one of the two drivers, would help her out. It didn't take much conversation to establish that computers were a passion and, yes, he'd love to have a job involving computers; he had matric but had only ever been employed as a driver; he had no formal computer training. I asked if he'd agree to go for an aptitude test. He did well, got an internal transfer to the information technology section and a year later was one of the staff who succeeded in getting one of the six training positions.

But Jurgens's story is the result of a chance observation, and my being in a position to follow up. The institutional workplace environment would not fundamentally change because of chance happenings. There had to be a more systematic approach to challenging workplace culture; that was what we needed to identify.

Out of the box thinking

I'd read Ricardo Semler's book *Maverick*. It's the story of a man whose father passes the reins of the family business over to him. The book describes an industrial company in Brazil – a 'southern' country, sharing our problems of development, and not some funky alternative company exploring different ways of being in Silicon Valley. Semler had never been happy with his father's business style. He took a deep breath, and risked offence to his bequeathing parent as he set about installing a different culture. He gives the lead that everything can be questioned. He challenges conventional norms such as office space (he gave his up!). Employees could choose the colour of their office walls; shop-floor workers could choose the colour of their overalls. These may seem cosmetic changes, but they are indicative of allowing workers to make decisions that affect them. The cosmetics of hierarchical status systems count because the bottom line is that we're all human irrespective of our current positions. Drivers don't like bosses who feel that it's beneath them to talk to the person who's driving them. Women having to wear a uniform in a workplace where men don't is a fair reflection of gender power relations. At a deeper level, Semler's factory workers discussed their working hours, check-in systems, productivity targets, and even debated the option of redundancy versus short time when Brazil hit a recession and company production had to scale back for a period.

Selected passages were drawn to the attention of participants in the consultation workshops. I made it known that any employee who wanted to read the rest of the book should buy it and he or she would be reimbursed on presentation of the receipt. Several people did, to the chagrin of the conservative accounts department who puzzled over how to classify these reimbursements. *Maverick*'s impact was to make me question the trappings of power. I moved out of the huge MD's office with its private toilet; the space could be better used. For some months I occupied what used to be the waiting room and painted it dusky pink – one splash of warm colour in a building of dark wooden panelling, beige, beige, more beige and green linoleum on the floor.

I was to learn just how many insecure or aspirant bosses wanted the cosmetic symbols of status and were unwilling to give up tokens, such as office size, by which society would judge them a success. I wondered why the status symbols mattered less to me than to many others. I wanted to be respected for quality of relationships and for achievements, and the status of power was all too often a disadvantage. Perhaps my parents' experience of being levelled by war taught me how tenuous current status can be – you never know what's in store to level you. My mother also influenced my attitude. During my teenage years she worked as a nursing sister and was intolerant of patients with 'high and mighty' attitudes. 'They all look the same when they're stripped down to their underwear,' she'd say.

But Semler's book is not only about workplace culture expressed in clothing, flexible hours, or choice of paint colour for the office you work in. It is also about turning around a business, securing a profitable enterprise, managing through economic down-turns, and making it a place that people want to work in. Semler's factories have 1200 applications for every vacancy. That was my dream – that the Land Bank would gain a reputation as a creative, human, profitable workplace. We would earn 'preferred employer status' and have the brightest, most able people queuing to join the team. And not only that, the underlying driver of the business would be the pursuit of the development ethic.

Unfortunately Semler's book did not identify a systematic approach to changing the nature of workplace relationships. His approach seemed to have depended on diffusion, whereas we needed fast-track change in twenty-six locations. We needed to identify a methodology that could be pursued with consistency. Our search was on. In the meantime we were able to identify some 'quick wins' which at least contributed to getting people into a state of greater acceptance that change could have positive effects on their working lives.

The first 'quick win' salvo

The internal consultative workshops run in each branch and the head office in 1997 had one session on 'What are we proud of? What are we sorry about?' There was a lot of pride in work done well, in reliability, in the personnel's knowledge of the agricultural sector they worked in. There was also frustration with twice-over bureaucracy and heavy centralisation: Price Waterhouse-Ebony (who were later to undertake the head office review) found a case of a request for the issue of a cheque for less than two thousand rands requiring thirteen signatures before reaching final approval.

The accounts were amalgamated; therefore business units were unable to have a clear sense of comparative efficiency. Yet there was an honesty that we were nowhere near the leading edge in our retail banking services. At each of the workshops I heard 'Why can't we . . .?' 'Why do we have to . . .?' 'Couldn't we . . .?' People complained that for years they had sent suggestions to head office where they disappeared as though into a black hole in the universe.

At the very centre of that black hole, the heart of darkness, which was how I felt about the Land Bank head office in my worst moments, there were cradled together two forces resisting change: the defence of power and the absence of a business drive. In other businesses the competitive ethos would have made efficiency proposals attractive. But the Land Bank, as long as it did not need to ask for additional state money, as long as it was ticking over getting out loans to white farmers, had considered that all was well. The key issue that appeared to have preoccupied many senior managers was their defence of internal fiefdoms.

The transformation consultants had earlier advised me to keep an eye open for 'quick wins'; find an action which shows that the change process can bring solutions – better for the personnel, better for the Bank. I asked branch managers to prepare themselves for a meeting at head office. They were to bring suggestions for amendments to the loan processing and decision-making system. I asked them to tell me who from head office needed to attend the meeting to secure agreement to proposed changes. There should be no loopholes for backtracking; I was given eight names of senior head office personnel and confirmed their availability.

At 10 am on 1 October 1997, the twenty-five branch managers met for the first time ever. Exchange of ideas among practitioners was not part of Land Bank culture. They were joined by myself and the eight other head office staff. Participation in the next four hours was uneven. Of the twenty-five managers half a dozen had come prepared with well thought out motivations – the others had sat quietly. The meeting was conducted in English, which may have been an inhibiting factor, but there were those who were concerned to make their contribution. They spoke Afrikaans to ensure clarity and translation was provided.

The proceedings were rather like an auction. The item for sale was one or other proposed change to one or other part of the administration of the loan application system. A branch manager would motivate the change; a debate then took place, sometimes with adjustments to the original proposal being accepted, and then a 'going, going . . . any last objections? Speak now or forever hold your peace . . . going, going, gone!' signalled its adoption. In four hours we dealt with fourteen proposals, some of which had been hanging in the stratosphere for several years.

It was a historic occasion. Keith Clowes, then the Pietermaritzburg branch manager, dropped me a line to say how delighted he was to be part of this meeting which in the space of a few hours had taken decisions promoting efficiency and cost savings. He reiterated that in his 'humble opinion and at the risk of stating the obvious', the decisions taken would:

- save thousands of pages of duplicated information;
- save many, many hours of unnecessary cross-checking;
- save on costs related to printing etc;
- release time to focus on training and marketing;
- heighten the sense of responsibility and self-worth among personnel because of the devolution of some decision-making powers.

It truly was a day for celebration – the indications were that the change process would bear fruit.

The participation and quiet supportive style of Dawie Maree, who was the general manager operations, was a surprise at first. Later I realised that over the years he'd had many ideas that had been squashed in a system that was overpowering. He told me: 'In the old days the MD decided everything. His word was final and there was no discussion.' He was enjoying a new atmosphere in which there was space to challenge. He was also genuinely concerned, as was financial adviser

Dr Jacobs, that change should not compromise business decision safeguards. Some rules had good reason for being and needed defending.

No leaders: no change

While a systematic approach to changing workplace culture was not yet clear, it was obvious that managers and managerial approaches played a determinant role. I began to look more closely at the managerial structure in the Bank, and the content of those jobs. I saw the four regional manager positions as gatekeepers, unnecessary sandwich filling between head office and the twenty-five branches; the added value of their function was unclear. They were not happy with the direction the transformation process was taking, as had been obvious in the 'quick wins' meeting; the nature of the decisions taken threatened their power base. Several branch managers continued their passive resistance to the change process, and resented the 'rocking of the boat' which the 'auction' meeting symbolised.

Following the historic 'fourteen decisions in four hours' meeting I asked to see the job description for the branch managers. It turned out to be essentially administrative oversight with signing-off duties, as well as supervision of a layer of middle managers who were themselves supervisors. I drew up a job description of what I really thought branch managers should be doing. It involved business planning (not a single branch or head office unit had a business plan), public relations, marketing, and a 'walk the talk' coaching-leadership function. I shared the draft job description with a couple of senior managers and incorporated their inputs. The two job descriptions, old and new, bore little resemblance to each other when placed side by side. I did not believe that one could simply ask the incumbents to scrap their old job description and accept the new one. My exposure to some of the managers left me with little faith in their having a conversion on the road to Damascus.

The human resources department advised me that in terms of Section 189 of the Labour Relations Act it was possible to declare the old positions redundant because of the imperatives of restructuring the business due to 'operational requirements'. The new posts (newly named 'branch directors') could be advertised. This would create the opportunity of bringing new blood into the organisation; the possibility of recruiting the first black managers into the retail network was especially attractive. We would then be seen to be recruiting blacks at senior level and not just entry level as had been noted and criticised by the Auditor General. This proposition was taken to the board of directors and given the go-ahead. The board shared the fear that without new leadership there was no real chance of securing change.

Karl Ehrenberg was the member of the old guard who was most helpful in 1997. When I needed to review job descriptions, he organised that I got them promptly. When I needed to familiarise myself with a Land Bank policy document only available in Afrikaans, he made sure it was translated with speed. Task teams needed co-ordination – he did it. Flattening of the regional branch management structure required face-to-face communication with all the personnel directly affected. Karl organised the meeting. He worked hard, humble but not subservient, truly committed to changes which he believed were good for the Bank and for the country. But he was squeezed in a vice between the old and the new. He was inundated with aggressive calls and visits from some of his lifelong colleagues. I was told that his wife was worried, and was pressurising him either to engage less or to retire. The strain of organising this meeting proved to be too much. He began to have chest pain, went for tests; his angina had reached danger levels. He was only fifty-seven and I had looked forward to at least another two years of working with him. I accepted his resignation with regret.

Fifty-two people were to be affected by the decision to cut out the regional management layer as well as the second-in-charge position at the branches. Regional managers had secretaries and there were regional agricultural economists. A board discussion culminated in the idea of a face-to-face meeting rather than sending 'Dear . . . We wish to advise you that your job will no longer exist' letters through the post. I anticipated the meeting with trepidation. It was not going to be easy to walk into that room of fifty-two people – but then as the strategic management team often said to each other: 'Working at the Land Bank is not for the faint-hearted!' We spent the money for all fifty-two people to come to Pretoria, covering travel costs, per diems, and accommodation. There wasn't a large enough comfortable space at head office for so many people. We rented a room at the Dutch Reformed Church's Synod building just a hundred metres down the street.

Was it worth it? I don't know. The tension in the air was so heavy; the bitterness so palpable. After a rough start there was some improvement. We had circulated by fax a copy of the proposed new job description. People worked in groups discussing it and then the amendments were pooled and a consensus on changes adopted. The new position was to be called 'branch director' to distinguish it from the old branch manager title; it symbolised the change towards a 'directing' activity – a move away from managing administrative oversight which had been the predominant focus of the redundant position. The advertising and recruitment process was discussed; and there were nominations for the head office personnel who should be included in the panel of interviewers.

What I learnt later was that we should also have distributed the very specific 'Dear ... We wish to advise you' letters. In terms of South African labour law, employees who may lose their jobs as the result of restructuring must be advised *in writing* of this possibility. We had written letters inviting people to the meeting, had explained why, and attached the draft job description, but in these processes the devil is also in the detail and there are word conventions to be complied with. We were later vulnerable to the accusation of possibly not having followed due process, even though we had spent thousands of rands on organising the meeting with all affected employees.

Of the fifty-two people, eleven were appointed as new branch directors and twenty-two were redeployed within the Bank. The remaining fourteen branch director positions went to seven internal promotions and seven successful external applicants of whom five were black. That left nineteen of the fifty-two unplaced. We were locked in a union disagreement over redundancy packages; if the nineteen people were to become redundant it would cost the Land Bank more than R30-million in severance packages and would create an unaffordable precedent. The people involved went on 'special leave' until eventually new positions were created to make the best use of their talents. They may not have been suitable for the new leadership positions, but they were senior personnel with years of technical experience.

It was great to welcome the new blood of the seven directors who were the successful external candidates – even better that five of them were black. They would enrich us with the experience that they brought from other financial institutions. It wasn't going to be easy for them. There was a lot of debate over the placement of Mmoloki Legodu to take over the Potchefstroom branch. Potchefstroom's reputation was that of the most conservative town, the heartland of the ultra-right wing Afrikaner Weerstandsbeweging (AWB) political party. But we needed to rattle the cages – to be upfront in our commitment to change. We estimated Legodu to be an energetic, able and diplomatic person – if anyone could handle this difficult situation it was him. He was the right choice. Eugene Terre'Blanche, the leader of the AWB, took the lead in extending a hand; after all, he wanted to borrow money from the Land Bank! He greeted Legodu with a 'Welcome, I don't care if you're black as long as you speak Afrikaans. My money speaks Afrikaans.'

I took early Christmas leave to spend time with my children who were going to be at home for only a few weeks. One day the Land Bank driver delivered post that had arrived in my absence and a large round tin. It contained layer upon layer of exquisite home-made biscuits, beautifully separated by lacy paper doilies. The card that came with it was from Petra Maree, the wife of the general manager of operations, wishing my family and me all the best. Tessa, Kyla and I enjoyed every morsel – the cookies tasted even better than they looked. On returning to work in the New Year I sent her a thank you card and a small bouquet of miniature roses. Later on the day they were delivered, Lettie told me that Petra Maree was on the line and wanted to speak to me personally.

'I want to say thank you. The roses are beautiful. I also wanted to say that if there is ever anything that I can do, please let me know. You are in my prayers that all will go well for you in the work you are doing.'

'But there *is* something that you can do for me,' I said, thinking of Karl Ehrenberg's angina and resignation. 'It's a strange thing to ask, but could you please make sure that Dawie is happy and relaxed at home? I'd be grateful.'

'But he is,' she said. 'He's never been happier working at the Land Bank than since you got there. I know it. I live with him. I can see it.'

Workplace redesign

The internal workshops held throughout the country formulated a set of desirables to be attained through a new Land Bank culture:

- effective two-way communication;
- understanding and empathy for cultural diversity;
- multi-skilling through training, knowledge and empowerment;
- a team-based approach to focus and motivate staff and maximise potential; and
- professionalism based on pride and integrity.

But how to get there? Every year I read the outcome of *Fortune*'s Top 100 Companies as voted by the employees. There's a lot of emphasis on workplace benefits and a little on workplace culture. But culture does not change through edict; it would be a matter of practice and the rooting of a new ethos. Our search was for something beyond management style that would ground a new workplace culture.

Steve Hobbs, the principal transformation consultant, spent a long time discussing the issue with me. He was way ahead in his knowledge of this area. As an organisational change specialist with a group of associates who were concerned with depth rather than cosmetics, he had links to an international network of consultants who specialised in the 'ecology of the workplace'. He told me about a particular group of practitioners who had been trained by an Australian, Fred Emery, who had designed a participatory approach for getting employees to rethink the systems of the place they worked in and their working relationships. The approach was grounded in the 1930s work of a German, Kurt Lewin, who on escaping fascism took refuge in the USA. He applied his intellect to the influence of society on the workplace. Lewin's 'direct experience of the horror of autocracy led him to a lifelong study of the potential of democracy – in society, in communities, in workplaces. People called Kurt Lewin the practical theorist because he considered theory and practice inseparable.'* I felt an enormous identification with his ideas.

Lewin is regarded as one of the originators of group dynamics, action research, and the field now known as 'organisational development'. Emery built on Lewin's ideas in his work with British coal miners in the 1950s and was linked to the London Tavistock School of Clinical Psychology. They used socio-technical analysis tools as a practical way to redesign work. I was more than curious about the Emery approach that was rooted in Lewin's work.

The board's handsome award of the R5-million transformation budget was enabling. There was money to be exploratory in finding a way forward. I was wary of scepticism and the need to get a larger group of employees, including the 'guiding coalition', to be part of choosing whether or not the Emery approach might be suitable for us. The decision was made to invite one of the international practitioners for one week, to listen to what he had to say, and to explore its applicability.

Tom Devane, trained by Emery, spent a week working with thirty Land Bank people. The mixed group, drawn from branches and head office, cut across race, gender and technical skills, and included typists, agricultural economists, accountants and IT personnel. We weren't going to leap into something on the basis of blind faith. It was November 1997 – an exciting week at the aptly named Sparkling Waters conference centre.

I got the chance to attend several of the sessions and saw people challenged by the ideas put forward. The first part was theoretical to reach a shared understanding of the principles, and then moved to an analysis of the status quo. In the second half of the week employees worked in small groups, pooling ideas on how the approach might be applied in the branches, at head office, and a new relationship between

---

*R Rehm, 1999, p.viii.

the two. They tentatively discussed changes that would be required to the delegation of powers, as some head office functions would be better done on a decentralised basis at branch level. There were sceptics in the group, and a memorable occasion when one person challenged another to get off the fence and make a commitment.

People once again worked hard and played hard – there was the most wonderful joke-telling session around a braai one evening. We were a mixed group of men and women, black and white, all of different status in the institutional hierarchy. We'd been unified by working on a common task – identifying a way forward that would affect all of us. On that starry November night, so conducive to romanticising, surely we could be excused for being tempted to feel that we were close to the best that the new South Africa could offer. Minds were opening – the future looked as though it would enrich both our personal and working lives.

At the end of the week of heated debate as well as humour, representatives of the group decided they would take the ideas to the December national consolidation conference. When they made a presentation at Klein Kariba the excitement of new possibilities of ways of working was infectious to other staff and those members of the board of directors who attended. Support from delegates for implementation was unreserved; for most there was little to lose and a lot to be gained – if it worked.

Designing redesign

The branch redesign process was rolled out in January and February 1998. Tom Devane was joined by two other US 'Emery practitioners': Nancy Cebula and Robert Rehm. They were joined by Clynt White from the transformation consulting firm we had contracted. Over one week they trained a brave crew of fifteen Land Bank employees, one from each of the nine provinces and six from head office. The selection criteria were: willingness, a demonstrated energy and participation during the previous year's consultation process, and the knowledge that they were highly respected by their fellow employees. We wanted to secure our own capacity and expertise; we were wary of fostering dependency on external consultants. We had to defer working at head office; there had been a decision to get in the expertise of business re-engineering specialists on this score, as the preliminary in-house work on restructuring indicated the possibility of a significant level of redundancies. The branches were different. They were the delivery end of the business and the mandate required an expansion of the client base. Short-term over-capacity was expected to end, and in the longer term there could well be an increasing number of jobs at provincial level.

Each workshop would take the best part of a week per branch. Time-wise, it was possible to compress the redesign process, but we took the option of including every employee, and yet we needed to keep the business running. Hence each day branch staff spent some time doing essential business both before and after the workshop sessions.

There were four parts to participative redesign:

- The first part dealt with BACKGROUND: a presentation of the ideas behind the approach, as well as a clarification of expectations; unreal expectations needed to be identified and addressed.

- The second part dealt with ASSESSMENT and set out the essentials of job satisfaction, with each participant's evaluation of their own 'as is' situation. It concluded with a mapping out of the 'as is' work flow and decision-making process.

- The third part dealt with REDESIGN. The managerial principles that inform different decision-making styles were compared. The new organisational values as stated at the December 1997 national consolidation conference were revisited. People then considered how to reorganise the work so as to make progress towards those values.

- The fourth part dealt with IMPLEMENTATION. The objective of attaining an integrated business process required teamwork. Team goals and training requirements had to be identified. Order had to prevail, albeit achieved through a different work style, but the demands for internal control and co-ordination of work in a banking environment were of paramount importance.

- A fifth part sprang up spontaneously at every single one of the redesign workshops, and it was the issue of career path and the alignment of pay with skills.

The business framework

We did not forget that the primary purpose was to restructure a business and not to fulfil a 'feel-good' mission. The existing systems looked as though they had been trapped in resin at least some twenty years earlier, and somehow we needed to escape that resin. The business specifications for the redesign process were taken from the board of directors' October 1997 meeting, and were referred to as 'The Framework'. They were:

- increase clients by fifteen per cent over three years;
- cost effective;
- no increase in operational costs;
- multi-skilled self-managing teams;

- cover skills shortage with training, adding skills wherever possible;
- flatter structure with streamlined administration;
- customer focus with direct customer delivery;
- branch and team empowerment.

Robert Rehm's book *People in Charge** features the Land Bank experience as a case study:

People had this information when going into the workshops:

1. The framework and design specifications are non-negotiable. No more layers of management; no more working in separate sections. There should be only two levels of structure in each branch – a branch director and self-managing teams. We want a different way of working that is more democratic, giving more responsibility to people doing the work. We want an open culture in the Bank where people can be brave, disagree, and contribute to the success of the business.

2. The Land Bank is overstaffed. We have a large staff relative to our current business. For now that means we have excess capacity that is available for training and for growing the business. We need different kinds of jobs, not different people. As the Bank identifies new types of business and modernises, new work opportunities will open up for people. Some jobs will become obsolete, others created. Retrenchment is the last option.

3. The salary system will change, but there will be no salary loss due to redesign. Pay and promotion will be based on skill and performance, not length of service. A bonus system will be developed to reward productivity. Regarding affirmative action, women and blacks have been held back in favour of white males too long. The Bank has had affirmative action for white males for years. Workers are encouraged to participate, join in the redesign, and find the right niche for themselves.

The affirmative action story was an ongoing sore point with the white males who for decades had been the powerhouse of the Bank. I patiently took the line of argument on the skills shortage in South Africa, the changing nature of work. I began to feel like a scratched record where the needle got stuck, jumped back and began to replay the same track over and over again. A specialist was brought in to give a seminar on the subject to the top fifty senior managers; he reiterated the theme: there's a skills shortage and room for all of us.

---

*R Rehm, 1999, p.59.

I never, however, shied away from the bottom line: if there was a vacancy and four candidates all competent to do the job – a black woman, a black man, a white woman, and a white man, then the award of the job would be in that very order. The Land Bank white male response was mostly: 'So there're no career prospects for us.' One day, exasperated, I retorted: 'Tough shit!' This was the comment that made the rounds of the Bank like wildfire – confirmation that the managing director was a heartless creature. 'Helena,' a friend advised me, 'you've got to remember that this job is like being on stage – every word you say, every move you make, takes on a life of its own. People discuss you and make their own interpretations – perhaps way off whatever you might have intended. It goes with the territory. Just watch what you say.'

Redesign under way

A major part of the redesign process involved mapping out the work flow on a flip chart. Both the consultative process and a review of the IT system had already shown that some pieces of work were done four times: at branch level records were kept both in writing and on computer. Head office then repeated the same work, again in writing and on computer. Whilst people complained that there were not enough computers, the low level of computer literacy was appalling. Typing pools still existed. A qualified LLB prepared a conveyancing report longhand and sent it to the typing pool. The typed draft was returned for correction and would go backwards and forwards until it was perfect.

I was at the Kroonstad branch in the Free State Province when they happened to be doing the part of the workshop where they map out their work flow and points of decision making. They got three quarters of the way through the process and stopped for a tea break. The beige walls were covered by a long continuum of flip chart paper. They stared at what they had set out so far. 'Is this really how we do it? We've never worked out how it all fits together before. Surely there must be a better way of doing it than this?'

The other problem with the loan processing system was that with the responsibility broken up between so many sections it was difficult to respond to a client who might enquire on the progress of his application. People tended to work in one section for several years and then move to another, but there was never integration of accumulated skills.

We got people to evaluate what are referred to in the Emery approach as the six criteria of productive work: (1) elbow room for decision making, (2) ongoing learning, (3) variety, (4) mutual support and respect, (5) meaningfulness, (6) desirable future. The scoring on the first three is between minus five to plus five, so zero is bull's eye – the balance is 'just right'. A plus five means an overdose of something – like a plus five for variety would mean there's so much of it that the person's head is spinning! The last three questions were scored out of ten. It would be an interesting exercise to undertake periodically; it would serve to evaluate what progress was being made.

When the Kroonstad staff members did this exercise, their results were consistent with scores in the other twenty-four branches. As Rehm writes: 'The scores indicate an organisation where decision making and goal setting are far away from the workers. Jobs are segmented and boring, particularly for typists and people handling paper work.'* The members of the loan approval committees, made up of some heads of sections and an agricultural economist, were the only ones who ever had a view of the composite outcome of all the work done.

At Credit Agricole in France I'd seen loan officers handle an application from A-Z, except for conveyancing (title transfer) which was outsourced. Our system seemed very inefficient. It might take some years to reach the Credit Agricole levels. I repeated to people how I'd been told that Credit Agricole had spent ten per cent of their salary bill on training every year for ten years when they'd confronted the same challenge that faced the Land Bank now. In the meantime, we needed to start somewhere; it seemed sensible to put a group of people together who between them possessed the complete set of skills needed to deal with a loan. The idea of each person handling a certain number of client accounts for improved customer service was also mooted.

In *First, Break all the Rules: What the World's Greatest Managers do Differently*, Buckingham and Coffman ridicule self-managing teams. They refer to a real-life experience of a hotel that did away with its managers, insisted on multi-skilling the employees to wait on tables, operate as front desk clerks, or do the housekeeping. Co-ordinators of the merry-go-round substituted for the managers. The outcome was a John Cleese 'Fawlty Towers' episode wherein the root problem was laid at the feet of the team focus: 'Each employee came to feel as though he were in the wrong role. He no longer knew what was clearly expected of him. He no longer felt competent, and with the focus on the team rather than individual excellence, he no longer felt important.'†

Job rotation was not what we understood by multi-skilling. For us it meant accumulating a set of related skills to be able to do an integrated

---

*R Rehm, 1999, pp. 13-18.
†M Buckingham & C Coffman, 1999, pp. 61-62.

piece of work, instead of just one part of it. The redesign process included an inventory of people skills, accumulated in the different sections they had worked in over the years, as well as a rating of the skill competency on a scale of low, medium or high.

For five weeks over January and February 1998 five teams of Land Bank staff, trained by the US consultants, worked their way through the branches. The first week they had the background support of a consultant coach – after that they were on their own. At the end of the five weeks each branch had mapped out their own way forward – if there were similarities it was by coincidence, not by prescription. The forms used might be the same, the computer software and the criteria for accepting or rejecting a loan application were standard, but the decision as how best to organise the work was determined by those responsible for doing it.

Life changes

By 1 March 1998 the redesign exercise had been completed in twenty-five branches, affecting the working lives of almost 900 employees. There were dramatic changes for some people – both in the workplace and at a personal level. Hope, at the Cape Town branch, had been employed as a 'sundry worker' – she cleaned and made tea. Nancy Cebula, one of the US consultants, recalls:

> I saw Hope . . . staring and frowning at the skills matrix. When asked if she needed any help, she replied that she did not know if she should acknowledge her accounting skills on the matrix as she was a tea girl, and black, to boot. She had been studying accounting at night school . . . However she was 'afraid' to mark the skills matrix in the accounting skills section. After a bit of encouragement she put a check mark in several of the accounting skills boxes and hurried back to her seat at the back of the room . . .
>
> Months later, I was visiting this branch and saw Hope sitting at a big desk, with a calculator and all the accoutrements that an accountant needs. One of her team members told me an interesting story. As the Land Bank had not finished changing its pay system, everyone was being paid the same wage they had earned before redesign. So, Hope was being paid . . . less than the other accounting team members were. When the branch was given its end of year bonus money, the accounting team voted to give all of their bonus money to Hope. They felt she earned it.*

---

*R Rehm, 1999, pp.236-237.

Typists in the Bank originally feared that general staff computer literacy would render them redundant. But Cebula encountered a different outcome. A typist told her that she had finally become 'a contributing member of a loan processing team . . . I had typed hundreds of loan applications in the past. Now I can work with people as they go through the application and approval process. I would rather use my head than just type what someone else has written. My future looks good now.'

'*Now I can use my brain at work*' was the statement that Cebula says she heard over and over again on revisiting the Land Bank, especially from black staff who moved out of sundry work. They began lives as apprentice loan officers ensuring translation for the new black clients if and when language difficulties arose. Several former 'sundry workers' became trained in the micro-finance scheme and left the offices for the first time ever in their working lives to proudly represent the Bank at workshops for potential clients. Many white staff members took African language courses; at worst it was in defence of their job security, at best it improved customer service and collegial relationships.

Bankies Malan was the gifted anchorman from the Land Bank liaising with the consultants. 'Gifted' is not an exaggeration. Rehm was to say that Malan had talent combined with natural understanding that catapulted him straight to a facilitator's skills level it had taken him, Rehm, years to attain. Unfortunately Malan is a highly experienced agricultural economist whose skills the Ops Division never wanted to relinquish. They 'lent him out' for other tasks with great reluctance. Malan concurred that whilst he liked the new work, he never came to terms with giving up his technical specialisation. Malan presented a paper on the Land Bank experience at the 1999 Ecology of Work Conference in Bonn. His last section recounts some of the behavioural changes noted by people.

> One of the fifteen employees, who was a provincial representative selected to be trained in the redesign methodology, reflected on the impact the redesign work was having on his personal life. 'You know,' he said, 'my relationship with my children has changed. When they used to bring me questions to do with homework or a school project, I would have told them – "Do it this way." Now, I ask them what they had been thinking as a way of tackling the work, and I listen to them in a way I never used to do before.'*

*Land Bank, 1999, 'People moving change: Change moving people', p.21.

The changes in the Bank reverberated in the families and communities that people came from. In 1997 when a black member of staff was requested to attend a workshop at the head office, he said: 'My family did not believe me when I said the Bank is flying me to head office in Pretoria. They said, "Man, you are black – they will not let you use an aeroplane." '

The first few months of teamwork experience

The first of March 1998 coincided with the launch of new products intended to cater to the needs of capital-poor black clients, as well as improve engagement with our traditional client base of white farmers. The implementation of the redesign therefore took place in a new and unstable environment. The slow pace of branch work that had prevailed for decades suddenly came to an abrupt end. There were now queues of potential black clients wanting appointments with loan officers.

We lost critical support capacity. In March 1998 our director of human resources went on special leave and was never to return to his job. In addition, shortly afterwards, the lead consultant on the work redesign project emigrated. We'd asked Wits University's Sociology of Work Unit to monitor our successes and failures in changing the workplace culture, but once the link with the HR department was broken this failed to take off.

With our local oversight capacity taking a serious knock the US consultants stepped in for three 'temperature visits' six months apart to provide assessment and advisory input, as well as engaging in e-mail discussions – but this could not fully make up for the lack of ongoing and on-site guardianship. We tried to compensate. We arranged meetings where people pooled their problems and began to share 'best practice' experience. For example, both Vryburg and Tzaneen were inundated with hundreds of new clients – why did Vryburg not have the queues that were frustrating the would-be clients in Tzaneen? The answer lay in Vryburg's adoption of a filtering and appointment system.

We needed to have figured out more precisely the rewriting of rules and the system of sharing best practice; otherwise too much depended on the quality of the branch leadership and managerial capacity. One clear feedback was the reiteration that 'freedom means rules'. Workplace democratisation meant a different set of clear rules, not an abandonment of rules. If decision-making powers were delegated to branch directors, these needed to be formally integrated into an addendum to the document on delegation of powers.

People's total lack of experience of relating to each other as adults in the workplace, as well as never having worked together in teams, provided new challenges. At the Bloemfontein branch I was told: 'It used to be that you could feel isolated. You saw the other people in their branch offices but you didn't know them. You didn't need to know them. Now our work depends on knowing and understanding one another, our strengths, weaknesses, personalities, and being able to work through any difficulties that crop up.'

The success of a self-managing team system depends on high levels of interpersonal maturity, discipline and the commitment of peer-group regulation. We needed a training programme to build life skills that were essential to the success of a democratised workplace, but which people didn't have: team skills, conflict resolution skills, and basic business knowledge. These issues required a systematic approach and could not be tackled in a haphazard way.

Another instance of synchronicity occurred. At a dinner table I had a chance encounter with Cy Charney. He was the designer of an on-the-job training approach that was being successfully implemented by South African Railways. He suggested that Land Bank people talk to the Railways people and take a closer look.

We bought the system called 'Peer Group Training' and, after first checking out which were the peak hours for customers, decided to open the branches one hour later every morning to permit one hour of training a day.

The best-run branches were those which kept to a training schedule. Others, feeling the pressure of overwork, abandoned the training for considerable periods. But for those who organised to stick with the training, the investment paid off with improved productivity and quality.

The unresolved question of a new remuneration policy was constantly on the agenda. It created obstacles in the attempts to raise the overall level of technical skills. Older staff members who had been in supervisory positions had been integrated into teams. Many were not so willing to pass on their deeper skills knowledge. The former supervisory staff was almost one hundred per cent white male. They feared they would be training black men and black and white women, whose career advancement might overtake them in the future. Many erstwhile seniors wanted a formal incentive scheme that recognised and rewarded their coaching role.

The need to align skills with pay needed resolution. Employees wanted reassurance at first that the move into multi-skilling would not damage their pay prospects. Then there was a sense among people that the more skills they acquired, the more pay they would qualify for. It had to be communicated that training would be provided according to business needs and payment would be for application, not acquisition.

Testing for skills competency was an outstanding issue. People who learnt a new skill needed to have it tested and 'signed-off'. A job grading exercise would be linked to competency testing. The competency level would determine whether people were qualified or not for certain decision-making responsibilities. Credit Agricole, for example, had four levels of classification among what we began to refer to 'business development advisers' (BDAs) – their classification determined the kind of loan application BDAs were allowed to handle and the limits of their decision-making powers. In the absence of a similar system, reflected in a new delegation of powers, we would be forever bound to the branch director's having to take innumerable decisions.

The other lacuna that emerged from the 'temperature visits' was that we had failed to convey the ethos of 'permission to revisit' the redesign. An old way of doing things had been replaced, but there was a tendency towards treating the new as also rigid and inflexible.

We were to learn just how deep historical workplace culture runs. One branch director spotted a problem, discussed with his staff a change to their original redesign and they reconstituted a special recoveries team. It worked – their recovery figures improved considerably – but they'd kept their change a secret. They thought they might be criticised for breaking away from the original plan. So what should have been a shared best practice was initially kept hidden.

Rehm had written a guide especially for the Land Bank, dealing with such key issues: *The Start-Up Guide to Self-Managing Teams.** Every one of nine hundred branch employees received a copy during the redesign roll out. We read it at the beginning, then put it aside as though we'd now learnt the traffic code, passed the driving test, and failed to look at the manual again – at least not until it was called to our attention in late 1999.

In retrospect, perhaps its title is wrong. *The Tracking Guide to Self-Managing Teams* would be more appropriate. If used on a continuous basis, it provides a check-in on the route you're taking. People's scoring on a satisfactory work environment needs to be revisited. Work systems and technology change constantly, so a basic tenet of the Emery approach is to inculcate readiness for yet another redesign when and as appropriate. *The Tracking Guide* told you all that and more.

---

*R Rehm, 1999, p. 95.

Management style and the race issue

An uneven management corps also made its impact with cumulative consequences over time. A real problem existed in trying to get people to understand that 'self-managing' does not mean '*laissez-faire*'. People often think of autocracy and *laissez-faire* as two poles of governance style with democracy somewhere in the middle. Kurt Lewin in 1945 and Rehm in 1999 are at pains to say that these are not points along a continuum but three distinct paradigms, better envisaged as the points of a triangle.

'The superiority of democracy in creating fair-minded and highly developed citizens is clear,' Lewin said.* Rehm emphasises qualitative changes in decision-making practices that mark the different paradigms, quoting Lewin again: 'An autocracy with a democratic front is still an autocracy.'

We had one branch where systems fell apart, which we discovered through our own internal audit process. In was a case of the manager adopting '*laissez-faire*' to the extent of creating a lack of order that provided a cover for fraud. We'd been dealing with accusations of racism in the branches. It was said that black people could be sure to get a loan at this particular branch when another of our branches had turned them down. I thought it might be a problem of the loan approval criteria being applied inconsistently. But there were rumours of an 'envelope system' operating – slip the bribe and the approval would be secured. Whenever rumours started at the Land Bank they were quickly embellished – the rumour became that not only was an envelope system in operation, but that there was even a publicly known tariff of bribes which worked on a sliding scale depending on the size of the loan.

Kurt Lewin had researched leadership styles with boys from the Iowa Boys Club in the USA. Under '*laissez-faire* leadership . . . the boys did whatever they wanted. They had complete freedom without any leadership participation. As a result, their behaviour was less work-centred; the boys were frightened, disturbed and had less discussion. Scapegoating occurred in the *laissez-faire* atmosphere, as it did in the autocratic. In *laissez-faire*, scapegoating occurred because no leadership or ground rules existed.'

These characteristics of *laissez-faire* disorder matched what we encountered in one situation. We had to pull this particular branch, both employees and systems, back from the brink of disorder verging on chaos. It was a delicate task and emotions ran high. Totsie Memela,

---

*Lewin quoted by R Rehm, 1999, pp.26-27.

general manager operations, and her retail network deputy, Veneta Klein, received anonymous, threatening phone calls. They were both black women, but came under attack from black farmers associated with the underperforming branch director. Farmers interviewed by journalists accused the Land Bank of having black managers who acted like whites. The branch director was black, so more than usual sensitivity was called for, given the potential to exploit the race card. It would have been an error to send in a white director to sort things out. It had to be done by our black directors. Working under a lot of stress, first Mmoloki Legodu, then Sbu Ngubane, then Martin Matutu performed brilliantly, putting systems and order back into place. But we'd had a glimpse of how far trust and employee relationships can break down, and also how employees had been scared to blow the whistle for fear of reprisal. We bought Deloitte and Touche's free-phone 'Tip Offs Anonymous' system. It provides a toll free number and ensures confidentiality to the person providing information on suspected fraud. We were a bank, a service business, and we needed to protect clients' confidence in us.

The issue of racism was one that the executive management both dogged and was dogged by. For the first six months, every black loan that any branch wanted to turn down crossed my desk for me to do the final sign-off on the refusal. Although we'd relaxed all the collateral rules for black entrepreneurs, there were still times we said no – we just didn't give one hundred per cent loans. We'd find ourselves being called racist. Some clients insisted that we were obliged to lend them money, they were black and had been disadvantaged, there could be no acceptable basis on which to refuse them a loan.

Reports of racism were problematic, more especially when statements were not supported by facts. Bonile Jack, our chairperson designate, mentioned at one board meeting that he had been approached about racism in the Kroonstad branch when he attended the annual maize show. It was impossible to follow up on hearsay that provided no detail such as where, who, what. On a visit to the Eastern Cape, I had breakfast with the provincial Minister for Agriculture, Max Mamase, who told me that he wasn't impressed with our Cradock branch. He'd walked in one day speaking Xhosa and pretending to be a farmer enquiring what the process and conditions were for getting a loan. He said he was told that the people who handled such enquiries were out for the day and there was no one else who could help him; understandably, he left dissatisfied. I cringe to think what I did at the next branch directors' meeting. I brought up the issue in front of the whole assembly – without first forewarning the Cradock branch director, Kobus Cloete. He wanted to curl up and die, as did I later when it dawned on me what a dreadful manager I'd been.

Reflection on these events led us to realise how complex the branch director jobs were, and the high expectations of them to be able to handle a wide range of issues – from business planning to accusations of racism. We began to think of the need for mentorship at a provincial level, and the possibility of creating a post that would be supportive, as well as take on board some of the difficult political encounters that seemed to be springing up.

Intangibles

'Best practice' can be inspiring, and sometimes frustrating too when you know that the intangible that's made the qualitative difference is a management style that can't be cloned. While there are several impressive redesign stories from different Land Bank branches, the Bethlehem branch was notable for evolving an effective and comprehensive workplace in which empowerment was balanced with strong internal controls. Rehm and Cebula were to say of branch director (BD) Dave Lessing:

> The backbone of this branch's team structure is the leadership of the BD. The BD took a positive and active role from the day of redesign, committing to a process of full multi-skilling. He engaged personally in a daily practice of training staff, and providing support for staff development. The BD displays some intangibles unique to the branch, such as humour, spirit, and motivational leadership. He keeps in close contact with the teams, intervening in conflicts when necessary, keeping an eye on quality, and maintaining a constant relationship with teams and staff.

This astonished me. I'd met Dave Lessing as a branch manager in Nelspruit two years earlier, a few weeks after starting my new job. He was one of the eleven redundant managers who'd made it through the selection process to become a branch director. We'd transferred him, as well as others, from one branch to another so that they could start afresh in their working relationships and not be haunted by patterns established in the past. I'd seen him in his Nelspruit domain, and at that time I'd had serious doubts about his capacity as a change agent. Maybe he didn't represent himself well at the time – he was recovering from a back operation. Maybe he was intimidated because I was the newly appointed and customarily feared managing director. Maybe my lack of Afrikaans and his then less-than-confident English meant that we couldn't narrow the culture and communication gap. I was once again reminded of the care needed with first impressions, especially in our society which is such a mix of different cultures that we can unwittingly miss signals or misread one another.

Some of the other reappointees did not turn out so well. They'd successfully acted their way through the theatre of the interview process. They mouthed the right words: participation, democracy, respect for cultural diversity, advocacy of affirmative action. But once back in the saddle they acted out both passive and clandestine resistance. There were stories of one branch director who spent hours playing solo on his computer, abdicating responsibility for his employees; after all, they were 'self-managing' now, weren't they? We desperately needed performance contracts and a performance management system; another reason for considering the creation of a provincial manager post. There was so much to do – and it was not always easy to create synergy between different activities.

Moving too fast

People kept giving me the Simon and Garfunkel line 'Slow down, you move too fast . . .' or more laconically 'Too much going on all at once'. I listened to US motivational business speaker Tom Peters address a conference. He'd become a speed freak preaching the need to chase innovation, thus relinquishing his 'pursuit of excellence' line. He quoted a well-known Italian racing driver: 'If you think you're under control, then you're not going fast enough!'

Eighteen months into transformation at the Land Bank we were in danger of a multiple pile-up. As a strategic management team bonding activity, there was a lunch and an afternoon at the Kyalami racetrack. An oiled, wet, rotating skidpad was the challenge: grit your teeth, drive over it and learn to stop the car going out of control. That was a skill high on our list of desirables. At the Land Bank we'd been going so fast; we really needed to know how to pull out of a spin.

The great thing throughout 1998-99 was that business continued to flourish. Client volumes increased exponentially. In the 1997 agricultural season we'd dealt with less than one thousand successful black loan applications. By mid 1999 the retail network had approved almost ten thousand new loan applications for that year, and more than half of those were for black farmers. More than twenty-five thousand people began using the Land Bank's new micro-finance scheme, 'Step Up'. Our first agribusiness applications were approved. The enormous increase in volumes created stress for staff. It was agreed that without the change in work systems the increase would not have been manageable. Even then, overtime became 'normal' for months on end in some branches. New IT systems were being introduced that required staff time for training. There were new credit products to handle. Peer group training was scheduled daily. We were hard put to keep all the plates juggling steadily.

Did we try to run before we could walk? Should we not have had more training and support in place before implementing redesign? In retrospect, a full-time organisational development person should have been hired at the outset for a dedicated driving and oversight responsibility. But in terms of securing the transformation process the redesign was Mission Critical – and the timing was everything. Peyrot, the French adviser, the sceptic when it came to much of the democratising 'soft-stuff' of human resources management exclaimed: 'Bravo!' He acknowledged the branch restructuring process as the cornerstone to the turnaround in the Bank's retail business. 'You took a risk – it worked. The old order has imploded. You have secured the change in the approach to business. Whatever happens it can never be the same again.'

SEVEN

HIRE SMART: WORK SMART: PAY SMART

A crisis in the making

On 16 January 1998 the chairperson designate, Bonile Jack, sent a letter to all staff members describing 1997 as highly challenging and dynamic. He expressed appreciation on behalf of the board of directors for the staff's 'enthusiastic participation in the transformation process'. He acknowledged the inclusivity of the approach taken, the extent to which not only had board members participated but also the extensive involvement of external stakeholders. It was true that head office alone had run workshops attended by dozens of stakeholders: agribusiness, farmers' associations, trade unionists, and departmental officials and representatives of other public entities.

Notwithstanding this shower of praise, the chairperson designate also signalled his awareness and concern about unresolved issues. A few weeks earlier Bank employees had demonstrated against several decisions taken by the board. Jack expressed his hope that in the future there would be a more positive and 'mature' approach to address areas of disagreement.

The unresolved issues centred on the never-ending promise of a new pay system, performance-linked bonuses, as well as the demand for clarity on the terms and conditions of retrenchment packages. Ever since the head office future search workshop in which participants calculated a staffing need of less than two hundred, rather than the three hundred currently employed, there had been heightened tension and insecurity among staff, irrespective of whatever negative or positive feelings they held as individuals about the change process as a whole.

At the January 1998 board meeting Jack, cognisant of the tension among employees, said the board needed to be self-critical of failing to make progress on the issue of remuneration in the preceding months, an issue that went back to 1994. He pledged that the issue was a priority for 'active engagement' in 1998. As chairperson designate, he affirmed the importance of appropriate levels of remuneration. The Land Bank needed to attract and retain a high calibre of staff, and could not afford to pay salaries that would attract only second-best employees. He also indicated that the remuneration of the board members needed to be addressed. At the same meeting Jack led the board discussion on the reintroduction of business class travel for board directors, and suggested the board consider renting a box for rugby and football. The board secretary was requested to get information from the different sports grounds. It was argued that sports occasions provided informal net-working opportunities, potentially of great value.

In the meetings I had with Jack, he repeatedly referred to the opportunity cost involved for board members running their own businesses. The amount of time they could afford to give to the board was limited – especially when the directors' fees were so low. Board remuneration was almost as much an issue to be resolved as employee remuneration.

Two consulting firms (FSA Contact and McGee) had completed remuneration policy proposals between 1994-97. During this three-year period the subject of a new payment policy was a recurring topic as the Bank engaged with union officials from SASBO and SACCAWU. Discussions held mid 1997 with the unions proved over-confident; the idea that the design and approval of a new pay system would be ready for consultation with them prior to a planned implementation by March 1998 was not going to materialise. The preparatory work required was greater than anticipated. It also made sense that the introduction of a new system should be tied into the restructuring of head office, which was expected to result in new jobs as well as retrench-ments.

The new deadline for implementation became November 1998. We were to tender for consultants to advise on head office restructuring, and a period needed to be factored in for board deliberation followed by union negotiation. November seemed a realistic possibility if all ran smoothly. There was pressure to adopt and implement the change in remuneration policy within the year to quell staff unhappiness. Pay issues had a protracted history of non-resolution that predated the appointment of the current board of directors.

The McGee proposal

Pay was the first 'in-your-face' problem that I was confronted with on arriving at the Land Bank. 'It will be your responsibility to implement this once it's been taken to the board,' said Van Staden, passing over to me a report representing two years of work undertaken since 1995 by a human resources consultant, McGee. 'You're going to have a tough time. It's not going to be popular with everyone. Some staff members will be very unhappy with the outcome.'

There were three problem areas, according to McGee: retention of good staff in technical and managerial positions, overpayment anomalies among administrative employees, and the unsatisfactory use of premium payments to compensate for an inadequate pay structure.

A two-hour meeting was set up with McGee during my induction period. He explained that prior to his arrival FSA Contact, a well-known South African human resources firm specialising in job profiles and pricing, had been contracted as consultants in 1994-95. FSA had used what is known as the Peromnes grading system to evaluate positions and propose packages. The proposal had not been accepted; there was obfuscation around the reasons for rejection, murmurings that certain staff were unhappy with the outcome on their own personal grading and had successfully manoeuvred to consign the FSA report to the archives.

McGee and Van Staden's rationale for the new study was 'the Land Bank being a unique institution that needed a tailor-made system that took account of its unique conditions.' The determinants of the uniqueness were never quite spelt out, but often referred to. Other occasions confirmed to me its use as an elusive defence against expectations that productivity and performance levels should match private sector banking norms.

McGee had spent more than eighteen months traipsing the length and breadth of the country interviewing staff on a one-on-one basis about their jobs and the skills used on the job. With his audit complete, McGee wrote a pricing proposal to fine-tune the current system as well as to address the two kinds of existing anomalies: overpayment and underpayment.

I did not doubt the validity of McGee's professional work. I already knew my driver earned the same as a senior lecturer, my secretary earned more than an associate professor. On the other hand, I was presented with data on how many agricultural economists had been poached by the commercial banks. The salaries for relatively mundane work were high in comparison to the market. This was explained to me as being the result of the 'notch system' of yearly increments for each additional year of service. On this basis two people doing the same job could earn significantly different sums of money because of the 'long service' premium. The payment was not for in-depth experience; the job was the same year-in, year-out, however many years you had been doing it. The salaries for technical professionals were constrained by some irrational limitation on the number of assistant manager posts; it was only once a person gained this status that they qualified for a car allowance which brought them a total package value that was nearer to their private sector counterparts. At a personal level I stood to gain handsomely from the McGee proposal. The new salary for the managing director was pitched at R828 000 per year. I had been employed on a total package of R580 000. The rise was equivalent to a forty-one per cent salary increase – not a bad rise in the first month of employment before proving even one iota of worth.

A revamp of the status quo

My first reaction was one of displeasure that Van Staden was leaving the implementation of this thorny issue in my hands. Why hadn't he brought closure to an issue that had been identified as a problem in 1994? I wished he'd braved the discomfort of a departure swansong; after all, he was about to retire into a life of golf-filled serenity.

On second thoughts, and for various reasons, I was pleased that the discussion of implementation would fall within the domain of the transformation board, and that I would be able to lobby for a review.

When I reread the McGee proposal thoroughly I was struck by its adherence to the current status quo. It was still firmly rooted in a concept of pay for rank, and two more ranks – i.e. nineteen instead of seventeen – were proposed. My gut reaction, after preliminary observation, was that there was something fundamentally flawed with this approach, out of line with best practice thinking in this area of human resources management. For example, I'd met several of the deputy general managers. Their jobs differed radically in terms of scope, responsibility and impact on the business. The deputy general manager of treasury could win or lose tens of millions of rands for the Bank, depending on his financial dexterity. The deputy general manager of wholesale finance managed the 'golden goose' of the Bank – we only made money on wholesale, not retail, business at this time. There were also four deputy general managers in regional positions, another one in head office who co-ordinated buildings, supplies and staff administration. Personally, I rated the jobs very differently and perceived that my views would be supported in the job market; a system that paid them the same because they shared the same rank title was conceptually suspect and deserving of review.

There was another niggling concern at the back of my mind. I could not see how the McGee proposal tallied with the Ministry of Labour's introduction of the National Qualifications Framework (NQF). Few Land Bank staff had tertiary qualifications. Most of their skills were the result of on-the-job training without certification. More information about the NQF should be considered prior to the board's perusal of the McGee proposal.

Return to the drawing board

The approaching July 1997 board *bosberaad* provided the ideal opportunity to bring in additional expertise, and listen to the board's views on pay and job grading. Enoch Gwala from the Development Bank of Southern Africa (DBSA) and Alan Taylor from the Public Service Commission agreed to join us. We listened to McGee. Gwala presented an overview of the job rating systems considered by the DBSA and the rationale for the choice they had made.

I was aware of Nyerere's reform of public sector salary policy in Tanzania; one of its intentions was to diminish the gap in earnings between top and bottom personnel. China had pursued a similar approach to capping top earnings. However, salary levels in the South African labour market are the outcome of free market demand, and supply and collective bargaining in some instances. There has been no move in South African society to restructure salaries in the interests of 'distributive justice'.* It would be idealistic to expect that the Land Bank could effectively operate with any different ethos outside of this dominant market reality.

The board discussed a preference for a standard rating approach and market-related salaries to be implemented at the Land Bank. There was dissatisfaction with McGee's 'Land Bank as a unique institution' argument. Discussion, however, comparing the Peromnes and Hay job rating systems as presented by Gwala raised questions about their rootedness in rank and qualifications. Taylor recommended we investigate an alternative rating approach called JE Manager (Job Evaluation Manager) as it accommodated the issues we faced of non-certificated training and assessment of the impact of the job on the business.

The old guard top managers were displeased with the board's decision to restart the remuneration review. They noted that they had already been adversely affected by a three-year delay, their under-remunerated

---

*G Standing, 1999.

status in relation to comparable market segments had been identified as early as 1994. The delays signified ongoing financial loss. Their complaints fell on deaf ears; concerns about productivity, inappropriate IT systems and lack of business planning made me feel that in mid 1997 we could hardly claim to be a market-performing institution deserving of market-related salaries.

Recruitment: affirmative action

The board agreed that we needed human resources expertise. McGee had two years earlier assessed the personnel section of the Bank as performing only a record-keeping function. We also needed to recruit a risk manager to comply with recommendations made in the Auditor General's performance report. Finally, to address the communication need identified by Kotter* as an imperative component of a transformation process, recruitment of a dynamic communications department was a priority.

The general manager finance handed in his resignation soon after the July 1997 board *bosberaad*, recognising that he would not be comfortable working within the new order. I was not sorry. As long as the financial adviser, Dr Jacobs, the deputy general manager of treasury and the chief accountant remained in place I welcomed a departure that opened up a top spot. This handful of new and vacant posts afforded an opportunity for affirmative action recruitment that would begin to change the race and gender profile of the top management of the Bank.

I contacted Moerane Maimane of the firm Equal Access Consulting; he had been engaged in the recruitment of managing directors for both the DBSA and the Land Bank. It appeared that the market-place perception was of the Land Bank being an unattractive place to work. This was a further problem to be addressed, to turn the Bank into a workplace with 'preferred employer' status. Yet I needed the cream of black professional competence to make a difference. We agreed to advertise simultaneously four human resources posts and three posts for communications and marketing.

The headhunting firm completed the shortlist for my review. With the communications position I found that all white candidates had been eliminated, irrespective of the strength of their CVs. This led to a discussion about the need for affirmative action recruitment, whilst building a team with a diversity in race and gender that reflected our population: an all black team was as unacceptable as the all white management had been.

Dan Matsapola, who was offered the human resources position at

---

*J P Kotter, 1996.

the rank of deputy general manager, was a clear winner at the interview. He was charming, with the most winning smile that lit up his rotund face as he spoke. He presented himself as working at the Commission for Conciliation, Mediation and Arbitration (CCMA), explaining that his family had found Cape Town a difficult place to settle down in. He had family in North West Province, and a chance to contribute to changing the Land Bank so that it would service the rural areas was attractive enough for him to make the move back to Gauteng. Another candidate was from the Pretoria City Council, a dynamo, but a job hopper. We were looking for at least a three-year commitment. Candidate Sam Mkhabela, who would two years later be appointed as the new chairperson of the board, was evaluated as highly theoretical. Dan was everybody's number one choice. 'Dan's the Man,' concluded Claude after meeting him in his first week at the office. 'He's ready for action. You can have confidence in his care-taking of the HR components of restructuring.' We were all wrong.

The next few months were filled with a flurry of recruitment. Dan, to my consternation, appointed three black people to fill his three positions. It was too late for me to do anything about my preference for diversity. He had sent off letters offering the jobs to the candidates that were legally binding, although this did not fall within his authority in terms of Bank regulations. I shared with Dan my concerns about the wisdom of the message he conveyed in setting up an all-black department; it went against the values being espoused in the transformation workshops. In response he just smiled.

The recruitment to replace the retiring general manager finance brought home to me the importance of succession planning. After a discussion with Timothy Thahane, the deputy governor of the Reserve Bank, I drafted a policy proposal for the board's consideration and approval. Thahane had suggested that I identify promising young black professionals and link them to executives whose departure was in the offing. The carrot for the departing executive was a golden handshake if they had successfully trained someone to replace them. I asked general manager operations Dawie Maree, who was approaching retirement, for his commitment to this concept. I then asked Totsie Memela, the board member from Peoples Bank, if she would be interested in a succession plan that should result in her appointment as general manager operations. The board gave their support.

Within almost nine months of my appointment in May 1997 the top management structure at the Bank had been significantly recon-figured. Of the newly appointed branch directors, seven were external appointments of whom five were black. Of the top eighteen in the newly defined hierarchy at the head office, nine were black and nine were white. There were six black men, three black women, five white men and four white women. It wasn't perfect, but we had come a long way from the day I walked into the Bank to find the top sixty-nine positions all occupied by white Afrikaner males.

Recruitment: pay issues

The recruitment of the risk manager was where the rubber met the tar in terms of the salary problem. A risk manager with seventeen years' employment in an international commercial bank was interested in the job but not prepared to take a significant drop in salary. DBSA had just employed a risk manager. I phoned managing director Ian Goldin to ask what they were paying and used this as my motivation to the board. The rank awarded was that of deputy general manager, but with a premium to bring his pay in line with the market.

The interviews for branch directors also raised the problems of job pricing. The complexity and risk of the business varied, depending on the location, and the number of staff per branch ranged from approximately twenty to almost ninety. The old guard came up with a weighting proposal and we reached consensus on three different salary ranges.

The issue of premium payments resurfaced in January 1998 when we recruited a general manager finance. The candidate from the head-hunter's shortlist with adequate experience and competence was a white male. In terms of cultural diversity, at least Adrian Toms was of English white origin rather than Afrikaner! He had had an offer that would pay him 33 per cent more than the Land Bank salary for the rank of general manager. It was customary for the Minister to sign the letters of appointment for the two general manager positions, even if not required by statute. This provided the opportunity to appraise the Minister of the difficulty of finding a suitable recruit at what had been the standard salary. Adrian Toms formulated the figure at which he was prepared to consider accepting the job, on the understanding that this was an interim arrangement pending the implementation in November 1998 of a new salary structure for all staff. The Minister signed the letter of appointment cognisant that the amount of the package made a break with the old salary scales and traditions. Toms countersigned acceptance of the job offer in February 1998 and was given confirmation that by November that year a new market-related salary structure would be operational.

After several months of successful mentorship Totsie Memela was confirmed in her position as general manager operations following the resignation of the able Dawie Maree. Minister Hanekom wrote to Memela, congratulating her. He acknowledged his awareness of the 'Board of Directors undertaking a comprehensive review of salaries and conditions of employment'. He indicated his understanding that the review would result in market-related, performance-based pay packages. In the interim he recommended her appointment on the existing package for the position of general manager, pending the implementation of the new policy.

Recruitment: interview problems

We faced a problem of lack of interviewing competence in the Land Bank. Over the course of a few days we had had three panels of Land Bank staff handling interviews to recruit for the twenty-five redefined branch director positions.

The hard lesson that had to be learnt was the gap between the applicant's self-representation and the reality of their performance. There was something amiss in our approach to interviewing that did not suss out the real competency level. 'Yes, I have worked with teams', or 'Yes, I have been a part of a restructuring, unbundling process', did not identify the role or responsibility undertaken in the experience.

We came unstuck with references. I found that people are circumspect in what they are prepared to say. There was a candidate who had been embroiled in conflict situations in her previous job. The referees suggested the cause was the company environment, not the person. With the hindsight of perfect 20:20 vision I now know it would have been better to ask for a contact, even at the first firm of employment, to ascertain whether or not it was a behavioural trend. 'It's very hard to think your input may be the basis for a person not getting the job,' was the very human response I was given when I once asked a person why he had been so reticent, and unintentionally misleading, in what he had been prepared to tell me.

It turned out that Dan Matsapola had not disclosed pertinent information to the Bank at his interview. Seven months after Matsapola's appointment, on 13 March 1998, I received a phone call from a journalist at *The Star* newspaper:* Did I know that Dan Matsapola, the human resources manager at the Land Bank, had been fired from his job at the CCMA? No. Had I checked references? Had I checked the veracity of qualifications? No. As we were paying a considerable fee to a headhunting firm I felt that we could safely assume that they would

---

*Peta Thornycroft, 'Official suspended for keeping mum on firing', *The Star*, 14 March 1998.

bring to the table only top-calibre people whom they had thoroughly checked out. The journalist would not reveal the source, but dispelled my belief that the informant must be one of the many conservative whites at the Bank. No, it was confirmed that the source was a black employee. Matsapola was eventually dismissed following a disciplinary hearing. He took his case to the CCMA, where the Bank was judged as having acted fairly.

A festering environment

This speed of change had the desired impact but also came at a cost; some people were alienated, and we made mistakes. Ever since the October 1997 head office future search workshop there had been tension in the Pretoria building. People's insecurities, compounded by the negative vibes of the emasculated old guard, developed into a poison which some actively tried to inject into the branch personnel.

The redesign process in the branches was making headway. The number of business transactions was escalating as thousands of black entrepreneurs got their first Land Bank loans. Staff worked harder than in all their years of service at the Bank. People wanted finality on the pay issue. They wanted equal pay for equal work. More experienced staff were going the extra mile to give fast-track training to younger, less-experienced employees. They justifiably felt that a salary review would recognise that they were no longer doing the same job that they used to.

There were problems arising from the group of nineteen employees who had not made it into managerial positions when the branch directors' posts had been redefined and advertised. Their experience as administrative managers was inappropriate to the new posts. They now occupied a debilitating limbo land called 'special leave', on which they had been placed pending resolution on redeployment.

While branch redesign was ongoing, the restructuring of head office needed resilience from the strategic management team. One could anticipate that it would be a formidable task. It was impossible not to feel bad about the negative impact that retrenchment might have on the lives of some employees.

The future search workshop on head office restructuring was described by its facilitator, Pam Pretorius, as 'the most difficult and challenging workshop' she had ever run in her life because of the levels of tension and anxiety. Some unflinchingly honest employees used razor-sharp scissors to cut to ribbons the current head office structure. Their appraisal suggested that the positions of over one-third of head office personnel should become defunct mainly because of decentralisation and the introduction of new systems. From this it was clear that resistance and demotivation were to be anticipated as decades-old fiefdoms disappeared. I was concerned that there should be no suggestion that the decisions on posts were the result of anything other than the best professional approach. With this in mind, it was proposed to the board that one of the 're-engineering' firms should be contracted to have a closer look and advise on the process for head office. There were almost thirty responses to the advertisement for tenders for the work. A Price Waterhouse-Ebony (PW-E) partnership won the bid; their work took four months and, meanwhile, you could cut the atmosphere in the head office with a knife.

In addition, there were mounting tensions among the newly recruited black staff. The human resources group wasn't delivering to deadline the drafts needed on new conditions of employment and other policy products that were essential to the transformation process.

Later I was to discover just how frustrated Matsapola's three deputies were with his leadership. The difficulties arising from handling the Matsapola case were exacerbated when I discovered that two other black employees had been aware of *The Star*'s information for a month. One of them indicated there was a dilemma associated with whistle-blowing on your senior. The other person was my own executive assistant. The reason she gave for not passing on the information was that she had difficulty coming to terms with a black professional letting the side down. 'I feel betrayed,' she said. The problem for me was that the choice of silence compromised the trust that is at the core of a working relationship between an MD and an executive assistant.

The timing of this breach of trust coincided with a cacophony of complaints about my executive assistant from a consultant, a black board member and a senior black contract manager. To cap it all, the strategic management team told me that the person's style was conflict-provoking and made good working relationships inordinately difficult. I was advised to start a counselling process, as well as register a verbal warning. The circuitous end result was resignation and another CCMA process with the ruling that the matter belonged in the labour court. There was, however, a further negative overspill that regrettably resulted in yet another resignation of a talented member of the human resources staff.

If I felt swamped with problems, there was still worse to come. In mid 1998 I was taken aback by the PW-E recommendations. Their minimalist approach resulted in a proposal for a head office with a staff of only eighty or so people. They contemplated redundancies as a result of decentralisation, new systems and outsourcing. Their structure looked anorexic to the point of being skeletal. Executive management and the board of directors spent a lot of time studying the proposal and expressing real concern.

Following extensive consultation – there were many hours of deliberation that included board, management and PW-E – the approved, refined restructuring proposal resulted in one hundred and ten jobs. More than thirty of these jobs were newly established positions which needed to be priced. The proposal was presented to the unions in diagrammatic form. Jobs that remained the same were boxed, jobs that were newly established were presented within oval shapes. If your name appeared within an oval shape, it meant that your job had been redefined and the choice was yours whether to opt for a redundancy package or whether to apply for the new post. It was made clear that employees in redundant positions who wished to apply for other posts would get priority over other candidates.

The PW-E restructuring proposal radically altered the structure of departments. With regard to the human resources department, the consultants' proposal, accepted by board and management, was very different from that conceived at the time of Matsapola's appointment. Two black managers thus found their names within oval shapes just one year after their appointment. They were perturbed and angry. More CCMA cases were to follow.

Meanwhile, the relationship with the two trade unions, SASBO and SACCAWU, was one of mounting tension. SASBO declared a dispute about the retrenchment package in relation to the nineteen persons who failed to get new managerial posts in the branches. At the end of 1997 the transformation board had rescinded the package adopted by the previous board in July 1996. The 1996 retrenchment package, according to the new board, was unduly generous, and unduly biased in favour of older staff. It was judged to be ten times more than the retrenchment package of private sector banks and as such was ill-conceived, unreasonable and poor business practice. To the current board's knowledge it had not been discussed with either union. The Bank files held no record of any agreement, and hence the board felt able to rescind it without union consent.

Dispute with the union held dangers. The Recognition Agreement with SASBO was seriously flawed in stipulating pendulum arbitration as the dispute resolution mechanism. Bargaining a compromise was not permitted; arbitration would decide in favour of one party or the other. The awful possibility was that if taken to arbitration and ruled in SASBO's favour, the ill-conceived 1996 retrenchment package might be legally entrenched. It was a 'winner takes all' and 'loser bites the

dust' approach, and an unsatisfactory basis for a constructive relationship with the unions.

Planning a way forward: clarification on trade union issues

It was gut-wrenching stuff. Publicly, I managed to project a positive
image and exude a modicum of calm; Joe had always applauded my
ability to appear unrattled at a time of crisis. But between one's body
and the subconscious there is a truth pact that refuses to be deceived by
the difference between public presentation and private reality. I would
wake with a hollow feeling in the pit of my stomach. I, who'd always
considered myself one of the healthiest people around, began to manifest
stress-related symptoms, high blood pressure and more. On bad days
the Yeats verse which inspired the title of Chinua Achebe's book would
do an unpleasant mantra inside my head: 'Things fall apart; the centre
cannot hold.' Head office restructuring, the industrial relations disputes,
the incomplete work on salary policy – all contributed to my angst.
There was a strange sense of oscillation; we were making strides forward
on business delivery, but at the same time being drawn back into a
quagmire of unresolved internal issues.

My guardian angel in mid 1998 came in the unlikely shape of Dave
Gillam. I'd been pouring my heart out to a confidante who advised:
'You need a top-class industrial relations adviser – someone who will
work well with your labour lawyers. A good understanding between
them is key. Ring your board lawyers, ask them for two or three
suggestions, track them down, and check that you're comfortable too.'
    Dave Gillam has had decades of South African experience. To meet
the man you'd think he'd stepped off the plane from England yesterday
– except his tan gives the lie to that. He's a stocky Cheshireman with an
accent that took me right back to the northern dialects of my childhood.
He has the most finely developed sense of fairness of anyone I know, an
ability to take the role of devil's advocate and insist that you look at
something from someone else's perspective, and a sense of humour that
would have me laughing even in some of the really bad moments that
were to come. He'd also be very straight with you about what he
considered your strengths and failings to be.
    I met Dave Gillam for an evening and laid bare an assessment of the
problems, as I understood them. Within three weeks, after perusal of
documents and more meetings, he asked for a special session at the
June 1998 extended board meeting. He was joined by Graham Damant,
the board lawyer from Bowman Gilfillan, a firm known for their

specialisation in labour issues.

Gillam spent the first part of an evening setting out his understanding of what ingredients were required for a positive relationship between employers and the trade unions as employee representatives. He explained why the principles embodied in a recognition agreement were so important, and flagged four areas of principal concern.

Issue 1: The need to renegotiate the recognition agreement with particular emphasis to remove the pendulum arbitration as a potential cancer that makes constructive resolution impossible.

Issue 2: The need to redeploy the special leave personnel. While they hadn't made it into the new managerial positions, they had accumulated technical experience. Special leave was inappropriate; their complaints that they felt humiliated were valid.

Issue 3: The need to make headway on the retrenchment and remuneration issues, because the positive strides we were trying to make were dogged by their non-resolution.

Issue 4: The need to get away from statutory regulations and allow collective bargaining to establish salaries and benefits.

A new factor had emerged in relation to the 1996 retrenchment package. SASBO claimed that they *did* have an agreement with the Land Bank after all. They produced a single sheet of paper stapled to the front of the July 1996 board document which carried the signatures of the MD's assistant and the head of the legal section, persons authorised to sign contractual agreements that were binding on the Bank. Damant was clear in his legal advice. It did not matter that Van Staden, the previous managing director, said he knew nothing of it. It did not matter that Dawie Maree, the general manager operations, knew nothing of it either. Whatever suspicions circulated around this piece of paper – of which there had been no copy in the Bank – it was likely to stand up as valid in court.

Gillam and Damant introduced a further consideration. The 1996 retrenchment policy had been distributed to all employees after the board meeting in June 1996 and could be considered as having been accepted by employees in that no objections were raised. This in itself could result in its being a binding commitment.

Gillam substantiated his reservations about the 1996 agreement. The issue of affordability lay at the heart of any retrenchment package agreement. The practice attempts fairness in that people who are to lose their jobs should be provided with financial cushioning while they look for another. On the other hand, it is important that the payments made cannot be of the magnitude that they jeopardise the future of the business.

The 1996 retrenchment packages were about ten times the industry norm; should the Land Bank make redundant all or most of its employees, the amount of money involved would dent the reserves considerably. These reserves were essential in the financial services industry for the Land Bank to continue its operations. If overly diminished, the Bank's credit rating would be affected and the conditions for its future business prejudiced.

Gillam did not mince his words. The Bank was in a pickle. The unions held the stronger cards. It would take tough discussions to persuade them to relinquish ground in the interest of the long-term business perspective. Yet short-term resolutions on current issues were required in the longer-term interest of the relationship. He was clear that he wanted board commitment and no prevarication. The slightest hint of equivocation or backtracking would precipitate his withdrawal.

Gillam joined the Land Bank staff as a part-time employee and became a member of management's negotiating team. The general manager human resources, Dan Matsapola, had just been fired. It was considered inopportune to headhunt a new senior executive into the current environment. Adrian Toms agreed to double up as head of human resources on top of his duties as general manager finance. Toms excelled as a negotiator, an important quality for the prospective period of head office restructuring.

Remuneration: clarification on policy intent

Bonile Jack was chairperson of the board remuneration committee; his 'active engagement' strategy on the salary issue led to regular meetings of the committee from early 1998. The late January meeting boasted full-house attendance of the nominated non-executive directors – Jack, Naidoo and Michel. The meeting discussed a new package structure as tabled by Komike Masekela, one of the Bank's new human resources specialists. Broad banding was proposed as the way to reduce the levels of hierarchy in the Bank. An important principle of restructuring would be the enhanced reward of technical skills; at that time only the managerial career path brought financial benefits.

It was agreed that the salary review should be holistic, including even the post of managing director which should not be considered in isolation. The Bank was to design a 'consistent policy'; its principles should apply to everyone. It was acknowledged that the retention of high-calibre employees required salaries pegged to market rates. Consistency also meant that both pay and benefits needed to be aligned; it would be inconsistent to use a mix of public service rates for salaries and market-related rates for other benefits. In the negotiations about the rights to carry over leave, the unions insisted that the appropriate comparisons were with commercial banks' norms. SASBO was a financial services workers' union, and the Land Bank was a financial services institution. SASBO stated that it was wrong to compare conditions of service and benefits with those of the Public Service Commission.

The HR personnel undertook branch visits to Middelburg, Rustenburg and Cape Town. Their findings confirmed the problem of salary differences between staff doing the same job, as well as overpayment anomalies, as had FSA Contact in 1994-95 and McGee in 1995-97. They drafted a reward strategy policy document for discussion. The January 1998 board meeting reconfirmed their commitment to new salary packages that would be market related. The union supported this perspective, aware that an anomaly management strategy and measurable performance bonus system would also be required.

An information-sharing session took place with the union representatives in March 1998. Evaluation, grading, salary levels, broad banding, salary structuring to optimise take-home pay, and performance management were discussed. The jargon concerning 'flexible' pay referred to a cafeteria system: employees would have a total annual package (i.e. cost to the Bank) linked to the post but would choose the make-up of each component of the package. Some staff members might want a vehicle allowance of twenty per cent, others only ten per cent or nothing at all. Tax advice would be made available so that employees could judge the implications of their choices.

The Bank would also have to take a decision about where in the range of market salaries it was prepared to make its pitch. There were basically three pitches to choose from, referred to as the lower quartile, the median, and the upper quartile.

If the salary you are earning is placed at the 'lower quartile', it indicates that twenty-five per cent of employees in this type of job earn below this figure; the rest are earning more. The 'median' pitch represents the midpoint; half the persons doing the same type of job earn more and half earn less. The 'upper quartile' figure indicates top payment; only twenty-five per cent of persons in this type of job earn more and as many as seventy-five per cent earn less. The figures refer to the total package cost of employment of a person by a company.

At the July 1998 board committee meeting Jack indicated his interest in a remuneration policy set at the median, with the caveat that in exceptional circumstances payment on the upper quartile should be considered. He requested information on this basis.

Toms duly presented a memo detailing the information from PE Corporate Services on median and upper quartile packages in the financial services industry. The managing director's median package was R1,08-million, and the upper quartile R1,3-million. The median for the position of executive general manager was R774 000 and the upper quartile R943 000. The median for the finance executive was R721 000 and the upper quartile figure was R870 000. The current Land Bank packages meant that the managing director earned 55 per cent of the market median, and the general manager finance 69 per cent.

A check was done that the figures were comparable with similar parastatal institutions. They were spot on. A headhunting firm provided information on the packages of recent parastatal placements, which further confirmed the above figures as correct. A new element was being introduced – the performance bonus. One of the parastatals retained a third of the potential total package. Its payment depended on perform-ance – split equally between an assessment of corporate performance and individual performance.

Jack confirmed his interest in this approach, and requested that a board policy proposal be drafted for discussion and approval. Three-year contracts for executive managers and performance-linked pay should be introduced. The upper quartile should be considered as a benchmark 'to serve as incentive for above average performance'. Jack also requested the preparation of a proposal to increase the remuneration of board members in keeping with the market-related philosophy that dominated the day's discussion.

At a personal level, the adoption of median level salaries would result in a magnitude of increase that I had not previously contemplated. I had always worked in the public sector, academic or NGO worlds, where salaries were comparatively modest. I had to confront the fact that the Land Bank was indeed performing in the financial services industry which was clearly our competition when it came to staff recruitment. Godfrey Masilela, the risk manager, had been recruited from an international bank; Totsie Memela had been poached from Peoples Bank. There had been applicants from the other private sector banks who had turned down our job offers on the grounds of insufficient remuneration. On the other hand, the Land Bank had a long history of its good staff being poached by the private sector.

Personal concerns aside about the wide disparity in income distri-bution, the fact that we were a competitor for scarce skills needed to run a bank was inescapable.

Personal qualms and personal philosophies had to be ruled out of the policy deliberations. The adoption of a salary policy that would attract and retain high-performing staff to achieve the new directives and goals set by the shareholder was the essence of the matter. I remembered the stories told by Joe's cousin in Lithuania of how the Soviet pay system had contributed to deep levels of demotivation and economic decline.

What I would do with so much money after giving back forty-five per cent to the taxman would be a matter for deliberation; my late husband, when earning as a Minister, had made donations. My own choices needed some serious thinking. My attitude to philanthropy would be tested.

At a later date, a financial media commentator noted that people in parastatals attained positions of seniority that they would not have been awarded in the private sector and, by implication, that the market-related salary was unmerited. The argument is spurious. The positions involve the care-taking of public resources without profit share incentives. They are no less stressful, and carry financial responsibility for billions of rands. They are often more demanding in terms of public account-ability. The turnaround challenges faced by many parastatals, not only the Land Bank, were and are gargantuan.

An ever-deepening crisis

The next step in the remuneration marathon was the drawing up of job profiles for every job in the Bank; the skills required could then be rated and this would result in a grading and, finally, a pricing exercise. The first tranche of job profiles would deal with head office. The PW-E proposals meant more than one hundred and fifty redundancies as well as some thirty newly established positions. Redundant employees would get first option to apply for the new posts if they were interested; obviously their interest would be influenced by the detailed job profile and the outcome of the job pricing exercise. The intent to assist employees who started service businesses in response to redundancies arising from the outsourcing of service functions, known as the 'business angel' approach, also required substantiation.

Every head office employee was provided with the board-approved PW-E document. Its release, in September 1998, collided with the ongoing discussion on annual increases and bonus payments. Emotions ran high. Fear of job loss was compounded by uncertainty about the actual basis of the retrenchment package. In October 1998 SASBO declared a dispute over not reaching an agreement on the 1 April 1998 pay increase.

The attempt at consultation to resolve the dispute failed, which resulted in the issuing of a Certificate of Failure to Resolve a Dispute by the CCMA commissioner. But an important achievement of the consultation process was that both parties had agreed to set aside pendulum arbitration and abide by the Labour Relations Act. Both parties thus gained the right to embark on protected (lawful) industrial action: the right to strike or go slow on the part of the union, and the right to lockout action on the part of management. The exercise of this right required each party to give the other forty-eight hours' notice.

The issue on which we had come unstuck at the conciliation hearing concerned the magnitude of annual increase; a lesser issue was the annual bonus. Most agreements taking place in the wider economy were not more than seven per cent. The union wanted an increase of ten per cent. Unlike the bonus, which is a one-off payment, any increase in basic pay has to be factored into the long-term salary bill and the compounding effect on the future had to be considered. The union position seemed to be influenced by shop stewards who were potentially redundant. These employees wanted to jack up their basic pay as much as possible as this would affect the value of their retrenchment payment.

The union gave its forty-eight hour notification of the intention to strike. They announced an initial one-day strike with follow-up go-slow action as a possibility. The strike was to be national, affecting both head office and all twenty-five branches. It would be the first strike in the entire history of the Land Bank.

We as managers had no experience of dealing with a strike. Dave Gillam worked overtime to ensure we knew the do's and don'ts of handling industrial action. We flew in all twenty-five branch directors. Head office managers joined the branch directors for several hours of briefing and discussion in the eighth floor Indaba Room. Acceptable and non-acceptable principles of strike action were explained: the right to picket, the right of the Land Bank to deduct salary from those who chose to strike, i.e. no work, no pay. Employees who came to work needed to sign in to ensure payment. Head office managers liaised with a designated province and the Indaba Room was turned into an Information Centre where all data relating to the strike action was registered.

It was a sad day in the history of the Land Bank. Many employees were ambivalent; they had torn loyalties between supporting a transformation process but some sympathy for the issues, real and hidden, in dispute. They also had long-established social relationships in the workplace which were important to them.

On the morning of the strike Tiene Vermaak, the driver assigned to me by the Bank, picked me up at six o'clock. No matter how early he needed to be, Tiene was always punctual and impeccably groomed. We arrived at work well before the picket line was established.

The stayaway varied from branch to branch – it was almost eighty per cent in some but there was virtually no support in others. As usual at the Land Bank, there was ugliness mixed with humour. At head office it was found that locks in the accounts department had been doctored with super glue – irritating but also innovative; we couldn't get to the cheque books that day.

The picket line was unusual. It sported protest placards, and a Guy Fawkes type effigy of me as the evil that had descended on the Bank. The media arrived, photos were taken; interviews were given to radio journalists.

At mid-morning on the kerbside opposite the Land Bank, which borders the gardens of Pretoria's City Hall, the picket line became festive. Music played and a braai was lit to cook meat and spiced sausages for the traditional Afrikaner boerewors rolls, and black passers-by attempted to teach the mostly white strikers to toyi-toyi correctly. Tiene Vermaak, his loyalties divided, joined the group for a couple of hours. He returned to work saying how much he had enjoyed his boerewors roll. His brief foray to the picket line cost him the day's pay. He protested, but the ruling was that he'd joined the strikers; if I had made an exception I'd be accused of favouritism. He took some teasing about the most expensive boerewors roll that he'd ever eaten in his life.

The strike placards were laden with anger, many of them personally directed.

QUESTION:	ARE YOU A BANKER?
DOLNY:	NO
QUESTION:	ARE YOU A FARMER?
DOLNY:	NO!
QUESTION:	THEN WHAT ARE YOU?
DOLNY:	CAPTAIN OF A SINKING SHIP

Many of the placards went back to taunts regarding the piglets advertisement, and the 'tough shit' comment I'd made one day in exasperation at people's unwillingness to come to terms with affirmative action.

Other placards expressed anger over management style and the decision that English would be the business language. Ironically most of the posters were in English! Other placards questioned whether or not I'd lost my heart somewhere in the transformation process.

AWAY WITH THE PIGS
GEE ONS PAKETTE EN SNORK VERDER VOORT
(Give us packages and carry on grunting)

A RETRENCHMENT A DAY WILL TAKE YOUR LIFE AWAY

AWAY WITH REVERSE RACISM AND DISCRIMINATION
PALE MALE OVER 50 – TOUGH
DOLNY SAID 'TUFF SHIT' [*sic*] TO OUR FUTURE

AWAY WITH AUTOCRATIC MANAGEMENT STYLE

KRAP AAN ONS TAAL, DAN KRAP JULLE AAN DIE LEEU
(You touch our language, then you touch the lion)

INSECURITY GIVES RISE TO DISLOYALTY
TIRED OF UNCERTAINTY
DOLNY – THE BUSINESS WOMAN WHERE IS YOUR HEART? –
DO NOT TAKE AWAY OUR BENEFITS

WORD WAKKER EN RUIK DIE PAP BRAND!!
(Wake up and smell the porridge burning!!)

In contrast, there were unequivocal messages of support from some of the branches, such as Rustenburg. Beaufort West had one hundred per cent attendance at work; in four others the stayaway was minimal.

But I didn't take the posters lightly. In Mozambique I'd frequently observed another side of a personality emerge when people became bosses, and I had to think about what was happening to me in trying to lead a difficult change process. How much was the stress affecting my equilibrium? My blood pressure told me that I was living on the edge; how much did that change the way I interacted with people? On the other hand, I'd console myself with the biblical story of the sacrificial scapegoat, and people's need to direct their guilt and anger at a selected target.

If you were leading a transformation process, it seemed impossible that you would not draw fire from one quarter or another. 'It goes with the territory,' would be one comforting remark from friends; other comments included: 'You don't make a cake without breaking eggs.' But I was deeply concerned. I couldn't wait for head office restructuring to be completed. Then those who worked at head office would be the ones who really wanted to be there and be part of a new Land Bank. And then perhaps a different atmosphere would prevail that would be healthier for all of us.

In the days that followed there were periods of go-slow. The head office building erupted on a couple of occasions into songs of protest and whistling. Employees gathered in the central stairwell of each floor and sang their demand for the Land Bank to pay employees their increase.

It was not clear how the deadlock could be broken. Undoubtedly it would take power or a return to sanity for the parties to resume negotiations. It was strange for me, the daughter of a factory worker, to be in a position where the possibility of a lockout was on the table with myself at the helm of management.

Operation Rescue: policy commitment and union agreement

Gillam was convinced that, while the dispute was about pay increases, the real driving force was the retrenchment policy and the ending of uncertainty. Somehow (and with SASBO now adopting a mature leadership role) he steered the negotiations back to these topics. The Labour Relations Act minimum for retrenchment is one week per year of service. The Land Bank/SASBO settlement agreed upon two weeks per year of service but with a minimum payment of fifteen thousand rands, irrespective of length of service.

Head office staff seemed relieved. Those people who were to become redundant at the end of March 1999 could now calculate the value of their package and begin to make plans accordingly. Those employees who were in 'oval boxes' could also weigh up the option of applying for one of the new jobs. But this decision depended on knowing what the salary package for the new jobs was going to be. This was what Adrian Toms and I were under inordinate pressure to sort out as fast as possible.

We'd contacted three consulting firms, briefed them and got back time frames and an estimation of costs. We settled on FSA Contact as appearing to have the best capacity to interview current managers and draw up the job descriptions for every head office post that was within the organograms of the PW-E documents.

Meanwhile, the remuneration committee prepared documentation and a draft resolution for consideration at the November 1998 board meeting, with the intention that the principles of remuneration policy should be clearly defined once and for all. At the December 1997 national consolidation conference the human resources task team had proposed that the Land Bank should seek to achieve Preferred Employer status and that salaries should be on the upper quartile, thus placing the Bank in the best payment league of financial service industry players.

The document submitted for the board's perusal differed from this recommendation and proposed payments on the median and not the upper quartile. Management were confident that this was the appropriate level at which we could attract and retain staff, especially given that performance bonus payments would be made in addition.

After debate, the formal resolution was passed and duly signed by Bonile Jack in his capacity as chairperson designate. The board resolved that the median was to be the norm for all Bank employees, and the upper quartile would be used in exceptional cases either to attract scarce skills or to reward staff who demonstrated excellent performance. FSA were therefore requested to provide both the median and upper quartile price for each position.

The problem was the battle against time: getting job descriptions right and evaluating the job rating needs to be done thoroughly since this determines the price for the job. It is time-consuming and there are no short cuts.

Once again we were failing to meet the agreed deadline. We were not going to fulfil our pledge made to employees that the new packages would be in place by November 1998. The whole PW-E process had taken more time than expected. The FSA process of drawing up job descriptions and job pricing was also to take longer than anticipated.

Retrenchments were scheduled for the end of March. The first of April 1999 signalled the start of the new year as the effective date for implementation of the outcome of salary and benefits negotiations.

Toms and I were sure that FSA would finish their job descriptions and pricing work by the end of January 1999 at which point employees would be able to visit the human resources department and peruse the descriptions of the newly established jobs and the associated annual salary package.

It seemed a fair and final promise that the new pay system would be ready for implementation on 1 April 1999.

Hiring smart

Whilst pricing was one issue to resolve, the other question to address was the quality of our selection approach. I was spending my reading time on different approaches to recruitment. We couldn't afford any more gaffes and filling the head of HR was now Mission Critical. I'd attended a seminar run by Tom Peters who'd spoken on how amateurishly most recruitment is done, and how expensive the error is if the person appointed doesn't work out. I couldn't have agreed more; one just had to add up the costs of making a mistake in recruiting an executive

– the adverts, the fees to headhunters, the lost months in which a perform-ance problem is identified, and then settlement – unless the performance improvement programme is successful. Peters had said, 'If there's only one book that you might ever read then it should be Pierre Mornell's *Hiring Smart*. The full title is *45 effective ways for hiring smart! How to predict winners and losers in the incredibly expensive people reading game*.'

It's an interesting book, and useful in its suggested approach to recruiting for a single executive post: pre-interview strategies, interview strategies, after interview follow-up suggestions, ensuring a better deal when checking references and so on. The author is a psychiatrist who helps companies large and small, public and private, to evaluate and select key people. It proved to be helpful as we interviewed, among others, Arnold Shkaidy, who was subsequently appointed as executive manager human resources.

However, the approach was not appropriate for the interviewing of literally a couple of hundred people for the thirty-something new posts in head office. The pre-interview and post-interview ideas on special assignments were useful, but the nub of our problem was the handling of the interview itself. There had been too many times when our questions were not good enough, and the impression we got in an interview did not later tally with our real-world experience of the employee. It worked both ways; some people turned out better than expected – but it's the failures that cause the anxiety.

Since FSA was the firm undertaking the job description and job pricing exercise, I asked for a discussion with Olof van Schalkwijk, their managing director, and put the problem to him. In a nutshell, I needed a squad of senior staff members who were trained in interviewing skills.

I wasn't looking for magic. I wanted something methodical and fact-finding that we could be taught, and which got us away from making intuitive and impressionistic judgements.

FSA introduced me to their interview training approach, 'targeted selection'. It is simple – once you've learnt it! Its attractiveness is that it's very 'learnable', especially when you're supplied with Hetta Bosart, one of the best trainers I've ever met.

First of all you need a developed job description or job profile. Secondly, you need to define what are the essential skills, or 'competencies' as HR fundis are wont to call them, without which it would be impossible for the job to be done properly. Thirdly, you draw up a set of questions around the key competencies. The questions are aimed at getting a set of answers that provide the members of the selection panel with a 'STAR'.

This 'star' is the memorable acronym representing certain identifiable components. 'ST', for example, represents SITUATION or TASK, hence the need for a question and answer that provides a context, such as: 'Tell us about a time when you have been involved in business planning.' The next component, 'A', probes the applicant's role and responsibility in the ACTION. 'Oh yes, I've often been involved in business planning,' isn't good enough; you're wanting to identify exactly what part they played in the process: major or minor, assistant or leader. The 'R' represents the RESULT. 'What were the results, positive or negative? Were your proposals implemented and if so what was the outcome?'

The training included a lot on the soft side of skills building; the care to be taken with body language, the need to be positive and empathetic, to boost the candidates' self-esteem, and get them to offer their best. It also involved mock interviews that were observed by the trainer and were quite nerve-racking. A debriefing session followed. We didn't all get our certificates. Some people just couldn't get away from introducing leading questions, or never managed to get full STARs on the competency that they were interviewing on.

However, there was now a group of people ready to do interviews. All we needed to do was the shortlisting. But we ran into another problem on the pricing that was to cause not only another major hiccup, but eventually unleashed an unexpected furore.

The pricing conundrum

There was no equivocation in the November 1998 board resolution that the norm of payment for Land Bank employees was to be the market median. I waited anxiously for FSA Contact to finish their job descriptions and pricing so that the outcome could be discussed with the union and the head office recruitment process could then begin in earnest. The branch implementation would be rolled out over a longer period, as a skills audit of every individual would be required in order to determine their salary. This was because there were only three or four job descriptions at branch level, but the range of individual competencies varied enormously because of the Land Bank history of people having done only a segment or two of the entire loan process.

When I got the FSA pricing it was not in line with expectations, nor did it appear to be aligned with known market-place, benchmark positions. Each member of the strategic management team had given me a pricing guesstimate based on their knowledge of recruitment within their field. I sat for hours checking figures, trying to avoid panic, frenetically working with a calculator. The lists included all jobs at head office, both old and newly established. Alongside were three columns:

Column One – the FSA pricing; Column Two – current earnings, if there was someone already in the job; and Column Three – managers' expectations of what they would have to pay to attract and retain good candidates in the vacant jobs.

According to the FSA figures, I was going to be handling a significant number of anomalies, and this included the pricing on the key middle and senior technical specialists. There were almost forty such cases out of a total of about one hundred and thirty jobs. Something seemed to be wrong. I phoned Olof van Schalkwijk and asked him for an emergency meeting with the strategic management team. Time was against us, so if something wasn't right it needed to be corrected – with speed.

The first part of our discussion focused on the job descriptions – had we got them right? If not, would this explain the discrepancy between the manager's valuation and that of the FSA consultants? The second part of the discussion centred on the data base used for pricing – was it appropriate for a financial services institution? How many firms and of what kinds of business had contributed to the data base?

Whilst work continued on the fine-tuning of some of the job descriptions, we approached the other national major pricing firm, PE Corporate Services, and asked them for their pricing of the same jobs. This was discussed with FSA – we didn't do it behind their backs. We were clear we wanted a second opinion, and if this confirmed the FSA pricing, we would just have to live through managing a very difficult anomalies situation. But so be it.

The results of the PE Corporate Services pricing exercise were about 15 per cent higher. We looked for the reason for the difference. The answer lay in the data base of company information used. FSA Contact used their national general remuneration survey. The data base used by PE Corporate Services was specifically geared towards the financial sector. It included 91 per cent of identified financial services or development finance institutions, while these comprised only 31 per cent of the FSA Contact survey. The PE figures were the more appropriate and accurate for the Land Bank.

We did one more piece of checking. We asked a headhunter to provide us with information about packages for posts they had recently been party to filling – without of course revealing identities. The information we received showed that, if anything, the PE median was modest. The headhunting recruitment was taking place on levels above the median. This seemed logical. Presumably you wouldn't be using a headhunter unless you were searching for a special recruit who was expected to be of such value to the company that payment would be above the median.

The data provided the per annum value of the package:

Managing Director	Medium size insurance company	R 2 800 000,00
Marketing Director	Medium size insurance company	R1 800 000,00
Chief Executive Officer	Parastatal	R1 750 000,00
General Manager	Parastatal	R1 050 000,00
Human Resources Director	Parastatal	R 900 000,00
Corporate Affairs Director	Corporate Company	R 950 000,00
Operations Director	Stock Market	R1 250 000,00

Board backtracking: the decision to be inconsistent

Although the implementation of policy is executive management responsibility, I wanted the board to be aware of the implications of the November 1998 policy decision, and their support for the decision to use the prices provided by PE Consulting and not those of FSA. We put together, for the board's perusal, a table indicating the Land Bank current salary and the median and upper quartile figures given to us by PE Corporate Services.* We included the upper quartile because of the board's November 1998 resolution that it was an option to be used when recruiting for skills that were especially scarce. The figures were in '000s of rands. The FSA figures illustrated the 'under-pricing' problem.

Job Title	L/Bank Actual	FSA Median	FSA UQ	PE Median	PE UQ
Managing Director	630	1046	1196	1411	1721
Exec Dir Operations	430	773	886	1053	1208
Exec Dir Fin & Admin	530	736	844	928	1075
Exec Man Corp Aff	380	556	639	688	805
Exec Manager HR	420	532	611	664	729
Manager IT	720	543	624	679	684
GM Branch Network	420	362	417	446	513
GM Treasury	450	417	417	N/A	N/A
Risk Manager	476	417	417	N/A	N/A
Manager Tech Sppt	410	285	321	312	362
Manager Com Accnt	250	225	256	271	314
Manager Sppt Serv	285	285	321	283	320
Manager Stakehldr	250	256	256	228	265
Manager Advert	210	192	226	243	278

*Katz Report, 1999. Annexure to the Jack letter.

The packages revealed the current state of the upper end of the South African labour market; the jump in salaries at the top levels was breathtaking, but reflects the operating reality of the South African job market.

The board discussion on 23 March 1999 was not easy. It seemed that some board members were realising for the very first time that the policy decision, while an essential step towards resolving anomalies and aligning with the market, would also result in large increases for senior management. I failed to understand the surprise. This had always been clear, not only from McGee's document two years earlier, but also from the information discussed by the board remuneration committee nine months earlier in July 1998.

Managers, Memela, Toms and I were asked to leave the room. On our return, Jack informed the meeting that the board's choice was to go with the FSA figures. I queried the decision, explaining it would be difficult to manage the anomalies situation and I feared staff loss if this choice was insisted upon. After further lengthy discussion the board came up with a compromise resolution. It was resolved that the PE median should be the basis of the Land Bank package norm; however, with regard to the top six executives there was an issue of conscience, and it was resolved that the PE lower quartile should prevail.

Another part of the discussion that was laden with tension was a concern, particularly from Kate Moloto, that the board did not have the right to take this decision, that it was a matter to be referred to the Minister for approval. This was something I had checked out earlier with Advocate Kügel, the legal specialist who had worked on the Land Bank Act with Department of Agriculture officials. I had been concerned that if this was the case, the difficulty of getting the Minister at a time when national election fever was beginning to grip the country would result in yet another delay in being able to settle with the unions and get on with the recruitment for head office. The legal view was clear: the Land Bank Act does not prescribe a role for the Minister in the decision-making process; the consulting partners for a decision to be brokered are the board of directors together with the managing director. This was the deliberate intention of the statute.

The ministerial role was to define the institutional mandate; the board was responsible for policy development and the executive management role was policy implementation. The minutes reflect that 'The Board acknowledged that the process had been properly mandated and executed. The Board acknowledged its mandate to approve remuneration policy changes in terms of Section 13(2)(c) of the amended Land Bank Act.' There was reluctance among some board members to accept this conclusion; they seemed to have difficulty acknowledging the parameters of their corporate governance responsibilities. Jack reassured them that a briefing would be given to the Minister and that the issue of the remuneration of the board members would also be raised.

I walked out of the meeting heaving a deep sigh of relief. The decision had taken this board almost two years, and was the culmination of a five-year process. Executives in other companies had been complimentary in their comments on the seriousness and thoroughness of the approach we had taken. I could not imagine that there would be objections from the unions; they were very clear how urgent it was that implementation should go ahead as quickly as possible and settle some of the festering concerns and uncertainties among employees.

However, some members of the strategic management team were extremely unhappy. The board decision was derogatorily referred to as the 'dog-leg' in terms of its use of the figures from the lower quartile column for the top six, and switching to the median column for the rest of the Bank's employees. It was an inconsistent policy and seen as insulting by some of those who considered they carried the greatest stress and responsibility. Those who were dissatisfied argued that they were not inferior 'lower quartile' performers, and that in essence the board decision constituted unfair labour practice. I was so relieved that we had a decision; the last thing I needed in my life was the submission of a dispute by executive management against the Land Bank board concerning unfair labour practice against its executives!

Implementation

The implementation of the remuneration decisions would have to be phased in and where appropriate there would be back pay. The recruitment to fill head office positions would occupy all the energies of the executive and senior management for the next few weeks. Only when this had been accomplished would we take the time to address the underpayment anomalies in head office, including those of the strategic management team. Leadership style matters, and it seemed important not to be pushing our own interests as priority, but rather to be seen as settling other employees' issues first.

A day after the March board meeting the unions sat down to consider the board resolution. They accepted its rationale and a new salary and benefits collective agreement was drawn up to become effective from 1 April 1999, thus when the underpayment anomalies were finally addressed the back pay would be calculated as from the date of the collective agreement.

Before settling into the recruitment drive the six-person strategic management team took a two-day getaway. Arnold Shkaidy had joined the Land Bank as HR executive manager, thus filling the vacant team position; we had long looked forward to a team-building opportunity.

It was a difficult meeting, as can often happen when a team is striving for honesty in the interests of a long-term future. One of the problems was that I raised the issue of hierarchy and significant salary differentials within the team. It seemed to me to go against the flattening of the management hierarchy in the rest of the Bank. The FSA job evaluation approach was traditional and conservative and philosophically went against the grain of the ethos I was trying to introduce of a shared executive responsibility amongst us.

To my way of thinking, there was interdependency in the group that meant that the whole was greater than the sum of the parts. Without operations there would be no Bank, and part of their effectiveness depended on communications and marketing. But without accounts and financial planning, operations could not deliver to customers, and if the IT system was not running smoothly this backfired on both operations and accounts. And the fundamental importance of good human resources management was so integral to success that it was beyond argument.

To the surprise of the group I suggested that we add up our six salaries and divide the total by six, and then each settle for the average salary. If the group was in favour of this approach, then I'd ask the new board to revisit the decision taken at the March 1999 meeting. The idea went down like a stone. I had really misjudged how important status was to some of the group members and their perception of fair and equitable reward. It didn't mean a thing that the main drop in salary would be mine. I was told later that those who considered themselves as senior within the group interpreted my proposal as showing a lack of confidence in them. I abandoned the idea. It was regarded as iconoclastic and people did not want to discuss it.

This was the kind of occasion on which I have to accept Gillam's criticism of me. He said I tended to go too fast in a new direction and then wanted everyone to be there with me. This was an example where I needed to have strategised and canvassed individually instead of putting the idea up front on the table.

I knew where I was coming from. I'd been reading the *Harvard Business Review* that had carried a couple of articles about today's executives pursuing lateral growth rather than over-specialisation. I wanted a modicum of substitutability – if we were a strategic management team, we should understand the principles of each other's work.

The idea was also rooted in those cartoons of the geese exchanging places in their flying formation and our ability to go further as a team because of interactive support. When I thought more about it, Totsie Memela and Adrian Toms had not been at the Bank during that first period of consultative debate. They'd joined later – and had jumped on to a moving train – and I'd not taken enough time to talk to them about the first part of the journey that they'd missed. They were in no way prepared or up to speed with my thinking with this proposal.

I also had to accept where they were coming from. They expected me, as managing director, to carry the can for both the successes and the failures of the institution. If something went wrong, I was expected to be answerable. This in their minds was the reason that managing directors got paid so much more than their lieutenants. They would concur with Viney* that

> The life of a business leader is not, to my mind, a particularly enviable one. It is characterised by complexity and the appearance of comfort is something of a chimera . . . To my mind they must also be compensated for the hardship of a working life which keeps them permanently on show to a range of interest groups which are not all supportive. Answerable to shareholders, a chief executive faces a far more hostile set of critics than the average manager and he is ultimately answerable on all issues all the time.

He goes on to describe the average life of a chief executive, a twelve-hour day followed by attendance at 'one of the many so-called "social" functions that go with the job, with little "quality" time with their families. They will probably come to know their grandchildren better than their own offspring!' On reflection, I had to admit that Viney described accurately the life I'd been leading for the past two years!

The ill-fated handover

The tenure of the transformation board was to end on 31 March 1999. Earlier in the year Jack had made a request, which I had supported, that the term of office of the board be extended – the rationale was continuity as we implemented head office restructuring. The Minister had replied unequivocally that a new board would be appointed by the end of March 1999; hence 31 March would constitute the end of the term of office as per the original letters of appointment.

For several weeks after 1 April 1999 the Bank operated without a board. It was only in late April that I received a copy of the cabinet

---

*J Viney, 1999.

memorandum announcing the new appointees. Memela, Toms and I would be executive directors; Michel and Moloto were to continue as non-executive directors. There were six new names, bringing the total to eleven. There was a vacant position; the list did not name a chairperson.

It was important to prepare a smooth handover. The status of a briefing meeting was not clear to me. The new board members were to gather and meet the outgoing members without a chairperson of the new board having been appointed. The opinion of Advocate Kügel, the Bank's adviser on statutory matters, was that the operation of the board without a chair was not legal, strictly speaking. However, a handover session needed to take place as soon as possible.

I tried several times to get the Minister's office to agree that he would attend a briefing session. Dinner on 11 May was finally agreed upon. Both old and new board members were to attend. The next day, 12 May, would be spent completing the briefing of the new members. Three days before the event I was advised that the Minister would not be able to attend because of party instructions that election campaigning was to take precedence over ministerial commitments.

There was an uneasy mood at the dinner on the evening of 11 May and to me it seemed a sad way to end a two-year relationship.

The uneasy mood matured overnight, and the atmosphere at the briefing meeting the next day was unpleasant. It seemed as though something had snapped inside Jack overnight. He usually projected himself as an affable character. In the days of the Strauss Commission he'd been relied upon to mediate differences between commissioners. But this day he was out of character. I had never seen him in this mood before. He behaved oddly. He claimed that the Minister had extended the tenure of the transformation board; this contradicted both the letter from the Minister and the cabinet memo. He complained to the new board members about how shabbily the old board had been treated by Minister Hanekom. Jack made reference to a fax he'd sent to board members indicating his concern that ministerial approval was required to confirm the board decision on remuneration policy. It became clear that only certain board members had received the fax and were aware of its contents; I was not one of them. I wanted us all to look at the fax he was referring to – but none of those who'd received it had it with them, and it was established that no copy had ever reached the Bank – either to myself, Totsie Memela or the board secretary.

Kate Moloto then asked if the ministerial briefing had been prepared. I was taken aback. I hadn't realised that a written briefing was to be presented. But it was a simple matter to rectify – the board documentation from March 1999 was comprehensive, and only needed the board resolution on the remuneration policy to be attached as an addendum. I apologised – perhaps in my busyness and anxiety over head office recruitment I had overlooked an instruction. When I glanced back at the March board minutes they were not clear on this issue, but quibbling would get me nowhere. It seemed better to be positive about a matter that was easily remedied; the difficulty would continue to be getting an appointment with the Minister before the elections. I asked Jack to forward a copy of the fax that had been received only by certain board members. If it was of concern then I wanted to familiarise myself with the contents.

I heaved another sigh of relief after the May 1999 'handover' meeting. Bonile Jack had behaved like an unguided missile. I'd held my peace, hoping it would be the last time he would negatively impact on my responsibility. I was weary of having a chairperson who was so begrudging of time given, who was inconsistent, and who had now misinformed people about an extended tenure of the board of his own invention.

In the days that followed the handover Jack never did fax me the letter of concerns on remuneration that he'd referred to. It seemed as though he could not be bothered with Land Bank business any longer. Surely if the fax was important he would make sure that Totsie, Adrian, the board secretary and I would all receive a copy? Meanwhile I was confident that the work done on the remuneration policy was within the board's mandate, and secure about the legal advice I had received. The Minister would be briefed at the earliest opportunity.

I immersed myself once again in the tasks arising from the restructuring of head office. Furthermore, it was time for business planning, and there was a meeting to be organised with the top forty managers of the Bank. It was the most important managerial meeting of the year, and needed wholehearted attention.

There was just one step outstanding with regard to concluding salary implementation for the members of the strategic management team. The board instruction was that I should make a proposal as to the exact salary that each was to receive. One of the details of the remuneration system was that there was a range of minus 15% to plus 15% around the lower quartile figure to allow some flexibility in cases of people coming into a job with uneven levels of experience and competence.

I did not want to be subjective. I preferred to set in place a performance appraisal as the basis for the determination of the salary. In early June 1999 I contacted Olof Van Schalkwijk again and asked for FSA assistance to draw up a performance agreement with each of the executives concerned. My own six-month performance plan was drawn up in consultation with the team, ready for presentation to the June 1999 board meeting. The appraisal was to apply to the forthcoming period July to November 1999. The results could then be shared with the board for a finalisation of where each executive manager would be placed within his or her range. In the interim there seemed no reason why people could not be placed on the minus 15% of the lower quartile in accordance with the board resolution. Adrian had been promised a market-related salary on his appointment almost eighteen months earlier; Totsie's letter of appointment made the same promise. I was aware that each of them had been house hunting in anticipation of receiving the salary increase with its accumulated back pay. I was trying to tie up as many loose ends as possible before taking a break with my younger daughter whose mid-year holidays were about to begin. I wrote the required memo to Adrian Toms requesting that the salary adjustments be made at minus 15% of the lower quartile figure for the six executive managers who made up the strategic management team, including myself.

I packed my bags hoping that when I returned I would be rested, and entering a new phase in the Bank's history that would be more positive and creative than the last year of restructuring had been. It seemed that the worst was over. There was a new atmosphere in the head office. Totsie and others were excited by the calibre of applicants for the new jobs. It appeared that our reputation as an innovative place to work, trying new things in pursuit of a development ethic, was beginning to filter through in the job market.

On return from my leave I intended to finalise the business planning process, to give support to the social accountability project that was now seriously starting its work. It was also critical that the nuts and bolts criteria for the equity finance projects to support black economic empowerment should be finalised. There was so much to be done that was exciting and challenging; perhaps at last the preoccupation with internal matters had run its course and more time could be dedicated to the delivery side of the business.

EIGHT

SKULDUGGERY

Something in the offing

The 1999 national elections came and went. In 1994 I had accompanied Joe to the historic and celebratory inauguration of Nelson Mandela as our first democratically chosen president. This time round, five years later, I did not receive an invitation to the swearing in of the new State President, Thabo Mbeki. I had heard that directors general and heads of parastatals were being invited, so my expectation of an invitation seemed reasonable. Nevertheless I hesitated to be pushy.

'Nonsense! Preposterous!' exclaimed Kader Asmal in his inimitable style when a friend told him I had not received an invitation. Asmal, now Minister of Education, was part of the inauguration organising committee. 'Helena would have received an invitation on either of two counts. Firstly, she's the head of an important state institution; secondly, she's the widow of one of the greatest heroes of our nation.' I'm not sure which one came first when he was giving this hearsay reply!

Suspicions that my star was on the wane were further confirmed a little later in the month. A 'Farewell Madiba'* banquet had been planned for 10 May 1999. I had received an invitation to this occasion and looked forward to the salute. It was then postponed on the very day – too many election commitments was the reason given. It was reorganised for the second half of June. On hearing that the new date had been set, I enquired if the prior invitation stood or whether there would be a reissue. The invitation list was being revised by the new president's office,

---

*Madiba is the clan name of Nelson Mandela.

I was told, but they could not yet tell me if I would remain invited. No invitation arrived – further confirmation that my socio-political mobility was on the down slope. I knew that relations between my late husband and the new president had been less than amicable, and had always felt that by association a certain coolness also extended towards me.

Meanwhile a new order was fast flexing its muscle in the Ministry of Agriculture. Thoko Didiza, formerly Derek Hanekom's deputy, had been appointed Minister. There was a new Deputy Minister, Dirk du Toit. Hanekom had been shafted and no longer figured in any ministerial equation. A friend informed me with his usual dry and irreverent humour of the rumoured existence of a 'hit list' comprising so-called 'Hanekom appointees', irrespective of race or gender. My name graced the hit list, so I was informed. I speculated about the truth of the rumour.

Official hierarchy aside, I sensed a triumvirate in power: the Minister, her trusted director general Bongi Njobe, and one of the deputy directors general, Masiphula Mbongwa – the combination did not augur well for me. I had little doubt that I was not Bongi Njobe's favourite person, in spite of our facilitation partnership in Lusaka and afterwards. We'd differed personally in our approach to the closing of the Agricultural Credit Board and in the parliamentary corridors she'd accused me of taking Hanekom's side once again. She'd differed with Hanekom on so many issues and I, from the time of my appointment as his adviser, had been classified as being in the 'Hanekom camp'. Masiphula Mbongwa had been consistently unfriendly since 1987, more especially after he wasn't appointed to the Strauss Commission. He'd been less than co-operative in the final stages of the Commission's work, blatantly saying he was too busy to meet to give any additional input on behalf of the Department of Agriculture. There was a fundamental difference in our approach to rural development as far back as the COSATU workshop on the economy in Harare in 1990. The new Minister was largely an unknown quantity as far as I was concerned. I had met her, sat next to her on a pleasant plane journey one time – but that did not give the knowledge of a person that comes with a closer working relationship.

On 21 June 1999 I received an invitation to attend a meeting with the Minister to take place two days later. The invitation instructed that a briefing on salient issues be prepared. Having been an adviser, I was familiar with the expected style of ministerial briefings: the need to be selective and economical, to make sure that the short time allotted would focus on the most important items. I chose the need to revise the Land Bank Act, the First National Bank challenge to the constitutionality of certain clauses of the Land Bank Act. I noted the progress made on restructuring:

the negotiation of the retrenchment package and the completed work on remuneration – and I attached documentation. In my cover letter I alerted the Minister to the outstanding need to revise the delegation of powers and rules and regulations of the Bank – both of these would require ministerial approval. Verbally, I intended to raise the issue that the Land Bank was currently operating improperly in the absence of an appointed chairperson. I prepared two copies, one for the Minister and one for the Deputy Minister.

The meeting was not what I expected. All the heads of parastatals who report to the Minister of Agriculture and Land Affairs were present, as well as Land Claims commissioners and the directors general; the room was crowded. We were asked, in situ, not to address pending issues as had been indicated, but to make a short overall presentation of our performance on delivery. This was the clarion call of the new Mbeki administration. There were more than half a dozen presentations made. I was asked to speak first. There was some supportive input from the floor in the ensuing question-and-answer session. But I left asking myself why I had an uneasy sense of having been picked on. Was I being paranoid?

With new personalities dominating the ministerial order I had qualms that this would affect my working life. Hanekom, the mandate established, had left things to the board of directors working with the executive management; I had good reason to believe that the civil servants in question had a more interventionist approach. But my sense of unease ran more deeply. Over a whisky with a friend the evening before leaving on holiday I was to say: 'I have a gut feeling that something is brewing, a sense of people plotting. I have nothing tangible to go on – but the feeling is there.' I wondered if I were to be called in and told by the Minister that she would like a black person to be in charge of the Land Bank. That was my own objective – to groom a black manager to take over from me. I needed at least one more year to ensure this, as well as to consolidate some of the things we were in the middle of implementing.

A few days after the 23 June meeting with the Minister my daughter Kyla and I left for the Maldives. It may not have been the best time in terms of there having been a change in board and Minister, but one has no control over the setting of dates for school holidays, and as Kyla was not living with me, this was my only opportunity to spend time with her.

One night while we were on holiday I was woken up by a bad dream. I couldn't remember the detail of it, except that the scene of the dream drama was the Land Bank, and that it was unpleasant enough to jolt me out of my sleep.

Toxic shock

It was Friday 16 July 1999. I'd fulfilled my family promise to learn scuba diving with Kyla. We had survived. I now had an open water diver's certificate – a major achievement for me as I nearly backed out on three occasions. (How is it that one can panic and feel claustrophobic in the vastness of the underwater sea?) Kyla, on the other hand, accomplished the whole course with ease and equanimity; her only problem was having to cope with her mother as her diving 'buddy'. We spent our last day in the Maldives 'island hopping' before getting our 1 am flight to Singapore. We were to have two nights there, and had planned what we wanted to do: visit the botanical gardens, tea at Raffles hotel, and an exploration of the shoe shops – we share a passion for shoes.

At 9 am Singapore time we'd just checked into our hotel room when the phone rang. It was my secretary Lettie who cried as she spoke: 'Helena, something terrible has happened. You are all over the newspapers, on the radio, on the TV. You are accused of racism, nepotism, mismanagement . . .' Her voice trailed off. I laughed with disbelief, told her not to worry, that everything would be fine. She told me that Totsie Memela and Adrian Toms would be phoning me shortly, which they did.

They told me of a letter, written by Bonile Jack in May to then president-in-waiting Mbeki that had been leaked to *The Star* newspaper. It appeared that its release had been well orchestrated. It was a half-page story with an enormous photograph and had been the front-page news item of every provincial paper belonging to the Independent newspaper group. It was the number one item on the South African Broadcasting Corporation's Channel 3 evening news.

A meeting between the Minister, Deputy Minister and the available board members had already taken place. Deputy Minister du Toit had immediately raised the very issue that had concerned me: the impropriety of the board acting in the absence of an appointed chairperson. The lacuna was immediately remedied; Sam Mkhabela, one of the new board members, was named as chairperson for the next two months.

Prior to the report of the Jack letter in the media Toms, who was acting managing director during one of the two weeks of my absence, had received a letter from the Minister. Her letter, addressed to me, headed 'Review of Salary Increases for Strategic Management Team and Staff' indicated that she had been informed that there was disagreement within the board, that the matter should be put on hold, and that she needed to familiarise herself with the issues. It seemed that neither she nor any of her ministerial staff nor the senior civil servants who reported to her had perused the documentation that was handed in to both her and her deputy at the briefing on 23 June.

Later I spoke to my brother Martin. He'd already been in touch with Pam Stein, an attorney at the firm of Cheadle Thompson & Haysom; it seemed as though I might well be in need of a lawyer. They had both spoken to the main journalist, Prince Hamnca. He said he'd had the story for a couple of weeks. Yes, he knew that I was due back on Sunday, and intended to meet me at the airport. But, he said, he got wind that another newspaper might break the story so he had to jump in first.

I may have been on a 'desert island' – and I'd joked about cellphones not working underwater – but Kuredu in the Maldives is an international holiday resort, online and accessible by telephone, fax and e-mail. On his own admission, Hamnca had been in possession of the Jack letter for several days, but he made no attempt to obtain any contact details, either through my family or the Land Bank. His action resulted in a public perception being formed that was to my detriment.

Kyla and I had several tense hours in Singapore trying to get on the flight that night. The last two days of our holiday were not going to be fun in the light of this toxic shock. Kyla took charge of me as delayed reaction set in. She made cups of tea while I phoned travel agents and airlines. We were told that our rescheduling could not be confirmed for several hours. Kyla took me to the shoe shops in an attempt to distract me. Those hours compete for first place in my list of the worst times of my life, in spite of my daughter's best efforts to calm me.

Media abuse

The Star media assault had been full blooded. They set the ball rolling on Thursday 15 July 1999, knowing full well that I was not expected back until the Sunday.

I had been raised to understand that the freedom of the press was an essential item of democracy; my parents noted the lack of it as evidence of things not going well under communism in the countries of their birth. As I read *The Star* report I wondered if there were rules that journalists needed to follow if they were about to publish a report that could be damaging to a person. I made a point of finding out about the codes of ethics designed to guide the journalistic profession. I thus discovered that *The Star*'s journalists had crossed the line; they broke the rules, both our national ones and those that are internationally respected.

The South African Press Ombudsman and Appeal Panel have a Code of Conduct by which they are guided in considering complaints. It includes the following clauses:

1.1   The press shall be obliged to report news truthfully, accurately and fairly.

1.2   News shall be presented in context and in a balanced manner without an intentional or negligent departure from the facts whether by:

1.2.1 distortion, exaggeration or misrepresentation;
1.2.2 material omission; or
1.2.3 summarisation.

1.3   Only what may reasonably be true having regard to the source of the news, may be presented as facts, and such facts shall be published fairly with due regard to content and importance. Where a rumour is not based on facts or is founded on opinions, allegation, rumour or supposition, it shall be presented in such a manner as to indicate this clearly.

1.4   Where there is reason to doubt the accuracy of the report and it is practicable to verify the accuracy thereof, it shall be verified. Where it has not been practicable to verify the accuracy of a report, this shall be mentioned in such report.

1.5   A newspaper should usually seek the views of the subject of serious critical reportage in advance of publication; provided that this need not be done where the newspaper has reasonable grounds for believing that by doing so it would be prevented from publishing the report or where evidence might be destroyed or witnesses intimidated.

1.10   In both news and comment, the press shall exercise exceptional care and consideration in matters involving the private lives and concerns of individuals, bearing in mind that any right to privacy may be overridden by a legitimate public interest.

With regard to ethical conduct, the American code provides the industry-wide, internationally accepted interpretation of the standards as outlined in the South African code.

The preamble to the Society of Professional Journalists' Code of Ethics incorporates four guiding principles:* *to seek truth*, *to minimise harm*, *to remain independent*, and *public accountability*. Good journalism is expected to play a key role in society in the belief that 'public enlightenment is the forerunner of justice and the foundation of democracy'. Such aspirations are to be achieved by 'Conscientious journalists . . . (who) strive to serve the public with thoroughness and honesty. Professional integrity is the cornerstone of the journalist's credibility.'

---

*J Black, B Steele & R Barney, 1999, p.6.

Expectations were developed for each of the four areas of the code, including:

Seek Truth and Report It
Journalists should be honest, fair and courageous in gathering, reporting and interpreting information. Journalists should:
- Test the accuracy of information from all sources and exercise care to avoid inadvertent error. Deliberate distortion is never permissible.
- Diligently seek out subjects of news stories to give them the opportunity to respond to allegations of wrongdoing . . .

Minimise Harm
Ethical journalists treat sources, subjects and colleagues as human beings deserving of respect. Journalists should:
- Show compassion for those who may be affected adversely by news coverage.
- Recognise that gathering and reporting information may cause harm or discomfort. Pursuit of news is not a licence for arrogance.

Act Independently
Journalists should be free of obligation to any interests other than the public's right to know.

Be Accountable
Journalists are accountable to their readers, listeners, viewers and each other.

Journalism, it was argued, did not lend itself to regulatory codes such as apply to other professions: the self-imposed integrity is therefore all the more important.

The absence of professional discipline makes journalistic codes more advisory than mandatory. That is in sharp contrast to the enforceable codes of the legal and medical professions . . . But it also means that journalists, individually and collectively, have a greater need for an articulated sense of ethics than do the more regulated professionals.*

The report, 'Serious allegations against Slovo's widow', with a very large photograph, occupied the entire top half of the front page of *The Star*, the main Johannesburg newspaper which sells 170 000 copies a

---

*J Black, B Steele & R Barney, 1999, p.18.

day. It was run as the top story in every one of the day's four editions. It was run in each of Independent Newspapers' stable of dailies countrywide: *The Pretoria News* 14 500 copies, *The Diamond Field Advertiser* in Kimberley 10 000 copies, *The Cape Argus* 79 500 copies, the *Cape Times* 50 700 copies (story title: 'Land Bank head accused of corruption'), the *Durban Daily News* 83 500 copies, the *Natal Mercury* 47 000 copies (story title: 'Slovo wife accused of corruption'), and the *Post* – also a Durban newspaper with a circulation of 51 000 copies. This newspaper chain calculates that each copy is read, on average, by four people; on this basis the lead story had a potential readership of more than two million on Thursday 15 July 1999.

Everyone reads the opening paragraph of an article that catches their attention, but they don't necessarily read the whole article, nor do they often check whether or not the introductory lines are substantiated. Hamnca's lead article for *The Star* started:

> Dr Helena Dolny, Land Bank managing director and widow of the late Joe Slovo, has been accused of corruption, mismanagement, racism, nepotism and trying to more than double her own salary.

Only three of these accusations were then taken up in the body of the article: salary, racism and nepotism; the words *corruption* (not a word used in the Jack letter) and *mismanagement* had been thrown in for good measure.

Chapter Four on 'Accuracy and Fairness' in the book *Doing Ethics in Journalism* reiterates earlier sentiments:

> Audiences deserve, and pay for, a reasonably accurate and unbiased picture of the world they live in. Every effort should be made to ensure that facts are correct and that information is presented in context. It is not appropriate to use deadlines, or competition, or personal excuses, or equipment problems, or staffing shortages, or any other reason to justify inaccuracies or bias.[*]

Much later I learnt that Hamnca had contacted the Land Bank two days before the article was printed and indicated that he was going to be doing a profile piece. In my absence, as well as that of the communications director, Adrian Toms as acting managing director requested our media consultants, the firm Horizon Strategy, to contact Prince Hamnca and ensure he had all the information he needed. Humphrey

---

[*]J Black, B Steele & R Barney, 1999, p.64.

Harrison from Horizon Strategy had immediately followed up with a phone call. Hamnca dissembled. He told Harrison that he was doing an article on parastatals and that all he needed was an organogram. In this context the Hamnca statement, 'Efforts to trace Dolny have proved fruitless and messages left on her cellphone have not been answered', was especially misleading. Hamnca knew I was on holiday overseas and could have surmised the possibility that the cellphone would not reconnect until I landed at Johannesburg airport. He had not tried to obtain either the phone number or fax number or e-mail address of the hotel where I was staying in the Maldives. It would seem probable that there was a preference for the story to be published without corroboration, and whilst I was still out of the country.

More worrisome, however, was what I learnt about the internal dynamics behind the publishing of the story at *The Star* newspaper. There is usually a late afternoon news conference which reviews the main stories for the morning newspaper. It is also the place at which judgement is made whether or not a story is at all problematic. In this case, it was not as though no one queried whether or not the facts had been checked, and whether or not efforts had been made to get my response. Patrick Bulger, the editor on duty to finalise the news stories, asked the questions appropriate to the professional code of ethics. It was confirmed that Hamnca had paid a visit to the office of the Minister earlier in the week. It was also clear that the facts had not been checked. Bulger's concern, voiced at the 17h30 internal news conference, was overruled by his seniors, editor Peter Sullivan and deputy editor Mathatha Tsedu. Reference was made to the *Mail & Guardian*'s having covered a spate of stories on black corruption and that the piece on me, a story of a corrupt white, provided a brilliant antidote.

While it was conceded that *The Star*'s standard investigation approach to corroborate facts had not been done, it was ruled that it was too good a story to be put on hold and that the newspaper would subsequently deal with any negative consequences – should these arise.

The guiding principles, 'to seek truth and minimise harm', were blatantly ignored. The accuracy of the information was not tested. There was a failure to diligently seek out myself as the subject of the news story to provide the opportunity to 'respond to allegations of wrong-doing'. Moreover, the reported lack of contact was expressed in a manner that insinuated that I might be in hiding, thus suggesting an awareness of an action of wrongdoing, rather than on the long-scheduled family holiday, which the journalist would have been well aware of.

Given the implications of what I was hearing, even if it was the same thing from different people, I decided to phone Peter Sullivan. It seemed only fair to get Sullivan's views first hand. I began the conversation by explaining that he might have heard that I was writing a book about the Land Bank.

'Yes, I believe I read about it somewhere.'

I explained that I wanted his comment on a couple of things that I understood were the buzz in the newsroom and among the subeditors at the time *The Star* broke the story. I told him I'd heard that there had been a decision to publish in spite of its being acknowledged that there had not been a corroboration of facts.

Sullivan responded: 'My memory is a little vague – time has passed – one of those things . . . feel slightly vague about it. From what I recollect it was just around the time that Mathatha had joined the paper and brought the story to me . . . From what I recollect, I was first given the story on a Tuesday. I said they should try every means to get hold of you. A couple of days passed – was told they were trying to get hold of you. Anyway, when four days passed and I was reassured that they had tried every possible avenue . . . I have no reason to believe that my staff lied to me . . . I decided that the allegations were on paper, written by a member of staff and that you would be called to answer them in due course . . . Decided to go ahead – wanted to do the story before the Sundays did it – was told that the *Sunday Times* had exactly the same story. I think we published on a Friday to get in before the Sundays . . .'

I interjected with a correction. 'No, Thursday. It was Thursday.'

I then asked him if he recalled a comment that this was a brilliant story about white corruption and exactly the kind of antidote needed to counterbalance the *Mail & Guardian*'s stories on black corruption.

'Not me,' he responded. 'Certainly I don't remember any comments like that. Mm . . . must say I never liked the story. I was always very wary of the story from the beginning. But the allegations had been made on paper, by a staff member, by the by what was his name? It was my duty to publish . . . what was his name?'

'Jack. Bonile Jack,' I answered.

Sullivan concluded: 'I must confess I was not happy in publishing it. I had rejected the story on three consecutive days . . . I don't know who the "they" is that you're talking about telling you these things . . .'

As he listened to my account of the conversation, another journalist observed: 'Sullivan avoided the issue of investigating the facts.'

As for 'every possible avenue' having been explored in the quest for my contact details before publication, I have yet to find evidence of any attempt. Tiyani Mongwe, responsible for secretarial duties at the

Land Bank on the critical days, kept the customary written record of all incoming phone calls and their subject matter. There was no record of a call from Hamnca. Totise Memela, acting MD in the week *The Star* published the story, has provided an affidavit that she was not contacted by Hamnca. Similarly, there was no contact with general manager communications Lauren Richer. The only enquiry from Hamnca that I tracked down was the apparently spurious one dealt with by Humphrey Harrison of Horizon Strategy.

The Star's code of ethics

Through my conversations with journalists I learnt that *The Star* has its own code of ethics that has been prominently displayed on the walls of its offices for several years. I obtained a copy.

Of the twenty-seven clauses of *The Star*'s code of ethics, several are of special interest to me in considering the quality of the newspaper's coverage as events unfolded.

> *Clause 1*: In its reporting and comment, *The Star* should be accurate, fair, honest and frank.
>
> *Clause 2*: *The Star* should aim to give all sides of an issue, by means of balanced presentation without bias, distortion, undue emphasis or omission.
>
> *Clause 3*: *The Star* should be independent of government, commerce or any other vested interest.
>
> *Clause 4*: *The Star* should expose wrongdoing, the misuse of power and unnecessary secrecy.
>
> *Clause 10*: Sources of news should be identified unless there is good reason not to.
>
> *Clause 11*: Facts should be checked carefully.
>
> *Clause 14*: *The Star* should report issues in an impartial and balanced manner. Every effort should be made to reflect all sides of a controversy, if not simultaneously, then in subsequent editions.

It is difficult to convince myself that *The Star* complied with its own code.

Tongue-tied

When I landed in Johannesburg early on the Saturday morning there was a message that the newly appointed chairperson would contact me later to do a full briefing but was unavailable until the evening because of study commitments. My friends took charge of me; the corporate affairs unit at the Land Bank was in a state of paralysis. There was no data at the ready to refute some of the allegations that had been made about non-delivery to black entrepreneurs – not even the basic list of media contact details was to hand. Some friends advised me that I should issue a press statement to refute the allegations. My concentration was poor and I needed their help. In a matter of a few hours they organised that I appear on the Sunday TV programme, Newsmaker of the Week, and that I do radio interviews at prime time as people travelled to work on Monday morning. They talked me through the key issues they thought I should cover.

There are a few critical hours after such media revelations that are important in the mind of the public as to whether a story settles and takes root or whether it is challenged. On Thursday morning Adrian Toms contacted our media adviser Humphrey Harrison to ask him what the Bank should do. By mid morning Harrison had faxed a reply. He considered *The Star* article 'a disgraceful piece of journalism . . . almost certainly libellous'. His advice to the Bank was:

> I would strongly urge you to marshal all available resources to contact Helena, whatever it takes. One of the most damaging aspects of the story is the insinuation that she acted deviously in seeking a salary increase and that she has gone into hiding. It doesn't say that she is on holiday, which it could have.
>
> . . . *The Star* should be contacted and made to feel distinctly uneasy about the story, on strictly professional grounds regarding unethical and scurrilous journalism. At the very least, the LB (quite distinct from Helena) in entitled to full and immediate right of reply. We must demand this and ensure that it is punchy and to the point.
>
> I understand from Lauren (general manager communications) that the thinking is merely to announce an enquiry into the allegations. If that is the only response, it would be akin to convicting Helena.

Precious hours were squandered phoning around to gather people together for a consultation with the Minister. To be fair, a chairperson to lead the board was only appointed later that day. The board, during those critical hours, was a body without a head. Meanwhile, the acting managing director and the communications general manager made no comment whilst the newspaper's second, third and fourth daily editions continued to roll off the press – and were picked up with the intended multiplier effect by the other newspaper groups. The lack of appropriate response was appalling.

The appointment of Sam Mkhabela as chairperson did not resolve the issue. If anything, his approach made things worse from my perspective. He mouthed words to the effect that the principles of natural justice must be adhered to: 'The facts must be availed to establish whether there is any substance to the allegations.' However, the first media release* read:

MEDIA RELEASE BY THE BOARD OF DIRECTORS OF THE LAND BANK

Allegations against Dr Dolny, Managing Director of the Land Bank

The Board of Directors of the Land Bank today decided, in consultation with the Minister for Agriculture and Land Affairs, to conduct an urgent investigation into the allegations against Dr Dolny, Managing Director of the Land Bank. It will report to the Minister, Ms Thoko Didiza, within fourteen days.

The Board met today in view of the widely reported allegations that have been made against Dr Dolny. It is satisfied that this matter will not affect the Land Bank's core mandate nor disrupt its operations.

ENQUIRIES Mr Sam Mkhabela
                 Chairperson of the Board of Directors of the Land Bank

The laconic style, the omission of a single supportive word and the total absence of any vote of confidence could only contribute to public suspicion that there might be truth in Jack's allegations. It went against the advice of the media consulting firm. It was in sharp contrast to the style with which the CCMA handled allegations leaked to the media against its director Thandi Orleyn a few weeks later, and as to how the board of Ntsika would later deal with the allegations against Kate Moloto.

Mkhabela briefed me late on Saturday evening. He told me of the decision to hold an inquiry to be run by a firm of lawyers – it must be established whether or not the allegations had any basis. A board meeting was to be held on Monday to select the lawyers. They were looking for a firm with the capacity to handle the matter with speed, and who would furnish a team with race and gender diversity. He advised me that it had been decided that he would be the only person to engage with the press. I informed him that I had already issued a press statement, and that I had commitments for TV and radio. I explained I had been advised that my silence would be interpreted as

*Media release, Land Bank, 15 July 1999.

guilt – and that I must at least make an initial reply. I told him that once these undertakings were over I would be happy for the inquiry to run its course and to refrain from further media engagement.

Shortly after the Monday morning radio interview I was phoned by Mkhabela, the sum of his words being: 'I have received phone calls from board members complaining about your media interviews. I thought we had agreed on no press engagement on your part.' I was taken aback. I thought we had amicably concluded that I would fulfil those engagements made prior to his discussion with me. I tactfully suggested that there might have been a misunderstanding between us. After that phone call I resolved to write down everything Mkhabela said in order to avoid further 'misunderstandings'.

Friends reminded me that Mkhabela was accumulating a reputation for backtracking. The Macro-economic Research Group expected him to take up a research post after completing his studies. He'd accepted a scholarship to do master's course at the School of Oriental and African Studies and duly started the course. His sudden return to Johannesburg to take up a corporate job embarrassed the course organisers who were left with the problem of explaining to sponsors the shortcomings of their selection procedures.

I was anxious to nurture a positive relationship with the new board chairperson and tried not to be unduly influenced by any negative statements I heard. But after our inauspicious start I had qualms about Mkhabela being straight in his dealings and forebodings about the future.

The media issue was raised at the Monday afternoon board meeting. The manner in which it was handled left me doubting the real intent of the instruction. I was asked to leave the meeting and it was discussed further. Later I received a letter from the chairperson formally noting the board's 'deep concern' about my media contact over the weekend and also noting that members of the board were not entirely satisfied with my explanations.

While media disengagement was laudably sold in the interests of avoiding 'trial by media', it was soon clear that there was a pair of hostile 'deep throats'* in direct contact with Prince Hamnca at *The Star* newspaper. Whilst I held true to the instruction to remain silent, it was debilitating

---

*'Deep throat' is the accepted reference to the existence of a confidential high-level source of information. The origin of the term stems from the Watergate Affair. Reporters Carl Bernstein and Bob Woodward used such a person in their investigation for the *Washington Post* in 1972-73.

to witness my own media assassination by *The Star*, to watch myself being hung, drawn and quartered. Yet I was trying to hold on to a job and the fear of dismissal for disobeying a board of directors' instruction loomed large in my mind. As part of a strategy of psychological disarmament the gagging order imposed upon me was effective.

In retrospect, I was to contemplate whether or not the instruction that I should not speak to the media about the allegations was a cover for a sinister strategy. Mkhabela was the only board member sanctioned to handle press queries. Yet in the weeks to follow, on more than one occasion, misinformation couched in terms detrimental to me was passed to *The Star* reporter. The 'source close to the Bank' could only have been someone on the board subcommittee dealing with the inquiry, or the lawyers involved. I was banned from making comment, and the board chairperson assiduously refrained from correcting the inaccuracies.

The members of the subcommittee set up to deal with all matters pertaining to the inquiry were Mkhabela as chairperson, Masiphula Mbongwa, Kate Moloto, and Jacob Modise. Mkhabela, with his evident political and corporate ambitions, could be expected to pursue a course of action that would ensure that he would continue to be well looked-upon by the powers that be. Mbongwa and I had a long, conflict-ridden working history, rooted in ideological differences of which colleagues were well aware. Kate Moloto recused herself from the subcommittee after *The Star* reported on a letter, again shared with them by deep throat, that spelt out that her position on Land Bank salaries was evidence that she could not be impartial. I respected Moloto for her withdrawal, and felt that Mbongwa, if he were principled, should have done the same. Jacob Modise's self-presentation was as the consummate corporate manicured man – a director on more than ten boards in addition to his full-time employment as the financial director of Johnnic, a black economic empowerment company in the midst of its own restructuring. In the months to come, his busy schedule would repeatedly prevent his attending meetings and giving considered attention to Land Bank board issues.

Three black men – hardly a well-balanced team in terms of race and gender and in stark contrast to the race and gender diversity that was being insisted upon with regard to the law firm. The signs did not augur well. I said nothing. I was trying to be co-operative – my long-term aim was to remain in a job that had become a passion – and I needed to maintain cordiality. If no other board member was prepared to express a reservation, then voicing my own concerns about the composition of the subcommittee would only add to the negative vibes.

A tense and hostile tenor emanating from this quarter immediately pervaded the board proceedings. I thought I was making a simple request: 'May I have a copy of the Jack letter?' 'No, that is not possible,' was Mkhabela's unequivocal reply. I would be permitted to read the letter written by Bonile Jack whilst on Bank premises and then return it to the board secretary as the other board members had done. In spite of a copy being in possession of a newspaper chain, it was considered confidential.

I queried the response. 'How am I to prepare myself to co-operate with the inquiry if I can't have possession of the letter of allegations?' I also asked about access to lawyers for advice. I was told that as a board member I could use the board lawyers from Bowman Gilfillan. This again seemed unreasonable. My preference would be an attorney from Cheadle Thompson & Haysom. The Land Bank had an account with both firms. If the board was prepared to let me be advised by lawyers, why this obstinacy to refuse to let me use the professional with whom I was most comfortable? Besides there was an inherent problem in my being told to use the lawyers who were acting on behalf of the board. A conflict of interest situation could arise.

My choice, Pam Stein, was a senior partner of the firm Cheadle Thompson & Haysom. Their reputation had been built on the defence of clients who had been at odds with the apartheid regime. Ironically, several of the current day clients were people with struggle backgrounds coming into collision with representatives of the new order. Pam Stein, blonde and petite, exuded calmness and determination. Her acceptance of me as a client was reassuring; I felt as though I was in good hands.

Compassion was not on the menu; I was obviously in for a rough ride. The tone being set by the chairperson and his subcommittee was unpleasant and obstructive rather than helpful. Pam Stein's first action was to persuade the board lawyers Graham Damant and Jerry Kaapu of Bowman Gilfillan to in turn persuade Mkhabela that my request for a copy of the Jack letter was reasonable. Permission was eventually granted – under the threat of disciplinary action should I dare to share it with anyone other than my lawyer. Again, why the secrecy? What was in the letter that the newspaper hadn't revealed? Eventually the entire Katz investigation report would be available to the public; it contains the Jack letter as an annexure. Five months later it would also become part of a High Court public record – so why the initial contrariness to a reasonable request?

The 'Jack Letter'*

P.O. Box 71056
BRYANSTON
2021

27 May 1999

Deputy President
Private Bag x911
PRETORIA
0001

Attention: Hon. Mr Thabo Mbeki
Fax: (012) 323 2505

Dear Mr Mbeki

REPORT ON CRITICAL ISSUES AT THE LAND AND AGRICULTURAL BANK OF SOUTH AFRICA (LAND BANK)

The government, through the Minister of Agriculture and Land Affairs, appointed me as the Chairperson Designate of the Land Bank in August 1997. Confirmation of my appointment as the Chairperson was supposed to have been effected as soon as the Land Bank Act was amended by parliament sometime in 1998. The Act was amended during last year and Mr Derek Hanekom, the Minister for Agriculture and Land Affairs did not communicate anything to me regarding the appointment. The amendment of the Act enabled the Land Bank to separate the position of Chairperson (non-Executive) to [sic] that of the Managing Director (currently Dr Helena Dolny).

To be exact, I strongly believe that the Board has had a fall-out with Dr Dolny and Mr Hanekom because we were not prepared to be rubber stamps for secret agendas that are prevalent in that Ministry. I would like to list a few that I believe are problematic in the running of any state/public institution that has a specific role to play.

1. After the appointment of the Board in 1997, we took a decision that we should consult all relevant stakeholders such as the farmers organisations (NAFU and SAAU), National Department of Agriculture, Department of Land Affairs, parastatals (DBSA, IDC, KHULA) and others.† We instructed Dr Dolny to invite the Deputy Minister of

---

*Annexure 6, High Court Case No. 34457/99.
†NAFU – National Agricultural Farmers' Union; SAAU – South African Agricultural Union; DBSA – Development Bank of Southern Africa; IDC – Industrial Development Corporation.

Agriculture, Ms Thoko Didiza, and the Director-General, Ms Bongi Njobe-Mbuli, to one of our meetings so that we could discuss roles and working relationship. She was reluctant until we had to push her to do that. On the day of the visit by these two senior agriculture officials, Dr Dolny did not hide her hatred for the two. After they had left the meeting, the Board expressed its displeasure to Dr Dolny at the tensions that would prevent the Land Bank and the department from working together.

It was decided that I should request Mr Hanekom (in writing) to convene a meeting that would include him, Ms Didiza, Ms Njobe-Mbuli, Dr Dolny and myself. The purpose of the meeting was to discuss ways and means of promoting co-operation between the Land Bank and the department. That meeting has never materialised. There was not even an acknowledgement of my letters by Mr Hanekom's Office. The Land Bank and the department have not worked together and, as a result, farmers who are supposed to be served have suffered severely.

2. An affirmative action programme was introduced by the Land Bank at the insistence of the Board. Various posts were advertised and black professionals were appointed (about six of them). Throughout last year (1998), the Board was inundated by complaints of racist treatment by the Managing Director, Dr Dolny, against black staff. I raised these concerns with her and she denied them. The problem came to a crisis point when she decided to chase Ms Moira Mokoena (Executive Assistant to the Managing Director and Board) out of the Land Bank because she did not like her. The Board disagreed with her actions on the basis that they were politically and morally indefensible. She decided to report the matter to Mr Hanekom and came back with a view that the Board was wrong and she was right (according to the Minister). We objected to that and I requested to see the Minister. Again he decided to avoid meeting with me.

By that time, Ms Mokoena was out of the Land Bank. The matter is currently with the Labour Court. As people who are expected to protect the rights of employees, (especially top management is the alleged perpetrator), we tried everything possible to normalise the situation. Instead Dr Dolny flushed more black managers out of the Land Bank. For example, Mr Tim Monare, Ms Berneditte [sic] Mosetle, Mr Ernest Khoza, Ms Komiki Masekela and Mr Dan Matsapola are no longer working for the Land Bank. That has happened within one year of their appointment. On the contrary all white new appointees (allegedly part of a liberal clique) are still there despite the fact that they had no relevant qualifications in banking.

3. Appointment of consultants has been biased towards white professionals some of whom are expatriates. These people have been appointed in a

clandestine manner and paid exorbitant amounts of money. The 1997/ 1998 Auditor General's Office raised a query on this matter in their report. They advised the Board to change the procedure as it was open to abuse and corruption. In some cases, consultants who are part of the circle of friends have been sent to community projects without consultation with the affected communities (see attachments). At the end of the day, these badly handled cases have had to be handled by the Board.

4. Of the R11 billion loan book of the Land Bank, only about R56 million has been allocated to black farmers. We have raised concerns as the Board regarding this problem without any co-operation from management. The problem relates to racism at the Land Bank branches and there have been complaints regarding this matter (see attachments). Dr Dolny's response has always been to blame the victims. In the Eastern Cape, for example, the MEC for Agriculture and Land Affairs, Mr Max Mamase experienced first hand racism in Cradock when he approached the Land Bank there (disguised as a black farmer). Dr Dolny knows about that and instead she has opted to treat the matter on a casual basis.

5. Recently, a company called Rutec was advanced a loan of about R10 million by the Land Bank although it does not meet the criteria. The bank went further to buy equity in the company. This is not provided for in the policies and procedures of the institution. This was reported in the papers without even informing the Board about it. When we enquired at the following Board meeting, Dr Dolny said 'there is always the first time'. An application by BAASA Holdings (Pty) Ltd (an empowerment company) was declined BY Dr Dolny on the grounds that I was a Director in that company. In the case of Rutec, they advanced the loan and equity for R10 million despite the fact that there was a Board member in that deal who happened to be white. Racism reared its ugly head in this case. Rutec is not even an agricultural business whilst BAASA is.

6. The Poultry Institute at the University of Natal was given a grant by the Land Bank of more than R300 000.00 whilst NAFU was flatly refused assistance. On investigation, the Board discovered that Dr Dolny's former husband runs the Institute and she never declared the matter. This type of information is often available to the public and questions are asked which the Board cannot answer. In situations like these, the Chairperson would be expected to discuss such irregularities with the Minister but no opportunity was ever availed. One ends up concluding that it would be a waste of time and energy to report such serious problems to a person who would find no problems with such behaviour.

7. During the restructuring process in 1998, Dr Dolny unilaterally decided to advertise the twenty-five (25) Branch Managers' posts at the Land Bank. The Board cautioned against advertising these posts whilst there are incumbents. She went ahead and appointed eighteen (18) people. The nineteen (19) incumbents were declared redundant. The case went to arbitration and the Land Bank had almost no chance to win it (according to legal opinion) and we were expected to pay R33 million towards settlement. We advised her to re-absorb them. The problem is still there.

8. The restructuring process of the Head Office has led to the retrenchment of about 250 of the 370 employees there. Of the 250 about 100 are from the cleaning staff and members of SACCAWU. We argued as the Board against the timing of this move (in May) just before the elections. Individual staff members and the SACCAWU have been phoning asking me to intervene but it has not been possible (see attachments). Some of these calls have been threatening. As a result, I have a guard at my home every night. I needed to discuss these problems with the Minister who was still not available to meet with me. Instead there were rumours spread that the Minister was not happy with the Board and was going to remove it before the elections.

9. The last straw in the relationship between Dr Dolny and the Board was at the meeting of the 24th March 1999 where management tabled a proposal for salary adjustments of everyone including themselves. The salaries of the top management were to go up by an average of 80%. Dr Dolny's salary, for example, was going to go up from R630 000,00 to R1 411 000,00 (123% increase), (see attachments) with immediate effect. Motivation by Dr Dolny was that the DBSA, IDC and others are getting more than that amount. The Board argued that we could not justify the increments whilst 250 out of 370 staff members are leaving the organisation (being retrenched). We also argued that the Minister, according to the Land Bank Act, appoints the Managing Director and the General Managers and their salaries are therefore the responsibility of the Minister and Cabinet. She was insisting that the Minister and the Cabinet have no role in this matter and that we should approve the increments. We decided that I should try and meet the Minister to discuss the matter. Again, I could not get him. Instead Dr Dolny told me that the Minister would be appointing a new Board that will handle the matter.

In conclusion, I wish to acknowledge the fact that the appointment of the Board is the prerogative of the Minister and the Cabinet. I, however, have a serious problem with the manner in which this process has been handled. It is even more problematic to appoint a Chairperson Designate of the Board (pending the amendment of the Act) and the Minister decide to change the cabinet decision without communicating with the person concerned. As far as the other Board Members are concerned, they were asked by the Minister's Office to indicate their availability to serve on the new Board. They all expressed their willingness to serve in the Board in writing. To everyone's surprise, at the Board meeting on the 12th May 1999, Dr Dolny informed us that a new Board has been appointed. There was no prior communication by the Minister's Office regarding this matter. For example, Mr Ugandra Naidoo, CA South Africa and others heard at the meeting that they were no longer Board members. That was a serious insult to the integrity of people who served the public so well. In my case, neither the Minister nor anyone in government has informed me of my position at the Land Bank.

It is very clear that there is no appreciation by the Minister of Agriculture and Land Affairs (and hopefully not government) of the sacrifices that the Board has made under difficult circumstances. The worst thing that one can accept is the open practice of racism that the Ministry displays towards black professionals. There is open contempt for the dignity and feelings of the black people despite their preparedness to contribute. If the government does not check Dr Dolny, the problem will soon explode on [sic] everybody's face. She is very insensitive and Mr Hanekom seems to shy away from the problem or maybe he supports her.

I am expressing my feelings on this matter and those of the recently terminated Board members. We would like to get clarity from the government as to why the change of the Board was handled in this manner? We would also like that there be serious attention given to the agriculture sector in this country. At the moment, it is held hostage by secret agendas, racisms, enrichment of friends and disregard for the role the African people can play in this sector. Any attempts by them to participate in the sector are being sabotaged. As for the Land Bank, the government needs to give urgent attention to the mismanagement and callousness that is being practised by the Managing Director with impunity.

Yours faithfully

BONILE JACK
CHAIRPERSON DESIGNATE: LAND BANK

Investigation interrogation

The firm of Edward Nathan & Friedland Inc (ENF) won the informal 'tender' to handle the investigation. In contrast to the Land Bank board's subcommittee comprising three black men, ENF were to field a team of one white woman, one black Indian man, and one black African male candidate attorney, with Professor Michael Katz, white male and one of the firm's senior partners, providing oversight of the team's work.

The approach fostered by the three-person board subcommittee was that I must co-operate with the Katz investigating team. The onus was not on Bonile Jack to come forward and provide proof for his allegations; rather that I must provide my defence of why they were false. This approach, added to the newspaper hype, made me feel as though I was being categorised as guilty unless I could prove my innocence.

In retrospect, my ordeal was only in its first stages. In the days that followed I began to liken myself to a detainee preparing for interrogation. With the help of colleagues and my attorney Pam Stein, I started to assemble a document of thesis proportions, complete with annexures, providing the factual basis to refute the allegations. As best as I was able, I continued to do my work as managing director of the Land Bank, and nudged along the business planning process for the year 2000 that dominated the third quarter of the year. I quickly became exhausted; the benefits of my annual leave obliterated.

In the midst of the preparations for the investigation Minister Didiza asked to meet with me. She was personable, and asked how I was. 'Stressed-out, high blood pressure, as well as other bodily foibles that flare up when I'm stressed,' was my reply. She shared with me an account of her similar experiences, and promised that she would try to ensure rapid progress with the investigation. She then spent the next forty minutes discussing the integrated rural development approach being promoted from the Deputy President's office and said that she'd like me to be part of the policy-making discussions. It felt good to have one hour of being treated humanely, empathetically and as a professional.

'How did your session with the Minister go?' a friend asked.

'I don't know,' I answered truthfully. 'Good, if it was for real. But maybe I was just witness to a politician's Oscar-winning performance.'

The Katz team was clear: they had no powers of compulsion to summons anyone to be questioned. The 'voluntary' nature of presenting myself for 'interrogation' by the team did not make it any easier. It was nerve-racking. I missed sleep, working through nights to prepare the statement that had become ninety-two pages long. There were two separate questioning sessions – a couple of hours on one day, and then a week later there was a marathon eight and a half hour stint interrupted only by a couple of short breaks. During question time I, who am usually articulate with good summary skills, found myself unravelling like a ball of wool. Pam told me to concentrate harder, to focus on the question. 'Don't tell the story. Figure out the point of the question and answer that point,' was her advice. But I was too exhausted, too close to the edge. I felt as though I was gaining a clearer understanding of the accounts I'd read of people breaking down in detention.

Weeks later when I read the transcripts of the sessions, they confirmed for me how much I'd underperformed; I didn't do the best for myself. There were important details that I forgot. When I read the transcripts of the other interviewees, I understood the extent of the flawed process I'd been subjected to. I read one person's transcript and circled 'L' for liar eleven times in the margin. I read another's transcript and pencilled in seven Ls. If this had been a properly instituted disciplinary hearing I would have been listening to these untruths and have had the right for my representative to undertake cross-questioning.

Every night I fell asleep instantly but then woke up three to four hours later, my mind buzzing with the latest additions to the unfolding odyssey. 'You don't have a sleeping problem,' my doctor told me. 'These are anxiety symptoms.'

I also began seriously to consider whether or not I'd been set up. The Katz team handed me a copy of a fax dated 8 April 1999. It was the letter that Jack had referred to at the handover meeting – the one he never sent to the Land Bank, only to some non-executive members of the board. Four months later I had it in my hands for the very first time. It stated that he'd received a 'legal opinion' (no mention from whom) and had now concluded that the decisions taken at the March board meeting went beyond the powers of the board accorded by the Land Bank Act. He proposed that a document should be prepared for the Minister's perusal and 'confirmation'. The penny finally dropped. I'd been puzzled in May by Moloto's insistence that the absence of a briefing document ready to hand was an example of a recalcitrant managing director. Presumably she assumed I knew of Jack's fax – the assumption was wrong. Nor had it ever been faxed to Totsie Memela as general manager of operations. Nor was it ever received by the board secretary for the purpose of complete official records of correspondence. It began to feel too strange to be coincidental.

My nightmare was compounded by the fact that the audio tapes of the March board meeting had mysteriously disappeared from the safe. Those tapes would have been of crucial importance for my representation as to what really happened at the meeting. People's recollections seem to have been subjected either to confusion or revision. Even the official minutes signed off by Bonile Jack as a true reflection of decisions taken were now being challenged. It seemed incredible, in terms of corporate governance, that minutes signed off by the chairperson after having been scrutinised in the presence of board members should later be questioned. Moreover, the board minutes from November 1998 – which included the policy resolution on remuneration – had also disappeared.

The plot thickened. It was the only copy of the resolutions that carried Jack's signature. We found them, inadvertently, when clearing out an office next door to mine that had been unused for ten months. It was difficult to believe that they hadn't been destroyed – everything else seemed to have been so well worked out.

One morning during this time Lettie arrived at work at 6.30 am, to squeeze in an hour of extra time. The collation of documentation to assist Katz had been time consuming and she was behind with her normal work. She found our office doors wide open – both hers and mine – and the filing cabinets in disarray. It seemed she'd interrupted someone; they must have heard the lift arrive. There was no sign of forced entry. Someone had keys. Who was it? What were they looking for?

Statute – a question of interpretation

The Katz team investigation seemed never-ending; the question of authority to implement the changes in salary was the one issue drawing major attention. I'd had Advocate Kügel's verbal input, but now I wanted the crème de la crème of legal opinion, in writing. Bowman Gilfillan approached Chris Loxton, a senior counsel considered an expert on interpretation of statute. His interpretation* set my mind at rest that I had indeed acted within the parameters of the powers granted to me by statute.

Loxton
Land & Agricultural Bank – staff – opinion
26/08/99

Ex-parte: LAND & AGRICULTURAL BANK OF
              SOUTHERN AFRICA   Consultant
In re: APPOINTMENT & REMUNERATION OF STAFF

OPINION

1. My advice has been sought on the proper interpretation of section 13 (2)(c) of the Land Bank Act, 1944 ('*the Act*') and in particular who is empowered to determine the '*remuneration, allowances, subsidies and other service benefits*' of '*staff*' of Consultant.

---

*Annexure 11, High Court Case No. 34457/99.

2. Section 13 provides as follows:

'13. *Appointment of staff* – (1) *The Minister shall appoint a suitable person as managing director of the bank.*

(2) The managing director shall –

(a) be responsible for –

   (i) the management of the day-to-day affairs of the bank, subject to the directions of the board; and
   (ii) administrative control over the staff appointed under paragraph (b);

(b) on such conditions as the board may determine, appoint general managers and other officials or contract with any person to supply such services as may be necessary to perform the work connected with the business of the bank;

(c) be paid and pay staff such remuneration, allowances, subsidies and other service benefits in accordance with a remuneration structure as may be determined from time to time in consultation with the board.'

   . . .

(10) Returning to section 13(2)(c) of the Act, it is in my view clear, by a process of elimination, that the determination of the remuneration structure in accordance with which both the managing director and the staff of the Consultant are to be paid is to be determined by the managing director.

(11) I agree with the views expressed by my instructing attorney in his draft letter to Consultant that logically the board cannot be the entity which is empowered to determine the remuneration structure, since it cannot sensibly consult with itself. Not only is the Minister not mentioned in Section 13(2), but it is in my view clear from section 10 that, as indicated above, the legislature intended that the Minister should determine the remuneration of members of the board but not of the managing director. In my view section 10 is a very powerful indication that the determination of the remuneration structure referred to in section 13(2(c) of the Act does not fall within the powers of the Minister.

(12) The only person who may determine the remuneration structure in terms of section 13(2)(c) of the Act is accordingly by default the managing director. It is true that that conclusion leads to the somewhat questionable position that the managing director determines his or her own remuneration. I agree however with my instructing attorney that the obligation of the managing director to

consult with the Board imposes certain objective limitations upon the remuneration structure which the managing director may determine. The advice of the board in this regard must be seriously considered and the managing director would not be entitled to depart from it materially on the basis of a mere whim or fancy. Furthermore, the managing director's fiduciary duties to the Land Bank would require that the structure determined by him or her should be in accordance with generally accepted criteria.

(13)   There are generally accepted methods by which a particular job size may be evaluated and the appropriate remuneration ranges determined. The discretion of the managing director to determine his or her own pay structure is accordingly limited by certain external and objectively ascertainable criteria.

(14)   In conclusion it is interesting to note that had the legislature intended that the remuneration structure in accordance with which the managing director and the staff of Consultant should be paid be determined by the Minister, it could have adopted provisions which exist in other Acts . . .'

Loxton was clear in his mind about the nature of consultation and the implementing powers of the managing director. His opinion confirmed the position of Kügel, also shared by Van Zyl, the Department of Agriculture's lawyer.

The Katz Report

On 30 August 1999, forty-seven long, drawn-out days since *The Star*'s revelation of selective parts of Jack's letter, Michael Katz, renowned senior partner in the legal firm of ENF, arrived at the Land Bank to address the board of directors on the findings of his investigating team. They had initially undertaken to report by 26 July. I had a dry mouth, cold clammy hands and my nerves were jangling. I made myself breathe deeply and steadied myself to listen to the presentation of the findings.

The whole meeting was tense. The Minister had expressed her dissatisfaction to Chairperson Mkhabela about the Katz team delays, and in turn Mkhabela had responded to enquiries from the press in a manner that blamed the delay on the Katz team. This angered people who had worked against time and late into the nights to finish as quickly as they could. They certainly looked tired and ragged on that Monday. Katz was strong in his diplomatic reprimand towards what he considered to be media indiscretion. He noted that the media comments about not respecting deadlines had been 'hurtful' as the Bank had set the deadlines without consultation. He explained: 'We have not responded in order to protect you. We have defended the dignity of the Bank by not replying.'

Katz introduced the team and then contextualised the report about to be distributed. Jack's letter comprised twelve allegations on which the Katz team had gathered evidence over six weeks. The Katz team – Mohamed Husain, Miranda Feinstein and Christian Ntuta – presented an eighty-five page report on their considerations.

They reviewed the Terms of Reference that required them to establish the facts concerning each of the allegations and to make recommendations. The conditions that had circumscribed their investigation were set out. The investigating team

> had no powers of compulsion . . . In view of the nature of the process and the time constraints imposed upon the investigating team by the Land Bank, the investigating team determined that it would merely put questions to witnesses who came to present evidence in order to clarify facts but would not undertake any cross-examination of those witnesses nor permit any cross-examination to be undertaken by any of the other witnesses nor Jack. The investigating team felt that it was vital that the process be such that there would be no right of witnesses to demand to be allowed access to evidence provided by other witnesses nor to counter any allegations made by other witnesses, nor to demand the right to cross-examine any witnesses. To do otherwise would have resulted in having to conduct a trial. This was not what the mandate required.*

The limitations applied to everyone interviewed, including myself and my legal representatives. The Katz team noted that: 'Each of the board members interviewed by the investigating team confirmed that the Jack letter was entirely his own initiative and had not been done in conjunction with any of them. Many of the matters raised in the Jack letter had never been raised in any form at board meetings and are only raised in certain cases years after the events. Some of the matters were raised at board meetings and disposed of.'

As a preamble to the presentation of their 'findings' the Katz team explained the possibility of imperfections in their 'findings'.

> The investigating team, as set out below, has made findings but with some diffidence, because: –
>
> • of conflicts in the evidence presented to the investigating team;
>
> • of the fact that a non-adversarial process was adopted, no cross-

---

*Katz Report 1999, Section 4.7, p.6.

examination was permitted, not all allegations were put to all witnesses etc;

- the critical minutes of the March and May board meetings are defective;
- tape recordings which could have clarified exactly what was decided at these critical March and May board meetings are either missing or were not made;
- the handwritten notes of the critical March and May board meetings were thrown away by Pienaar after she prepared the minutes;
- most, if not all, of the witnesses interviewed had unclear recollections of many material issues and tended to blur the March and May board meetings and matters which arose subsequent in time.
- The findings have of necessity in the circumstances had to be made based on a preponderance of the evidence given to the investigating team and the probabilities having regard to documentary evidence made available to the investigating team.
- Against this background the investigating team had the agonising task of making findings and recommendations which the investigating team fully realises are of great importance to the Land Bank and the lives and reputations of the individuals concerned.
- The investigating team was not required to make conclusive findings. Its mandate required an investigation of specific issues raised in the Jack letter. Where, therefore, this report refers to the 'findings' of the investigation team, this must be understood within the context of the mandate and the procedure followed. Such 'findings' as have been made were purely for purposes of making recommendations.*

ALLEGATION 1: Dolny fall-out with the Board and secret agendas in the Ministry†

The Jack letter alleged: 'I strongly believe that the Board has had a fall-out with Dr Dolny and Mr Hanekom because we were not prepared to be rubber stamps for secret agendas that are prevalent in that Ministry.'

The Katz team interviewed two executive board members (myself and Memela) and five non-executive members: Jack, Cronje, Moloto, Naidoo and Philip. Michel and Matthews were not available.

The Katz 'findings' noted: 'Each board member interviewed by the investigating team, other than Jack, was strongly of the view that not only was the board not a rubber stamp'; on the contrary, it was asserted

---

*Katz Report 1999, Sections 8.1 to 8.5.
†Katz Report 1999, Sections 11.1.3, 11.1.4, 11.1.8, 11.2.2, and 11.2.3.

that the board 'had played a very active and vital role in giving strategic guidance to the Land Bank on a monthly basis at a critical time for the Land Bank when it was involved in a very difficult and traumatic process of transformation'. Moreover, 'board meetings were characterised by long and lively debates'. Some non-executive members described me as headstrong and as having 'refused on occasion to heed independent and considered advice from the non-executive directors'.

With regard to the allegation of 'secret agendas': 'No evidence was placed before the investigating team to demonstrate any secret agendas in the Ministry involving Dolny. The investigating team finds that there was disagreement on a number of occasions at professional level between Dolny and representatives of the Ministry, including the Minister, specifically regarding the requirement of the Ministry that that Land Bank take over the business of the defunct Agricultural Credit Board.'

With regard to the fall-out between the non-executive directors and executive directors concerning the disciplinary case of Mokuena, the Katz team found that 'once the matter had been referred to the board (and this was done by Dolny, notwithstanding that she might not have been obliged in fact to refer it) Dolny ought not to have disregarded the advice of the board and unilaterally consulted the Minister without first clearing that with the board.' In mitigation, 'The investigating team finds that Dolny was acting in the best interests of the Land Bank in seeking to avoid setting an unacceptable precedent by making an extremely large settlement payment to Mokuena after only 4 months of service with the Land Bank.'

ALLEGATION 2: Poor working relationship with Ministry officials affecting business with black farmers*

The Jack letter alleged: 'On the day of the visit by these two senior agriculture officials, Dr Dolny did not hide her hatred for the two (Deputy Minister, Ms Thoko Didiza and the Director General, Ms Bongi Njobe-Mbuli). After they had left the meeting the Board expressed its displeasure to Dr Dolny at the tensions that would prevent the Land Bank and the department from working together.'

The Katz 'findings' with regard to the alleged display of 'hatred' state: 'No other board member can recall this behaviour on the part of Dolny. Some board members indicated that there may have been some tension between Dolny and officials from the Ministry, but do not believe that

---

*Katz Report 1999, Section 11.1.6.

this affected the operations of the Land Bank.' With regard to the alleged 'board displeasure', the investigating team found that 'The minutes of the board meeting do not reflect any such censure. Dolny says there was no such censure. None of the other directors who were interviewed . . . and who attended that meeting namely Cronje, Philip, Moloto and Memela specifically remembers any such censure or expression of displeasure.'

Furthermore Jack alleged: 'The Land Bank and the department have not worked together and, as a result, farmers who are supposed to be served have suffered severely.' The investigating team found that 'No person interviewed supported this allegation nor was any evidence adduced in support of it.'

ALLEGATION 3: Board inundated by complaints of racist treatment by staff, the 'flushing out' of black managers, and appointment of white employees despite lack of qualifications because they are allegedly members of a liberal clique*

At his interview Jack named employees Colvin, Richer and De Klerk as the three employees allegedly without appropriate qualifications.

The Katz team considered the allegations of racism and 'flushing out of black managers' on my part. The team observed that 'allegations of racism which are unfounded' are 'equally undermining of an organisation' (as is the racism itself); that 'the Board was not inundated with complaints of racist treatment by Dolny of black staff'; that certain complaints made were not instances of racism and that it was irresponsible of Jack to portray them as such; that the investigating team could not find that I was actuated by racism; that while there were still pockets of racism in the Bank, I was not the cause of, nor did I support this.

'It goes without saying that racism in any organisation is unacceptable but the more so in a parastatal, the shareholder of which has directed it to transform from a bastion of white apartheid to reflect the policies enshrined in the constitution.'

'Jack's use of Matsapola as an example of Dolny "flushing" black managers out of the Land Bank was unjustified and improper in view of the board's decision that this was not an instance of racism. It would have been setting a very poor precedent in the Land Bank were an employee such as Matsapola to have been retained. The investigating team finds that it was irresponsible of Jack to rely on the example of

---

*Katz Report 1999, Sections 13.1 and 13.2.

Khoza as an instance of Dolny "flushing out" black managers.' Khoza was an employee on a one-year contract; he took up a job promotion in Mpumalanga.

Evidence was presented that I was *'equally tough with white as well as with black employees'*. With regard to a certain employee, Masekela, the Katz team found me to have been *'highly insensitive'* and that there were times when my behaviour may have been *'misconstrued as racism'*, that some of the employees who had left the Bank were so embittered that they were unwilling to accept plausible explanations for some of the events that had occurred. The Katz team mentioned a witness who said he didn't find me *'difficult'* or *'racist'* but then on reflection said I was a *'very subtle racist'*. Another witness made a statement to the effect that, no, he'd never found me racist but *'naïve'*.

It's terrible to read pages and pages of conclusions about oneself based on evidence that one didn't hear, that one didn't have the possibility to cross-question. In particular, whilst acknowledging that I made mistakes, the Masekela incident is not one that stands out for me in my private *mea culpa* listings. Unbeknown to me, Mokuena had told Masekela to attend a strategic management team getaway. I disagreed that a person in an acting capacity should join the event. I would counter that the situation had been manoeuvred and manipulated by Mokuena who was angry about a counselling process she had been asked to partake in.

With regard to my having employed white people who supposedly did not have appropriate qualifications, the Katz team 'finding' was that 'Jack was unable to give any details as to why these people were not suitably qualified . . . or why they were members of a liberal clique.' I was able to cite the qualifications and the appropriateness of the previous experience of all three employees as the basis for their appointments.

ALLEGATION 4: *Appointment of friends as consultants in a clandestine manner, and paid exorbitant amounts of money**

The Jack letter alleged: 'Appointment of consultants has been biased toward white professionals some of whom are expatriates. These people have been appointed in a clandestine manner and paid exorbitant amounts of money. The 1997/1998 Auditor General's Office raised a query on this matter in their report.'

---

*Katz Report 1999, Sections 13.2.12 and 13.2.13.

The Katz 'finding': 'The investigating team finds that there is no evidence that the appointment of consultants was done in a clandestine manner. The investigating team finds that where a tender process took place, the fees by definition must have been market related.'

They recorded: 'Dolny indicated that in regard to all the overseas consultants, she negotiated their standard rates downwards, quite significantly in certain cases . . . Dolny has furnished an extract from the report of the Auditor General which reports that the consultants are mainly appointed by Dolny which is in line with the powers delegated to her by the Land Bank.

'The Auditor General recommended that more than one person should be involved in monitoring performance of consultants and that there should be a formal tendering process although the Auditor General recognised that tender processes could not usually be used successfully for specialist consultants.

'Dolny confirmed that following the recommendation of the Auditor General consultants are now required to give overviews as different sections of their work are completed. It is also clear that Deloitte & Touche, the external auditors of the Land Bank, performed a due diligence exercise in regard to the appointment of consultants.'

The investigating team found that 'Jack never raised the issues that the appointment of consultants was racially biased or that they were paid exorbitant fees at any board meeting.' Furthermore, 'no evidence was placed before it which suggested any impropriety in racial mix of the consultants appointed by the Land Bank. There is no indication from any of the board members . . . that there was any concern about the appointment of consultants.'

ALLEGATION 5: Limited size of loan book to black farmers*

The Jack letter alleged: 'Of the R11 billion loan book of the Land Bank, only about R56 million has been allocated to black farmers. We have raised concerns as the Board regarding this problem without any co-operation from management.'

The Katz 'finding' after perusing the figures on the changes to the Bank's business and the numbers of new black clients was that 'there is no basis for the inference that the Land Bank is not making proper allocations of resources to black farmers.'

---

*Katz Report 1999, Section 13.2.14.

ALLEGATION 6: *Racism in the Land Bank branches**

The Jack letter alleged: 'The problem relates to racism at the Land Bank branches, and there have been complaints regarding this matter. Dr Dolny's response has always been to blame the victims.'

The Katz team found that 'steps were instituted by Dolny to eradicate racism at branch level but it is inevitable that this will take time in view of the history of the Land Bank.'

ALLEGATION 7: *Legitimacy of loan to Rutec*†

The Jack letter alleged: 'Recently, a company called Rutec was advanced a loan of about R10 million by the Land Bank although it does not meet the criteria. The bank went further to buy equity in the company. This is not provided for in the policies and procedures of the institution.'

The evidence presented to Katz clarified that no loan had ever been made to a company called Rutec. The loan referred to was in fact made to the Mineworkers' Development Agency (MDA), a not for profit non-governmental organisation set up by the National Union of Mineworkers, to create rural jobs for redundant mineworkers.

The Katz team 'finding' was that 'the Act in general concerning the usages to which the funds of the Land Bank could be put is on the face of it extremely wide . . . There seems to be no limitation in the Act that investments can only be made in companies etc. involved in the agricultural industry. Accordingly the investigating team finds that even though Rutec may not have been predominantly an agricultural business, the Land Bank was probably entitled to invest in it.' And finally, 'although the Act permitted equity investments to be made by the Land Bank and no criteria in this regard had been formulated, the board of directors was willing for these proposals to be considered by management.' The minute of the board meeting of 24 November 1998 is referred to as support for this statement.

ALLEGATION 8: *Award of Rutec loan: as a further demonstration of racism*‡

The Jack letter alleged: 'An application by BAASA Holdings (Pty) Ltd (an empowerment company) was declined BY Dr Dolny on the grounds that

---

*Katz Report 1999, Section 13.2.15.
†Katz Report 1999, Sections 13.2.18 to 13.2.20.
‡Katz Report 1999, Section 13.2.17.

I was a director in that company. In the case of Rutec, they advanced the loan and equity for R10 million despite the fact that there was a Board member in that deal who happened to be white. Racism reared its ugly head in this case.'

The Katz team found that Section 21(2) of the Act 'would prohibit a loan by the Land Bank to BAASA whilst Jack was a director of both' and accordingly 'there is no substance in the allegation by Jack regarding the loan application made by BAASA.'

It was further verified that a loan was granted to MDA whose CEO was Kate Philip – the white member of the Land Bank board referred to by Jack. There had been doubts about whether Section 21(2) was applicable in the case of the MDA loan application; Kate Philip was not a shareholder of MDA and did not stand to benefit personally. Legal opinion was solicited.

The Katz team did 'not necessarily agree with the opinion furnished to Dolny by Kügel in regard to the position of Philip as a director of both the Land Bank and the MDA, but finds that Dolny was entitled to rely on that opinion.'

ALLEGATION 9: *Nepotism in award of grant to the KwaZulu Natal Poultry Institute: Refusal of grant to NAFU**

The Jack letter alleged: 'The Poultry Institute at the University of Natal was given a grant by the Land Bank of more than R300 000.00 whilst NAFU was flatly refused assistance. On investigation, the Board discovered that Dr Dolny's former husband runs the Institute and she never declared the matter.'

'With regard to Jack's allegation that an investigation had been required to uncover nepotism on the part of Dolny in relation to the grant awarded to the Poultry Institute', the Katz team found that 'there had never been such investigation as referred to by Jack.' The team discovered that the minute of the board meeting of 25 November 1997 'reflects the fact that the grant to the Poultry Institute had to be ratified by the board because of the size of the grant and that it was so ratified. The minute further reflects a "recusal because of possible conflict of interests: Dr Dolny-KwaZulu/Natal Poultry Institute".'

The team found 'that it was highly improper of Jack to make an allegation that it required a board investigation to discover that Dolny's

---

*Katz Report 1999, Sections 14.1.2 to 14.1.6 and 14.2.2 to 14.2.4.

former husband runs the Poultry Institute and that she never declared the interest. On the contrary Jack was at the meeting when the disclosure was made. When Jack gave evidence he acknowledged this . . . Dolny's (former) husband does not run the Poultry Institute but is an employee. The investigating team further finds that there was no impropriety in the making of the grant to the Poultry Institute; it was precisely the kind of institution to which it was normal for the Bank to award a grant.'

The membership of NAFU (National African Farmers' Union) comprises black entrepreneurs. With regard to Jack's allegation that there had been a flat refusal to award grant money to NAFU, the Katz team recorded: 'Evidence was produced to the investigating team that several grants were made to NAFU namely R150 000.00 in May 1998, R25 000.00 in November 1998 . . . and R96 000.00 in March 1999. In addition Dolny advised that NAFU affiliates . . . were given grants over a period totalling R60 000.00.'

The Katz team concluded that 'Jack's allegation that NAFU was flatly refused assistance was completely without substance and improper in the circumstances.'

ALLEGATION 10: Mismanagement: Unilateral decision to make posts redundant thus incurring liability of R33 million *

The Jack letter alleged: 'Dr Dolny unilaterally decided to advertise the twenty-five (25) Branch Managers' posts at the Land Bank . . . nineteen (19) incumbents were declared redundant. The case went to arbitration and . . . we were expected to pay R33 million towards settlement.'

The Katz team recorded: 'Dolny and many of the directors interviewed stated that the transformation of the Land Bank, which was a bastion of apartheid, was an extremely difficult and trying process.

'Dolny was expected to accelerate the transformation of the Land Bank, inter alia by having a more balanced staff complement. Bearing in mind that prior to the transformation process the staff complement of the Land Bank was almost exclusively white male, it would have been impossible for her to achieve this transformation objective without advertising these posts in order to bring in black employees.'

The Katz 'finding' was that: 'the impression that Jack gives in paragraph 7 of the Jack letter that it was Dolny's conduct which resulted in a case being brought against the Land Bank to claim R33 000 000.00 of damages is an unfair impression and not factually correct. The

---

*Katz Report 1999, Sections 14.1.8 and 14.2.5.

investigating team finds there was no impropriety or mismanagement on the part of Dolny.'

ALLEGATION 11: Mismanagement: Retrenchment at the time of elections*

The Jack letter alleged: 'The restructuring process of the head office has led to the retrenchment of about 250 of the 370 employees there. Of the 250 about 100 are from the cleaning staff and members of SACCAWU. We argued as the Board against the timing of this move (in May) just before the elections.'

The Katz team 'finding' was that: 'The factual allegations made by Jack are not correct in many respects. The investigating team finds that in view of the transformation imperative which was a policy decision of the Ministry which the board was mandated to carry out, Dolny had no choice but to implement retrenchments. The investigating team finds that the board impliedly authorised this in January 1999. The investigating team finds that the board was incorrect in this instance to allow the election process to become a consideration in regard to the operations of the Land Bank.'

ALLEGATION 12: Salary increases – Insistence that Ministerial approval not a prerequisite†

The Jack letter alleged: 'At the meeting of 24th March 1999 . . . management tabled a proposal for salary adjustments of everyone including themselves. The salaries of the top management were to go up by an average of 80%. Dr Dolny's salary, for example, was going to go up from R630 000.00 to R1 411 000.00 (123% increase) with immediate effect . . . We also argued that the Minister, according to the Land Bank Act, appoints the Managing Director and the General Managers and their salaries are therefore the responsibility of the Minister and Cabinet. She was insisting that the Minister and the Cabinet have no role in this matter and that we should approve the increments.'

The Katz team recorded that: 'Dolny sent a memorandum to Toms on 10 March 1999 regarding decision-making powers concerning remuneration. Dolny referred to section 13(2)(c) of the Act in her memorandum.

---

*Katz Report 1999, Section 14.2.6.
†Katz Report 1999, Sections 11.1.4 and 11.1.16.6-7, 11.2.10, 11.2.4, 11.2.12.1 and 11.3.8.

She stated in that memorandum that she considered section 13(2)(c) of the Act to be "clear and unambiguous" [based on the legal advice given by Kügel]. Section 13(2)(c) of the Act provides *inter alia* that the managing director shall "be paid and pay staff such remuneration, allowances, subsidies and other service benefits . . . as may be determined from time to time in consultation with the board".'

The Katz team further noted: 'The board ultimately agreed in view of the insistence by the executive directors as to the necessity for urgency regarding the top 6, despite their concerns that the benchmark was inappropriate, to use the PE lower quartile as the reference point for the salary adjustments for the top 6.'

Furthermore, 'It was agreed that Dolny would prepare a motivation as to the levels at which the increases for the top 6 would be pitched. This motivation was to be taken by Jack and Dolny to the Minister.' The Katz team recorded that there was no agreement among the directors interviewed as to the purpose of the motivation. 'Dolny and Toms understood it to be for information only whilst the non-executive directors understood it to be the basis upon which the Minister would make his decision.'

The respective powers of the Managing Director, the Board of Directors and the Minister was what Jack put in question in a fax which he shared selectively with some board members – prior to his drafting his letter to the then Deputy President Thabo Mbeki. When the matter arose at the gathering of old and new board members in May 1999, Jack referred to his fax of 8 April – but no copy had ever been received by either the executive directors or the board secretary, and as no one present had a copy the discussion was curtailed. Jack promised to fax a copy immediately but failed to do so. Memela and I advised the Katz team that we had never seen that fax prior to a copy being shown to us by the team.

The investigating team found that 'Dolny's recollection of the decision at the May board meeting as well as the minute of the May board meeting are not correct in view of the independent evidence namely the fax of 8 April 1999 addressed by Jack to the board members (other than Memela) and the letter sent by Moloto on 28 June 1999 to the then Minister. The investigating team finds that it is probable that the directors resolved that the approval of the Minister to the increases in salaries of the top 6 had to be obtained. However even if this is not the case bearing in mind that there is no tape recording or contemporaneous note of what was said at the May board meeting and bearing in mind that there are conflicting views between Toms and Dolny on the one hand and the non-executive directors on the other as to what was decided at the May board meeting, at the least the investigating team finds that it was clear to Dolny that there were serious misgivings on the part of the non-executive directors regarding the implementation of the salary increases for the top 6 which had been voiced at two consecutive board meetings, and that it was incumbent on a managing director in view of those serious misgivings, as a matter of good corporate governance, not to have implemented such salary increases, particularly her own, without again raising the matter at a board meeting and getting clear instructions in that regard.'

'The investigating team is of the opinion that the provisions of section 13(2)(c) of the Act are not so clear and unambiguous as considered by Dolny. The section permits the managing director to determine her own salary in consultation with the board. There is a dearth of case law interpreting the phrase "in consultation". In the view of the investigating team, the correct legal interpretation of this section is that the managing director has to agree the levels of remuneration with the board. The position would have been different had the section referred to "after consultation" instead of "in consultation". Accordingly the managing director did not have the authority alone to make a decision after having heard the board's views on the issue of remuneration.'

Hence the Katz team concludes, 'on a proper interpretation of the provisions of section 13(2)(c) of the Act Dolny did not have the authority unilaterally to determine the remuneration of the top 6 but instead required the approval of the board'.

The Katz team's recommendation regarding this one outstanding allegation was: 'No further implementation of the salary increases instructed by Dolny in regard to the top 6 should occur until the board has determined the salary increases in consultation with Dolny.'

Acknowledgement*

The investigating team acknowledged that 'the incidents which form the basis of the investigation took place at a very difficult time in the history and transformation of the Land Bank specifically and the country in general. A number of (persons interviewed) referred to the very hostile environment which came overwhelmingly from the old guard white staff, because of Dolny's marriage to Joe Slovo and her political affiliations. Thus it was not simply "business as usual". This in itself gave rise to very difficult complications of a human and personal nature.'

---

*Katz Report 1999, Sections 13.2.3.1 and 13.2.3.2, and 13.2.4, and 13.1.2, and 8.6.

'The Land Bank has over the last two years been through a cataclysmic conversion from:–

an almost wholly white organisation committed to serving only the interest of white farmers to an organisation with a mission to set right the injustices of the past perpetrated on black farmers;

a bureaucratic state organisation run without any appreciation of business principles into one run on the same principles as a private sector bank.'

They elaborated: 'Such a conversion cannot be achieved overnight, nor cannot [sic] it be achieved without intense pain being suffered. The incumbent white employees of the Land Bank naturally felt threatened that their jobs would be lost to black employees and found it difficult to change their philosophical outlook which had been the previous apartheid mission of the Land Bank. Black employees came into an organisation which was at the least suspicious of them, their motives and capabilities and at worst distinctly hostile. Aside from this, these employees now had to run the Land Bank on economic principles, which in itself was a dramatic and revolutionary concept. This alone would have resulted in difficult and trying times for management. Dolny's position was indeed an invidious one – both the white employees and the black employees unsure of their own standing in the organisation considered her to be biased towards the other group; she had to balance the demands of the Ministry that the Land Bank be run both as a commercial organisation and at the same time fund black farmers who were not always able to meet the credit risk requirements which a commercially run bank would have imposed; the transformation had to be carried out as a matter of urgency; and finally it cannot be lost sight of that Dolny was introduced to head up an organisation which had always been the exclusive domain of male managers. The difficulties faced by her from traditionalists unwilling to have a woman as a boss cannot be overlooked.

'From the evidence presented the investigating team finds that Dolny, in the most trying circumstances, with the backing of a very supportive board did an effective job in the transformation process of the Land Bank . . . In general considerable progress seems to have been made in the transformation of the Land Bank and this is to the credit of the parties involved.'

Following Michael Katz's conclusion of his overview of the report, there was a question-and-answer session between the board members and the

Katz team. Katz was asked: 'How should this process be taken forward?' He responded that a basic challenge was to ensure the truth should out to avoid the 'damage that rumour-mongering is creating'. He spoke of the need to 'manage an effective healing process' and strongly advocated: 'Get this out of the minds of the public. Straighten the record.' With regard to the salary issue, the recommendation was for the new board to reconsider the matter.

I asked if there was any basis for a disciplinary inquiry. The answer was 'No.' Modise asked Katz if the report was 'judicially defensible' and later said that the board members should be careful to reserve the right to question the Katz conclusions. Katz reiterated that they had tried to draw up recommendations that were constructive, and decisions needed to be made in the best interests of the Bank. He noted that the team might have erred in one way or another; no one, he noted, could 'profess a monopoly on wisdom'. Clearly the 'findings' of the inquiry did not have the benefit of a judiciary process involving a public hearing and the opportunity for cross questioning.

'Cruel, wicked and improper'

I was taken aback by the lack of equivocation on the part of the Katz team with regard to the salary increases. Notwithstanding some factual inaccuracies in their report, their confidence in their own interpretation of statute seemed misplaced when it differed so radically from that of Loxton, the country's renowned legal specialist in the field of statute.

I felt they should also have considered the possibility of a set up. On the basis of their own investigation, they had rejected eleven of the twelve allegations made by Jack. They had found him culpable of distorting facts and making improper accusations – clearly an unreliable witness. There was a host of other considerations that were cause for concern – who removed the tapes of the March board meeting about which there was such controversy, and divergence in recall. Was it not oddly coincident that the November board documentation containing the new remuneration policy also went missing? Was it not an overly strange coincidence that the three persons in the Land Bank head office who should have been recipients of the Jack fax of 8 April never received it?

Other facts had also been discounted. What about the letter from the Minister on the appointment of Totsie Memela which clearly indicated his awareness of the impending change in salaries? What about the briefing pack provided to the new Minister within days of her appointment but which her officials had failed to read?

And surely I had proven that I took the 'serious misgivings' very seriously indeed in that I implemented salary increases for the strategic management team only at the lower quartile level as per the March 1999 board resolution. Up to then all board discussions had focused on the need for a consistent remuneration strategy; the board had broken with this and I had respected their decision. If I had gone ahead and implemented the executive increases on the median level, disregarding the March 1999 board resolution, then I would accept that I had indeed failed to heed 'serious misgivings'. But this was not so. I had, moreover, carefully instituted an objective performance evaluation process as the basis on which to set the final level of the remuneration of executive management.

Within a few days of the Katz team delivering their report, two newspapers carried stories based on leaks. The *Business Day* article headed 'Report clears Dolny's name' drew accurately on the Katz text. In contrast, *The Star** ran a story, once again written by Prince Hamnca, stating that Dolny 'is expected to face an internal disciplinary inquiry'. Prince, it seemed, had a line to a deep throat who was a step ahead of the board.

A *Business Day* journalist[†] commented that '*The Star*'s consistent negative bias in its coverage, by a black journalist apparently guided by a senior with a strong black consciousness background, smelt more and more strongly of an anti-Dolny vendetta. This was at its most glaring when the paper reported Katz's exoneration of the Land Bank MD on the main charges in a smallish story near the bottom of the front page, after earlier stories were splashed in page one leads. From the report's almost exclusive focus on findings unflattering to Dolny, it was hard to fathom why Katz should have cleared her at all.' I was advised to contact a defamation lawyer, and that 'Anyone can see there's real malice.'

The actions of *The Star*'s 'source close to the Bank' went against the advice of the Katz team that an 'effective healing process' had to be managed. One of the team bumped into one of the board members on the morning that *The Star*'s article suggested a disciplinary inquiry had been recommended. The team member referred to the article as 'cruel, wicked and improper'.

It was suggested that the board chairperson should issue a statement to stem the conjecture. Mkhabela's response was: 'The Board has not formed an opinion. The Board of Directors has not yet finished its deliberations on the report. Any press reports at this time are purely speculative.' And that was the public status quo of my fate for several weeks to come.

---

*P Hamnca, 'Dolny set to face internal investigation', *The Star*, 1 September 1999.
[†]D Forrest, 'Nonracial politics suffers a blow', *Business Day*, 7 September 1999.

NINE

THE NIGHT OF THE LONG KNIVES

Accentuate the negative: eliminate the positive

I got many congratulatory phone calls from people who understood that the Katz team had cleared me, but *The Star* report suggesting that I would be facing a disciplinary hearing was unsettling. The board had not reached such a conclusion, so from where was this line being pushed? Was this the thinking behind the scenes in the ministerial office, with Masiphula Mbongwa as the messenger on the board subcommittee now mandated to follow through on the Katz report? Both Dave Gillam, the industrial relations consultant, and my attorney Pam Stein consoled me with the advice that if a decision was reached to go ahead with a disciplinary hearing (regarding my implementation of the salary increase of which the Katz team had been critical), it would provide the proper process through which to clear my name. I would have the chance to be represented, to call and cross-examine witnesses – which had not been possible in the Katz process.

The board subcommittee agreed with the Minister that they would prepare a summary of the Katz report and propose the actions to be taken. Two weeks later they presented their first draft to a sitting of the full board. What we were given to read was a lesson in the art of butchery. They had undertaken the most skilful deboning, filleting job possible, with the intention to accentuate the negative and eliminate the positive. They indeed recommended a disciplinary hearing with regard to the salary increase implementation. The press release they prepared was remarkable – the praise embedded in the Katz report was ignored. The statement recorded the need to 'root out remaining pockets of racism', 'deal with misconduct', 'repair and enhance corporate governance' and 'accelerate the process of transformation' – not a word of criticism of Jack, not a word of acknowledgement for achievements.*

The suggestion to *'accelerate* transformation' was written from a position of ignorance. The subcommittee members were all new board directors. They had not yet taken the time either to learn the Bank's business or to familiarise themselves with the crazy pace of trans-formation under the guidance of the previous board. All of the 'transformation board' members, except Jack, had spoken to Katz about the speed and difficulty of transformation. The pace of change we'd attempted had threatened systems – how was it possible to go any faster?

It was frustrating to witness the acquiescence of the majority of board members who I knew were unhappy with the selectivity and tone of the statements as well as the proposed course of action. Katz had spoken about the need to be constructive, and the 'management of an effective healing process' as the necessary next step. This advice was being blatantly ignored.

'Why do you go along with this?' I asked some of them. 'Why do you allow this subcommittee to be so overwhelmingly powerful?'

'Because when they speak, it is as if they speak with the voice of the Minister,' was the answer. When the Land Bank received the itemised invoice from the law firm the frequent consultation over the weeks between the lawyer Jerry Kaapu and Mbongwa, the Minister's deputy director general, confirmed him as the main driver on the board's subcommittee.

However, it seemed the Minister had some doubts about the proposed disciplinary hearing. She replied to the board within two days on 8 September, then fifty-six days since *The Star*'s release of the Jack letter. Her reply, in a letter† addressed to the chairperson Sam Mkhabela, recorded her reservations:

> Thank you for your report on the above matter. I have studied carefully both the actual report and your proposed actions. It is however not clear for me what you as the Board are recommending on the overall findings, bearing in mind that the investigation of Katz was conducted in a manner that is restrictive and severely qualified by themselves.
>
> This may have an influence on the weight to be given to both the factual findings as well as the recommendations of the Katz report. This is

---

*Media Release by board of directors of the Land Bank, 10 September 1999.
†T Didiza, 1999, Annexure 13, High Court Case No. 34457/99.

especially true with regard to the question whether disciplinary proceedings regarding the implementation of the salary increases must be instituted. In this regard I would appreciate hearing from you how you suggest motivating and formulating the charges for instituting disciplinary proceedings. I must emphasise that I am of the opinion that applicable labour law must be followed scrupulously in this regard . . .

I would appreciate a response not later than Monday the 13th of September 1999.

Mondays 13, 20, and 27 September came and went, as did the Mondays of 4, 11, 18 and 25 October. There was no formal board subcommittee response to the Minister to the knowledge of the rest of the directors. The question 'What, if anything, was to happen?' hung suspended in mid-air.

Low intensity warfare

Those few weeks were a torturous limbo period. As for the proposed disciplinary hearing, nothing happened. Nothing at all. Mkhabela announced that he was taking up a position as human resources manager for the African region at the company 3M, and that he would have little time available for board activities. To start with, he absolutely refused to meet anyone for the next two weeks of his new job – his overseas bosses were to be in town. It set a tone for a board that rapidly became non-functional. Board subcommittee meetings were called off at the last minute because late cancellations meant they would not be quorate. This was demoralising for board members who'd spent several hours travelling in from the provinces to attend.

But the limbo period was also a period of attrition. Several proposals put forward by the executive directors were obstructed, and the obstruction was undermining of both confidence and operations.

A resolution to resume settlement negotiations with the Banking Council concerning our preferential creditor status was rejected. The legal opinion that I'd received advised me of the unconstitutionality of the clause and that we would probably lose at the constitutional court – in fact a challenge to a similar provision in the statutes of the North West Agricultural Bank succeeded.

The request for a board of directors' strategy statement was ignored week after week even though the three executive directors pleaded that this was of crucial importance. The new Minister avoided a policy statement opportunity when she failed to attend the main session of the presentation of the 1998 Annual Report. She arrived only when the media had departed. Later she made a statement in passing at a major public meeting, the Agricultural Job Summit in October 1999, that the mandate of the Land Bank needed to change, but without spelling out how. Such statements were unsettling for our investors. In the absence of a clear policy and strategy commitment from the board, combined with the ministerial comments, investors were showing signs of reticence in buying Land Bank paper on the money market. The irony was that whilst we were now heading for the best ever financial results in the Bank's history, our treasury department was nervous and forecast a cash flow shortage. We were a bank, but we were about to run out of money to lend.*

There was an executive management resolution concerning the liquidation of the Northern Transvaal Cooperative (NTC) that needed a decision from the board. It was technically insolvent. We were losing hundreds of thousands of rands in unpaid interest. We had spent months giving them time to draw up a resuscitation plan, but a convincing proposal had not emerged. If another creditor were to step in before us, we would lose the right to appoint the liquidator of our choosing. We wanted that choice; it was important to salvage maximum value and look for empowerment opportunities for the parts of the NTC business that were in fact a going concern. The chairperson did not seem to understand either the basis for or the urgency of the decision.

Then there was the most bizarre discussion about the advisory nature of the relationship between the board and the executive directors. During the tenure of the transformation board I had on occasion asked for their advice even on a managerial matter that fell within my decision-making competence. I had valued the board's input. The new board's ruling was that if the managing director requested advice, the board's conclusion should be regarded as an instruction and acted upon as such. This was notwithstanding that the request might be on a matter not requiring consultation according to the delegation of powers.

I protested: 'If one is going to be obliged to follow advice as if an order has been given, surely that will make one think twice about asking for advice in the first place?'

'Precisely. If you don't want to follow advice as an instruction, then don't ask for it' was the outcome of this discussion.

I began to feel that the foundations were being laid for a culture of

---

*D Greybe, 'Saga must end, Land Bank is told: Short-term paper no longer highly sought after in money market, says financial adviser', *Business Day*, 14 October 1999.

subordination; the executive directors would be subordinate to the non-executive directors. So much for the King recommendations on a unitary board as the best approach to corporate governance!

Meeting after meeting scheduled for the board subcommittee on remuneration was cancelled. This exacerbated another problem: our urgent need to fill the vacant post of information technology manager. We were paying expensive consultancy fees, and for many other reasons wanted an employee, not a consultant, in place. But we could not proceed without addressing the suspended resolution on the salary levels for the top six positions.

The cancellation of meetings was chronic. I began to be concerned about what the Auditor General would say about corporate governance when the external audit completed their review of the functioning of the board committees. Whilst the board subcommittee dealing with the Katz report mouthed words about the need 'to repair and enhance corporate governance and to speed up transformation', our de facto experience of the new board's malfunctioning was itself a travesty of corporate governance.

Unbearable suspense

Was this a concerted attrition process meant to push me to the wall to hand in my resignation? And what about the threat of the disciplinary hearing hanging over me? The Minister's request for a reply by 13 September remained unanswered. Was this a psychological approach that was meant to wear me down?

Would there or would there not be a disciplinary hearing? One morning I received a phone call from a *Business Day* journalist. 'I don't want to talk to you about the Katz report or anything. I know you're banned from speaking – but I've got some news for you that should make you feel happier. We've been trying to get a statement from the Minister for the whole of the last month since the Katz report was submitted. There's been no response to a repeated number of calls. So we got fed up, sent a fax that we would be writing a story on their lack of response. This morning the Minister's spokesperson phoned to say that the Minister is ready to issue a statement. You'll be delighted to know that they are not going ahead with the disciplinary hearing. But the Minister's in a cabinet meeting now, and afterwards she's seeing Mbeki. The spokesperson indicated that he would confirm everything later today.'

Early that evening I got another phone call from the same journalist. 'Very strange. The Minister's spokesperson withdrew everything that was said to me in the morning. It seems that the discussion with Mbeki has changed things. If the disciplinary hearing goes ahead then it seems he's partial to this course of action.'

Still nothing happened. The suspense was unbearable. On 15 October 1999, some thirty-eight days since the subcommittee handed in their report to the Minister, and some ninety-three days since Jack's letter was published, I asked Pam Stein to write to the board attorneys. In my mind the uncertainty I had to contend with, drawn out over an unreasonable length of time, amounted to an unfair labour practice. The letter* spelt out my predicament fairly and squarely:

> In many respects, the inaction of the Board over the past five weeks, and the complete failure of the Board to state to employees of the Bank and the public in general, that our client has been cleared, has had the result of placing our client in a position where:
> > rumours abound concerning her and her future at the Bank;
> > her ability to perform her functions properly as Managing Director of the Bank is made increasingly difficult;
> > the respect that she should command from employees of the Bank is being undermined.
> The situation has been exacerbated by the Board's instruction to our client that she may not divulge or discuss the contents of the Katz report with anyone. The unreasonableness of this instruction is questionable, given the complete failure to make public a statement in which it declares the Jack allegations as unfounded, and more importantly indicates its confidence in the Managing Director.
> The Board's failure to deal fairly, responsibly and timeously with this matter is creating an extraordinarily difficult working environment for our client, given the uncertainty, the lack of public exoneration and the absence of any words of support from the Board.
> The actions of the Board of the Bank are inexplicable, unreasonable and unfair on our client and in fact appear to be designed to create a working environment intolerable to our client.
> It is our client's wish to bring these matters to the attention of the Board, with a reservation of her rights.

Attrition intensified

The attrition was not confined to the workplace. It may be that the following events were just a series of strange coincidences, one after the other, but the net effect was rattling. If indeed there was a concerted

---

*Annexure 14, High Court Case No. 34457/99.

effort being made to jangle my nerves, then it succeeded.

There had been threats during the head office restructuring process earlier in the year: 'Why don't you let us arrange a hijack?' 'Why don't you just dump her in Soweto township?' were the ill-humoured proposals put to Tiene Vermaak, the Land Bank driver. There were also unpleasant incidents concerning other members of the strategic management team: not only threatening phone calls, but also the golf ball that shattered Dawie Maree's lounge window late one night. We presumed that Dawie had drawn anger from Afrikaner staff who regarded his contribution to the ethos of the new Land Bank as treason.

Since the time of the industrial unrest, the phone calls and window breakage, I not only had a driver but also a bodyguard escorting me to and from work. One evening in September we left the head office building around 9.30 pm. On the highway we found ourselves being shadowed by two identical cars travelling alongside, keeping pace with us. We slowed down; they slowed down. We speeded up, they did likewise. We weren't however planning to complete our normal route. I was dropping in to see a friend on my way home. We took an off-ramp and lost them in the suburbs. I'd jotted down the number plates. The security firm checked them the next day; one didn't exist and the other belonged to a different make of vehicle, not the one that had shadowed us the night before. 'Chase plates, that's what we call them in the trade,' commented the bodyguard. Another day, another incident: it seemed as though someone was trying to force us into the oncoming traffic.

Then one evening a bullet chanced to make its way into my kitchen at home. I was making supper for my mother, my brother Martin and sister-in-law Elmori. It was a special occasion – the last evening of a visit from my mother and I was making what she liked best of my cooking – beef roasted in mustard and parsley. Everyone was sitting around the kitchen table whilst I stood by the stove slicing the meat, and waiting for the vegetables to finish cooking. I was just about to serve the food on to the plates that were stacked at the ready when there was the sharp sound of glass breaking and something hit the kitchen floor. I turned round expecting to see a fallen glass, but I couldn't see anything.

Elmori got up to look. The floor was dented; a small metal object had ricocheted and now lay next to the cabinet.

'It's a bullet!' she cried. 'Where there's one, we can expect another!'

There was confusion. What to do?

'Switch out the lights!' we all shouted.

My demure, sweet-talking sister-in-law had an instant metamorphosis into chief boss: 'Get on the floor,' she instructed.

We didn't know where the bullet had come from – all we knew was that we were sitting ducks in a well-lit room with glass sliding doors and no curtains. I flicked off the hot plate switches and crouched down on the floor.

'Closer over here,' said my mother who got down fast in spite of her arthritis. 'Here is the safest place – you must have it. I've lived my life, now you must have yours.'

'Press the panic button!'

'Where's the cellphone?'

I crawled back towards the table in front of the sliding doors, feeling desperately vulnerable and exposed. I tried to hook the cellphone off the table with the end of my mother's walking stick. I knocked over a wine glass that shattered both itself and our nerves.

I began making phone calls while we lay on the floor. My brother crawled out of the kitchen to press the nearest panic button. There was another sharp crack of something exploding. We couldn't work it out. Where were the shots coming from?

'Someone's in the tree.' It was a windy night, half lit by the half moon – easy enough to imagine anything in the branches of the trees.

Another sharp explosion. This time a feeling of warmth crept up my thigh. Isn't that what they say? That when you're hit you don't always feel pain – you feel heat?

By now Adrian Toms was on the phone reassuring me that the body-guard was on his way. 'The shots are getting closer!' I cried. 'Tell him to come quickly. Please come quickly!' Then there was yet another sharp sound like another shot.

The security guard arrived and shone neon torchlight into our kitchen. We shouted hysterically: 'Don't shine the light at us! Shine it into the trees!'

The house was soon swarming with people. It turned out that there was only ever one real shot. The other explosions were plates breaking. In turning off the hotplates I'd accidentally turned on the one that the plates were standing on. The warmth I'd felt on my thigh was the heat of a broken piece of plate that had flown through the air and landed on me.

Afterwards, we poured shots (!) of whisky and laughed ourselves silly in hysterical relief.

And the one real shot? Someone, somewhere close by, cleaning a gun that went off and the bullet just happened to fly through our kitchen skylight? Or a deliberate shot with the intent to intimidate?

The charge sheet, 'special leave' and legal costs

On the evening of Friday 22 October, on day one hundred of my trauma, I met the chairperson to discuss a couple of matters. When I'd tried to arrange a time he told me he was extremely busy and could avail himself for no more than one hour at the most. I suggested the end of the Friday rather than making an arrangement over the weekend. My house seemed the most convenient place to meet.

Business done, he began to chat about his daughter who is of a similar age to mine; he told me proudly that his daughter wanted to become an engineer and what his thoughts were on the merits of various universities. Why was he suddenly trying to be friendly? Salving his feelings of guilt? The week before the Minister had held a press conference, publicly released the Katz report, and mentioned the intention to have a disciplinary hearing. I'd heard rumours that I'd get the charges for the hearing any day now; I'd seen the lawyers arrive earlier in the week for a hurried meeting with the subcommittee during an interval in our board meeting.

What was Mkhabela up to? Was he now going to start up a good cop, bad cop routine with himself in the role of good cop and Masiphula Mbongwa as the bad cop? I didn't appreciate his timing for this apparent overture of friendliness. He was the one who'd said 'I can avail one hour only' with his customary peremptoriness and air of self-importance. I needed this meeting to end. I had half an hour to shower, change and get ready to go to a wedding anniversary celebration. I requested closure, explaining the reason why I was in a hurry. 'When do you expect to arrive home?' the chairperson enquired. 'There should be something in your letter box on your return.'

I was back at 10.30 pm. Sure enough, there was a hand-delivered envelope in my box. I sat down at my desk to read the contents. It was the charge sheet* concerning the disciplinary hearing:

CHARGE OF MISCONDUCT

1. By the power delegated to the Board by the Minister of Agriculture and Land Affairs, you are charged with the following misconduct:

1.1   Contravention of your fiduciary duties in that:-

1.1.1 you unilaterally and without approval of the Board determined the remuneration of Managing Director, Financial and Administration Manager, Corporate Affairs and Marketing Manager, Information

---

*Annexure 17, High Court Case No. 34457/99.

Technology Manager, Human Resources Manager and Operations Manager ("the top six") contrary to the provisions of Section 13(2)(c) of the Land Bank Act;

1.1.2   on 10 March 1999 you instructed the implementation of the increase of remuneration of the top six or part thereof without actual authority from the Board to make such implementation and/or

1.2   You acted in breach of the Board's decision taken in the May 1999 Board meeting relating to the increase of remuneration of the top six that the approval of the Minister had to be obtained . . .

1.3   You acted in breach of your duties as Managing Director and/or in breach of good corporate governance by implementing the salary of the top six despite serious misgivings on the part of the non-executive directors and without again raising the matter at the Board meeting and getting clear instructions in that regard . . .

4.   You are advised to take special leave from the date of receipt of this letter to enable you to prepare your case in response to the charges that have been brought against you. The special leave shall be valid until the disciplinary enquiry has been completed.

5.   You will be entitled to the following during the disciplinary enquiry:

5.1   an opportunity to state your case in response to the charges, including hearing of evidence and cross-examination of witnesses; and

5.2   external legal representation at your own cost . . .

What fiduciary duty? It was my job to make sure that the Bank was able to attract and retain competent people to run a business dealing with billions of rands! The phone on my desk rang, startling me at that late hour. The phone was not my family number but a Land Bank line used for business calls and known only to a handful of people. I picked up the receiver. 'Hullo?' Silence. I had the eeriest feeling of someone checking that I had indeed arrived home and had received and read the charge sheet. Did they expect me to sound distraught?

The charge sheet 'advised' that I should take special leave in order to prepare for the disciplinary hearing. 'Advice' from the Land Bank board, as had been so unequivocally made clear to me, was to be regarded as mandatory, an *instruction* to be followed. Hence, over the weekend I rang my colleagues to arrange a handover meeting of issues that would need their continued attention in my absence. At 7.40 am on the Monday morning the phone on my desk rang again. As on the Friday evening, the response to my greeting was silence. What was this about? Was it to check up to see that I'd stayed home on this Monday morning and hadn't defied the 'advice' to take special leave? Was someone playing mind games?

I understood the 'special leave' as psychological warfare. It effectively removed me from the daily rhythm of work and the people support base that sustained me. Home alone was meant to be isolating and debilitating. On the third day of my special leave I met Jacob Modise for an extended lunch. It seemed he had been tasked to sound me out about how I would feel about being paid a settlement to leave the Bank. I wasn't interested; this was the job I'd lived for, day in and day out, for the last two years. The worst of restructuring was over and I now wanted to enjoy the next period of creative consolidation.

I questioned Modise on the rationale for the obligatory nature of my special leave. 'But I didn't understand it would be mandatory,' he said. 'The way it was put to me is that it would be offered as an option. But then I didn't see the final draft of the letter you received.' Modise's observation confirmed for me that he was a fellow traveller and not the driver of the subcommittee.

Much of the charge sheet was incomprehensible both to my attorney and myself. A request for clarification concerning the charges was in order. I needed an advocate to represent me. Pam Stein teamed up with Derek Spitz, who was already familiar with my case as he'd been approached for advice on my pursuing defamation proceedings against Bonile Jack and possibly *The Star* newspaper.

The poor formulation of the charges resulted in a great deal of work for Pam and Derek to prepare the 'Respondent's request for further particulars to the Charges of Misconduct'.* So loose were the charges and so confused in terms of the powers of the Land Bank Act that the request for further particulars submitted to the Board attorneys was a sixty-five-page document. My eyes stood on stalks as I read through and initialled each one of the pages. I was impressed by the thoroughness of the questions and the precision of response demanded. There were thirty-one preliminary questions relating to 'misconduct', nineteen questions on the definition of 'fiduciary duties', twelve questions concerning the issue of so-called 'unilateral' decision making, twenty-five questions about 'the approval of the board'. It was an intimidating document, the work of lawyers acting to the best of their professional ability in my best interests. The document was submitted within a week,

---

*Annexure 21, High Court Case No. 34457/99.

and then we settled back into what in exile we referred to as the 'Hurry Up and Wait' mode; everything was always urgent, but everything always seemed to take forever.

'Tell me what keeps you going?' asked Pam one day, as we entered the fourth month of this never-ending saga. 'Where do you get the strength to hang in?'

It took me some time to consider and come up with a reply. 'It's more than wanting to clear my name. I think in part it's because I don't have citizenship by birthright; but I was so proud the day it was granted. I chose to be here. I chose to bring up my children here. I want to have confidence that there's a future for them. It's important to take a stand on issues of principle and governance. If principles cannot be upheld, and if governance is abused then I lose my hope in our country's future and my children's future. So I have to hang in.'

At the end of October 1999 the board chairperson sent a letter informing us that the disciplinary hearing would be on 10 and 11 November, that the 'further particulars' would be provided timeously, and that a well-known black woman advocate, Kgomotso Moroka, would preside over the hearing.* I had made a request for financial assistance towards my legal costs – the board, after all, had run up a bill of several hundred thousand rands on the Katz team, the board attorneys and now advocates. It was their choice, not mine, to hold a disciplinary hearing that engaged legal professionals external to the Bank. My legal expenses already totalled one hundred and fifty thousand rands. The board chairperson indicated there was no obligation on the part of the Bank to assist me financially, but awarded me the miserly sum of fifteen thousand rands.

The day after I'd sent the letter requesting financial assistance I received a phone call from Moira Mokuena, my ex-assistant who had resigned in a huff almost eighteen months earlier. She appeared to be especially well connected with the board subcommittee dealing with the inquiry in that she knew of my letter of request written only two days earlier.

'Helena, how are you? I hear you're in need of some legal assistance.' Her deep voice glided slowly over the words, giving the impression of someone who was gloating. 'As one woman in support of another woman, I'd like to offer you mine.'

'Moira,' I replied, 'I have heard from various sources that you assisted Bonile Jack in drafting the letter to Thabo Mbeki, and then personally

---

*Annexure 19, High Court Case No. 34457/99.

delivered it to Mathatha Tsedu at *The Star*. On that basis, thank you, but I would not be able to trust your assistance.'

'My pleasure,' she commented, and I put the phone down shaking with disbelief.

Attempted conciliation

There was a lobby of people interested in trying to resolve the matter outside of the disciplinary hearing process. The Minister, director general and deputy director general, they argued, wanted their own person in my position. I wanted a period in the Bank to consolidate. Perhaps a compromise could be brokered – just as Geoff Budlender, the Land Affairs director general, had agreed to shorten his contract and not serve the full term of five years. Moeketsi Shai, a strategy consultant we had employed on several occasions, was interested in brokering conciliation. His assessment was that a one-on-one meeting was needed with the Minister.

'Your problem is not Masiphula driving the subcommittee of the board; it's not Mkhabela – he's too busy with his new job. Masiphula is the leg man, but Masiphula is only a leg of the octopus. You have to get to the head of the octopus – that's the Minister.' He explained to me that he'd heard that the Minister had been displeased by my television comment to the effect that I didn't know her, but was looking forward to working with her. He told me that in African culture disclaiming that you know someone can be interpreted as offensive.

I explained why I had made the remark. For years I'd lived with someone 'famous' and again and again would come across people who would claim to 'know' Joe Slovo on the basis of the briefest encounter – and that kind of personal history made me cautious about claiming to 'know' someone.

The Minister responded positively to the Moeketsi overture. She agreed to meet with me and set a date and a time, midday on 4 November. It seemed we were in business. If misunderstandings could be clarified and she could be reassured of my political fidelity to pursue the policies that she would want the Land Bank to fulfil then perhaps some way forward could be mapped out. On the very day of the midday meeting, Moeketsi phoned me at home – I was still on so-called 'special leave'. He told me: 'Don't leave for Pretoria until I confirm with you, there are moves afoot to cancel.' Thirty minutes before the meeting I received the definitive phone call. 'It's off. I couldn't get to the Minister's inner sanctum. I couldn't get to speak to her directly. Everything was done through Masiphula Mbongwa with Bongi Njobe in attendance. It seems that they persuaded Minister Didiza against the meeting.'

The lawyers take over

Derek Spitz wanted to work with a senior counsel with impeccable professional credentials. Feelers were put out to a few people; much depended on their availability not only for preparation at short notice but also for the days of 10 and 11 November that had been set down for the hearing. One such senior counsel who was contacted regretted his conflict of interest; he'd been approached by Katz to give advice – advice that had not been wholly accepted. The Katz report did Helena Dolny 'the most grave injustice,' he commented. When I heard that comment I had one of the worst days in the entire trauma. If the Katz team had taken the advice surely things would have turned out differently, and my living hell would have ended weeks before, on 30 August.

I phoned George Bizos, tracking him down to a hotel room in Holland. 'I can do it,' he said after consulting his diary. 'I'll be back on Saturday. Have the background documentation delivered to my house. And,' he added, 'keep your chin up.'

When I met George on the Monday morning he'd had time to familiarise himself with much of the documentation. He was effervescent: 'I started reading, I couldn't stop. I read until three thirty in the morning. The more I read the more indignant I became on your behalf, about what you have been subjected to. These accusations of Bonile Jack are scurrilous!'

I drove home that lunchtime feeling over the moon. George's indignation was such sweet balm to my soul. I felt I could happily put a bumper sticker on my car: 'I love George Bizos!' When I got home I looked up the word 'scurrilous' in the dictionary – it had such an expressive feel to it: '*scurrilous adj. – indecently abusive and unjustifiably defamatory*'. There couldn't be a better choice of adjective.

When word got out that George Bizos, South Africa's famous legal activist, was to be my senior counsel it seemed to provoke anxiety among the board subcommittee and their attorneys and advocates. Out of the blue a letter postponed the disciplinary hearing scheduled for 10 and 11 November. A scratch around for new dates when all the legal eagles would be available settled on November 27 and 29. The pathetic excuse given for postponement was the unavailability of documentation – pathetic because everything had long ago been given, in its entirety, to the Katz team. The real reason was probably the inability to answer the request for further particulars, the realisation of how poorly the charges had been formulated, and how strong my case was after all.

Besides George's instruction to 'keep your chin up', his other advice was, 'I want you back at work.' Pam Stein had already prepared a letter to the board attorneys thanking them for the special leave, explaining that I'd now had all the time I could usefully use pending the delivery of the further particulars and that I was resuming my contractual obligations.* The intention was to make them suspend me correctly, if that was what they wanted to do, but that they should not get away with this 'special leave' – a cheap euphemism for suspension. Masiphula Mbongwa was furious. 'We made a mistake,' he told a fellow board member. 'She was never supposed to go back to work.'

It was good to be back within the dull beige-green confines of the Land Bank building on Visagie Street. I had truly become 'at home'. I walked the stairs, to be visible, to reconnect with people. *Vasbyt* (hang in) was the Afrikaans word I learnt that week as people greeted me and welcomed me back to work.

Meanwhile I had finished the painstaking preparation of a seventy-six-page document for George Bizos, starting at day one of my employment in the Land Bank and recording every single meeting or discussion about remuneration policy. George, for his part, scrutinised the Katz report; found areas he was dissatisfied with and began his own research. Derek Spitz and Hamilton Maenetje scoured the archives for judgments providing precedents which defined 'fiduciary duty'. George discreetly went off to see Mervyn King, the author of the King Report on Corporate Governance. George had his own doubts about the Katz 'finding' that I had acted with 'poor corporate governance'. He shared his thinking with King who agreed to come to the disciplinary hearing as a witness to be questioned by Bizos. I was sworn to secrecy; this was to be our surprise witness, Mervyn King on corporate governance. Things looked good. The days passed. The response to our 'request for further particulars' was still not forthcoming. There were strong rumours that the advocates appointed by the board were unsure of the case.

Then, over a weekend, there was a strange flurry of activity to further test my interest in settlement. I got a call from Quadafi, an acquaintance from exile days who I had not heard from in several years. 'Let's get together and talk about what you've been going through.' Strange. I asked where he'd been, what he'd been doing, and what he was doing now. It turned out that he'd just been appointed as adviser to the Minister. 'Oh, which Minister?' I asked, being a bit slow. 'The Minister of Agriculture,' came the answer.

Dave Gillam received a call from board attorney Graham Damant. 'Do you think Helena would be interested in a settlement offer?' The

*Annexure 22, High Court Case No. 34457/99.

Deputy Minister of Agriculture, Dirk du Toit, phoned to tell me that he'd now been mandated to have a discussion to see if we couldn't sort things out differently, rather than pursuing the disciplinary hearing. On the same Saturday Pam Stein switched on her cellphone to find several messages from Maserumule Incorporated, the firm of attorneys appointed to handle the disciplinary hearing. They, Maserumule and Khumalo, insisted on meeting her that afternoon – again, the question was posed: would Helena be interested in a settlement to leave the Bank?

On Monday morning, 15 November, just eleven days before the rescheduled hearing, George Bizos, Pam Stein, Derek Spitz, Hamilton Maenetje and I gathered to review the diverse contacts. During our meeting, Maserumule and Khumalo phoned and announced their wish to have a 'without prejudice' discussion. They arrived within a few minutes.

Bizos later recounted the meeting, which naturally excluded me. In high style, Bizos had told Maserumule and Khumalo: 'My client has been publicly vilified and needs to be publicly exonerated. The hearing must be public. Settlement is dependent on either the hearing or a public statement that clears her name.' Settlement figures were tabled verbally by Maserumule, but Bizos insisted that 'Settlement is secondary to the restoration of my client's good name.'

The next evening another attorney from Maserumule Incorporated arrived at the house of my new personal assistant, Brendan Pearce; the two knew each other from their law student days. The discussion, supposedly informal and referred to in the trade as 'without prejudice', was worrisome. The attorney said he had been briefed by Masiphula Mbongwa on behalf of the board subcommittee.

'Your boss has got to go,' my assistant was told. 'The board is prepared "to go far" to ensure she is out. It can be argued that there's an irreparable breakdown in the working relationship. If your boss insists on going forward with this hearing, it will be perceived that she is taking on the Minister, that she is fighting the African National Congress. Talk to her about settlement.'

The report back of this conversation hit me below the belt. I was being expected to forgo clearing my name to cover up for the poor judgement of the board subcommittee and the Minister, and what's more there was an attempt to guilt-trip me, that this would be expected of me as a loyal ANC member. I learnt this of myself: there are limitations to my party loyalty; this so-called ANC behaviour did not merit loyalty.

Dave Gillam tried to prime me to accept that my departure now seemed inevitable. He kindly wrote his perspective out on paper; if I didn't want to hear him now, his argument was set out for reference. Gillam's starting point was that I needed to accept that there are occasions when people lose without deserving to. He reminded me of the earlier incident when the Minister's spokesperson told *Business Day* 'no action to be taken' and six hours later rescinded this statement. Why? It must have been pressure from the top. There are some tough knocks to be taken in life, said Gillam, and I was faced with one of them. He wrote:

Question: Can workers cause a perfectly innocent management member to be fired?

Answer: Yes. Over time concerted grievances and complaints with false witnesses and/or industrial action will bring about dismissal.

Question: Can management cause a perfectly innocent employee (whether MD, shop steward or any other employee) to be fired?

Answer: Yes. Over time concerted complaints and ongoing borderline 'unreasonable' requests/instructions/expectations will bring about dismissal.*

The disciplinary inquiry was couched in terms of a charge of 'misconduct' with the intent to justify dismissal. Our many pages of questions requesting clarification on the charges was causing consternation. Their failure to win the case would not help their cause; it would make the next attempt to get rid of me more difficult.

The board then looked to strengthen its legal team; senior counsel Martin Brassey joined Maserumule and Khumalo. I heard there was a search for an alternative to the disciplinary inquiry brainstormed on the Sunday afternoon by Brassey, the Minister, the board chairperson, the leg-man Mbongwa and Advocate Maserumule. At the board meeting the following evening, after I was asked to leave the room, the board was told that settlement discussions had come to nought. It had moreover been agreed that the Katz team had indeed reached a conclusive finding and that the board had been remiss in not acting. The lack of action was couched as a lapse of fiduciary duty on the part of the board. The board was told by the subcommittee that an alternative to a disciplinary inquiry would be pursued – apparently the outcome of Brassey's advisory input.

I was soon to learn what the alternative was. Pam Stein received a

---

*Gillam to Dolny, personal correspondence.

letter,* delivered on Tuesday 23 November, now only three days prior to the start of the long-planned disciplinary hearing. In short, it sought to bypass justice through the bypass of a proper hearing. The letter informed us that the disciplinary inquiry had been cancelled, that my guilt had been established beyond doubt, and that I should arrive at the Land Bank for a two-hour meeting in two days' time to receive my punishment. I would, however, be allowed to make representation in mitigation.

23 November 1999

Dear Madam

THE LAND AND AGRICULTURAL BANK/DR HELENA DOLNY

The Honourable Minister of Agriculture and Land Affairs and the Board of the Bank, represented by a sub-committee appointed for the purpose, have jointly sought legal advice on the need for the impending disciplinary enquiry against your client. On the basis of the advice, they have each formed the view that it would be undesirable to permit the enquiry to proceed. The merits of the charges against your client were canvassed in the ENF investigation, which concluded that your client had acted improperly in precisely the manner contemplated by the pending charges, and the manner of sanction can, in the view of the Bank and the Minister, be entrusted to a purely internal enquiry to determine.

The present enquiry has, in consequence, been terminated, and Advocate Moroka will be notified accordingly.

The sanction to be imposed on your client, if any, will be considered by the sub-committee to which I have already referred. The committee will meet for the purpose at the Land Bank Head Office at corner Visagie and Paul Kruger Streets, Pretoria on Thursday 25 November 1999 from 15h00 to 17h00. Your client is invited to make representations in her defence at the meeting, but they must be confined exclusively to questions of mitigation. At the hearing she will have the right to legal representation.

Yours faithfully,
R Khumalo for Maserumule Incorporated

Application for a High Court interdict

Pam Stein faxed the letter through to my office, and it was hand delivered to me at a conference I was attending. I phoned Pam and paced up and down as I expressed the disbelief that she shared. The letter was the equivalent of a 'Do you still beat your wife?' question. It

---

*Annexure 2, High Court Case No. 34457/99.

was premised on prior acceptance between both parties that I had done something wrong.

Copies of the above, soon to be infamous, letter were faxed between legal offices with urgency and later Bizos came on the line: 'You cannot go to this sanction hearing. I will not let you be a sacrificial lamb. To let you go to the sanction hearing, without putting up a fight challenging the legitimacy of such a hearing, is to throw you to the lions.'

The lawyers decided that we must attempt to stop the meeting from taking place. Pam wrote a letter to Maserumule Incorporated indicating that their invitation to a sanction meeting was a violation of my constitutional right to a proper hearing. We would be applying to the High Court for an interdict to stop the proposed meeting taking place, unless they voluntarily withdrew. They did not grace us with any response.

The hours and hours of work needed to prepare the necessary documentation began; it was a race against time. On Wednesday evening, the day before the scheduled sanction hearing, we gathered at the offices of Cheadle Thompson & Haysom Attorneys. There was a whoop of delight when Hamilton Maenetje found a case similar to mine that had been heard in the High Court; up to that moment it was feared that the appropriateness of our choice of courts might be challenged. As the preparation continued into the evening there was a phone call which seemed to indicate an interest to make the first formal settlement offer. I was asked via my attorney to set out the money value of my salary and benefits to the end of five years' service. It seemed a reasonable request for information; an official in the public service had earlier informed me that settlement discussions often centred on the pay-out of the remainder of a five-year service period. I sat down with a calculator and arrived at a figure of R2,3-million.

Deep throat (by now the deep throat contact had been narrowed down to one of the board advocates or board subcommittee members) must have immediately contacted Prince Hamnca. The next morning *The Star* published his latest derogatory story.* Facts were embellished: apparently not only had I demanded R2,3-million but also two luxury vehicles, one of them a Mercedes Benz.

That Thursday morning I had woken up feeling terrible. I hated the morass of conflict that my life had become. And yet it felt so important to me to hang in, clear my name, and make a stand against political machinations.

When I got to the lawyers' offices, Pam Stein, Derek Spitz and George

---

*'Dolny holds out for R2,3m payout from bank', *The Star*, 26 November 1999.

Bizos were still busy. Pam informed me that they had received a fax containing a settlement offer for the sum of one and a half million rands if I left the Land Bank immediately. She told me that she had a duty to advise me, as her client, to consider the offer seriously. There was no certainty that the interdict application to the High Court would be judged in my favour. If my application failed, the sanction hearing would go ahead with its obvious intention to fire me. Should that be the outcome, I would be looking for a job under a cloud, and in the meanwhile how would I cover my household expenses, my children's school and university fees, and so on?

I felt dirty. I felt as though I was being bribed. Going to court would be a nerve-racking experience. I could avoid it by bowing to the pressure to take the money. I had to listen to Pam. However right we might feel we were, there was no guarantee that a judge would see it the same way. But there was a strong feeling that we should go to court and expose this attempted abuse of power. I had no money to fall back on, however, if things went against me. I paced up and down again, making phone calls to friends to get their assurance that they'd lend me money if necessary. They were willing to stand by me.

Pam confirmed: 'So we're going ahead and completing the application. I'm not sending a reply to the fax regarding the settlement. The offer is open until 13h00 – they can wait and wonder if there's going to be a response!'

Pam then asked me to begin reading the tens of pages of the affidavit that had to be signed by myself and a commissioner of oaths before its official submission. As I read it I remembered something I'd just been told during one of my phone calls: 'By the by, one of the friends that I was just talking to says that the Minister was interviewed on television and radio this morning. Apparently she said that the disciplinary hearing would not take place as planned because it would take too long and cost too much money.'

'What!' exclaimed Pam, following this with an expletive. What I'd just mentioned in passing as one more outrageous comment was of import for our case. 'Get the transcripts – both radio and television. We must have them as annexures* to the affidavit.'

It was raining when we finally drove to Pretoria at midday. I was nervous; the decision to go to court had not been taken lightly. I recalled that the day we'd buried Joe it had rained endlessly, and I'd been told that in African culture rain is a good omen.

---

*Annexures 28, 29, 30, 31, High Court Case No. 34457/99.

Pretoria's High Court had a sombre, dour interior, dark corridors, and lots of wooden panelling – it was even less hospitable than the Land Bank. The judge accepted the urgency of the application but needed to finish another case first. Hard benches lined the walls of the corridors and we sat, uncomfortably, for the hours of waiting. We finally began at a quarter to five and would only leave the courtroom at eight thirty that evening. Each party was to be asked to present their argument and then the Judge would deliver his decision.

Bizos – activist lawyer

George Bizos prides himself on the selectivity with which he chooses the cases he is prepared to defend. 'Mr Bizos,' he was once asked in an interview, 'you seem to have spent your life defending unpopular cases – what do you say to that?' 'On the contrary,' retorted Bizos, 'I have spent my entire life in defence of popular cases!'

Bizos retired to dress himself for the court appearance and emerged swathed in robes that were too big for him. I didn't know it before, but apparently advocates lend each other robes to pass on luck – if they've just had a good case, or for any other subjective reason. Bizos is a short and somewhat round man with a surprisingly deep, resonant voice. On this occasion he had been lent robes by the tall Karel Tip, a fellow advocate. The robe-lending was a good luck gesture. Karel and I had been going to the same tai chi class on Saturday mornings for the last four years.

Bizos made the opening request as to the urgency of the matter. 'We request interim relief from a hearing which says another body found our client guilty and she may only reply in mitigation.' He read out the letter that called me to the special hearing, and argued why this was contrary to the administration of justice. The judge answered: 'My understanding is that the matter is sufficiently urgent and is enrolled.' Bizos, wishing to accommodate the judge, asked: 'I understand that Judge Coetze is overworked and may wish to adjourn to tomorrow morning.' 'No,' replied the judge tersely. 'I prefer to hear now, would like to finish now.' The judge listened intently for the next three and a half hours, interjecting only with brief questions in the interests of clarity.

What I witnessed was a revelation to me. I'd heard that so much in our law depends on what precedents exist from earlier similar cases; in the next hours I watched a tennis match, the lawyers for each side engaged in their professional combat. The 'aces' that they aspired to depended on knowing, choosing and arguing about the applicability of points from previous cases to the one 'on the stand'.

Bizos and his team had selected two cases in which it was found that the failure to permit a hearing that included the opportunity to cross-question constituted an unfair labour practice. The proposed sanction hearing, it was argued, was of the same order.

As background, Bizos built up a description of me as an exemplary character. Jack's allegations were 'scurrilous' – and the Katz findings had rejected all but one of the allegations. With regard to the salary issue, Bizos noted: 'The applicant acted in full consultation with the remuneration committee. She was mindful of her salary and the lacuna in the Act and obtained legal opinion. The formula was agreed to by the board. In April and May she tried to get to the Minister. On arrival of the new Minister she provided a written briefing. The figure implemented was the lowest figure on the scale; the action was supported by the legal adviser. There is evidence that, throughout her tenure, she took steps to prevent unnecessary expenditure. Where is the bad governance? Where is the lack of fiduciary duty?' The Jack fax of April 1999 was not circulated. It was contended that Jack, and possibly others, were 'cooking up a case'.

Bizos continued:

> The applicant maintains that she has done no wrong, no wilful wrong. The applicant welcomed the disciplinary inquiry – as indicated in clause 8.15.8. The applicant does not accept the accuracy or correctness of the Katz conclusion.* The welcome of the disciplinary inquiry was not based on the presumption of guilt!
>
> The applicant was gagged not to talk to the media or employees – therefore the Minister's suggestion that Dolny never denied the conclusions reached by Katz is not appropriate in these circumstances.† Ministers have to rely on the good information of others. I therefore contend that the Minister was not properly briefed.
>
> An employer has rights, but also has obligations. The employer in this case is a statutory body, and an organ of state. An employer has responsibility to employees. The authorities say organs of state have special responsibility. The applicant's right to administrative justice is protected in the constitution. With regard to the employee there is a question of status, a question of dignity, which must be protected when improperly attacked.
>
> We do not maintain that a managing director has special privileges; the lowest worker is entitled to this dignity. But where there has been a campaign, where the applicant has been publicly vilified, it is important that the applicant be entitled to a proper process. The wrongful act is not proved. The wrongful act is not admitted. To deny the applicant an interdict for this mitigation inquiry would be manifest injustice.

---

*Document 2, Founding Affidavit, High Court Case No. 34457/99.
†Annexure 9, High Court Case No. 34457/99.

There is a rule, known as the *audi alteram partem* rule, which requires that the person accused of wrongdoing be sufficiently heard. My reasonable expectation, 'to be heard', was now being denied. 'It is important (to note),' said Bizos, 'the board minutes promised an inquiry, instituted an inquiry, took steps to start up the inquiry, and then for no reason, except that given on the radio by the Minister about time and money, such inquiry is terminated and another process begun on the premise of guilt.

'To go ahead and expect the applicant to plead in mitigation is beyond anyone's imagination who has a respect for legality. The sanction hearing must be prohibited.'

Brassed-off

Just as Bizos had spoken well of me, so Martin Brassey argued the opposite, making me out to be a recalcitrant and avaricious character. I was uncomfortable listening to him, because of his derogatory references to me, and also because of his style. He approximates a British upper-class manner of speaking which carried me back to a deeply embedded childhood prejudice. Brassey's line of argument rested on the fact that the Katz hearing fulfilled the requirement of the *audi alteram partem* rule, and that according to legal precedent no employee had an unquestionable right to a disciplinary hearing prior to dismissal. Moreover, he was at pains to point out that my constitutional right to appeal against any sanction in the event of my disagreeing with my punishment would remain intact.

Brassey indicated that he would confine himself to four points: Had a case been identified? Was there a case of irreparable harm? Was there no satisfactory alternative? What was the issue of proper remedy? He also intended to explore the requirements of the *audi alteram partem* rule, and finally, he asked rhetorically: 'What constitutes a "fair hearing"?'

He indicated that his proposition number one was that there was no automatic right to a hearing prior to dismissal. For a definition of whether a 'fair hearing' has been accomplished prior to the taking of a decision, Brassey indicated that the English case of Russell and the Duke of Norfolk was pertinent. I was amazed that some case between the landed gentry and an employee some fifty years ago could be pertinent – the importance of precedent in legal argument was brought home to me.

He then expounded: 'Natural justice is not engraved in stone (but) depends on the character of the decision-making body and the statutory framework in which it operates. There must be flexible emphasis, not a rigid rule.' He continued: 'There is never a stereotype of natural justice

. . . What constitutes a fair hearing depends on the exigencies of the case.' The 'content of the *audi alteram partem* rule depends on the scope of operation; in a more complex situation it may not be appropriate to accord the full right to be heard'.

Brassey argued: 'The Katz investigation, conducted over a protracted period of time, came to a certain "finding" – and on this basis my client relies . . . and has on the basis of this reached a conclusion of what must be done with this managing director.'

The judge interjected: 'Katz does not use the word "misconduct".'

Brassey, unfazed, continued that Katz had needed to review several allegations and that there was no need of a formal charge; it was sufficient that the facts had been investigated to reach a conclusion. He then presented the Katz 'findings' on the salary issue as unquestionable; he contradicted Bizos's account, casting aspersions on the truthfulness of it as having been 'based on consultation with Ms Dolny'. He referred to my having had the 'effrontery' to go ahead with salary increase implementation despite 'serious misgivings', and that it was appropriate for 'a tribunal to reach a decision' and consider the 'options on punishment'. He affirmed that the requirements of the *audi alteram partem* rule did not afford a right to a public hearing, no right to further particulars, no entitlement to legal representation, no right to cross-examination, and no entitlement to make oral representation.

Brassey concluded, therefore, that the Katz investigation sufficed as a substitute for a hearing: 'Your Lordship doesn't have to find that Dolny was guilty. Katz was right; Katz made inquiry and drew conclusions of propriety and this suffices the employer to administer sanction. It was not a "disciplinary inquiry" as we know it, but an investigation into facts, and Katz cast light on the want of judgment. I am saying, my Lord, that through the investigation process, Katz fulfils the *audi alteram partem* rule and concludes "misconduct". The Bank is entitled to act.' He motivated that the sanction hearing should proceed and that 'if Dolny was not satisfied with the outcome, she could take herself to court and institute a *de novo* hearing'.

The judge tersely requested clarification from Brassey. Was he to understand that the power of sanction included the power to dismiss, and that if the sanction was not acceptable to the applicant 'You are saying that then Dolny can come to court and get remedy on *de novo* inquiry?'

Brassey confirmed: 'It is very important, my Lord, to appreciate, it is utterly crucial to appreciate here, that there would be no constitutive effects on Ms Dolny's rights, on her ability to come before the courts.

She can request damages, can request reinstatement. That court considers the matter wholly afresh.'

It was hard for me to listen to him. I accepted that I was probably oversensitive, but his language in referring to me was offensive through- out – even allowing for the theatrical manner with which some counsels approach the courtroom. It was difficult to believe this was the Brassey with a reputation as a clever, progressive lawyer, who in the apartheid years had partnered Pam Stein in many cases defending trade unionists. I understood his need to represent professionally the client whose interests he had accepted to defend, but nevertheless there still remained a question of style.

Brassey concluded why there should be speedy closure through the sanction hearing. 'The Land Bank is embroiled in litigation (which) spins out Ms Dolny's entitlement to draw a salary. My client (the Minister) questions not honesty but judgement. Ms Dolny is not a fit and proper person to be a Land Bank chief executive.' He stated that the 'managing director's position is one of trust', implied that this had been lost and that it was not appropriate that 'Dolny each day draws her salary'. He defended the two-day notice of the two-hour hearing: 'Is it fair to deal with it in forty-eight hours? Is it fair to cap the time? There is no entitlement to legal representation; a customary position is that questions of internal disciplinary hearings are dealt with internally. If she doesn't like it she still has her remedies in law.'

With regard to the cancellation of the long-planned disciplinary hearing, Brassey confirmed that 'the services of Maserumule and Advocate Moroka are withdrawn', and 'nothing can be said that that withdrawal was improper'. With regard to the Minister's radio and television statements, he dismissed them as 'hardly of consequence'.

His finale cast further aspersions on my character. With barely disguised reference to the settlement discussions, his closing comments were: 'There's an industry developing (wherein) recalcitrant and fractious employees' use a situation that 'provides a lever to extract settlement' and seek 'deals far beyond her entitlement. There must be an end. There must be finality. I request to dismiss this application.'

Spitz: closing argument

The judge then asked if Spitz, the junior counsel to Bizos, would like to add anything by way of closing argument. Spitz's effectiveness lay in his calm, concise presentation, which conveyed an uncomplicated conviction of the moral right of his case. His style was in sharp contrast to the clever cut, thrust and parry of Brassey's wordsmanship and sophistry to defend the indefensible. Spitz simply stated that with regard to time pressures 'The delays have been at the instance of the Bank and not the applicant.' Furthermore, Brassey, he said, had failed to address the issue of 'legitimate expectation' of a disciplinary hearing. Whilst it was not an agreement, it 'was a promise made, and an expectation created', and 'for inexplicable reasons withdrawn'. The minutes of the board themselves indicated the reason for an external hearing with an independent chair.

With regard to the argument concerning the requisites of a 'fair hearing', he said, 'I submit there is no fixed formula', but argued that Katz himself noted the qualified nature of the investigation and 'findings'. Spitz argued moreover that I had been subjected to trial by media, while under gagging orders, and that itself should suffice as persuasion that cross-examination was an appropriate ingredient of a 'fair hearing'. Brassey had cited Baxter's case of the employee Russell and the Duke of Norfolk to argue that there was no entitled right to a hearing and cross-examination. Spitz, with a wonderful and quiet touché, also cited a section in Baxter which indicated that in certain situations 'cross-examination may be necessary to secure a fair hearing'.

He added that Brassey had omitted consideration of the public dimension, the Land Bank as an organ of state. Section 7(2) of the constitution indicated the obligation to protect rights; section 34 of the constitution conferred the right to a public hearing – not just a hearing by a subcommittee of the board limited to mitigation. He argued that I would be irreparably harmed by sanction, that Brassey's reassurance of right to appeal was no consolation. There was a question of personal dignity at stake that no amount of damages could salve. He questioned Brassey's plea about the time frame – his aspersion that I undeservedly continued to be paid a salary. The proper disciplinary hearing was scheduled for two days' time; it was the Land Bank that had controlled the pace of the process.

The Judge picked up his papers to leave, saying: 'Judgment will be given at 9 am. Tomorrow morning. Courtroom B.'

Another night of anxiety. In essence, Brassey had argued that the Bank had a right to deal with me as they wished and that if I didn't like the outcome I could go to the Labour Court. Bizos and Spitz had argued that the proposed sanction hearing was an abuse of power, that a proper disciplinary hearing was a fair expectation.

Which way would the judge rule? Next morning, with nervousness, we first made it to the wrong courtroom, having failed to remember a change of venue. We almost missed the beginning of the delivery of judgment.

I listened, overawed by the fluency of an uninterrupted delivery. Whilst I had tossed and turned all night, my mind churning to no avail, Judge Coetze had ordered his thoughts.

Judgment*

IN THE HIGH COURT OF SOUTH AFRICA
(TRANSVAAL PROVINCIAL DIVISION)
PRETORIA

CASE No.:	34457/99
DATE:	1999-11-25

In the matter between

HELENA MARIA DOLNY   Applicant

and

THE MINISTER OF AGRICULTURE AND OTHERS   Respondent

JUDGMENT

COETZE AJ : This is an urgent application for the following relief.

1. *Interdicting and restraining the respondents from holding a meeting on Thursday 25 November 1999 at 15:00 or at any time thereafter, at which meeting the respondents intend to give effect to their decision: "to consider the sanction if any, to be imposed on the applicant at a meeting of the third respondent which is to be held on Thursday, 25 November 1999, or at any other time", which meeting the respondents intend to convene on the basis that "the merits of the charges against your client were canvassed in the ENF investigation which concluded that your client had acted improperly in precisely the manner contemplated by the pending charges and the matter of sanction, can in view of the Bank and the Minister be entrusted to a purely internal enquiry to determine" and to which meeting "your client is invited to make representations in her defence at the meeting but must be confined exclusively to questions of mitigation".*

---

*High Court Case No. 34457/99: Judgment.

2. *The interdict set out in prayer 1 above is to operate as an interim interdict pending the launching of an application reviewing, setting aside and correcting the decision set out in paragraph 1 above, which application will be launched within a time period which this honourable court deems is appropriate.*

The applicant, Dr Dolny, is the managing director of the Land and Agricultural Bank of South Africa. She was appointed in that post during May 1997 and is presently still employed by the Bank and is performing her functions and duties in terms of her contract of employment. She is also the chairperson of the board of directors. When this matter was called respondent took issue with the alleged urgency of the application. I ruled in favour of the applicant on the question of urgency. Respondents' counsel informed me that their clients did not wish to deliver answering affidavits and I then heard counsels' arguments on the merits.

During September 1997 the applicant proposed to the then Minister of Agriculture and Land Affairs that the roles of chairperson of the board and managing director of the Bank should be separated and that Mr Bonile Jack should be appointed to act as the chairperson of the board of directors. The proposal was accepted and Mr Jack was appointed as the chairperson designate of the board during November 1997. On 27 May 1999 Mr Jack wrote a letter to the then deputy president, Mr Mbeki, in which letter defamatory and baseless allegations were made against the applicant. The Bank was also criticized in this letter. During July the letter was leaked to the media, it was published in various newspapers and was also brought to the attention of the public through television and radio broadcasts. The letter became known as the "Jack-letter".

The judge then cited the terms of the appointment of the attorneys Edward Nathan & Friedland, and their undertaking to 'deliver the report to the board by 26 July 1999'. The judge further noted that

The "Katz investigation" as this investigation became known, received extensive media coverage and the applicant states that she was subjected to what amounted to a trial by the media . . . The investigation was not an enquiry of a disciplinary nature. This appearance from the investigation team's own view of their mandate . . .

The Katz investigation team executed their mandate and filed a report. The applicant states that, during the course of the investigation not all allegations were put to all witnesses and that its proceedings were non-adversarial. It made findings but qualified the nature of its findings . . .

As far as the applicant is concerned the investigation was mainly directed towards her alleged unilateral and unauthorised decision to substantially increase the salaries of herself and five other top employees of the Bank.

The judge quoted the Katz 'findings' on this matter and commented:

The Katz report does not find that the applicant's proposal to implement the salary increases constitutes misconduct. Neither does it recommend that disciplinary action be taken against her. Professor Katz, subsequent to the filing of the report on 30 August 1999, told the board of directors that he did not recommend that disciplinary steps be taken against the applicant.

The judge continued:

The second respondent was instructed to draft a report of the board on the Katz report. This report was put before the board and approved of. It was then handed to the Minister. The board recommended that disciplinary proceedings be instituted against the applicant, and stated that there is prima facie *evidence of wrong doing, warranting disciplinary proceedings being instituted. The appropriate way for that to be dealt with, so they opined, was through a disciplinary enquiry so that evidence can be properly tested and a final finding on the facts be made. The applicant was instructed by the chair of the second respondent to refrain from discussing the allegations against her with the media . . .*

It appears from a transcript of a radio report that the first respondent stated that the inquiry was called off because it would take too long and would be too expensive.

In my view it is crystal clear from a reading of the letter of 23 November 1999 that the third respondent had found the applicant guilty of improper conduct. It informed the applicant to appear and plead in mitigation. That certainly means that the first leg of the disciplinary hearing namely the consideration of the applicant's guilt or innocence has been finalised. The basis for this finding is the alleged conclusion that the Katz committee allegedly came to namely that she had acted improperly.

That is not what the Katz investigation team found. It was of the opinion that, because she had acted in breach of the board's decision and because of her failure to heed the serious misgivings of her colleagues about her actions, her conduct did not constitute good corporate governance. That is a far cry from a finding that she acted improperly.

Before it can be said that an employee acts improperly it must be shown that he or she acted wilfully or negligently. The word impropriety connotes blameworthiness. The applicant's contention is that section 13(2)(c) of the Land Bank Act 1944, empowers her, in her capacity as the managing director of the Bank, to determine her remuneration and that of the other employees of the Bank, in consultation with the board. She disputes that she required the authority of the board to fix her remuneration and that of the Bank's employees. When she took the decision to increase the salaries of the top six officials at the Bank, she thought that she was acting in accordance with powers conferred upon her by the Act. Such action cannot be labelled as improper conduct. Even if she had misconstrued the provisions of the Act or misunderstood the March decision of the board, that does not necessarily mean that she acted improperly.

The third respondent, in my view, committed a serious and a material misdirection in the process of considering her guilt. That misdirection vitiates its decisions and is liable to be set aside on review. In my opinion the third respondent also acted irregularly and contrary to her constitutional right to lawful and procedurally fair administrative action. It found her guilty without having heard her. It failed to comply with the audi alteram partem rule and the provisions of the Constitution.

The respondent [the Minister] argues that she was heard by the Katz investigating team. I do not agree with that submission. The Katz committee did not conduct a disciplinary hearing. It was not mandated to do so and its proceedings certainly was not of such a nature. She was never charged by the committee nor was she told that it might pronounce upon her guilt or innocence. These are fundamental requirements for a disciplinary hearing.

I have no doubt that, should the applicant apply for a review and setting aside of the proceedings and decisions of the third respondent referred to in the letter of 23 November, she will succeed. Any sentence imposed by the third respondent would for these reasons be a nullity. Furthermore, I am of the view that the fact that the second and third respondents reneged on the arrangement to afford the applicant a proper hearing constitutes unfair administrative action as envisaged by the Constitution. That is a further ground for a review and in my opinion, on the probabilities, a successful review.

In my view it would be pointless to require of the applicant to attend a hearing which will come to nothing. It was contended that *her remedy is to attend the meeting, to take her punishment and then to bring the proceedings and decisions, including the decision on sentence, on review. In my view it would be unfair to expect of the applicant to subject herself to the degrading exercise of pleading for mercy whilst the conviction was irregular and improper. The argument also loses sight of the fact that this exercise will involve considerable expense which the applicant will not be able to recover from the Bank.*

In my opinion the applicant has made out a prima facie *right if not a clear right, to the relief that she seeks. The applicant has in my view also proved the other requisites for a temporary interdict. An appearance at such a meeting as envisaged in the letter of 23 November 1999 and the imposition of a sentence, whether it is a dismissal from employment or a mere reprimand, will be injurious to the applicant's good name and reputation and will probably count against her should she leave the employ of the Bank and seek work elsewhere. Employers who employ people of the applicant's calibre would most probably prefer to employ a person without a history of improper conduct at the work place.*

She also has no other satisfactory remedy. The injury that she will suffer should she be compelled to attend this meeting, plead for mercy and be punished, cannot be corrected by a claim for damages. In the light thereof a claim for damages cannot be a satisfactory remedy.

The balance of convenience also clearly, in my view, favours the applicant. The inconvenience that will be suffered by the second and third respondents, should the enquiry be temporarily postponed, is negligible.

In the result I find for the applicant, and I make the following order:

1. *The meeting referred to in the letter of attorneys, Maserumule Incorporated, dated 23 November 1999, annexure HMD2 to the applicant's founding affidavit, which was scheduled to take place at 15:00 on 25 November 1999, and which was postponed by agreement to 10:00 today, is postponed.*

2. *The respondents are interdicted and restrained from conducting such a meeting or any meeting of similar nature, dealing with the alleged improper conduct on the part of the applicant pending the determination of an application to be launched by the applicant within 30 days from the date of this order, for an order reviewing and setting aside the proceedings and the decisions of the third respondent referred to in the aforesaid letter.*

3. *Should the applicant fail to bring such an application within 30 days from the date of this order, this order shall lapse.*

4. *The first, second and third respondents are ordered, jointly and severally, to pay the costs of the application. The costs include the costs of two counsel.*

My side of the courtroom broke into smiles all round. 'Pure poetry,' was Pam Stein's whispered comment. We tried to maintain orderly decorum until we were outside the courtroom where several Land Bank staff who had come to listen to the verdict gave me a warm embrace.

Outside there was a flank of journalists, cameras, microphones, and the challenge to put together the right diplomatic sound bite. I managed to say how much I regretted having had to come to court, how it was the first time I'd been afforded the opportunity to state my case publicly and be listened to. I concluded that much would now depend on the maturity of the parties concerned to resolve the issues.

We walked the few blocks to the Land Bank. The news had already reached my office – they'd had the radio on, waiting for the news flash. Driver Tiene Vermaak looked at Pam and then at me, smiled wryly and commented: 'They took on the wrong blondes.' For once I didn't put down a criticism of the 'blonde' jibe. This was too sweet a moment to spoil. One of the branch directors congratulated me for the stand I'd taken. He, too, was limited by his social conditioning in the comment he found most appropriate: 'Hey lady,' he said, 'I can't think of another way to say it, but – you got balls!'

Running on empty

That over-the-moon feeling of victory could last only for one interminably sweet evening. I savoured every moment of that 'high'. I was realistic enough to reckon on the possibility of having won a battle but lost the war. Such realism was to be deferred until daybreak; the intervening time of celebration was a precious interlude. The congratulatory phone messages piled up, intensifying the moment of sweetness. Glasses of whisky chinked as they met to toast our success in blocking an injustice, albeit with the regretful recognition that the abuse of power had been mandated by erstwhile comrades, now the elected representatives of the new democratic order.

This time round *Landbouweekblad* came up with a cartoon of myself and Didiza in the boxing ring, with her groaning about how difficult it was proving to knock me out.

The morning after the night before, I acknowledged my battle wounds. I was running on empty; even my adrenalin was in short supply. The day of the High Court judgment had been a Friday, with just a weekend before the Minister was to leave for the international trade talks in Seattle. The advocates and attorneys met with the Minister. I received mixed messages through the grapevine: 'If only Helena and the Minister could sit down and have a heart-to-heart discussion I think they could sort this out between themselves.' I thought back to the meeting that Moeketsi had brokered weeks earlier and that Didiza had called off at the eleventh hour. I felt that my scepticism was reasonable. The contrasting comment from the board attorney summed up as: 'There's unfettered hostility, the best option is to seek settlement.'

It seemed to me that I listened to a thousand inputs of advice and I tried to sift through them. My days were a continuing nightmare, and when night finally arrived my mind insisted on a video replay of the nightmare without the pause or stop functions being operational. I was strung out and wondered how much more strain my resilience could take before finally snapping like an overstretched elastic band. 'The job will never be the same again,' commented Gillam.

'Helena, you don't have to continue,' said one confidante. 'I know you want to have your name cleared publicly, but you've hung in so long – people are now saying that you've obviously got nothing to hide or be ashamed of, otherwise you would have quit long ago.'

'Hi, Helena – just a solidarity phone call. Well done and hang in. If it's any comfort to you, it's happening to other people in other workplaces – though not on the same scale and not with the same publicity. It's so important that you remain solid and hang in,' advised another acquaintance, a senior employee of the Department of Land Affairs.

Almost two weeks after the hearing, I had a phone conversation with George Bizos just before he left on a lengthy overseas trip. His comments were sobering and almost brought to an end my ambivalence towards the settlement proposal. Afterwards I mulled over the sum of his comments mixed with my own thoughts.

'We may have won a battle but we have not won the war. They have shown that they don't want you – to the extent that they were prepared to be unconstitutional to get rid of you. Yes, you can go on to the disciplinary hearing in the New Year. Yes, you may well be cleared by the disciplinary hearing – that's what they were afraid of and that's why they tried to circumvent it. And then what? They'll fire you anyway. They'll say there was an "irretrievable breakdown of relationship". You'll be out on the street without a job, waiting your turn in a ten-month queue for the labour court. You'll win the case of constructive dismissal – but will you want to go back to a job that has been filled in the meantime? Sure, it's a job you loved and you put everything you had into it with a passion – but it would not be the same any more. Do you wish to continue working with this Minister and this board who have displayed such a lack of support? Why would you wish to continue working with people who have reviled you? Is that the way you want to spend the year 2000? You don't need this in your life; better to stomach the idea of settlement. Walk away. There will be life again after the Land Bank. Get on with the rest of your life.'

The Minister returned from Seattle, and settlement discussions proceeded in earnest. It was a strange process. Again, as in the court case, it was like being a spectator at a theatre production of one's own life. The lawyers and industrial relations adviser were embroiled in discussions, each arguing what was 'fair', 'just' and 'an acceptable market practice for departing executives'. I was provided with information updates and occasionally asked for comment. I was faxed a draft of an agreement. I asked for the words 'amicable settlement' to be erased; I refused to be party to dishonesty. I'd become stuck between a rock and a hard place after months of psychological intimidation, nights of poor sleep, and the ensuing physical depletion. The temperature of amicability in those negotiations was minus thirty below zero. This settlement was not amicable; it was a 'hostile buyout'.

The eve of signing the settlement agreement coincided with my going out to supper with the Afrikaner counsellors who had worked in the Bank for the last eighteen months. They were horrified by my state of mind. They assured me of the support I enjoyed amongst staff and farming clients. 'You are strong,' they said. 'You have support. You are in the right. You are strong enough to survive.' They talked to me about Beyers Naude, whom they had worked with for many years, how he was steadfast in his beliefs and made the difficult choices which alienated him from the Afrikaner community he had been born into. I argued back feebly. 'Yes I may have support – but from people who do not have a voice, not with the politicians. The support is not articulated – it's not enough to get me through.' I was in no mood to be persuaded towards the idea of heroism.

But the words of the counsellors shook my earlier resolve; my confidence in the decision-in-the-making took a knock. Another night of tossing and turning. 'You're a coward,' one brain gremlin told me. 'Don't call me a coward, not after all these months.' 'Then why don't you go the extra mile?'

Towards that dawn time of surfing in and out of short sleep waves, the observations a friend made some three months earlier surfaced: 'The danger is that you end up in situations that are too consuming. There are some things that you have no control over. You need to back off and walk away from conflict. You are very insistent. You stick with things until they are worked out. But people around you are directing their anger towards you. Turn your back on it and put your energy elsewhere. It's as though the more you do the worse it gets. Be careful not to get too deeply involved in a conflict that is a black hole. If you continue to be involved in situations of deep conflict it will impact on your health. You need a retreat for six months. You need to step back.'

Pam Stein called me late mid morning to tell me that the final settlement papers were to be delivered for signing shortly, and that I should make my way to the office. I practised breathing deeply, and drove slowly and with extreme care. I had already had three minor accidents in recent weeks. I vowed to myself that I would be calm and that I would not cry. But as I sat and initialled one page after another page after another page, tears brimmed over the wet eyelashes and began to flow down my cheeks. It was as though the floodgates were being lifted and all the tears that I hadn't shed in the last months were now streaming through the sluices. The witnesses to the signing arranged stony expressions on their faces and left the room as quickly as possible.

'You don't have to go through with this. We can tear this up,' Pam told me.

Between sobs, I explained: 'With my head I know that signing is the right thing to do – but my heart? My heart feels as though it's going to break.'

Aftermath

I found no peace, there was no relief at having signed. I'd written a statement days before which was released to the press. I got a phone call the next evening from one of the board members that stunned me.

'I'm really angry with you. I heard that you've decided to leave.'

'But I thought you were party to the whole settlement initiative?' I protested.

'No, it was the subcommittee. The rest of us were not consulted. You know I've stood firmly behind you. I really tried to do my best for you. I wanted you to carry on.'

'I know, and I'd like to thank you for your support. But in this case, your best wasn't good enough. They are just too strong. The Minister is behind them.'

I watched the news on television, and was angered by chairperson Sam Mkhabela's falsity. How could he so shamelessly mouth words about 'amicable settlement' when precisely that phrase had been scotched from the settlement agreement? The ANC spokesperson, Smuts Ngonyama, then talked about 'the ANC' being glad that the situation had been 'resolved'. More anger. You call this resolution? To squeeze someone out of a job that they are doing well? We have such a dearth of talented, competent people and yet in several ministries we'd been witnessing the exodus of those who for one reason or another had fallen foul of the politician in charge. This was no longer the ANC that I joined in the early eighties, that pooled all talents, whatever people had to offer, in the interests of the liberation struggle.

I floated through Christmas Eve, Christmas Day, Boxing Day. On the surface they were pleasant days filled with family, friends and phone calls, but below the surface there was turmoil and the setting in of grief. I also had to face up to my last three days at the Land Bank, writing handover memos and packing up my office. They were awful days. Employees came to my office shaking their heads. 'It shouldn't have ended this way. You didn't deserve this.' It was as if someone close to me had died and this was the time for the receiving of condolences – but in this instance the 'death' was my own and I the living witness to it. Bouquets of roses arrived, one from a Bank branch with the message 'You made a difference'. Lettie cried and cried and cried. Dr Jacobs brought champagne to toast me on my way – and somehow there was a little laughter mixed in with the tears.

Whatever possessed me to agree to a TV interview during those awful three days? I was in such poor shape. I'd read the *Business Day* editorial, 'A sorry episode': *

> The resignation of Land Bank MD Helena Dolny brings down the curtain on a sorry episode which does no credit to the Land Bank's board, Land and Agricultural Minister Thoko Didiza and perhaps even President Thabo Mbeki. Mbeki likes to operate by remote control. Given Didiza's in-experience and the controversy around the Dolny affair, there can be little doubt about his involvement . . . What one might call smiling assassination has become the hallmark of Mbeki's leadership. He gives no hint of his displeasure – until, without warning, the guillotine descends.

I'd read the Democratic Party's accusation that the team that Hanekom put together was slowly but surely being axed. I thought back to the teasing of my friend after the new Minister's appointment: 'I hear there's a hit list – and you're on it.' During the weeks of the never-ending saga,

---

*'A sorry episode', *Business Day* editorial, 28 December 1999.

he would call occasionally and, with irreverent humour, ask: 'Dolny, tell me, how's the process of ethnic cleansing going?' He'd always somehow manage to make me laugh – no matter how bleak I felt. I was grateful for the laughter – it sustained me.

Now, as I was being interviewed and asked what I thought of the editorial and the DP statement, ill-timed facetiousness popped up like a true gremlin: 'Some people call it ethnic cleansing,' I quipped ironically.

Did that phrase really slip out? It was only my nearest and dearest who knew the origin of the quip; even so, my teenager said: 'Mom, you didn't really say that, did you? Not in public? Not on television?' But yes, I did, and for Joe Public the remark was taken at face value. It was broadcast over and over again in the Christmas to New Year interlude when there seemed to be a desperate shortage of other news. The SABC hauled out the analysts on ethnic cleansing. The journalists had a field day.

Taken at face value, it was really the most outrageous remark. In collegial gossip, however, the words referred to the 'Hanekom appointees' – a group of people black and white (Budlender, Goldblatt, Johnson, Lund, Nhoca, Nkosi, Simbi and others), perceived as sharing a common view of rural development, who were being systematically marginalised or rooted out of positions of responsibility. It is easy enough for a spin to be put on the departures (e.g. one resigned, one wasn't performing, another's contract was coming to an end, et ceteras) by the ministerial spin-doctor whose very job was to convince us to conclude: 'What a relief! There's no witch-hunt.' This was the tongue-in-cheek comment by Hogarth,* satirical columnist in the *Sunday Times*. However, the reality of the convergence of the continuing departures appeared to be more than 'just an innocent coincidence'. It is regrettable that resolution of ideological differences was not attempted; the preference was to put scarce talent and intellectual capital out of service.

Nevertheless the error in framing the remark as I did was mine alone. After six months of gruelling trauma, there was exhaustion, exasperation, and a damaged capacity for diplomacy. Notwithstanding these mitigating factors, irony was and is an inappropriate form of expression for television sound bites. There's a responsibility prerequisite in our race-sensitive South Africa for a more careful choice of words.

Mea culpa. I retreated into self-flagellation mode. My Catholic upbringing had its own field day. Self-flagellation mixed with grief was a devastating blend.

---

*Hogarth, 'Ethnic cleansing or just dirty politics', *Sunday Times*, 9 January 2000.

My friends rescued me from myself, and through their efforts the pieces that I had broken into were picked up and slowly glued back together.

'Helena,' said a Robben Island comrade, 'you have a reputation as an honest activist. If you made a mistake, it should never have been handled in this way.'

Another comrade interjected: 'Yes, but other people can make the most whopping mistakes and get away with it.' Everyone knew he was talking about Minister Maduna's mistaken accusation of Kleuver, the Auditor General, which unnecessarily cost the taxpayer some R30-million to investigate.

Another comrade quipped: 'But Helena didn't need to make a mistake; they'd have invented one.'

A young woman phoned me to tell me she'd just spent a month with her parents in their Transkei village. 'People on the ground know how the Land Bank changed since you took over. In my parents' village people have Land Bank loans for the first time ever. Remember those successes. No one can ever take that away from you.'

I was in London at the beginning of March 2000 when I got a phone call from a journalist asking me what I thought about the Land Bank executive salary hikes having gone through – and backdated to April 1999 into the bargain. What's more, the inconsistency of the resolution taken at the March 1999 board meeting was to be revisited. The revised decision taken almost one year later to the day, at the end of March 2000, was that the median was to be the price basis for all jobs in the Land Bank including the top six executive managers; again with back pay! On that basis, my successor would now earn a package of R1,4-million, or twenty-five per cent more than the R1,1-million approved by the transformation board in March 1999.*

Of course I felt vindicated. It proved that the furore about the increase was but a smoke and mirrors act to conjure up a charge against me – but once I was out of the way, the logic and sound governance policy of allowing the pay rise to go through was unassailable.

---

*D Greybe, 'Land Bank officials get huge increases', *Business Day*, 3 March 2000.

TEN

A QUESTION OF GOVERNANCE

A damaged business

It would be simple to dismiss the problems experienced at the Land Bank as the result of political intrigue and interference. I think of such a response as one of analytical abdication. It begs the question of what we should expect from corporate governance. The Bank saga is a testimony of what can unfold when the exercise of governance is below par.

In January 2000 a journalist wrote: 'Behind Helena Dolny's ouster from the top spot at the Land Bank lies a tangled web of political friendships gone wrong, ideological fall outs over land reform, bitter rivalries and undisclosed relationships between some of the actors . . . Dolny was in reality a minor player in these disputes . . .'*

Asked to comment, Sam Mkhabela, the chairperson of the Land Bank board said: 'Alleged personal and ideological relationships and rivalries are unknown to me, nor were they the basis of the board's decisions. The board sought to safeguard good corporate governance . . . and to ensure that its executive was above reproach in carrying out its fiduciary duties.' Therein lies the rub. My own view is that if there had been effective corporate governance at the Bank, events would not have turned out as they did.

The public saga sparked off by *The Star*'s coverage of the Jack letter lasted six months. The damage it caused was cumulative over time – precisely because of the way it was handled by the board. Staff, manage-

---

*Howard Barrell, 'A Struggle Rooted in the Land', *Mail & Guardian*, 7-13 January 2000.

ment and executive management was distracted by the continuing tension and cloud of irresolution, and this took its toll on the restructuring of the business. Transformation stalled, the unbundling of the branch network did not receive the attention it required. The development of the criteria and operational rules for new intermediaries and franchises slowed down. Problems emerged with the implementation of the new information technology system. In normal circumstances these would have been picked up on earlier and become the focus of dedicated management attention. There were problems in reconciling accounts, and several months of delay in the provision of year end figures to parliament. And yet the figures would show that, in spite of the problems, the Bank had in fact enjoyed its best ever financial year. The continued attrition was damaging to staff morale. A few key staff members eventually left as a result of their disenchantment and lack of confidence in the performance of the new board of directors.

Such damage incurs financial costs. Investors were hesitant and the Bank began to pay more for the purchase of its funds, reflecting the market assessment. This naturally impacted on the bottom line of the business resulting in less surplus revenue to put into development spending. The Bank also ran up legal bills amounting to several hundreds of thousands of rands, which the Auditor General, with a stringent eye, might well classify as 'fruitless expenditure'.

There were some precarious weeks when we became a bank that was almost out of money to lend.* We were consumed with anxiety as we struggled to manage our cash flow. Our internal crisis coincided with a period in which several of our investors' commitments were due for re-payment; if we could not persuade them to reinvest we would be in serious trouble. In the pipeline there were loans approved but not yet disbursed. We were doing a balancing act that was barely under control. The day the head of the wholesale finance unit declared that he needed an extra two hundred million for a large loan to a cooperative, we balked. If we said yes, we'd be close to an empty till. We racked our brains about how we would say no without provoking a spate of whispering in the market environment about our financial troubles.

The damage at the Bank was of an order which in other circumstances would possibly have ended in its demise. There have been instances where a fall in investor confidence has led to a withdrawal of funds,

---

*D Greybe, 'Saga must end, Land Bank is told: Short term paper no longer highly sought after in money market, says financial adviser', *Business Day*, 14 October 1999.

which has then brought the institution to its knees as a result of cash flow problems. The woes of FBC Fidelity Bank, weeks earlier, were precisely exacerbated by a liquidity squeeze after a run on its deposits and led to the appointment of a curator in October 1999. The Land Bank appeared to be veering towards the same fate in early November 1999. There were late night phone calls with high ranking government officials to ensure that the R1,6-billion of promissory notes held by the Public Investment Corporation would be renewed later in the month. If those promissory notes had been in the hands of private investors, and not renewed, the outcome would have been catastrophic.

The link between the problems the Bank experienced and the corporate governance problem has to be acknowledged. One of the primary requirements of good corporate governance is the ability to resolve crises with speed, before too much damage is done. It is doubtful that such a crippling process would have been allowed to run on for such length of time in a private sector business. Directors of a private company are all too aware that their responsibility is to take care of company assets and that vacillation in dealing with a problem will affect the bottom line and hurt the shareholders' pocket.

In private sector businesses it is often the case that directors hold shares in the company. Mervyn King, South Africa's foremost expert on corporate governance, addressing a business school forum in September 2000, stated that he is in favour of directors investing their own money in businesses for which they assume governance responsibility, commenting: 'It focuses the mind somewhat.'* The possession of shares secures the alignment of the directors with the interests of the company.

The problem with public sector companies is that the shareholder is ultimately the country's citizenry represented by the minister of the portfolio under whose jurisdiction the public entity belongs. The minister stands neither to gain nor to suffer materially from the performance of the entity. Similarly, the board of directors of a public company stands to lose nothing if the enterprise underperforms. It is increasingly common for the remuneration of executive directors to be linked to a performance agreement. There seems to be no reason why the same should not apply to the non-executive directors, whether such performance is measured in financial terms or according to the accomplishment of development objectives. In the meantime, the issue of leverage over non-executive directors' performance in state-owned companies remains unresolved.

---

*Mervyn King, 'Developments in Corporate Governance', presentation and discussion at the Gordon Institute of Business Science, 18 September 2000.

What recourse is there when a board of directors fails to perform – yet underperformance is not recognised by the politician as the shareowner representative of the public interest?

A not uncommon public sector experience

Effective governance produces better business results according to an investors' report carried out by McKinsey, a worldwide consulting firm. So while people often think of the value of good governance as being abstract, the reality is that it affects the bottom line. The McKinsey survey showed that 'the great institutions of the world practising positive corporate governance attract better and cheaper investment, as do the countries whose corporations employ it.'* Governance standards provide the basis for confidence in investment. The level of confidence finds expression in the price paid (i.e. the rate of interest) by a country for the funds it needs to borrow. At a company level, the market also makes a judgement through the pricing of funds in the domestic market. In the case of the Land Bank, the results were tangible; investors began to demand that we pay them more to borrow their money for our onlending purposes.

South Africa's private sector corporate governance is rated as one of the best among emerging market economies. However there are problems of governance in several of South Africa's public entities; the Land Bank's experience is not unique. There have been problems at the South African Broadcasting Corporation, the Mpumalanga Parks Board, and the Mpumalanga Housing Board. A litany of unsavoury governance anecdotes is provided by the dealings that have taken place over the power to award cellular phone licences, the debacle over the privatisation of Sun Airways, the problematic privatisation of the state forestry company SAFCOL, and in connection with the purchase of new planes by South African Airways, besides irregularities in the award of contracts for the purchase of weapons and defence machinery.

The problems have varied between different public entities, but in their totality they call for greater respect between the parties involved as to their different roles, as well as adherence to fundamental principles of corporate governance. There are instances where problems between the board and the minister as political stakeholder have been exacerbated by public servant interference. There have been privatisation initiatives in which the ministerial advisers, public servants, and externally appointed transaction advisers have pointedly ignored the board of

---

Business Day, 2 October 2000.

directors, thus effectively emasculating them in respect of their responsibility for governance.

Political interference in the work of a number of public sector boards has sapped their effectiveness like a cancer. There are boards whose performance has been adversely affected to the extent that the proper accomplishment of their fiduciary duties has been compromised and they have resorted to seeking advice on the possible juridical liability of their failure to adequately safeguard the value of the assets. In at least one public company civil servants appear to have done a behind-the-scenes deal with trade unions and presented a *fait accompli* to the board of directors. As a result, the absorption of employees who were formerly in the pay of a government department will cost the company extra millions of rands in an increased wage bill, thus affecting future business prospects.

It is not uncommon for directors of state-owned companies to complain that both ministers and civil servants fail to understand the principles of corporate governance. A more critical view is that they do not wish to acknowledge the principles because the confusion created then allows the minister and his or her surrogates to repossess a delegated power. By this light, even though the minister-as-shareholder may have appointed a board of directors as the caretaker of governance it emerges that he or she subsequently informally relegates the powers of the board. Such relegation, downgrading, is even more likely, due to possible mistrust, in the case where a minister inherits an existing board on taking office. The relegation of the board takes place through a process which allows power to be usurped by transitory advisers and government officials, some of whom are enamoured of their licence to play god with public assets worth hundreds of millions of rands. It should not happen, but in practice board members have passively acquiesced or succumbed to intimidation, and therefore failed to take a stand against political interference.

Shared clarity between the board of directors and the government is of paramount importance to safeguard the exercise of good governance. Indications of failure by either party to accept the clearly defined roles constitute a danger signal. In October 2000 a newspaper report noted:* 'A controversial proposal by the board of the SABC (South African Broadcasting Corporation) to refer senior appointments to the Cabinet for approval is likely to be challenged in Parliament.' The issue at stake is independence – one of the cornerstones of governance. One of the SABC's

---

Mail & Guardian, 6-12 October 2000.

transformation objectives defined after the 1994 democratic elections was to ensure that it would cease to be the state broadcaster and rather become the public broadcaster, independent of the party holding power. The Freedom of Expression Institute commented that if cabinet were to have final powers of appointment of the top three executives 'it could lead to interference in the affairs of the Corporation and compromise the integrity of the board'. If cabinet were indeed to approve appointments the question would need to be asked: Does government really understand governance? The defence of good corporate governance in the public sector depends on all the involved parties having a fundamental commitment to respecting its principles.

In September 1999 the Minister of Public Enterprises confirmed the need for state-owned companies to adhere to the King Commission recommendations and emphasised: 'We need clearly defined roles for management, the board and government as the shareholder so that we do not run into collision with one another.'* It may be observed that the respective roles have long been defined; the issue is not one of definition but rather of the need for the parties concerned to understand and respect the defined roles.

King I, and *King II* and I

The divide between the theory and the practice of corporate governance was of great import to my existence as managing director of the Land Bank. As South Africans, we own a code of corporate governance that was published in 1994 just after the establishment of our new democracy, and which is highly regarded internationally. It was developed by a committee under the leadership of Mervyn King, a Senior Counsel, former judge of the Supreme Court of South Africa, and a successful businessman – a man whose credentials for the task were clearly impeccable. He is currently President of the Commonwealth Association on Corporate Governance. The 1994 code, known as the 'King Code', goes beyond the Cadbury Code developed in the United Kingdom in its tailor-made recommendations to deal specifically with our need to establish boards of directors that reflect our new non-racial state.

The King Code 1994, referred to here as *King I*, laid out in considerable detail what is required of a board of directors in regard to a range of aspects including the process of selection of members, their skills and qualities, their tasks, and the respective roles of the shareholder, the

---

*Jeff Radebe, Budget vote address to parliament, 14 April 2000.

board and the executive management. The recommendations were drawn up with the expressed intention that they should apply not only to private sector companies but also to large public, i.e. government-owned, entities including the Land Bank.* In 1999 the new Minister of Public Enterprises reiterated that government would 'seek a vigorous implementation of the Corporate Governance Principles laid down by the King Commission'.

In 2000 the King Commission was reconstituted as *King II* and a revised code is expected to be published by April 2001. The need for revision has arisen from the acknowledgement of the changing characteristics of the business world as we begin the twenty-first century. The challenges are interesting. While the four pillars of corporate governance – fairness, accountability, responsibility and transparency – remain unassailable, new issues have emerged.

The issue of transient ownership gives rise to questions on accountability. The profile of the listed shareowners of a company changes daily as trading takes place on the stock exchange. The increasingly fluid nature of ownership in the private sector produces its own conundrum. The conceptual foundation that initially provided the *raison d'être* of creating boards of directors was that of 'guardianship'. But to whom is the board accountable nowadays when the shareowners are themselves constantly changing, and who guards the guardians? The primary duty of the board of directors is less and less one of accountability to an amorphous mass of shareowners, but rather the guardianship of the long-term sustainability of the company. The performance of the board in this role is critical.

Other challenges lie in the changing nature of companies.† The boards of directors used to function as caretakers of the financial asset – yet we live in a world in which the non-financial assets of a company, its skills base and intellectual capital, are now often of greater value than the financial assets. Technological advancement has revolutionised commerce. E-trading will come to dominate, requiring an updated regulatory environment. Multinationals are unquestionably powerful and carry extraordinary importance within national economies. In Holland, Shell represents forty per cent of the country's market capitalisation. The financial power wielded by a multinational can significantly affect the destiny of a country and has called into question the true power of a government elected to carry out the will of the people.

---

*King I, 1994, Chapter 3, clause 2.
†Issues in the following paragraphs were cited by Mervyn King at the Gordon Institute of Business Science presentation, September 2000.

The operating environment of any business is also changing. It used to be that the board of directors was primarily concerned with taking care of the bottom line for their shareowners and that involved overseeing management's implementation of strategy. However, the strategy for a company now has to consider the wider operating environment, and take serious heed of the stakeholders whose lives are affected by company business. The stakeholder definition goes beyond those whose business or communities are directly affected and includes pressure groups who are increasingly effective in lobbying for change when they are dissatisfied. Animal rights groups have successfully persuaded pension companies to disinvest in drug firms that test their products on animals. Their tactics include making directors the target of discomfort; names and telephone numbers have been published to assist an effective lobbying campaign.

Whereas the original concept of governance focused largely on the financial assets and the duty of directors to pronounce on the viability of the company, there is now a set of non-financials that directors must report on in fulfilment of their duties. Such non-financials include: innovation, learning and training, identification of stakeholders, reciprocal relationships, management credibility as perceived externally, the ability to attract and incentivise talent, and ensuring that the company has an appropriate level of technology in line with that of its competitors. There is no doubt that *King II* will be a more sophisticated product, more suitable to our twenty-first century operating environment.

The problems arising in South African public sector companies are basic and the result of an inadequate application of the principles so clearly set out in *King I*. At least this was my first line of argument when I tried to analyse 'So what precisely went wrong with corporate governance at the Land Bank?' I began to set out the deviations from *King I* that had occurred, thinking that if only the King recommendations had been adhered to things would have turned out differently. But that is not the conclusion that stayed with me. Whereas *King I* is intended to be applicable to both private and state-owned companies, I found myself increasingly debating the difference between them which stems from the differing nature of the shareholder. The power and political character of the single statutory entity as shareholder is the root cause of many of the problems confronted by the directors of public companies.

The transposition on to public entities of a governance model designed for private sector companies would appear to be taking strain. Questions arise about the applicability of the model of a unitary board as recommended by *King I*. There is an emerging opinion that *King II* should tailor-make some recommendations for state-owned companies that acknowledge the difference in the nature of the shareholder between public and private sector business.

Issues of independence and balance

Up until 1995 the Land Bank board comprised the managing director and eight full-time directors who were selected from the Afrikaner farming community. Under the hegemony of the National Party the alignment of its policies and the institutional implementation of benefits to a select portion of the populace was seamless. In respect of corporate governance at the Land Bank, there was no question of the independence of the directors to act in the best interests of the company. White farmer well-being took precedence over business considerations, as reflected in the subsidised rates to this historically advantaged minority. The comfortable white apple cart was upset in 1994 and the new democratic order demanded a revision of board membership of public entities to break the outdated hegemony. In the case of the Land Bank, during 1995 two additional board members were selected from among the Strauss commissioners. Bonile Jack and Daphne Motsepe were not only the first black directors but also the first truly non-executive directors of the Land Bank board in that, unlike the other full-time board members, they had no management role and did not receive salaries – they earned fees only for their attendance at board meetings. Another change took place – the ministerial-shareholder jurisdiction of the Land Bank fell to the Minister of Finance, but in December 1996 cabinet decided that the Minister of Agriculture and Land Affairs would more appropriately attend to the required new direction of this public entity.

A new Land Bank board, specifically chosen to support institutional transformation, and thus referred to as the 'Transformation Board', was appointed to take up its duties on 1 April 1997 for a specified period of not more than two years. There was a startling switchover to a board consisting entirely of non-executive directors, apart from the managing director.

The Cadbury Code recommendation was that for good corporate governance to have a real chance there should be at least three independent non-executive directors of sufficient calibre for the weight of their independent judgement to be influential. A proposed modification, bearing in mind that the size of a board may vary was: 'The company board shall consist of a minimum of one third non-executive directors, the majority of whom should preferably be free of any other business, or financial connection, with the company, apart from their share-holdings.'*

This is not what happened at the Land Bank. The ratio of non-executive directors to executive directors was 10:1. My instinctive concern that problems might arise from this imbalance was correct. After a year of creative endeavour we hit on an issue on which there was complete disagreement between the executive management, represented by myself as the sole executive director, and the non-executive directors. The issue was a difference of opinion over how to handle a disciplinary matter involving the board secretary. This is not normally an issue which would involve the deliberations of a board – but in the case of the Land Bank we were still working with outdated statutes, first drafted in 1947, which were premised on the continued existence of a full-time board with prescribed managerial responsibilities.

What emerged was the obvious necessity for the revision of statute. But, more important it seems to me, a board that is so unequal in its balance between executive and non-executive members is faulty in various ways. Firstly, there are not enough board members with a serious day-to-day understanding of the business able to make a significant contribution to deliberations. Secondly, a sole executive director is placed in the onerous position of representing the entire executive management and becomes vulnerable to the personalisation of disagreements, should they arise.

King I observed that if the appropriate check and balance of the executive directors is to be ensured, then the membership of a board should comprise 'at least an equal number of executive and non-executive directors'. The Land Bank statutes provided for a board of directors of up to twelve members. A composition of seven non-executive and five executive might have resulted in better corporate governance than the 10:1 configuration that I inherited on 1 May 1997 when taking up the position of managing director.

Conflation of roles: managing director and chairperson of the board

It used to be more common that a managing director of a company was also the chairperson of the board of directors, more especially in companies that had their roots in a family business that had extended its ownership by issuing shares. It is however strongly advised and generally accepted

---

*N N G Maw *in* S Crane (ed), 1995, p.1055.

that it is better to separate these two roles: 'The two jobs are wholly different. The chairman is there not only to supervise the proper and efficient conduct of the board meetings; his or her task is also to encourage, question and evaluate and (sometimes) kick management.'*

The governance literature also argues the merits of the board chairperson being a non-executive director. *King I* assigns to the chairperson the responsibility of ensuring the rapid integration and effective contribution of new board members. Furthermore, it falls to the chairperson to ensure that the composition of the board of directors is balanced in terms of the numerical representation of executive and non-executive directors. *King I* expects the chairperson to have sufficient knowledge of the business to determine the agenda for a meeting, and 'The Chair must ensure that all board members are as fully informed as possible on any issue on which a decision has to be made. The Chair must ensure that executive directors play not only a management role, but fully participate in the governance of the company.'†

It was a surprise to me that my letter of appointment congratulated me on becoming both the managing director and chairperson of the board. This was another gremlin emerging from the continued use of an outdated statute. While Cadbury and *King I* provided the intellectual rationale explaining the difference in roles and positing that better governance would be achieved by separation, my concerns about the conflation were more practical. I soon found it humanly impossible to drive a transformation initiative, begin the process of building a supportive internal executive team, and simultaneously meet the very onerous responsibilities assigned to a chairperson.

The transformation board of the Land Bank took its role seriously and its members were putting in the time to meet every month. The chairperson's preparatory role with regard to the agenda, and ensuring that all board members were up to date on issues when they had missed meetings, proved too much to handle. I asked the consultants working on the drafting of amendments to the Land Bank Act what might be done pending a change in legislation. They proposed the idea of a 'Chairperson Designate'. I approached the Minister to field this idea, and formally wrote to him expressing my concerns and suggesting the appointment of a chairperson designate. In November 1997 Bonile Jack received, and responded positively to, the invitation from the Minister to take up the position.

---

*N N G Maw *in* S Crane (ed), 1995, p.1056.
†*King I*, 1994, Chapter 7, clause 3.

Confusion over role and function

The *King I* code of corporate governance is clear that the definition of the mandate is the shareholder's responsibility. The board's responsibility is to define the strategy to fulfil the mandate. Management responsibility is to implement the strategy.

King I gives its assessment of what makes a good board: 'There are three keys to a good board. The members understand and agree on what are the proper functions of the board; the board is composed of people of integrity who bring a blend of knowledge, skills, attitudes, experience and commitment to the job; and finally the board is led by a capable chair who brings out the best – individually and collectively – in the directors.'

Besides the responsibility for strategy, *King I* is clear that a board of directors will operate with committees who will spend time dedicated to issues such as the audit oversight, remuneration policy and affirmative action.

In light of the Land Bank debacle over the implementation of re-muneration policy, it is interesting to note *King I* on this subject: 'A remuneration committee will not necessarily reflect the view of the shareholders: At the AGM the Chair of the Remuneration Committee should motivate the remuneration decisions. In discussing remuner-ation the committee and shareholders must be mindful of the fact that a director's remuneration is a reward for enterprise so that there should be an incentive for superior performance but likewise there should not be rewards for failure. The shareholders are entitled to openness and disclosure in regard to directors' earnings so that they can see that the directors are being fairly rewarded . . . and that the executive directors are further remunerated if they surpass the expected results of properly performing their tasks. They need consistent reports so that they can compare year on year remuneration and a breakdown of earnings. Having said this, it seems unnecessary for the needs of the shareholders to disclose and discuss each individual director's remuneration in detail.'

On this basis *King I* would not expect a board to be involved in discussions with the shareholder on the remuneration of the executives. In the case of the Land Bank, the shareholder representative being the Minister, the expressed preference by some board members that salaries should be discussed with the Minister indicates a failure to truly assume governance responsibility, thus permitting a confusion of roles. Once the confusion is created a snowstorm effect with impaired visibility ensues, with deleterious consequences. Minister Didiza's intervention in June 1999 to issue an instruction to executive management with regard to salaries was entirely beyond her responsibilities either in terms of the Land Bank statute or according to the recommendations of *King I*, which government purports to wish to follow.

The chairperson's communication role

The leadership and communication roles of the chairperson cannot be overstated. These are important not only for determining priorities and setting the agenda for board meetings, but also include the task of ensuring a common understanding of the important issues by the entire board. In the words of *King I*: 'The Chair must also ensure that all board members are as fully informed as possible on any issue on which a decision is to be made.'

The Land Bank remuneration policy was the result of months of discussion and homework by the remuneration committee. The committee's work was undertaken on the basis of the board's expressed policy intention that salaries be pegged to market norms for the financial services industry. In June 1998 the comparative earnings of individuals in similar public enterprises, as well as the private sector, were discussed – the implications that there would be significant increases for top management were clear. A resolution on remuneration policy was comprehensively elaborated and formally adopted in November 1998 at a full board meeting. For some non-executive directors to have expressed surprise months later at the magnitude of increases for the directors in keeping with the policy they had approved, indicates a lack of communication from the board chairperson. This proved to be of special importance when members had missed board meetings at which crucial policy decisions were taken.

The communication issue was rooted in two problem areas: the time constraints of the chairperson and the remuneration of the non-executive directors. There was expressed dissatisfaction with the amount of time that Land Bank duties consumed, especially by those members who were drawn away from their own business interests. They said that the time they sacrificed was not adequately compensated, leading to an unwillingness to dedicate more time. In this regard, non-executive directors draw sympathy from King, who has stated that the common payment of R15 000 to R30 000 per year for board members is a paltry sum when the time requirements and levels of responsibility are seriously considered.

A problematic selection process

King I presupposes a continuing board with a modicum of turnover and recommends that the entire board makes nominations for any vacancy. In South Africa's public entities the practice is that the Minister, as shareholder representative, puts forward nominations for cabinet consideration and approval. Whether or not there is any consultation with the chairperson or board is entirely the Minister's prerogative. Acquaintances who serve as board members on public entities tell me that it is not uncommon for a new member to arrive at a board meeting, selected by the minister in question, without forewarning to the existing board members.

This practice flies in the face of accepted good corporate governance. The Cadbury Committee states: 'Given the importance of their distinctive contribution, non-executive directors should be selected with the same impartiality and care as senior executives. We recommend that their formal appointment should be a matter for the board as a whole and that there should be a formal selection process, which will reinforce the independence of the non-executive directors and make it evident that they have been appointed on merit and not through any form of patronage. We regard it as good practice for a nomination committee to carry out the selection process and to make proposals to the board.'

King I argued against nomination committees tasked with the purpose of proposing new board members, and presented a case for why this should be the responsibility of the entire board:* 'Nomination committees will not improve incorrect selection processes. The selection process in the past has been wrong. It is seen as part of an "old boys' network" of "cronyism". Usually the board knows of a retiring director and the chair proposes the new appointment. It is usually someone well known to the chair or a senior board member. There is some discussion about their being a "good chap" and they are duly appointed. Further, in the past in South Africa, the appointments have usually been male and white.'

The term of office for the Land Bank's transformation board was for a maximum period of two years. Fifteen months into the completion of its two-year term, the board carried out a workshop which examined the skills required within a board, and the support required for it to fulfil its responsibilities adequately. The conclusions reached in this workshop were presented to the Minister with the intention that the selection of the next board be informed by these considerations. The

---

*King I, 1994, Chapter 9, clauses 3 and 4.

recommendations included a proposal that the next board comprise seven non-executive and five executive directors. There were also suggestions about particular specialisations that might be especially useful on the next board. For example, discussions on the need for a social accountability approach to the Land Bank's business were under way; a non-executive director attuned to this business approach was considered to be especially valuable. Other considerations were also tabled; the concern over time availability led to a recommendation that no person who was already a member of five other boards should be appointed.

In early 1999 Bonile Jack wrote to the Minister requesting that the board's tenure should be extended by three months to end in June 1999. This proposal was not accepted. Instead the Minister sent a request to the non-executive members to indicate their willingness or otherwise to serve as members of the new board which he intimated would be appointed by the end of March to take up office with immediate effect.

That enquiry was the beginning and the end of any consultation process by the Minister with the directors. A copy of an approved cabinet memo received by my office in April 1999 indicated that the Land Bank was currently operating without a board of directors, hence the urgency to take a decision on the membership of a new board. The approved membership comprised eight non-executive directors and three executive directors – myself, the general manager operations and the general manager finance. The rationale for the Minister's choice of eight non-executive members seemed to have been based on constituency considerations. There was a person who represented the interests of the established commercial farming/agribusiness community. Another worked in a grassroots NGO and represented the interests of the historically disadvantaged. There were three persons directly representing ministerial interests. One was a deputy director general in the Department of Land Affairs. Another was a deputy director general in the Department of Agriculture. The third was an adviser to the Minister of Finance. Another person was the CEO of a public entity dealing with the provision of training to support small business development. The financial expertise was embodied in a person drawn from a black empowerment company. I discovered to my dismay that he was already a member of more than ten boards; my qualms that he would not have sufficient time to attend meetings proved well founded. Another person was drawn from a private sector company and had recently acquired human resources management experience. As far as I could tell from his CV, he had no previous experience of serving on the board of directors of a business enterprise.

I was a deeply concerned managing director when I learnt of the appointment of the new board. My fears were various. I feared factional interests on the part of the public servants, and my anxiety was later vindicated. I am told that there used to be a ruling that public servants could not be appointed as members of (parastatal) public entities because of reservations about their independence and possible vested interests. It would seem that in the peaceful revolution which overturned the entire cabinet membership of the country there was a loss of institutional memory and this important consideration was forgotten. The Land Bank is not the only state-owned development finance institution with civil servants on its board of directors. The same practice is true of the Development Bank of Southern Africa and the Industrial Development Corporation.

King I sets store on the integrity, skills and independence of the non-executive directors chosen to serve on a board: 'Each board member must, of course, have absolute integrity.' Furthermore 'All directors, both executive and non-executive are bound by fiduciary duties (i.e. duties of loyalty) and duties of care and skill.' An additional invocation is that 'a board should not be dominated by an individual or individuals, so as to ensure that an objective and intellectually honest collective mind is brought to bear on decisions.'

The Land Bank experience substantially supports these former reservations about the possible lack of independence of public servants, and also the power they may exert because of the special link to the politician shareholder. Once the non-executive board member Masiphula Mbongwa, deputy director general of Agriculture, was identified as the right hand man of the new Minister, his influence dominated the outcome of board deliberations. He also became the link person with the lawyers who acted on behalf of Minister Didiza in the events leading up to the high court interdict hearing. His undue influence was acknowledged by other board members. 'When Masiphula speaks it is as though he speaks with the voice of the Minister,' I was told.

My greater concern, on learning who the new appointees were, was to assist an effective handover process from the outgoing board to the incoming board. There were two non-executive members who were continuing for a second term of office, but the other six appointees were coming in cold. *King I* states: 'It usually takes a year for a non-executive director to become familiar with the business of the company and they usually serve an apprenticeship for six months to one year, while they are absorbing all that is happening around them. Consequently we believe that a three year term of office is too short, but equally why should a five or ten year term be correct?'*

Three, possibly four, of the new members had little experience as board members of other companies. *King I* reiterates that directors have 'awesome' responsibilities and must be properly prepared to carry out their duties. The chairperson should give letters of appointment to new board members that define their duties. Each new board member must have proper internal training, i.e. must undergo a proper process of induction into the company's affairs. If a new director has no prior board experience, training should be provided before the board responsibilities are assumed. 'Such considerations,' says *King I*, 'need to be uppermost in the minds of boards in making new appointments.'

A further stipulation of *King I* is that it is the responsibility of the chairperson to facilitate the integration of new members to secure their 'effective and rapid contribution'.† The chair is also tasked to clarify expectations concerning roles, give briefings on individual liability, indicate the responsibilities of any committee on which the new director may be required to serve, and finally to ensure that training is available should it be needed.

I was left with a conundrum: how to secure an effective board handover process, while noting the legal advice that I received insisting that a board required a chairperson for legal constitutionality. Bonile Jack had indicated his unwillingness to serve another term of office on the board of directors. The cabinet memo named eleven members of a twelve-person board. The top spot of non-executive chairperson remained vacant. We were a board without leadership. A member of the Minister's staff assured me that the lacuna was intentional. The Minister was hopeful that after the 1999 elections, a person of exactly the appropriate calibre might be free to take up the position.

A schism in continuity

King I does not anticipate the needs of a handover process. The recommendations assume a continuing board with a modicum of turnover due to resignations or because there might be a stipulated maximum term of office.

My attempts at a successful handover were stymied by the election activities under way. Bonile Jack expressed his wish that the Minister be present for part of the induction meeting. It was a fair expectation; a

---

King I, 1994, Chapter 6, clause 10.
†Ibid, Chapter 9, clauses 8.1 to 8.4.

similar meeting had taken place when there was a change in the board of directors of the Agricultural Research Council. The occasion would provide a board debriefing for the Minister and double as a briefing for the new members on the important policy issues that the outgoing board had grappled with. There were difficulties over setting a date, but finally the Minister's office agreed to an evening including dinner on 11 May 1999. The old board would continue its meeting with the new board members for the whole of 12 May to fast track bringing the new members up to speed. Unfortunately, as I was to learn, the ANC's general secretary Kgalema Motlanthe intervened and issued an instruction to cabinet ministers that they needed to postpone their ministerial engagements and pull out all stops in the election effort. Three days before the agreed upon evening meeting the Minister cancelled. His insufficient compensation was to send the director general of Land Affairs as a substitute to offer his thanks and welcome.

I knew that some of the outgoing board members would be disappointed that their term of office was not being renewed. I had suggested to the Minister's secretary that she send letters of thanks to the outgoing members, and offered to draft such letters on an individual basis because of my familiarity with the persons and the roles that they had played. The draft letters were e-mailed to the Minister's secretariat but, for whatever reason, they were never typeset on letterhead and sent. The painful outcome of this was that some of the members of the outgoing transformation board only learnt that their appointments had not been renewed when they arrived at the dinner. They assumed they were coming to a briefing of the Minister and that, not having heard to the contrary, they were continuing in their duties. The dinner was dominated by emotions of hurt and anger. Notwithstanding the pressures of elections, people felt they had given of their best for two years and were being treated shabbily and deserved better.

It was an inauspicious start for the new members as the malignant mood carried over into the next day's induction session. When it came to the reports of the board committees by the non-executive chairpersons, only Izak Cronje gave a thoroughly prepared presentation on behalf of the audit committee. Other presentations were given short shrift and were indicative of the dominant negative energy. Jack spoke highly of the work undertaken by the outgoing board and, with no holds barred, expressed his dissatisfaction with the lack of a relationship with Minister Hanekom. Hours of hard work had gone into the preparation of briefing packs and a slide presentation to the new board by each of the six executive managers. We had done a timed rehearsal the previous day. The value of this effort was overshadowed by the negative emotions. It was one of those days when the best-laid plans come to nought. To describe executive management as disheartened would be to understate their disappointment.

Again, the Land Bank is not a lone example; other public entities have experienced board changeover problems. The Independent Development Trust changed its board composition on 31 March 1998. On that very day the outgoing chairperson, Mamphela Ramphele, issued a press statement announcing the dismissal of three members of staff – a hot potato that the incoming board eventually decided they would rather drop than run with. The board of directors of the SABC, newly appointed in 2000, similarly experienced setbacks to a smooth transition. Newspaper reports covered the axing of the SABC's then chief executive, the Reverend Hawu Mbatha.* The story covered the criticism by the KPMG auditing firm of Mbatha's fiduciary controls, and also corporate governance concerns around a controversial extension of Mbatha's contract of employment which the new board was to challenge.

A similar situation of a new board overturning the decisions of the outgoing board also occurred at the Land Bank. The new board, on the basis of minimal consideration, rescinded the transformation board's decision to seek a settlement with the Banking Council of South Africa on the issue of the Land Bank's preferential creditor status. After months of deliberation we had judged as fundamentally unconstitutional our statutory right to be first in the queue to repossess the goods of an indebted farmer, leaving other creditors to pick at any leftovers. The new board persuaded itself that it was a privilege that a development finance institution deserved, and against the advice of executive management they instructed the pursuit of an expensive defence against First National Bank (FNB) in the constitutional court.† The court ruled in favour of the FNB claim that the Land Bank statute was indeed unconstitutional.

The problems arising over the formal ending of the term of office of one board and its replacement by a new board, which may or may not have a minority element of continuity, must provoke questions on the efficacy of this practice. Such schisms in continuity do not occur in the private sector. An international board on which I served had a maximum term of office per member, and carefully planned the entry and exit of its

---

*B Streek, 'Conflict as SABC refers posts to cabinet', Mail & Guardian, 6-12 October 2000.

†J Wilhelm, P Honey & A Roberts, 'Banks: Land vs Commercial – When bankers are seized by the issue of power', Financial Mail, 1 October 1999.

members so that in any one year there would not be more than one-third change in the turnover process. *King I* is silent on the issue of board continuity; perhaps this is a subject that merits the attention of *King II*.

The importance of effective chairing

The twelfth vacant spot on the Land Bank board was never filled. In June 1999 when the new Minister was appointed I alerted her to the fact that the board was without a chairperson. A month later when the Bonile Jack letter was published, the headless board of directors was at a loss how to respond. The new Minister then announced that Sam Mkhabela would become the new chairperson of the board. As far as I was aware this was the first time that Mkhabela would be serving as a director on the board of a commercial enterprise, and he was being asked to occupy the position of chairperson with little experience to fall back on. It was a tall order.

King I is expansive in its detail on the expectations of a chairperson, concluding that *in toto* the time requirement and skills expected are considerable: 'Theirs is to be a far more demanding involvement than that of other directors, and consequently they are usually paid more than other board members. An engagement with the executives is required to prepare the meetings. The effective use of the time allocated for the board meeting will depend on the skill of chairing the discussion. The role of the chairperson demands a monitoring responsibility to identify weakness among board members, and action to resolve such problems.'*

In my view, Mkhabela proved to have three areas of weakness: his inability to be decisive when steering a discussion towards conclusion, poor time-keeping skills, as well as a shortage of time. One unforgettable evening Mkhabela accepted a request for an emergency board meeting. But then a full two hours was spent in debate on the status of the meeting about to begin. The chairperson proffered the following question for discussion: 'Was the occasion to be constituted as an extraordinary meeting of the board of directors or was it to be defined as "an extended meeting of the board ad hoc subcommittee dealing with the investigation" to which other board members could be invited?' A transcript of the ensuing two-hour discussion would provide any scriptwriter with unique resource material for the theatre of the absurd.

The time management problem proved to be chronic, and resulted in a consistent failure to deal with board business in the allocated time. A meeting scheduled to last from 9 am to 4 pm only finished at 7 pm.

---

*King I, 1994, Chapter 7.

In terms of completing the agenda as drawn up by the chairperson, we had covered only the items that were supposed to have been completed by lunchtime. This situation repeated itself from one board meeting to the next with items continuously carried over. One consequence was that the draft statement on 'Strategic Direction' was submitted to four consecutive meetings without being discussed. This was in spite of executive management pointing out that such a statement was of crucial importance to investors who were awaiting a clear strategy commitment following the appointment of the new Minister and the new board.

A career move on the part of the chairperson led to his frequently indicating a time constraint problem. This impacted on the functioning of the board committees. Meetings were scheduled and repeatedly cancelled. At the end of August the Katz investigation team recommended that the issue of executive management remuneration be reconsidered afresh by the new board of directors. In the next four months the remuneration committee repeatedly set meetings which failed to materialise. Either there was an unwillingness to confront the issue, or a genuine problem of time availability on the part of the non-executive directors or, as has been mooted, it was an intentional strategy to create an environment of attrition to push me towards resignation. Whatever the cause, the non-functioning of the board committees did not constitute good governance.

A weak skills base

King I notes concern over South African ability to comply with the Cadbury recommendation that each company board should have at least three non-executive directors of calibre. The *King I* reservation is that while the Cadbury Code was 'undoubtedly correct in principle, in South Africa the question arises as to whether there is a sufficient pool of trained and experienced people available to serve as independent non-executive directors'.

A recent review of new black economic empowerment companies confirms that directors have had to grapple with inexperience in tackling their corporate governance. Business Map, a South African consulting firm, points out that it is precisely the companies that have clarified their business strategy and secured their overseeing of internal controls that have performed best as companies, proving the business efficacy of good governance.*

---

*Business Map presentation to the Consultative Conference of the Black Economic Empowerment Commission, 29-30 September 2000.

The lack of experience among the non-executive members of the new board was telling. Several members were completely new to dealing with a financial services business. They had difficulty understanding the funding mechanisms of the Bank's business. Concepts of promissory notes and Land Bank bills were new to them. Executive management's anxiety about a liquidity squeeze and cash flow crisis was not comprehensible to some of them. Another problem for some was a failure to understand the function of the Bank's reserves. They were unfamiliar with the concept of capital adequacy ratio as a prerequisite of a banking operation. One member clearly regarded the Bank's reserves of R1,7-billion as a huge development fund to be tapped into. Our in-house Development Finance Fund, topped up annually from internal transfers based on a tax and dividend imputation, was regarded as insufficient and judged as indicative of a failure by executive management to commit the institution to a substantial development programme. At a more basic level, some members simply had difficulty reading the balance sheet.

Effective business practice was hampered by non-executive directors who did not understand its dynamics. For example Totsie Memela, the general manager operations, and Adrian Toms, the general manager finance, had reached the decision on the necessity to proceed with the liquidation of Northern Transvaal Cooperative (NTC). Such action required the provisioning of possibly up to a hundred million rands or more to cover our losses and required board approval. There had been regular briefings on NTC's precarious financial situation for more than two years. It was felt that every avenue that might have resulted in improvement and resuscitation had been explored and exhausted.

Toms was adamant that we had reached a critical juncture and time was now of the essence, not only in terms of not incurring further losses to the Bank, but because we were only one of many creditors. If we were the first to pull the rug, we would be able to choose the liquidator. We considered this to be important; our choice would be informed by a commitment to salvage some of the better performing NTC business units with the intention of identifying black economic empowerment opportunities. The chairperson's comments, scrawled over the resolution as submitted for board consideration, was that the NTC directors were acting 'in bad faith', that our proposed liquidation would let them 'escape their obligations', and that further deliberation was necessary. The subsequent prevarication and delay before a shared understanding was hammered out was an exasperating experience for executive management.

Executive directors who are part of the everyday running of a business obviously possess a different level of knowledge from that of the non-executive director. The non-executive partakes in discussions a few times a year, and most of their information about the business is based on reading while, if inexperienced, they are learning as they go along. They are tasked to bring objectivity and independence to the discussion. It is acknowledged that executive directors are so close to the business that they may not see the wood for the trees. But there are dangers to having a board in place that is overwhelmingly non-executive; decisions with far-reaching consequences are then made on a few days a year by a group of people hardly connected to the business and who may have a very shallow understanding of the issues.

An under-represented group of executive directors expected to operate with a larger, weak group of non-executive directors proved to be a problematic combination that made the smooth running of the business impossible.

The board's weak base of experience affected the manner in which it dealt with the publication of the Jack letter. One of the hallmarks, and indeed expectations, of a performing board is its capacity to deal with or avert a crisis. The Land Bank's drawn-out handling of the crisis attracted public criticism both in parliament and the media. 'Damage by Dithering' was the description coined by *Business Day* in their editorial* after publishing an account of the Land Bank facing a cash flow crisis and paying an extra R500 000 per month for the additional premium on its purchase of funds.

A lawyer's considered opinion was that the inexperience of the board contributed to its susceptibility both to accept poor advice and become wrong-footed by the hype of the media coverage. The criticism levelled is that the original notion of the Katz investigation was ill considered, let alone the delays that took place after its completion. It is argued that good governance does not permit the leisure of time for such a lengthy process. The board was responsible for the guardianship of a financial institution. Serious accusations had been levelled at its top official. The situation required a rapid response. Jack, it was opined, should have been interviewed immediately to substantiate the basis for his allegations. Within two or three days there should have been a decision as to whether or not a disciplinary hearing was in order and, if so, be duly undertaken with speed.

---

*'Damage by Dithering', *Business Day* editorial, 18 October 1999.

So where to?

In the private sector business arena there is preoccupation with the *King I* recommendations: are they sufficiently onerous in light of a spate of business failures of listed companies? There are also regular problems of insider trading, accusations of company takeovers based on an under-valuation of assets, misrepresentation of financial information presented to the annual general meetings of shareowners, irregular practices affecting remuneration and share awards to directors. *King II* is expected not only to deal with the consequences of the new operating environment of the twenty-first century but also to look at recommendations that might provide more stringent guidance on these issues.

The problems that emerged in the Land Bank's governance were basic: the process of selecting board members and the availability of effective training, the calibre of the chairperson, time availability, the benefit of a formal process of evaluation, and the question of the remuneration of non-executive directors.

Selection and training

King I views the board of directors as having responsibility for the selection of the managing director or chief executive officer, a view that is commonly shared in international business circles. 'A board is responsible for seeing that the company has the highest calibre CEO and executive team possible and that certain managers are being groomed to assume the CEO's responsibilities in the future'. Furthermore, *King I* advocates that the nominations for new board members should be the outcome of deliberations undertaken by the whole board. The problems associated with a handover process due to radical change in board membership are not anticipated.

The public sector does not follow this process. The selection of the managing director of the Land Bank was carried out by a panel appointed by the Minister as politician shareholder. In this case the panel included only one of the members of the board in place at the time. Similarly, the selection process for the board members is also the domain of the politician, who may or may not decide to consult the current board members. Sometimes boards of public entities have been selected by a call for public nominations, and a chosen panel has then interviewed the nominated candidates. The prerogative of politicians to select board members has not been questioned, but surely it should be. What is the rationale for a different approach to selection of board members for the oversight of governance of a public sector company? Why should the process deviate from the recommendations of *King I* to which the government has said it intends to adhere more closely?

Whatever the process, the consequences emerging are several. There has been disruption when one board has replaced another. Independence has been compromised when public servants were selected to serve on a public entity. There has been a failure to adequately consider the skills a candidate possessed or, in the case of a novice director, a failure to insist that the person complete a directors' training course immediately after accepting the position.

Although the McKinsey Investors' report rated South Africa as performing well on corporate governance among emerging market economies, their criteria are unlikely to have included performance on race and gender representation. *King I* affirmed concern about the shortage of experienced black and female directors as a consequence of the domain of directorship traditionally having been peopled by white males.

Clearly the commitment to affirmative action, to ensure race and gender diversity among directors, requires that for an interim period it will be necessary to select people on the basis of potential rather than proven experience. But the acquisition of the relevant skills assumes such importance that the suggestion of obligatory certification does not seem unreasonable. A waiver system could be designed for those people who have a clear track record of serving as directors. The skills and experience required to perform as an effective director may be likened to the process of learning to drive. It is not legally permitted for a learner to drive alone until both theoretical skills and the practical exercise of road manoeuvre have been tested. Access to the steering wheel of a company should similarly be denied unless there is proven competence. The idea of 'candidate membership' is suggested for consideration. Where a board vacancy is to occur in several months' time, an incumbent who may be judged to have potential but not experience could be identified and serve a non-voting apprenticeship.

Business School professors have been heard to complain that they cannot get sponsorship to run courses for non-executive directors, but there are director courses that are run periodically by some institutions. My exposure to these has resulted in wariness about what can be achieved when the teaching is compressed and mainly theoretical. The teaching requires a problem-solving approach, rather than that of providing a half-day overview of *King I* and an exercise in how to read a balance sheet. It would seem appropriate to establish a Sector Education and Training Authority (SETA) dedicated to specialised training on corporate governance. The SETA could appropriately be financed through a non-refundable levy on business.

Grooming chairpersons: specialised training and mentorship

There is an increased corporate consciousness of the need for board composition to change to be more representative of the race and gender demographics of our country. The commitment is clearer in the state sector. The proportion of women directors has risen from almost zero to one-fifth since 1994. The comparative figures for the private sector are lower and resulted in a *Business Day* editorial* suggesting that there be an 'amendment to the Companies Act requiring publicly listed companies to report changes over time in the gender composition of their boards' with the idea that 'Regular exposure and embarrassment can be a potent force for change.'

While initial progress may be slower than desirable, the expectation is that there will be greater commitment to the placement of black and female directors, and as black empowerment takes root this will mean not only board membership but also their appointment as chairpersons. Such fast track changes need special supportive measures, especially for the task of chairing a board.

King I is adamant that chairpersons require skills in addition to those expected from the ordinary non-executive director. Cadbury was un-equivocal about the weight of responsibility on the chair to secure proper board functionality: 'It is a basic error to suppose that if you sit competent people of goodwill round a boardroom table, they will function as a board. Effective boards do not simply happen; they are the result of hard work by their members and particularly by their chairmen.'

Some of the skills required by the chair are more tangible than others. The ability to chair a meeting with a firm hand on the discussion to maintain efficient time-keeping is essential. But above and beyond such competencies the role of the chair includes the obligation to take on a specific leadership role.

King I indicates that once a chairperson has ensured a balanced composition of the board, that the members are well informed, that there is good participation from both executive and non-executive directors, the remaining role of coaching and team-building should not be overlooked.

The chairperson is also assigned the important responsibility of leading the process through which board performance is assessed. This may be either an assessment of the whole board, or of its individuals, or may apply to both levels. This would extend to calling to account those

---

*'Boardroom Chauvinism', *Business Day* editorial, October 2000.

board members who are failing to perform either due to poor board attendance, inadequate preparation, or a failure to participate.

A leading company in the UK, whose business is to headhunt suitable directors and provide support to company boards, has reached the conclusion that mandatory training is appropriate, as well as the practice of providing one-on-one mentorship. With regard to the commitment to demographic change in the composition of South African boards, such a conclusion, based on many years of specialised experience, should be taken seriously.

Appraising boardroom performance

A *Harvard Business Review* (HBR) article begins: 'There's little argument about the modern board's responsibilities . . . First, it is responsible . . . for ensuring that a strategic planning process is in place . . . Further the board must monitor the implementation of current strategic initiatives to assess whether they are on schedule, on budget and producing effective results.' The second responsibility pertains to the selection and grooming of the executive management. 'Third, as the ultimate oversight body, the board must be sure that the company has adequate information, control and audit systems in place to tell it and senior management whether the company is meeting its business objectives. And it is also the board's responsibility to ensure that the company complies with the legal and ethical standards imposed by law and by the company's own statement of values. Finally, the board has responsibilities for preventing and managing crises – that is, for risk management.'*

The authors note that while companies regularly have in place performance assessment mechanisms for individuals, work teams, business units, or senior managers, 'one contributor usually escapes such review, and one that is arguably the single most important – the corporate board.'

The same HBR article refers to a Russell Reynolds survey in 1997 which found that while sixty-nine per cent of boards had a performance process in place to evaluate the chief executive officer, only twenty-five per cent had a process in place to evaluate board performance, and as few as ten per cent had a process in place that embraced a holistic evaluation of the CEO, the board and its individual directors.

The HBR authors suggest a three-stage process. Firstly, the annual board objectives should be set at the beginning of the fiscal year. Secondly, the board secretary should take responsibility to collect and disseminate

---

Harvard Business Review, 1998.

information and secure adequacy of resources. The third phase is for an interim assessment of performance-to-plan that takes place in sufficient time before the end of the year so that corrective action can still be identified as needed.

Performance and non-executive directors' remuneration

The final issue arising in the quest for better board performance is that of non-executive directors' remuneration. I came across a very blunt statement: 'The most important factor in determining if a board will be effective is whether there is a small group of directors that has a substantial ownership stake in the company, enough so that it hurts them personally if the company is underperforming.'*

UK businesswoman and public-spirited politician Baroness Linda Chalker made similar remarks when addressing the Commonwealth Business Conference held in Johannesburg in late 1999. The ownership of shares in the company, she argued, serves as a lever on performance as well as promoting a better exchange of information between executive and non-executive directors.

King, in his address to the Gordon Business Institute Forum in September 2000, noted that there has been a tendency to undervalue the importance of the guardianship of good governance reflected in the practice of relatively modest payments to non-executive directors. He also opined that directors varied in their contribution and he supported different payments to different directors in keeping with the responsibility they exercised within the board. Not only might they have different functional responsibilities (according to their serving different board committees), but it was acknowledged that some board members prepared themselves much more diligently than others, and offered a higher level of participation in the proceedings. His practice, through his experience of chairing several boards over the years, is to engage on an individual basis with each director at least once a year to discuss their performance.

Obviously share ownership is not a factor that comes into play as a leverage mechanism when dealing with the governance of public entities. It is also to be noted that the rate that ministers set for non-executive directors of state-owned companies is often less than the going rate in the private sector due to a perception that a spirit of public service should prevail. My own experience is that altruism is difficult to sustain,

---

*Golub, *Harvard Business Review*, 1998, p.142.

and that non-executive board members whose time at meetings is at the expense of time otherwise dedicated to the pursuit of their personal business interests have passed sharp comments about the inadequacy of remuneration.

In the absence of share ownership, perhaps the way forward in the public sector is through performance contracts. The Minister of Public Enterprises has voiced the intention to put in place performance agreements between the ministry as shareholder and the board as mandated to act as shareholder representative.* There is no reason why such an agreement cannot be translated into tangible financial and non-financial targets; a basic payment could operate throughout the year with the possibility of a variable bonus according to an assessment of the quality of performance.

State versus private: acknowledging dissimilarity

Even if all the above issues of selection, chairing, evaluation and remuneration were resolved, I do not think that would be the end of governance problems in the public sector. Of the issues arising, the discussion of selection and remuneration indicated the need for specific deliberations by *King II* on how to secure quality and efficacy in the public sector. There is, however, an emerging debate among directors serving on the boards of public entities that has begun to query the wisdom of transposing the *King I* recommendations on to public sector companies. The code was heavily influenced by private sector considerations, so perhaps additional specific recommendations are in order which would accommodate the specificities of the public sector.

The debate on the total appropriateness of *King I* to state-owned companies begins with a simple review of the accumulated complexity that emerges through the corporate graduation from the one-person family business to the common company structure owned by shareholders. The difference in the character of the shareholder and the consequent differing application of shareholder power between private and public sector companies is then spelt out. This is the crux of the argument as to why the public sector requires a moderated approach to accepted best practice in the corporate governance of the private sector.

In a one-man show the person is the board, the shareholder, the self-employed manager, all rolled into one. At first, as business expands the owner/self-directing manager operates simply as staff members are

---

*J Radebe, Budget vote address to parliament, April 2000, p.9.

employed: each individual is paid a salary and any profits revert to the sole owner who has absolute decision-making power over the disposal of profits and assets. As soon as several partners own the business, decision-making over business strategy and disposal of surplus revenue becomes more complex.

Once the owners of the business expand its ownership through the issue of shares, things change radically. A four-tier structure comes into operation: shareholders, or shareowners as they may otherwise be described, a board of directors, the management and the staff members. The Companies Act sets out the compliance expectations of directors and the fiduciary duties they must fulfil. There may or may not be an overlap between tiers. Shareowners who purchased shares at the stock exchange will have nothing to do with the daily running of the business – their participation will be limited to questions that they may wish to pose at the annual general meeting. It is common, however, for both executive and non-executive directors, and even senior management, to be offered shares in a company as part of their incentive package. Whatever the composition of share ownership, it falls to the board of directors to assume guardianship of the best long-term interests of the company on behalf of those shareowners.

Peculiarities emerge in not for profit companies and non-governmental organisations. The mandate of the shareholder may be difficult to define, the stakeholders may be dispersed, almost ephemeral, and the end result can be that in practice the directors are answerable to none but themselves – another challenging situation for the application of good corporate governance. The exercise of governance in the public service is the subject of another ongoing debate – should politicians be responsible for the appointment of top civil servants? The UK model is based on a professional civil service independent of the party in power. The US model identifies certain key posts over which the party in government has the power to make appointments, but there are checks and balances in that nominations have to be approved by the Senate. This is not the case in other countries, and has caused concerns about impaired effectiveness due to disruptive changes when ministers change portfolios and are uncomfortable with the appointment choices of their predecessor. The failure to spend 78.5 per cent of budget allocation in the 1998/99 financial year (which included poverty relief funds) by the Ministry of Social Welfare was blamed on the turnover of senior officials provoked by a change of ministers.* There

*E Randal, 'Welfare Spending in the Doldrums', *The Sunday Independent*, 10 September 2000.

are many such interesting tangential considerations when the debate over governance is explored more widely. The following discussion limits itself to an exploration of the dissimilarities between the public and private sector that may be said to have contributed to governance problems.

State versus private: the essential dissimilarities

There are at least five essential public versus private dissimilarities which impact on governance: the political nature of the shareholder, the basis of selection of the non-executive directors, public servant intervention, the consequences of an imbalance between executive and non-executive directors, and finally the elusiveness of continuity.

The whole edifice of modern capitalism is premised on the existence of shareholders who are able to articulate their business interests. King has noted the problems arising when share ownership is widely dispersed and transient. It becomes more difficult for the shareowners to issue a mandate to the board of directors who are then tasked with the identification of strategy and overall guardianship of assets and ethics. Public sector companies have only one shareowner, i.e. the government acting on behalf of the country's citizens. An elected politician is appointed as minister and inherits a portfolio which may include responsibility for a public enterprise linked to the sectoral interests of that ministry.

The special nature of the sole shareholder as politician may contribute to various problematic outcomes. Firstly, the politician/shareholder concerns may be complex, yet not necessarily commercial. This may also mean that shareholder objectives are less easily articulated. Secondly, it may prove too difficult to get a commitment to long-term enterprise goals; the public nature of a state-owned company means it is exposed to the changing policies of changing politicians. The policy changes cannot be anticipated and are subject to vagaries over which neither directors nor management have any control. Thirdly, the shareholder does not have an owner-business interest, or any real knowledge of the public company. His/hers is essentially a political interest. It may have the result that there is not a great deal of realism or practicality in the ideas concerning the implementation of policy. The political concerns tend to overrule other considerations; the qualifications of a politician do not necessarily include business knowledge and insight.

It is common practice in South African public entities that the overwhelming majority of board membership comprises non-executive directors. On several such boards the managing director is the lone executive director. Board appointments are the result of a process controlled by politicians that does not necessarily or sufficiently take the skills requirements of the public entity into account. Where political and constituency considerations have dominated the selection criteria, the possible weak skills base and lack of relevant experience may compromise good governance.

A possible solution from the *King I* perspective would be to classify more members of the company's top management as executive directors in attendance at board meetings as full participating members. While this might achieve some improvement, the problem of the board as a strange hybrid would remain – the group would now be a mix of company executives and the cabinet-appointed members whose selection has been informed by a variety of considerations: skills, experience, political loyalty and constituency representation. The persisting problems can be anticipated as follows:

- The political and constituency representatives are unlikely to possess knowledge of the functional business matters. It can be argued that training could solve this issue; this assumes that the non-executive director will commit to the time necessary.

- The inequality and disparity between the executive and non-executive members of the board may cause tension and even result in mistrust. The executive directors will by virtue of their full-time employment have an in-depth knowledge of the subjects to be discussed. If the non-executives fail to dominate the content of the matter, then it is possible their decision-making would be based on feelings rather than business logic connected to confirmed policy positions.

- The appointment of non-executive members to safeguard the political agenda of the government shareholder may result in the boardroom becoming the theatre within which politics are played. Political objectives may be pursued without concern for the effects of these actions on the commercial imperatives.

- It is possible that a dominance will emerge from the person or persons perceived to wield the greatest political clout due to their relationship to the politician shareholder. It would be a remarkable coincidence if such clout were to coincide with the necessary commercial skills.

A further problem is the elusive goal of maintaining continuity when there is a change of portfolios among ministers. Then even those non-executive members who were politically connected to the former minister may be wrong-footed. Their term of office began under one political ministerial reign and when this changed, even the political representatives may find themselves out of alignment with the new minister exercising the power of the shareholder.

The ANC as the ruling political party has stated that ministers must conform and adhere to ANC policies, thus indicating that ministerial changes should not result in significant policy shifts unless there is an approved change of policy. Such a statement should provide the comfort of a commitment to continuity. However, practice has proven otherwise. Continuity has proved itself to be a mirage as board switchovers and policy swings due to changes in ANC cabinet appointments have caused turbulence.

The relationship between the minister as shareholder representative and the board of directors mandated as caretakers of company governance can get complex and messy when ministers use advisers as their communication intermediaries. The opportunities for misunderstanding in both directions increase. Much is dependent on the quality of the adviser's interpretation of the minister's wishes, and the nature of the adviser's report of his or her subjective perceptions of the board. Advisers have proven transitory. Public sector companies dealing with privatisation have had to interact with at least three different ministerial advisers in three years. The inconsistency is frustrating and yet the ministers have allowed advisers and even their senior public servants to exercise a level of authority that has usurped the board's governance responsibility.

The quest for an alternative

Variations in the above mix of possible problems provide the opportunity for a lethal cocktail capable of paralysing good governance. Unfortunately the numbers of board members of public entities who find it easy to identify with the problems as set out are more than is desirable.

King I considered the three common approaches that dominate governance styles in different parts of the world. The Anglo-American style is to use a unitary board that integrates both executive and non-executive directors. The German model is two-tiered, comprising a supervisory board and a management board. The Japanese system currently retains the concentration of power in the hands of the chief director and an executive committee with few appointments of external directors.

King I is clear in its preference for unitary boards to be the standard corporate practice in South Africa. Recommendation 6.1 states: 'The unitary board is appropriate in South Africa especially with affirmative action programmes as the unitary board results in new board members interacting with experienced board members dealing with such matters as enterprise, intellectual honesty, strategy, planning, communicating with stakeholders, etc, rather than having a monitoring function only as supervisory board members.' The premise is that the integrated board comprises executive and non-executive members of equal standing. 'A situation is to be avoided in which the non-executive board members perceive themselves to be the "checkers" of the executive directors as the "doers". The intention is that a unitary board, in its deliberations, has the advantages of the (involved) executives sitting around a table and putting forward their views directly to the less involved (non-executive) directors for probing, analysis, debate and decision.'* The notion of a unitary board with a balance of executive and non-executive directors regarded as having equal standing is especially important if and when there is a single shareholder. As soon as a director, whether executive or non-executive, has a 'hotline' and non-transparent relationship to the single shareholder, the ethics of good governance stand to be manipulated and compromised.

My abiding reservation is that the *King I* recommendations appear to have been drawn up with a primary focus on the private sector, and these may not be entirely appropriate to the public sector. The specificity of state-owned companies as a unique business entity was not contemplated in *King I*. At best, public sector governance works with ad hoc levels of comfort sometimes smoothed and soothed by social relationships; at worst, it may be said to be failing.

South Africa operates in both a new business environment and a new political environment. This impacts on the governance of public entities. For decades there was stability in the hegemony and alignment between the apartheid political masters and their institutional servants – whether as civil servants or directors of state-owned companies. The notion of 'independence' did not exist. The model once operative is patently no longer workable. The contemporary rough and tumble experience gives rise to serious doubts about the possibility of a successful transposition of the *King I* corporate governance model on to a public entity.

When in 1994 *King I* stated that the UK model of a unitary board provided the best model for South Africa, it was with only the briefest reference to the alternative governance models such as the German two-tier model with a supervisory board, and the Japanese model with a minimalist inclusion of non-executive directors. In 1995 UK political journalist Will Hutton† criticised the Anglo-Saxon governance approach exemplified by the unitary board, pointing out that the German and Japanese models were proving more effective in promoting investment

---

*N N G Maw *in* S Crane (ed.), 1995, p.1055.
†W Hutton, 1995.

and riding out crises; the takeover by German firms of flagship British companies like Rover, Morgan Grenfell makes the point, and the trend continues. Both the German and Japanese models have a stronger sense of accountability to stakeholders. The German supervisory board includes workers. In the Japanese model, although non-executive directors are few, they are usually major stakeholders; hence the involvement of the Sumitomo bank was important in the rescue of the car firm Toyo Kogyo which makes Mazdas. Hutton claims that governance models designed to exact greater accountability and stakeholder involvement have been resisted by the British as 'they challenge the citadels of power of gentlemanly capitalism', with negative consequences to the economy. The link between the performance of governance and business success is confirmed once again.

Perhaps *King II* could amplify its deliberations on alternative approaches to governance which received little coverage in 1994. It may be worth reconsidering the applicability to public sector governance of the two-tier approach used by the Germans. There has been a rejection of the two-tier model by South Africa's private sector, but it may provide a better operating model for governance in state-owned companies. Constituency representation of differing socio-economic interests is popular in a country that is focused on correcting historical injustices. Perhaps there could be a separation of political and constituency representatives into one board, and the effective running of the business would be the domain of a separate management board. It would seem to be worth a try. Or perhaps *King II* can produce specific recommendations on public sector governance that address the problems identified. The *King II* review is eagerly awaited, with the hope that the combined wisdom and deliberations of the committee will succeed in charting out an approach that results in a more constructive experience in public sector governance in the future.

The unfettered continuation of the status quo is awful to contemplate. The sum total of state assets is worth tens of billions of rands. The imperatives of a developmental state committed to resolving the iniquities and inequities of historical injustice require that not all public entities will be privatised in the short term. Hence the issue to be confronted is the continued governance or misgovernance, management or mismanagement, of those assets. Public sector governance should not be tainted by personal rivalries and failure to adhere to the principles of governance; and if it is allowed to be so tainted, that surely constitutes a sad betrayal of public interest.

ELEVEN

LOOKING BACK

The redundant wardrobe

The doors of my wardrobe were wide open. I sat on the bed staring at the contents. I needed to choose something to wear. It was early January 2000, and it should have been a normal working day, except that I wasn't going back to my job. What stared back at me was a rack full of formal outfits that I would not need for a while.

The unneeded clothes held their own stories. There was the navy pinstripe trouser suit that I bought in May 1997, immediately after my appointment as managing director. It was the suit I had hidden inside when I was interviewed for the weekly magazine, *Finance and Technology*. The cover photograph showed a smiling person, apparently self-possessed and confident – such a lie. I was scared of the job I was taking on. The years of drama lessons stood me in good stead to cover up my real feelings. It was said that I was a political appointee. I had been uncomfortable with the label. I'd spent my working life striving for professional excellence in each and every one of the diverse jobs I'd undertaken. My nervousness was because of the magnitude of the job I was to start, the high expectations, the fear I would not make it.

There was the double-breasted black jacket and skirt, with its sixteen gold button, four pairs on the front and a row of four on the cuff of each sleeve. A corporate suit, so elegant, but awful to wear. I'd felt stiff and trussed-up whenever I wore it.

A blue Swazi *seshweshwe* skirt and white blouse hung together as did the calf-length taupe linen skirt and black shirt. These were the outfits I wore when I attended meetings in rural areas and thought that my city clothes were inappropriate.

Alongside were the coloured ensembles, now beginning to fade, the ones acquired later but worn more often. I'd bought them when I'd begun to relax and wanted to wear clothes more in keeping with my sense of self. My vulnerability had retreated as I'd come to grips with the task. The more I felt at ease and confident that a good job was being done, the less willing I was to submit to the formal, dark, corporate wear that made me feel as though I were in a uniform or in disguise.

I smiled at happy memories. There was the pale apricot summer jacket and skirt, not too short, but short enough to show some good leg. 'If you've got legs, wear them!' Totsie and I had said laughingly to each other on our skirt days, except that mine were fewer. I felt disadvantaged enough being white, blonde and blue-eyed, without creating additional problems for myself.

The raspberry two-piece – not yet thrown out! I really had enjoyed wearing it, but then it had the car accident. Ravenous but rushed, I'd stopped to buy prime junk food. I lined up long, fat chips on top of the charred beef patty, replaced the top of the bun, squeezed it together and drove off. At every red light, I sank my teeth in. Pink sauce dribbled down, missed the napkin and landed in my lap. Heedless, I carried on eating. But now I'd have to swing by home and change before I could go to my next appointment – so much for a timesaving takeaway. I'd left the skirt to soak. The grease stains soaked out but metal stains from the buttons soaked in. It really was beyond rescue. I needed to admit defeat and throw it away.

I wasn't sure how many of those clothes to cast aside. I wasn't sure which of them I would ever wear again.

I'd relinquished my corporate job. My decision to leave was not made within a professional career plan, but precipitated by external forces.

My head was in a turmoil, I had no clue what I would do next to earn a living.

My settlement would allow me to pay my way through six months of unemployment, with a 'future uncertain' at the end of it. The only definitive was my current indecisiveness.

It was thus too early to add the clothes to the boxes already stacked in my garage, destined for the next worthy jumble sale. For a while I'd just have to tolerate those suits taking space and reminding me of a former life.

Looking back on 'leading change'

I had six months to sit, to think, and to write. I valued the opportunity to deliberate on the Land Bank experience and more. I was glad I'd taken the advice to take the time; if I'd rushed into another corporate job I don't think there would have been quite the same reflecting or the healing.

So many people have asked me: 'What did you learn most from your experience? What do you think your mistakes were? What lessons are there for those of us engaged in change processes?'

As I've written I've tried to stand back and consider: What worked? What didn't work? What lessons can be drawn? The learning curve was so steep – and sometimes I felt I was acquiring skills for a situation that I'd prefer never again to experience; for example, the enervating task of downsizing the Land Bank's head office. In April, May, and June 1999 more than one person walked into my office and the sum of their words was effectively: 'I want to say goodbye and thank you. The last two years of my working life here have been the most interesting, and when I learnt the most. I'd hoped there might be a job for me in the new Land Bank – but it hasn't turned out that way. But I do want to say thanks, and good luck for the future.' The personal consequences of business restructuring were hard to deal with.

There was one departure that I found especially difficult. Piet Moolman, a lawyer in what became a defunct legal unit as a result of restructuring, had dedicated himself heart and soul to transformation. He'd been part of the original communications task team, then one of the members of the workplace redesign team, and finally one of the facilitators of the leadership, alignment and development workshops that took place in head office and every branch. So many nights away from home had been hard on his family, and yet Piet had given of his best unstintingly. He came to see me on his last day, and took the opportunity to tell me that he hadn't always agreed with decisions or the approach taken, but that he was leaving with respect. I thanked him for his contribution, expressed my regret that a restructured head office did not accommodate him, and choked as we shook hands and said goodbye.

If I were to do a full circle and find myself part of leading a change process again, what would I do differently, given the chance? Sharing the introspection with former colleagues has been invaluable in identifying the weaknesses and the strengths. The objective of the discussions has been that whatever any of us do next in our lives, whilst we expect ourselves to be human and to make mistakes, let them not be the same ones!

There's nothing that I've since read, or that any corporate trans-formation or change practitioner has told me of in the interim, that would deter me from using Kotter's eight-stage approach to 'Leading Change' again. In fact, I'd consider giving a weighted importance to some of the stages, after thinking over some of the weaknesses in our Land Bank change process.

His eight stages were:*

#1 Establishing a sense of urgency
#2 Creating the guiding coalition
#3 Developing a vision and strategy
#4 Communicating the change vision
#5 Empowering broad-based action
#6 Generating short-term wins
#7 Consolidating gains and producing more change
#8 Anchoring new approaches in the culture

Our principal areas of weakness were #4 'Communication,' and #6, 'Generating short-term wins'.

Underperformance: communicate, communicate, communicate!

In the first few months we did well at communicating internally. We had excess operational capacity at head office, and even though most people received very little training, they did really well at creating a sense of engagement in the process at every level of the institution, in each of the twenty-six locations. It was after the national consolidation conference, when we got into the technicalities of human resources policy, and the quagmire of restructuring head office, that our internal communication dynamic faltered. Perhaps fatigue contributed, as well as a lapse in remembering just how important that face-to-face human interaction is. Circulars are no substitute. Videos don't provide the opportunity for dialogue. My former colleagues have taken up the 'road show' style again, especially to explain new human resources policies, and there's no doubt that there's nothing to beat personal interaction in winning people over.

External communication was always a problem. The land issue was never an attractive media subject until President Mugabe's actions and

---

*Reprinted by permission of Harvard Business School Press. From *Leading Change* by J P Kotter. Boston, MA, 1996, p.21. Copyright © 1996 by John P Kotter. All rights reserved.

land invasions in Zimbabwe caught public attention. The reform of the Land Bank, a stodgy apartheid institution, was of even less interest than general land issues. It proved difficult for the communications department to capture media interest, except when the Bonile Jack letter hit the headlines. It would have required a superior communications strategist with connections to the media world to possibly make a difference.

Underperformance: falling short on quick wins

In 'generating short-term wins', we managed reasonably well in terms of new products for clients. The 'bonus for on-time payment', the Step Up micro-finance scheme for the poorer client, and the special mortgage bond for the aspirant black landowner met some key customer demands.

We fell short in failing to resolve human resources issues speedily enough. In retrospect, I think it may well be important to opt for an imperfect solution, if it allows you to make progress whilst permitting adjustment for improvements in the future. A tangible example is needed here for this to make sense. For instance, at the beginning of 1998 we decided not to use JE Manager (see Chapter 7) as a job-grading tool in the branches as the basis for introducing a new salary structure. We opted for a circuitous 'perfectionist' route in pursuit of fairness, and at a time when we were still fearless of exploring innovative approaches. The long route towards attempting something more fair meant that Arnold Shkaidy and his HR team valiantly led a process which required them to:

- create 'job families' in the Bank's branch network;
- identify the competencies/activities required for each of the job outputs;
- rate the complexity of each activity;
- translate this into an accepted HR scoring base;
- convert this to a Patterson grading;
- determine the appropriate rand value of the job being done through the use of pricing consultants.

The above process, accomplished with considerable employee participation, ranks as a major achievement – but it took almost two years from conception to implementation. In the meantime there were high levels of staff frustration. In retrospect, maybe we should have used JE Manager as an interim alternative. The 'short-term win' would have been to gain the confidence of the employees that there was a real commitment to resolve outstanding dissatisfaction on the approach to pay, whereas the long route option we pursued was invisible for a great part of the preparation time.

The lesson for me was not only about confirming the importance of 'short-term wins', but also the strategic wisdom of contemplating an imperfect solution, and not to be so quick in rejecting the less than perfect route as a possible way forward.

Getting it right 1: Creating vision and a guiding coalition

When I arrived at the Land Bank people did not debate; branch managers had never met to exchange ideas and learn from internal best practice experience. The business planning session we held in Irene in June 1999 was a highlight for me. People set out their hopes for where they wanted the Land Bank to be in three years' time. It was an exciting exercise with a high exchange of energy.

But this was not 'blue sky' dreaming. The vision translated into tangible financial products that reflected the expressed intentions of targeting different customer groups. A risk analysis assessment was initiated for each province and then people were asked to put forward business targets which were challenged by the rest of the group when considered overly modest.

What I want to convey is the positive affirmation of sharing a three-day session with twenty-five people that was like-minded, stimulating and productive. It was a far cry from the first lonely months when I felt like the extraterrestrial being whose space capsule had come to land in alien territory.

On a daily basis, the strategic management team was strongly functional. We were an interconnected group whose complementary specialisations were essential to the smooth running of the Bank. There were *six* of us. *Operations* is everything because unless you can assess and evaluate the loan applications, then it's irrelevant whether or not there's money to be lent. But operations without *communications and marketing* may stumble; people do not buy unless they know that you have the product they are looking for. *Human resources management* may retain an administrative function, but strategically one hopes that it will strongly contribute to the emergence of the new culture, and deal with employment equity issues and fast track career advancement. The *finance* department can be creative or merely pedestrian, depending on whether or not the bean-counting function is complemented by analysis of the accounts to provide strategic management information. And everyone is dependent on *information technology*, especially operations, human resources and finance. We needed to mature as a team, but I was confident of the strategic interconnectedness of our components and valued the collegial interaction and support. I looked forward to developing the ethos of the *managing director* as the team coach.

Getting it right 2: Accepting our past into our future

We live in a country with a shameful history in which social relations have been deeply damaged by racial injustice. The Land Bank is only one of many institutions that is required to confront its past in order to make the transition to a different future. I think what we did well was not to make the past invisible behind an opaque amnesia, but nor did we single out individuals as scapegoats, or require people to make penitential confessions and request absolution.

The 'proud' and 'sorry' sessions that were a part of the consultative workshops in which every staff member took part in the first months of transformation were salutary. They allowed participants to speak of pain and regret without singling out individuals for blame. It was a process of institutional acknowledgement of wrongdoing. For many participants it seemed to provide the life jacket for their crossing of an internal Rubicon that allowed them their private commitment to the aims and objectives of the new Land Bank. My gut feeling is that if the process had been individualised, the emotional pain and humiliation would have caused an alienating level of trauma.

Similarly, while we were not able to take a reconciled report to the Truth and Reconciliation Commission, the exercise clarified how far we needed to go to resolve our different perceptions of history. The fact that we did not try to shy away from this, and produced the dual report for public scrutiny, proved to be the right thing to do to win people over.

Getting it right 3: Fostering a new workplace culture

Kotter's Stage #8 in his approach to leading institutional change is 'anchoring new approaches in the culture'. There are many inter-pretations of what new approaches might mean. The business appraisals of GEC's Jack Welch make him out to be the unrelenting tyrant when it comes to driving out unnecessary bureaucracy in GEC's business.* Such a campaign against bureaucracy should obviously result in efficiency

---

*S Crainer, 1999. Chapter 8: 'Kill Bureaucracy'.

gains; it may also challenge the power fiefdoms that people sometimes cultivate under the guise of 'needing formalised systems of checks and balances'.

There's no denying that by the end of the 1980s GEC was a leaner and fitter organisation. Any complacency that may have existed was eradicated. In retrospect, Welch's greatest decision may have been to go in all guns blazing . . . 'Shun the incremental and go for the leap' is Welch's advice.*

One of the intentions of the workplace redesign initiative described in Chapter 6 was to shake people out of their boxes in thinking about their working relationships. Changing culture is intrinsically a longer-term initiative, with expectations of both progress and reverses. It will continue to be an ever intriguing challenge to combine the rules and authority levels required for a financial services business whilst pushing empowerment.

At the Land Bank, our challenge to workplace culture, however imperfect and incomplete, was more fundamental than the pursuit of efficiencies, and for many people irrevocably changed their own vision of the possibilities that their working life could offer them. I kept true to the pact that I'd reached with myself. As a young researcher, I noted the parallels between my father's experience as a factory worker and that of the Mozambican state farm workers; I vowed that if ever I was to be in a managerial position, I would try to create an environment that opened up possibilities for people.

Another focus was to create an environment of 'continuous learning'. This had not been fostered in an institution in which many of the elders in control had never formally studied after completing secondary school. We introduced several initiatives, ranging from breakfast seminars to getting middle-aged branch directors with a school-leaving certificate to start studying for a management degree.

The breakfast seminars were an attempt to create a thinking senior management group at head office. Once every six weeks we had either an internal or external speaker. One time it was a presentation on the implications for agriculture of South Africa becoming party to World Trade Organisation (WTO) agreements. Another time there was a report back from one of the executives who had attended an African banking conference; another time the social responsibility team shared not only their future perspectives but also reported back on their participation in an international conference. It seemed worthwhile making an effort to

---

*S Crainer, 1999, p.11.

create intellectual capital, and get people to think beyond the narrow confines of their line function responsibility.

It was also important for people to get formal recognition of the skills that they had acquired through in-house training. Ten agricultural economists completed the valuation course and obtained certification.

We wanted to catalyse the branch directors' management style towards the business driver ethos. We got several branch directors to enrol in a UK Open University distance education programme 'Capable Manager', locally available through the University of Pretoria. It proved arduous but its assessment by participants was unwaveringly positive. Kobus Cloete, the Cradock director, studied in a caravan in the late evenings so that he was not disturbed by his family as they watched television. Abe Botes, the Pietersburg branch director said if there was ever one thing that the 'new' Land Bank had done right, it was getting people to study. His whole management attitude changed. Earlier I remembered him being teased by a colleague for 'fence-sitting'. Later, not only did his own branch staff rate him highly, but he proved invaluable with his 'can do, how to' attitude.

Getting it right 4 : Attracting and retaining employees

The restructuring of head office had wins and losses. It afforded the opportunity for some fast-track promotions of black personnel and women who had been employed at very junior levels in the Bank several years earlier. Some people discovered their wings in the change process and left the Bank to spread them. Letitia Erasmus, who had joined the communications team, became confident enough to decide to try her hand at her own business. Hope Babili followed a career opportunity in a private sector company.

It became clear that raising skills levels internally improved career mobility, and again underlined the necessity of getting the right material and non-material conditions conducive to attracting and retaining staff for the running of a successful business. It proved to be a long, complex and controversial process, but when fully complete and in place, the bleeding of skilled technical and managerial staff due to comparatively poor remuneration packages was halted.

Getting it right 5 : Rooting a business ethic

In retrospect, my finding an overriding lack of business sensibility at the Bank seems incredible.

I arrived shortly after the new Rustenburg branch office building had been completed. It had cost a cool seven million rands, and cast in stone an office space structure that reflected the decades-old organisation of segmented work and hierarchy. It was, at the time, every branch manager's dream. Cost accounting, imputed rental charges, and calculations on net income terminated those dreams and for the first time made people face the reality of running a business. The business planning cycle became part of Land Bank culture, and the margins on different financial products was a key topic of heated debate. The right pricing of what one sells, added to quality of customer service, makes all the difference. It was exciting to watch people learn and grapple with this process.

Getting it right 6: clarification of the development intent

Within two years Land Bank employees understood that the development character of the Bank was its *raison d'être*. If there was not significant delivery on the development mandate then there was little reason for its existence. The thousands of commercial farmer accounts that we dealt with were important, but I reckoned the majority of farmers would survive as clients of the commercial banks if the Land Bank were to go out of existence. They might have more difficulty, but I had no doubt about their overall survival.

Whilst our development mandate was paramount, the symbiosis between our customer groupings was also clear. We would run the commercial portfolio as efficiently as possible, whilst retaining the special customer relationship that the Bank had fostered with many of its commercial clients – the willingness for a partnership attitude, the foul-weather friend approach which was manifest in the reluctance to foreclose with speed when farmers were facing difficulties.

But we did not view the commercial portfolio only as our golden goose to create surplus that could be directed towards black economic empowerment activity. We had longer-term aspirations that we would be a positive influence on the way people farmed commercially and therefore seek a developmental impact even with our commercial clients.

Ruminations

Kotter's eight-stage approach may prove to be generic; it certainly provided a useful guide for the Land Bank experience. However, I found myself ruminating on additional issues that need consideration when discussing approaches to change, especially in South Africa when dealing with changed mandates, corporatisation or privatisation of public sector companies. I've chosen four additional 'issues' that I think make an impact on the chances of a change process being effectively carried through. There are the questions of *politics, engagement with adversaries, an alignment between statute, strategy and governance*, as well as *race*, that ineluctable issue that lives with us.

Issue 1: 'Politics, man, politics'

Joe made me laugh with his descriptions of the security police raids on the family home in the Johannesburg suburb of Emmarentia. Each time they found a copy of Stendhal's *The Red and the Black* they confiscated it. As Joe put it, the book's title, in the eyes of apartheid's police, combined the two most subversive factors imaginable. Joe once asked the police what they were looking for. 'Politics, man, politics,' was the answer.

And that was the very mistake I made in settling down at the Land Bank. I got engrossed in the job, let down my guard and forgot to keep eyes in the back of my head on the look out for the politics! It was brought home to me in no uncertain terms one day early on in the saga set in motion by the Jack letter.

Towards the end of a rare morning of quiet desk-work, my secretary Lettie told me that there had been a call from the security personnel in reception. 'The police are here to see you.' What now? What more? There had been letters from the Public Protector earlier in the week. They seemed to want to do their own investigation concerning the Jack letter in parallel with the Katz team.

'Fine, I'll see them.'

I heard the lift doors open and the sound of heavy boots approaching the reception room. My eyes came to rest on a familiar face, a comrade friend from Lusaka days who I rarely saw since we both took on our stressful jobs. He greeted Lettie with feigned professional severity. The tall black man, flashing his official police card, successfully intimidated her. We stepped into my office and as I closed the door a warm, teasing smile broke over his face. I laughed with relief; this was obviously not a visit to launch some unpleasant new salvo.

'How could you do this to me? Do you know how on edge I am?'

'It was the surest way to get to see you immediately. I was passing. I had time. I've been thinking so much about you.'

We spent a little time talking about how I was coping, and where things were at with the investigation, and then the gist of the conversation went something like this:

'So tell me – what have you been doing with your time in the Land Bank these last couple of years?'

'Working.'

'Working?'

'Yes, trying to turn this place around into something that will deliver.'

'You're a bloody fool.'

'What do you mean that I'm a bloody fool?'

'Exactly that. This is a political job. The Helena that I knew in Lusaka was a political animal not a technician. To survive in a job like this you've got to have political allies. I mean, look at Bongi Njobe and the way she operates. The day of election results at Gallagher Estate, she's there. On the occasion of the announcement of the new cabinet ministers, she's there, hovering in the background. And you? Where are you? Who do you keep contact with? Who do you consider to be your political allies?'

The conclusion to our conversation did not augur well. Hobnobbing generally gets a low priority rating from me. Among friends I'm inclined to refer to certain people as *gat kruipers* (the Afrikaans term for those who bow and scrape) in a fairly derogatory tone. There's a fine line between public relations and 'sucking up' in the interests of career advancement.

A while later, having given me some advice, he left me to mull over our conversation. He was right, of course. I had been internally focused with the Land Bank's transformation, trying to make sure that we had the right products lined up for new mandate clients, that the working environment changed for the better, that systems were upgraded to deliver an efficient and cost-effective high standard of service. I'd ignored the public relations politics at my peril, and was now paying for this neglect. My biggest mistake had been to fail to take sufficient heed of the political dynamics and their tentacles that reach deep into South African business activity.

Issue 2: Engage your adversaries

Another evening, I spent a couple of hours with a friend who had been a Robben Islander. He's not one of the favoured, but is perceived as a survival strategist. He made a pot of tea and we settled down with pen and paper to talk through my problems and strategise a way forward.

'Tell me about the board members, the provincial ministers for agriculture, the top departmental officials. Who are your allies? Who are your adversaries? Who is neutral?'

We went through each one of the personalities listed. 'You need a strategy,' he said. 'You need to be interactive with those who you can win over, and to undertake damage control with those who you think are being primed to think adversely of you. That's what I do. When I hear rumblings on the grapevine, I don't ignore the rumblings, I make it my business to meet up with the people concerned. I don't necessarily confront the issues head on. I may skirt around them. But the intent of the engagement is to spike the rumours, create the dialogue and ensure that it's not so easy for the rumblings to continue.'

He suggested that I draw up a plan for the next few weeks to travel in the provinces, meet up with the provincial ministers, invite the board members individually for lunch, a drink or whatever. At that time he was still convinced that I'd make it through the imbroglio. It was therefore imperative that I lay the foundations for survival in the future.

He was so right. I had not been astute in my handling of 'rumblings'. I was aware, for example, of the relationship problems with a couple of significant senior personnel in the Department of Agriculture. They were not especially of my own making; one was caught up as a minor player in a bigger scenario of personality clashes and ideological differences. But it had been unwise of me simply to 'get on with my job' and ignore the dissenting murmurs. A better strategy would have been continuous engagement in dialogue, to seek to minimise differences, to search out the possibilities of common ground and thus avoid false polarisation. The strategy might still have failed but then it wouldn't have been for the want of trying.

Issue 3: Legalwise

Alignment between statute, strategy and governance is essential; we slipped up on a few occasions in the Land Bank change process because we didn't get our ducks in a row. The transformation board directors undertook a steep learning curve as we grappled to understand agreements and legislation that circumscribed a change process. This included our trade union agreement, the outdated Land Bank Act, and labour law governing a restructuring initiative. In retrospect, at our very first transformation board *bosberaad*, it might have been wiser to have taken a more in-depth review of agreements and statutes and thus avoided some later surprises:

- The collective agreement with the two trade unions operating in the Bank was a poorly conceived document in terms of considered best practice. We should have spotted the pendulum arbitration clause earlier. We probably required a more detailed briefing than was given to me by the union on my arrival; for example, the 'turning up' of the union agreement on retrenchment packages was not the way that one should have discovered its existence.

- The Land Bank Act was originally drafted in the 1940s for use by a full-time executive board. We didn't scour it thoroughly enough when we had the chance to make amendments pending a full revision. We should have noticed the problematic clauses that required the board's involvement in personnel management matters, which is entirely inappropriate in terms of governance. We were, in those early days, so focused on changing the clauses that facilitated the change of business so as to be able to deliver on our new mandate, that we missed the chance to make what would have been other positive adjustments.

   Business imperatives drove the choices made on what to change. The lawyers did not want to fiddle with too many bits of the statute in light of plans to move towards something more akin to the Companies Act within the next two years. It is only hindsight that affords 20/20 vision!

- An understanding of Labour Law, especially what is known as Section 189, is a must for any business, private or public, that is undergoing restructuring. The due process required is exigent, and any mistake can be costly in financial terms. Here we benefited from good legal advice; the lesson we learnt was that general human resources practitioners cannot be relied upon to have a detailed understanding of the technicalities of the law, and that money spent on specialist lawyers is money well spent.

One of the pieces of advice that I did not take up on being appointed managing director was: 'Employ a legal adviser – at your side.' The problem was the many legal specialisations applicable to different parts of the business. Dealing with the Banking Council on the dispute over preferential creditor status needed one set of legal skills; negotiating with the union over the collective agreement needed a different specialisation. I opted for an 'as needed' selective approach. In retrospect, having an oversight adviser on a retainer basis would have been a wiser option.

Issue 4: 'Managing' racism

When I arrived at the Land Bank it was the subliminal racism that was notable, such as the comment by an old-guard manager about the staff component being made up of a third men, a third women, and a third blacks. And I felt, on occasion, an implicit racism in the reasons given for turning down a black applicant. A black farmer wanted to buy a farm in Komga in the Eastern Cape. My approval that the application be turned down was requested. The proposed rejection was based on a conservative estimation of cash flow together with a comment that the person didn't have entrepreneurial experience. I disagreed. The man had twenty hectares of arable land in the Transkei, a two-thousand-bird poultry unit, two tractors and a bakkie. He was obviously a go-getter who had succeeded at a time when the odds were stacked against small black business. The need for Land Bank loan officers to have a better understanding of the dynamics of the black rural economy was manifest.

Later there was a tendency for black applicants who were turned down to make accusations of racism when the assessment had been made by a white loan officer. Their dissatisfaction was born out of frustration. Increasingly, loan officers bent over backwards to approve loans, but rejections were inevitable. Bank employees were obliged to assess risk and approve only loans that were judged to be repayable. The answer lay in the Land Bank's providing comprehensible and accessible information that explained the basis for approval or dis-approval to avoid the accusations of racial bias.

In Tzaneen we had an abuse of procedures governing the granting of loans. The person responsible was black, and had a close relationship with certain members of the black farmers' union. Our professional responsibility to deal with corruption was greeted with accusations of racism. The two most senior members of the operations unit, both black, were appointed to handle the matter. The problems discovered were serious enough to warrant a year-long police investigation.* Even so, members of the black farmers' union interviewed were reported as saying that the Bank's black managers 'acted with white skins'.†

We also had the insidious poison of racism being actively stirred by an employee with a black consciousness background. She asked a fellow employee, also black: 'How come you're so comfortable working with these whites?' referring to myself and another white Land Bank employee who, by the by, had been an ANC member for more than twenty years. I watched the damage inflicted with amazement. It was like a successful application of the principles of guerrilla warfare; you need only a few selective hits to create a disturbance that played on our years of emotions rooted in apartheid history.

This kind of poison acknowledged no boundaries; it attacked viciously

---

*Tefo Mothibeli, 'Land Bank acts against corruption. Firing of 12 officials said to have saved R30m; some cases referred to police for investigation', *Business Day*, 14 November 2000.
†Louise Cooke, 'Farmers march on Land Bank office', *Business Day*, 14 October 1999.

without any ready antidote being available. In October 1999, the *Sunday Times** ran a review on women bosses, reporting on a US survey of 2500 managers in 450 companies. The published study found that women bosses were better than men 'by a long chalk'. 'It found that women were more sympathetic and were also more adept at planning, teamwork and technical tasks.' A *Sunday Times* reporter rang people who worked with three 'women bosses' – myself, the entrepreneur Wendy Luhabe, and Foreign Minister Nkosazana Dlamini Zuma. In my case they spoke to Mmoloki Legodu of the Land Bank's Potchefstroom branch. 'Working with Helena is a nightmare – she's so driven and she's a workaholic,' he joked. 'She wants me to work at the same pace she does and I can't. She's a very nice person and a very good manager, but if you don't comply with what she wants she makes you feel very guilty.' An ex-employee of the Land Bank, Moira Mokuena, open about her grudges, rang Mmoloki and said: 'You must stop your support of this white woman. You are impeding the advance of the black nation.'

The race issue began to colour every aspect of management, especially deliberations on how to handle personnel situations of underperformance by black professionals. The fear was that a negative appraisal of a black employee by a white manager could be misconstrued as racism. There was a case of one black manager who had oversight of a project that was key to the Bank's long-term development future; he was not giving it the attention required. The strategic management team discussed the transfer of this responsibility out of his hands. The first option of additional training or support was considered but rejected for various reasons. Totsie Memela advised me: 'Don't do this, don't take away his responsibility, not now when emotions are running high.' It coincided with the Tzaneen problem. 'If you take this action, it will be interpreted as the marginalisation of another black manager. You'll be criticised yet again.' So there was the dilemma of facing criticism for unpopular action or facing the consequences of the non-performance of a project that was essential to fulfilling the development mandate of the Bank. I hesitated. I took Totsie's advice, but felt I was compromising my professional integrity.

A few months after my departure Totsie, as acting managing director, did exactly what she had advised me not to do; she removed the locus of project supervision from the underperforming employee. Her blackness seemed to afford her greater latitude. When interviewed on her appointment as acting managing director she commented on just how

*'The truth about women bosses', *Sunday Times*, 3 October 1999.

difficult it was to handle the race issue, how she longed for the day when such tensions had healed, and how she intended to drive for performance from employees irrespective of their racial origin. One of Totsie's assets was her uncompromising intolerance towards attitudes of entitlement from non-performing black employees who felt they were owed promotion on the basis of their skin colour. Her arrival at the Bank had been such a healthy experience after my having been burnt by the black brotherhood attitude among certain employees who had opted to shield the first black HR manager whose appointment had been based on misrepresentation.

Being white in a leadership position in which the expectation is to transform a white-dominated apartheid institution is tough. When racial tension is being actively fomented the going gets even tougher. It is possible to succeed only if you have the unequivocal backing of your board of directors, and an ethos of non-racialism as the walk-the-talk of top management. Once there are cracks in your support, it creates the gaps for unsubstantiated and opportunistic accusations to be given a life. After the Bonile Jack allegations and the new board's manifest lack of encouragement, I eventually felt that my ability to continue to manage a transformation process was compromised. If the board is not vocal in its expression of confidence in you, and not seen to be standing behind you, your vulnerability becomes too high.

In the year 2000 discussion of the race issue in South Africa was catapulted on to the front page by the Human Rights Commission overview of race in the media. I've thought over the last twenty-five years of my working experience and realised that I've never at any other time felt so white as I did at that moment. I thought back on the different jobs I've held and the locus of the race issue in those jobs.

In Mozambique the issue didn't surface in quite the same way. Perhaps it was because of the avowedly socialist line of economic development pursued by the FRELIMO government. For example, the Ministry of Agriculture employed me in the Department of Collective Production. The team members had both technical skills and political commitment. Mozambicans, black and white, were mixed with people drawn from the left of various nationalities. My non-Mozambican colleagues were Brazilian, Portuguese and Chilean. Membership of the department meant you were a trusted cadre, and you worked on state farms with project teams comprising Cubans, Chinese, East Germans and Bulgarians. Commitment to an objective superseded any race considerations.

When I moved to the cooperative department I spent days in villages. The acknowledgement of racial difference was always there; children were often curious to touch soft *mulungu* hair to know the feel of it. But race was not a frontline issue. And there was the comradeship of working together towards the same socio-economic objectives.

Perhaps the overriding factor was that the commanding heights of the economy did not remain in the hands of whites because almost all the white Portuguese abandoned Mozambique in fear of the FRELIMO regime. The abandonment of many enterprises, some sabotaged by their owners prior to departure, resulted in a national reconstruction effort that embraced any person of any race willing to put their shoulders to the wheel. FRELIMO's choice of a socialist approach to reconstruction denied black capitalist empowerment opportunities for many years. In retrospect, there has been much criticism of the economic approach; one of its up sides, however, may be that it was enabling in terms of more positive race relations.

A quarter of a century later, South Africa's black economic empowerment drive pursues a capitalist agenda. Many of the black comrades who were in exile have now clubbed together and started empowerment groupings that naturally exclude their former white comrades with whom they worked for many years. An underground, special operations project meant, for example, that comrades of different race groups worked together. Race issues, like personality differences, had to be subjugated; lives depended on the trust of working as a team. Those very same comrades are now separated.

The importance of black economic empowerment is unquestionable. The greatest part of the institutional change effort in the Land Bank was to create an enabling environment for black entrepreneurs involved in agriculture and associated economic activity. At the Land Bank, however, as in other South African institutions, there is a real challenge to balance the confirmation of power in the hands of blacks whilst maintaining the continued contribution of participating whites.

All over the world businesses face the twenty-first century challenge of competing in a global environment; transformation is a business imperative. There's no room for complacency; what may be successful in one period may soon become obsolete due to innovation. In this context, the challenges facing South Africa are particularly demanding.

One of the proven critical success factors in business worldwide is the education of workers and entrepreneurs. Significant training budgets are therefore required to compensate for underspending on professional development during the apartheid era. The need for fast-track training opportunities for historically disadvantaged black personnel is obvious, but the Land Bank showed low levels of training, even among its white employees. The apartheid legacy less often talked about is the current day cost of its past isolation and a protected environment in which business could survive without real investment in personnel. Credit Agricole in France told me in 1997 that when they decided to get themselves into a turnaround state of real market competitiveness in the 1970s, they dedicated an equivalent of ten per cent of the salary cost to training for a period of ten years. South African companies' expenditure on training is generally less than three per cent of their salary budget.

South Africa's social transformation is also a business imperative. Racism and patriarchy have been responsible for businesses not tapping into the human potential of the majority of the population. Gender sensitivity training was one of the recommendations of the Strauss Commission. The more problematic transformation challenge is the race issue and the need to harness the talents of all people, of all races. The Land Bank story is testimony to both the creativity that can be achieved with a diverse group of men and women occupying senior positions, as well as the damage that is possible when tensions are unresolved.

We are not an integrated society. Many black people harbour anger towards whites. Some have noted the symbolism of the fact that whites do not bother to learn an African language; they see it as indicative of a lack of real commitment to our country. Many white people, on the other hand, are fearful of the rise of black political and economic power. The business hearings of the Truth and Reconciliation Commission set out to solicit acknowledgement and apology from the business community for past actions. Perhaps if the top one hundred companies as well as the public service were to invest in communication literacy – setting aside resources and time for language training – it would be an act of conciliation that invested in the future, far more meaningful than the expression of regret for the past.

South Africa is rich in the cultural diversity of its people. The success (or otherwise) of its economic reforms will be determined by its ability to unleash the creativity that is possible when synergy succeeds and results in an outcome wherein the whole is greater than the sum of the parts. It is not an easy challenge, and it requires the courage to engage in debate and confront disagreement. This was South Africa's strength in 1992-94 as it searched for a path towards a peaceful transition to democracy. The proof is there for us; 'creative discomfort' is the only way to secure a positive way forward for our society and economy.

TWELVE

MOVING ON

Silver linings

There have been real silver linings to my life since *The Star* published its report on the Jack letter. The bonds with my children, family and friends deepened as the ordeal progressed and as we talked through, and dealt with, the emotions during its different stages. When adversity promotes bonding in personal relationships, then the strength forged feels formidable, and in spite of the trauma I had a sense that I was being offered something precious in my life. There was empathy, solidarity, support, and professional assistance beyond the call of duty.

I was humbled by the generosity of support. The ethos of give and take is strong in my family, and I felt that for the last couple of years I'd been only a taker. I'd become totally enveloped and consumed by the Land Bank change process. I'd neglected my personal relationships; it would take me weeks to return personal phone calls – if at all. Friends would tease me and say that if they wanted to know where I was, whether or not I was in town, then their best bet was to phone my secretary. And yet they pulled out all stops in my hour of need.

Grief

Allowing oneself to become all-consumed by a job came with another cost; the loss of it was devastating. For months I had tried to be stoic and put on a brave face. But afterwards it was as though I was disintegrating. There was the day that my best friend had time off, and we decided to enjoy the decadence of a movie on a weekday afternoon – not that it should any longer have seemed decadent to me, given my state of unemployment. Gonda and I bumped into four lots of acquaintances who I hadn't met for several months. They all made comments about my having been through the mill, how proud they were of the way I had handled it, and so on. I found the sympathy to be my undoing; my voice wavered as I spoke.

The only time in my life that I've cried as much as I did in the early months of the new millennium was exactly five years before, when Joe died in January 1995. It seemed to be an unreasonable parallel, that the loss of a husband and the loss of a job should be placed in the same league of emotional response. I had to accept that the job had come to occupy an abnormal place in my life. Grief as an emotion was perhaps not inappropriate in the circumstances.

In the end I accepted the grieving unashamedly. Time, the healer, would run its course. So I stopped attempting stoicism. When people asked me what I was doing I replied, 'Convalescing.' I needed time to do very little, very slowly, and regain my equilibrium. I also knew that I needed to think about what such equilibrium would be made up of in the future. Life at the Land Bank, for all the stimulation and sense of achievement that it had offered, was not a way of living that one should want to go back to. It is not that I'd never want a job again that might provoke engagement, but I'd like the involvement to be less intense. I'd want to secure the space for those personal relationships that sustained me through crisis. I never again want to subordinate my personal life the way I did for those two and a half years.

But besides the grief over losing the job, I was generally upset with the story as part of contemporary history. I was puzzled over just how deeply shaken I was, and confided to a friend: 'I don't understand why I'm so upset. I've lived close to politics most of my adult life. For years I lived with a high-profile politician. I know, from close experience, just how dirty politics can be. So how can I justify being so upset?' The answer was consoling and reassuring in terms of personal values: 'Because you still care. Because you haven't become so cynical as to cut off your feelings.'

I began writing. I liked the patient crafting of words; I had always found it calming. I thought of writing as the making a piece of furniture by hand, and from scratch. There was the need to do a design, assemble materials, and then undertake the tasks of measuring, sawing, gluing and nailing pieces together, sanding, and polishing. I was also intrigued by the writing process, how even if you thought you had a plan, you would find thoughts being written down that you didn't know were inside you, and couldn't have guessed you were going to write. So there was also a sense of undertaking a mysterious journey. You weren't quite sure what would happen on the way. I hoped the writing time would prove valuable. I'd have the time not only for stocktaking, but also to settle on what to do next to earn a living.

Diffidence

As the weeks progressed, I seemed to be clearer on what I didn't want to do, rather than gaining any positive outlook on future possibilities. I appreciate that I've had extraordinary opportunities in life, the people who I have been fortunate to know closely, and the work opportunities that came my way. Nevertheless in the last five years in our post-apartheid South Africa, there'd been hard knocks quite unlike anything that had previously challenged my confidence. The trauma that brought my Land Bank tenure to an end left me temporarily disabled. I realised that I'd now be much more circumspect about a frontline job that engages the nerve-endings of our country's transformation. I felt I should wisely add diffidence to my character.

I didn't consciously think about diffidence until I was approached by a professor who was a member of a university search committee. Their job was to come up with candidates for the new posts of executive deans. One of the vacancies was as executive dean of the faculties of commerce, management and law. 'Would I be interested in applying?' My ready response was affirmative. It was a new post. It would have its own peculiar difficulties; I'd been reading press articles about concerned academics who felt they might one day be held hostage by such management deans. But I would be capable of doing the job and empathetic to the academics. It would be another job with a public service spirit. It was easy to persuade oneself of its merit; our educational institutions need to be a cornerstone in building society.

But I balked at the thought of another potential powder keg. It would be another one of those risky jobs. I thought of the university's contro-versies in recent years. There was still so much volatility in the air.

'Helena, please don't even think of considering it,' a dear friend told me. 'You just need to be picked on, for some arbitrary reason or another, and you'll find yourself under attack. And where would your political support be? Listen to me, please. Don't consider.' He was right, of course. I'd reached that conclusion on leaving the Bank – you only do those 'on the line', tightrope walking jobs if and when you have solid backing. That was the lesson; if you lose the backing – bail out fast.

But I thought twice, thrice, day after day for a week about the university proposition. I now knew only too well the limitation and vulnerability of being my colour in the rough and tumble of transformation. I couldn't face it again, at least not so soon. I felt sad as I reached this conclusion. I felt in danger of approximating closure to a part of my personal history.

Later I dwelt on what was in reality a much longer conversation. I thought back to a young woman who slept with tracksuit and running shoes next to her bed in Maputo, ready to grab her child Tessa, then still a toddler, and run when there was a telephone alert that the *Boers* were in town. I'd been a relatively insignificant person, but part of a lofty and noble cause; I'd been, alongside so many others, ready to risk my life to bring down a hateful, inhumane racist regime. Identifying 'the enemy' wasn't difficult. The white perpetrators were readily identifiable: P W Botha, Craig Williamson and their black partners, such as Matanzima and Mangope, equally obvious and odious.

Now ten years after the unbanning of the ANC, in the sixth year of our fledgling multiracial democracy, there was a speed chase to form and be part of a new elite that overturned previous allegiances. It had become a time of confusion. Those who one might venture to identify as 'conservative' were now so diverse in their racial origins and political histories that it was hard to reconcile their current day commonality. Liberation movement activists abandoned long-held ideals. Red diaper babies, brought up in exile, now worked hand in hand with former puppets with chequered histories who had enjoyed high-ranking civil service positions in the bantustans. My new diffidence towards this new and confusing order bordered on being scared. Being physically scared of the *Boers* was one kind of scariness – being turned upon by people who avowedly share the same politics is different, and worse.

My new diffidence is accompanied by regret. People tend not to speak their minds as they used to; to do so might thwart their ambitions. Or when they have, even at a Sunday lunch gathering of old acquaintants, I've witnessed criticism of the ANC being met by accusations of disloyalty. Mamphela Ramphele, the former Vice-Chancellor of the University of Cape Town, has spoken about potential threats to our fledgling democracy, the pervasive reticence of blacks to 'criticise government because of misplaced loyalty'. She noted the added difficulty and fear for whites who 'no longer speak out on issues of national concern because they will be labelled racist'.* She concluded: 'A culture of silence is putting democracy at risk.' Her words struck home deeply; for me to submit to silence would be to negate that part of my life given to fighting injustice.

In Charlene Smith, 'Is our African Dream just a fantasy?' *Saturday Star*, 14 May 1999.

Like others, I've read political assessments of what a miracle we are, what an inspiration to other countries embroiled in political strife, of how we have achieved our political transition without civil war. I've read the analyses about how our cautious economic policies have earned us international respect and protected our financial rating. It is indisputable that we have a lot to be proud of.

And yet I also have such a strong sense that we've lost something. The more open-minded debate of the early nineties has gone; criticism of economic policy has been unceremoniously squashed from the top. Sycophancy and kowtowing are in vogue as the path to promotion or the award of business contracts. There's been a growing intolerance towards those who dare to criticise; some of our finest minds have either found themselves marginalised, assigned to the parliamentary back benches, or have opted out of politics. So many comrades, of all races, who were initially proud to put their talents into the service of the new defence force or government departments have left those jobs. There's something amiss in our fledgling state.

Personal damage: public damage

On a personal level I'd say I'd survived. I lost my job, but the hostile buy-out afforded me the opportunity of a six-month sabbatical which I've treasured as a precious, unexpected gift. Although I spent long hours writing, it was a different pace to the intense daily pressure of corporate management life.

The reason for survival was the support offered by those close to me, and their absolute disbelief in the accusations against me, not only because they had known me for years but because of their doubts of the source and motivation. I like to think that I take criticism seriously, but much depends on where it is coming from, and what depth of information it is rooted in. The criticism I take most seriously is that which comes from friends and professional colleagues who have worked with me and know what they're talking about. Holding on to that important consideration provided an anchor to rein in emotions that might otherwise have been unbearable. I'm not saying that I became immune and was never upset; I was. The importance of locating and evaluating the source of criticism allowed me to read the Jack letter as well as unpleasant media reports without it hurting too much. But whilst I survived at a personal level, on the public level I felt damaged, most certainly.

There are many thousands of people who read and believe *The Star* chain of newspapers. *The Star* cast their reportage of events in the most unfavourable light possible, and moreover chose to limit their coverage when there were facts to be reported that were in my favour. The positive parts of the Katz report were largely ignored; Judge Coetze's verdict at the High Court got but a few lines on page two, compared to comprehensive coverage in other dailies such as *The Citizen* and *Business Day*. Reportage on the implementation of the new salary policy at executive level in the Land Bank just a few weeks after my departure was avoided.

People's uncritical reading of newspaper reports has been confirmed for me by Horizon Strategy, a media training consulting firm. They have used *The Star* newspaper report of 15 July 1999 in their courses. They confirm that when they hand out the newspaper cutting to be appraised by trainees what is distressing is that the initial response of nine out of every ten is that the report is good. It is only when the lecturer takes them through the article and asks questions that they stop to reconsider. What about corroboration? What about the relationship of the accuser to the accused – was there a score to settle? The lecturer notes that in fact the KwaZulu-Natal Poultry Institute is precisely the kind of outfit that the Bank would be likely to give a grant to – and that the reference to my 'former husband' (presumably divorced due to a breakdown in the relationship) works as a red herring.

In early October 2000 it was with bemusement that I read Mathatha Tsedu's weekly opinion column in *The Star*, 'Black Eye'.* That particular week he was reflecting on the transformation trajectory of the SABC. He noted the early positive steps taken and then expressed regret that at a certain stage 'political agendas and monetary gains superseded the noble ethics of journalism', and competent people were edged out. I could not help wishing that he, too, had upheld 'the noble ethics of journalism' on the afternoon of 14 July 1999 when he himself was party to the sanctioning of *The Star*'s report on the scurrilous Jack letter.

There are people who try to console me and tell me that the attempted defamation didn't stick, that the abiding public memory is that I was unjustly shafted. But the body public is a large body. What lingers on in the memory of part of the general public is that I tried to get a salary hike by sleight of hand. It has even been insinuated that the figures were a personal thumb-suck drawn up without reference to the business world.

In April 2000, ten months after *The Star*'s coverage of the Jack letter, *The Sunday Independent* carried an article on the setting of corporate salaries and the way consultants are used to recommend salaries.

---

*Mathatha Tsedu, 'Good News from the SABC', *The Star*, 2 October 2000.

Journalist Jamie Carr* proffered his comment on where he reckoned I had gone wrong. 'Helena Dolny could have saved a ton of hassle by paying a decent firm of consultants to tell her to double up her salary, rather than just up and doing it herself.' His comments are presumably based on his memory of the media story; he, too, did not follow the professional advisory code about journalists' need to check the facts. The Land Bank employed consultants on four different occasions – FSA Contact in 1994/95, McGee in 1996/97, FSA Contact again in 1998 and PE Corporate Services in 1999. Carr's reference is insulting; there was a serious professional effort to make sure we were getting it right.

I refuse to accept that I may be oversensitive about my sense of damage; there's evidence to the contrary. My child was in an accounting class at her new school – she has a different surname to mine so the teacher was unaware that I was her mother. 'Careful,' he told the pupils as they copied figures down from the board. 'Careful to write down the figures correctly. Be careful not to make a mistake. Remember that lady at the Land Bank and what happened to her when she tried to increase her salary.' Needless to say the inference hurt my child; she discussed with her classmates what she should do about the incident. It took her almost a week before she told me, because she knew the hurt I'd feel. There was also a mother's guilt that events in my professional life should carry over into hers and cause pain.

People at shopping malls and airports, ask me: 'Don't I recognise your face? Ah, the Land Bank. Yes, I followed that story closely.' Their associated thoughts are of me as a 'controversial personality', whereas I consider myself a straightforward, albeit unusually determined, professional who built a team to carry through a creative change process.

Moving on slowly, but moving

Thenji Mtintso, the deputy secretary general of the ANC, dropped in unexpectedly one afternoon bringing me beautiful flowers. She had phoned that morning out of the blue, and picked up a low in my voice. We talked about how unusual the Land Bank had been as a workplace for me, in that it was a job that used a composite range of skills that I'd accumulated over the years. We acknowledged the passion that had been at the core of my taking on the job. I'd loved that job, I couldn't ever imagine having the opportunity to do something quite so satisfying again. She commented: 'It wasn't just a job, it was a calling.'

---

*Jamie Carr, 'Delicious details of directors' pay packages bound to whet public appetite', *The Sunday Independent*, 7 May 2000.

My strength has been to bite the bullet, to take decisions and live with them. I've done it over and over again – sometimes at unforeseen cost I've taken personal decisions that proved hard to live with. In getting to grips with the task of the transformation of an institution that was so unquestionably a bastion of the apartheid system, it was precisely this bite-the-bullet attitude that was effective in securing an unswerving change trajectory. Kotter's observation on leading change was: 'If top management consists only of cautious managers, no one will push the urgency rate sufficiently high and a major transformation will never succeed.'* A *Financial Mail* article reviewing my performance quoted a fellow development financier as pointing out that 'it takes a certain kind of person to wrench an institution as conservative as the Land Bank out of the seventies. A forthright approach, a bit of arrogance, come with the territory.'†

The decision to write the book was true to character in that once again I am aware that I'm putting myself on the line. As much as I've enjoyed the crafting of words, the time for reflection, there is something intimidating about committing words to paper which, once written and published, afford no backtracking. I expect criticism of some of the approaches we took in our change initiative; that would be fine. There's a chance of learning from the critique. I also hope the chapter on governance will provoke debate; I would see that as an achievement. The account I've offered is intended as a contribution to the ongoing debates on the contemporary history that we are all part of. Institutional change is a fact of life that confronts many of us on a daily basis, as are the issues of race, pay and performance. My hope is that there will be some positive spin-offs from this ugly saga in at least three areas: a more constructive view on the salary issue, greater care taken by the media in their reporting of defamatory allegations, and the challenge to rethink approaches to corporate governance.

My time at the Land Bank granted me the opportunity of an invaluable learning experience that goes with me into whatever my future turns out to be. And maybe I can temper this strength of mine, and tone down that part of my character referred to as 'headstrong'. But as I kept saying at the Land Bank when faced with an audience that didn't like the straightness of my answers, I was not in the running for a place

---

*Reprinted by permission of Harvard Business School Press. From *Leading Change* by J P Kotter. Boston MA, 1996, p.43. Copyright © 1996 by John P Kotter. All rights reserved.

†Adrienne Roberts, 'The Bank that Dolny Built', *Financial Mail*, 17 September 1999.

in the popularity listings. Besides, being headstrong was a part of my character that landed me in South Africa in the first place. I don't want to change too much. I hope that the hard knocks won't dent my courage to ask awkward questions, or to take up difficult challenges, or speak on issues that I feel spirited about. I want to be able to retain the ability to do all those things. And if that's the case, I'd better learn to take the punches on the chin or, better still, improve my tai chi so that a practised twist of the body will convert that would-be punch into a mere glancing blow!

I'm still on the journey of moving on. There is no going back, and nor is there a simple way forward. I miss my colleagues. I'm jealous of their continued engagement; there are so many people in the Land Bank giving of their best in the effort to consolidate. It turned out to be a rare working experience in terms of the richness of working relationships, and the unusual bonds forged as a result of navigating difficulties together.

Would I go back, were the impossible to happen and I was offered the possibility? I don't know that the answer wouldn't be a yes, in spite of everything that's happened. I'm still in transit, the moving on process not completed; my mind has continued to grapple with the issues we were dealing with, especially because of these months now spent thinking and writing about them. At this moment, I'd still say, I'd love to be doing the job again; I know I'd do it better now than before. There's a difference in perspective after having had half a year to take stock and evaluate strengths and weaknesses, not only of myself but also the process and the business. I'd also be curious to see if I could meet the challenge of balancing the work and maintaining the personal space that I failed to do before.

It has proved difficult to disengage from 'unfinished business', and moving on means my bringing full closure to this chapter in my life. Parts of the book have been difficult to write as it meant reliving the emotions, but with time these have lessened in their intensity. There are days when I simply appreciate that I'm out of the morass that life had become. Another life, post Land Bank, is slowly being woven into place, at least on the personal level that I'd so much neglected.

Two steps forward, one step back

There have been wobbly moments. I'm probably not quite thick-skinned enough, but nor do I want thickened skin calluses to the extent that the strengths derived from sensitivity may be blunted. Inevitably there have been times of vulnerability in the aftermath of such a trauma when one's self-confidence has been knocked about. During this time of convalescence, when some remnant shards of vulnerability have poked their way through the foundations of my confidence, I've reached for Maya Angelou's spirited antidote, and drunk a shot of her sassy strength. She's made me smile as I've read, and reread:

STILL I RISE*

You may write me down in history
With your bitter, twisted lies,
You may trod me in the very dirt
But still, like dust, I'll rise.

Does my sassiness upset you?
Why are you beset with gloom?
'Cause I walk like I've got oil wells
Pumping in my living room.

Just like moons and like suns,
With the certainty of tides,
Just like hopes springing high,
Still I'll rise.

Did you want to see me broken?
Bowed head and lowered eyes?
Shoulders falling down like teardrops,
Weakened by my soulful cries.

Does my haughtiness offend you?
Don't you take it awful hard
'Cause I laugh like I've got gold mines
Diggin' in my own back yard.

You may shoot me with your words,
You may cut me with your eyes,
You may kill me with your hatefulness,
But still, like air, I'll rise.

Does my sexiness upset you?
Does it come as a surprise
That I dance like I've got diamonds
At the meeting of my thighs?

*Reproduced by permission of Virago Press, an imprint of Little, Brown & Co. (UK), from *The Complete Collected Poems* by Maya Angelou.

Out of the huts of history's shame
I rise
Up from a past that's rooted in pain
I rise
I'm a black ocean, leaping and wide,
Welling and swelling I bear in the tide.

Leaving behind nights of terror and fear
I rise
Into a daybreak that's wondrously clear
I rise
Bringing the gifts that my ancestors gave,
I am the dream and the hope of the slave.
I rise
I rise
I rise.

(Maya Angelou 1978)

I'm not so sure about the 'I rise' bit of the poem. It seems safer to stay close to the ground for a time, as the crosswinds in the higher stratosphere remain contaminated with poisonous vapours.

In May 2000 I was elected on to my neighbourhood ANC branch executive committee. It wasn't something that I'd planned. I'd gone down to Hofland Park community centre on a Sunday afternoon to be part of making sure that there'd be more than fifty members – the requirement to validate a branch annual general meeting. When nominated, I couldn't think of a reason for saying no, and there was good reason to say yes. When you've been accused of racism there's something sweetly seductive in being voted for in a roomful of people who are majority black. Besides, so many comrades had stood by me in the last few months that I felt indebted; it was right that I should begin to give something back.

I'd hardly lived in my neighbourhood since I'd bought the house in 1997. My home served mainly as a dormitory where I arrived to sleep before leaving for work again. In the meantime inner city poverty had spilled over into the Johannesburg East branch areas that cover Troyeville and Malvern. The problems being faced right under our noses keep the discussions down to earth. I'm one of fifteen, and not an office bearer; the others are more skilled and experienced than I in this domain. The politics are healthy. The group works hard, debates seriously; there's a pervasive humour. It's fun.

I'm not rising. I'm inching my way forward, one tentative step at a time, but no longer balancing on a tightrope. I'm not trying to put the past behind me, as some people advised; I'm working out how best to take it into my future. I'm on the ground, in good company, and it feels right.

The chance to make a difference

People have asked if I was thinking of leaving the country, or even heard it rumoured that I had done so. Why on earth would I want to stay when I'd been subjected to this level of trauma? I don't think of myself as a masochist; I ask myself what binds me. I have no ancestral land. I have no business interests. I have less family in South Africa than most other people. My children are grown, now deciding on their own path of self-determination as they begin their adult lives. Their needs of me are different; the daily logistical support is obsolete. I have saleable professional skills, in demand in other countries. I am mobile.

There are four lines of a García Lorca poem that have stuck with me since those teenage years when I studied Spanish at secondary school. My lay person's rough translation left the following in my memory:

> There was a thorn in my heart
> I could feel the pain
> I took out the thorn
> I could no longer feel my heart

There lies the answer. I could lead a different, possibly safer, life elsewhere; my fear is of what I would lose. There would be too much about this country of ours that I would miss: the energy, the engagement, and the complexity as we grapple with trying to construct a different future for those who will come after us. My overseas visitors have spoken of their envy of meeting so many South Africans seeking a space within their profession in which they can make a contribution. They contrast this with the passivity and cynicism they witness in their own countries.

Southern Africa has been for me the source of inordinate gifts, of having a chance to love and live 'on the edge' at both a personal and professional level. I have much to be grateful for. South Africa is a hard place in which to live on a daily basis, the uncomfortable contrast of opulence with poverty, the daily locking of car doors that you forget is obsessive until you are overseas and people comment when you follow the same routine there. The ties that have encircled my adult life in Southern Africa are tightly bound, but they are ties that have been enriching; they are not constraining ties that would want me to contemplate their severance. The discomfort of the last six months of my tenure at the Land Bank did not spike so many thorns into my heart as to make me consider leaving. I'd long since decided that taking the rough with the smooth in life means at times living with thorns as part of the deal of having the privilege of passion.

The work at the Land Bank combined professional fulfilment and personal engagement. It proved to be exhilarating, stressful, humbling, and there were some amazing moments of gratification, of being inspired by people. It was a life – just a different kind of life for a while – somewhat unbalanced. There was a vigour and ebullience about it all, encapsulating the best and the worst of South Africa. I'm glad to be searching for a new space, but on looking back I feel that I was extraordinarily fortunate.

It may be written off as just another story of a business turnaround with a corporate assassination plot thrown in for good measure – something that happens all the time the world over. But the Land Bank story is peculiarly South African – all the joy and the ugliness of it, the potential for fundamental change in tango with the potential for failure. Business success, democratisation, black economic empowerment, radical change in racial relationships versus patronage, mediocrity, racial tension, black entitlement. Except the daily schedule is not polarised in such a simple way – it's an ongoing messy mixture and for those who live here, in the words of Chilean singer Victor Jara, 'we're part of a story without knowing the end'.

I often think of all of us as only cogs in the wheel of history – or as players with bit parts in the larger theatre of life. But the end of our story isn't written, and our roles may be bigger or smaller in different scenes of the play. However, as we're part of an unfolding story, the way we act out our roles may make a difference to the direction that the plot takes. And isn't that what drives so many of us – the chance to make a difference?

REFERENCES

Academy of Management Executive (2000). Vol.14, No.1. 'The next frontier: Edgar Schein on organisational therapy'. Interview by James Campbell Quick with Joanne H Gavin.

Auditor General (1997). Report of the Auditor General on the Performance Audits completed during the period 1 January 1996 to 31 December 1996. RP 39/1997. Pretoria, RSA: Government Printer.

Belasco, James A & Stayer, Ralph C (1994). *Flight of the Buffalo: Soaring to Excellence: Learning to Let Employees Lead*. USA: Warner Books.

Black, J, Steele, B & Barney, R (1999). *Doing Ethics in Journalism*. USA: Allyn & Bacon.

Branson, Richard (1998). *Losing My Virginity: the autobiography*. London: Virgin.

Buckingham, M & Coffman, C (1999). *First, Break all the Rules: What the World's Greatest Managers do Differently*. UK: Simon & Schuster.

Coetzee, G, Mbongwa, M & Pheeha, M (1999). Salient results from the evaluation of the state assisted loan scheme for small farmers. Paper presented to the AGREKON Conference.

Conger, J A, Finegold, D & Lawler, E (1998). 'Appraising Boardroom Performance', *Harvard Business Review*, January-February 1998.

Crainer, S (1999). *Business the Jack Welch Way*. UK: Capstone Publishing.

Crane, S (ed.) (1995). *The Financial Times Handbook of Management*. Part 4: 'New Elements in Management – Corporate Governance' overview by Nigel N Graham Maw, pp.1052-1060. FT Pitman Publishing.

De Klerk, M (1984). 'Seasons that will never return: the impact of farm mechanisation on employment, incomes and population distribution in the Western Transvaal'. *Journal of Southern African Studies* 11 (1).

De Villiers, Marq (1990). *White Tribe Dreaming*. London: Penguin Books.

Dolny, H (1992). 'Land and Agrarian Reform in South Africa: Land Ownership, Land Markets and the State'. Unpublished doctoral thesis, Open University.

Dolny, H (17 July 1999). Press Statement by Dr Helena Dolny, Managing Director of the Land Bank of South Africa.

Dolny, H (23 December 1999). Press Statement.

Food Studies Group, Oxford, UK (1996). Unpublished mimeograph 'Effects of Farming Subsidies'.

Gonella, C, Pilling, A & Zadek, S (1998). 'Making Values Count'. Report published by the Association of Chartered Certified Accountants (ACCA), UK.

High Court of South Africa (1999). Notice of Motion in the High Court of South Africa (Transvaal Provincial Division), Case Number 34457/99: Documents 1-2, Annexures 1-31, and Judgment.

Hutton, W (1995). *The State We're In*. Vintage Press.

The King Committee (1994). The King Report on Corporate Governance. The Institute of Directors in Southern Africa.

Kotter, John P (1996). *Leading Change*. Boston: Harvard Business School Press.

Land Bank (1998). Prospectus.

Land Bank (1998). 'Black Economic Empowerment Initiative'.

Land Bank (1999). 'People Moving Change: Change Moving People'. Paper presented to the Ecology of Work Conference, Bonn.

Land Bank (15 July 1999). Media Release by the Board of Directors of the Land Bank.

Land Bank (10 September 1999). Media Release by the Board of Directors of the Land Bank.

Marcus, T (1989). *Modernising Super Exploitation: Restructuring South African Agriculture*. London and New Jersey: Zed Books.

Nathan, Edward & Friedland Inc (1999). Report of the Investigating Team at Edward Nathan & Friedland Inc concerning allegations regarding the Land and Agricultural Bank of South Africa ('The Katz Report'), with Annexures A-R.

O'Meara, D (1983). *Volkskapitalisme. Class, Capital and Ideology in the Development of Afrikaner Nationalism 1934-1948*. Johannesburg: Ravan Press.

Radebe, J (2000). Budget vote address by Minister of Public Enterprises.

Rehm, R (1999). *People in Charge – Creating Self-managing Workplaces*. UK: Hawthorn Press.

Schein, E & De Vries, K (2000). Academy of Management Executive, Vol. 14, No. 1, p.33.

Seers, D (1977). 'The Meaning of Development', *International Development Review* 19 (22), 2-7.

Semler, R (1999). *Maverick! The success story behind the world's most unusual workplace*. Arrow.

Sender, J (2000). 'Struggles to escape rural poverty in South Africa'. Working Paper Series No.107, Department of Economics, School of Oriental and African Studies.

Standing, G (1999). *Global Labour Flexibility: Seeking Distributive Justice*. London: Macmillan.

Strauss Commission (1996). Interim Report of the Commission of Inquiry into the Provision of Rural Financial Services, RP 38/1996.

Strauss Commission (1996). Final Report of the Commission of Inquiry into the Provision of Rural Financial Services, RP 108/1996.

Suttner, R & Cronin, J (1986). *Thirty Years of the Freedom Charter*. Johannesburg: Ravan Press.

Viney, J (1999). *Drive: What makes a leader in Business and Beyond*.